The Romantic Worl
of Puccini

The Romantic World of Puccini

A New Critical Appraisal of the Operas

IRIS J. ARNESEN

McFarland & Company, Inc., Publishers
Jefferson, North Carolina, and London

I would like to acknowledge the support and encouragement of the readers of my performing arts publication, *The Opera Glass*. Their enthusiasm for that project has made work on it, and on this book, a great joy, and I sincerely thank them. I particularly want to thank Trude Raymond, who opened a door that otherwise would have remained closed to me.

LIBRARY OF CONGRESS CATALOGUING-IN-PUBLICATION DATA

Arnesen, Iris J., 1955–
The romantic world of Puccini : a new critical
appraisal of the operas / Iris J. Arnesen.
p.   cm.
Includes bibliographical references and index.

ISBN 978-0-7864-4482-3
softcover : 50# alkaline paper ∞

1. Puccini, Giacomo, 1858–1924. Operas.
I. Title.
ML410.P89A66   2009   782.1092 — dc22   2009021372

British Library cataloguing data are available

On the cover: Cristina Gallardo-Domas, right, as Mimi and Marcello Giordani, left, as Rodolfo, in *La Bohème*, 2005 (AP Photo/Keystone, Eddy Risch)

Manufactured in the United States of America

McFarland & Company, Inc., Publishers
Box 611, Jefferson, North Carolina 28640
www.mcfarlandpub.com

To Fred Woodworth, who makes all things possible

Table of Contents

Preface

DUKE: For women are as roses, whose fair flow'r
      Being once displayed, doth fall that very hour.
VIOLA: And so they are; alas, that they are so!
      To die, even when they to perfection grow!
                — *Twelfth Night*
                William Shakespeare

The operas of Giacomo Puccini have rarely inspired much respect from critics. Even those who admit to liking his music and who grant his appeal to the audience tend to deprecate Puccini's works as sentimental tearjerkers—slightly hysterical melodramas that for two hours or more appeal entirely to the emotions, while leaving the intellect twiddling its thumbs.

The standard against which Puccini is often measured and found wanting is Giuseppe Verdi, whose operas tend to feature big and masculine subjects, such as the conflict between the individual and the state, or between personal desire and the demands of conscience. Compared to the monumental goings-on in such Verdi works as *Don Carlo*, *Aida*, or even *La Forza del Destino*, Puccini's subjects can appear hopelessly trivial.

And then of course there is the sadism. Even Puccini's biggest fans among the critics acknowledge, with more or less nervous laughter, how much delight the composer took in torturing his heroines, those "frail and gentle creatures," before he crushed them; how he reveled in the death agonies of his pathetic butterflies, broken on the wheel. The only trouble with these characterizations of Puccini, his operas, and his heroines, is that there isn't a word of truth in them. What has caused Puccini's works to be so badly misunderstood is the great complexity and oddness of their librettos. Of all opera composers, it was Puccini who most needed an exciting libretto to stimulate him musically, and unfortunately for him there was only one subject that really excited him. That's why it was so difficult for him throughout his career to find suitable libretto material.

As a result, Puccini's operas, which on the surface appear to stand as completely independent works, are actually very closely linked. Whether by design or by necessity, Puccini's works form what could arguably be called a cycle, not unlike that of Richard Wagner's Ring Cycle.

This thesis no doubt sounds incredible. While Wagner's massive operas tell an obviously continuing story of the theft of the Rhine gold and the eventual Twilight of the Gods, complete with characters and musical themes that recur throughout the cycle, Puccini's little works seem to have nothing in common but the style of Puccini. How could the events of his first opera, *Le Villi*, be the start of a continuing story that concludes forty years later with what happens in his last opera, *Turandot*?

If the answer could be given in a few sentences, Puccini's cycle would have been identified long ago. The connecting material of Puccini's cycle is so personal, so complex, and so obscured by the operas' engaging surface plots and ravishing music, that until now no one has detected it. I was able to detect it because I have studied literature most of my life, and so was able to identify the basic genre of the librettos, and to recognize and understand the significance of the recurring allusions, symbols, metaphors, and character types. Having also studied music, I was uniquely positioned to see the links between the operas' musical and literary elements.

Part One of this book provides the initial outline of Puccini's operatic cycle, describing the nature and substance of its connecting material. I have called it the Rose Cycle, in honor of the immensely powerful soprano heroines who until the end of the cycle carry flowers, usually the red rose, as a symbol of undying love. Part Two contains a new critical appraisal of the operas contained within the cycle, which include all of the operas that Puccini wrote, with the exceptions of *Edgar* and *Gianni Schicchi*. While elaborating on the material of the cycle, this appraisal gives special attention to the literary details and stage directions of the librettos, and to the composer's use of rhythm and recurring music to unify his scores.

These chapters on the individual operas address such subjects as the use of fire imagery in *La Bohème*, the plethora of musical labels assigned to people, places, actions, and thoughts in *Tosca*, the Japanese code of *giri* as employed in *Madama Butterfly*, the importance of Dante's book *Vita nuova* to the libretto of *La Fanciulla del West*, the use of the triplet rhythm in *Le Villi*, *Il Tabarro*, and *Turandot*, and the use, in *Manon Lescaut*, of music to depict acts of sexual intercourse — one of them explosively successful, the other ending in humiliating failure when the musical erection collapses. Discussed in both Parts One and Two is Puccini's borrowing of several major scenes from Richard Wagner's *Parsifal*, for use in the librettos of *La Rondine*, *Suor Angelica*, and *Turandot*. To the best of my knowledge, no previous writer has ever addressed any of this material. Puccini has been long and widely charged with the careless, even sloppy, use of recurring music. I believe these chapters will refute those accusations, which were based on insufficient analysis, and will prove that the composer almost always employed recurring music with the hand of a master craftsman.

This book was many years in the writing, and during the course of those years I developed a deep respect for the immense and utterly unique talents of Giacomo Puccini, who is simultaneously the best loved and most under-appreciated opera composer the world has ever known.

PART ONE

1

Genre

Giacomo Puccini was far from being the only artist of his age to associate women with flowers. Despite the advance of Modernism, Romanticism maintained a strong grip on the popular arts throughout much of Puccini's career, which began with the premiere of his first opera in 1884 and ended with his death in 1924, and the association of women with objects from the world of nature was extremely common in the arts. Another very typical equation of the time, one that Puccini makes in almost every one of his operas and which is equally as important as the flower association, is his identification of his soprano heroines with the moon.

During the closing years of the 1800s, in the period known as the *fin de siècle*, the artwork of Western Europe was awash with images of woman-as-flower, and woman-as-moon goddess, not to mention woman-as-animal, and woman-as-mythological creature.[1] What causes Puccini to stand apart from his contemporaries in his portrayals of women, despite his use of some of the same images, is the unusual attitude he expresses in respect to his female characters' dignity and sexuality. Puccini lived during a time of great repression of women in the Western world — of social, economic, political, and sexual repression. If we can judge them from their work, most male artists of the time, including writers and those who worked in the graphic arts as well as opera composers, were at best dismissive of the very idea of the independent woman, and were often simultaneously obsessed with and disgusted by the idea of the sexually independent woman.[2]

But in company with a few other prominent and liberal minded men, generally socialists like George Bernard Shaw, and one-of-a-kind individuals such as John Stuart Mill and Henrik Ibsen, Puccini was an exception. If we can judge him from his work, Puccini absolutely loved the liberated and sexually powerful woman.

Most *fin de siècle* artists who employed images of women as flowers and moon goddesses and the like seem to have been suggesting a romantic, passive, innocent beauty — one that was primitive, natural, unthreatening, and devoid of human intelligence. Primitive beauty was also suggested in portrayals of women as, or in connection with, animals—cats and snakes were favorites—and as mythological creatures, such as water sprites and sphinxes, but this beauty tended to have something unnatural and menacing about it — something that suggested secret knowledge, and malice.

While the flower and moon women tended to be chaste, these latter creatures exuded a strong and murderous sexuality. The flowers and moon goddesses could perhaps be safely played with, but those other, sexual creatures would surely drag a man down to depravity, insanity, and death. To put it in contemporary terms, a man had a choice between a sexless madonna and a devouring whore.

The sexual woman can be observed at her evil work in such operas as Bizet's *Carmen* and Saint-Saëns' *Samson et Dalila*, in which the initially virtuous heroes are tempted by

dark-haired vixens into sexual debauchery and the betrayal of all moral and religious principles. Even when the sexual woman is a sympathetic character, such as the title roles in
Massenet's *Thaïs*, Catalani's *Loreley*, and Dvořák's *Rusalka*, her spellbinding beauty, throbbing sexuality, and general witchery invariably turns men into helpless victims, doomed
to die. Even in the more slice-of-life operas such as Mascagni's *Cavalleria Rusticana* and
Leoncavallo's *Pagliacci*, women who attempt sexual independence simply breed death for
the poor males they entrap.

The majority of opera critics have consistently misunderstood the male/female dynamic
in Puccini's operas. Beginning perhaps with noted biographer Mosco Carner, whose highly
respected study of Puccini and his works first appeared in 1958, critics have almost invariably described Puccini's heroines as pathetic, helpless, frail creatures who suffer and die for
love.[3] This is so far removed from reality that one can only wonder whether these critics
have ever read the librettos.

Puccini's heroines are in fact incredibly powerful women — not just sexually, but emotionally, and sometimes even physically. Other artists of Puccini's time were as obsessed by
the strong and sexual woman as he was, but their heroes were horrified at being in the
clutches of such a creature (or at least, they claimed to be), while Puccini's heroes are frankly
overjoyed at it. Without a flicker of reservation Puccini presents his strong female characters in an entirely positive light, and his tenor characters do not in the least mind having
their girlfriends elbow them aside and take charge — as they invariably do. If there are any
important decisions to be made during the course of one of Puccini's Rose Cycle operas,
any vengeance to be taken, or any rescuing to be done, it is a woman who will do those
things.

Before we can understand the Rose Cycle — why it is called that, and what its connecting material is — we need to be acquainted with the genre in which it was conceived. Puccini's operas are usually labeled as either verismo or melodrama, but they actually rely very
heavily on the traditional elements of the *romance*. This is not simply to say that Puccini's
operas feature love stories, but rather that they follow a literary tradition that grew out of
the medieval poems and songs of courtly love, as popularized by the French troubadours
of the 12th century. The late 18th century saw a huge revival of interest in all things
medieval — a fascination with knights and castles and crumbling monasteries and quests
for the Holy Grail and so on — and so it was that the themes sounded by the troubadours
found their way first into the literature, then into the opera librettos, of the 19th century.

Courtly love is a genre with complex origins. In part it was inspired by the erotic love
lyrics of the Roman poet Ovid, who lived at the time of the Emperor Augustus and wrote
quirky poems in which love was depicted as a war in which the God of Love was the general, men were soldiers in his army, and women had supreme power over their lovers.

Ovid's poem *The Art of Love*, which gives all sorts of silly instructions as to how the
languishing male lover is supposed to behave — he doesn't eat, doesn't sleep, turns pale,
falls ill, goes mad, etc.— is believed by some to be a parody of the technical treatises that
were popular in Ovid's day, but whether the author was joking or not, the poem's enthusiastic promotion of sensual, extramarital relationships, in which the man ideally behaves
toward his beloved like a devoted, if scheming, slave, found an eager audience in 12th century France and England.[4]

An equally strong stimulus to the development of the literature of courtly love seems
to have been the writings of the powerful French abbot Bernard de Clairvaux (1090?–1153),

a celibate monk (and eventual saint) who promoted an erotic conception of the relationship between God and the soul, and an erotic veneration of the Virgin Mary.

Memoirs and letters from the period suggest that many women were highly attracted by the abbot's promotion of what came to be called Bridal Mysticism: a conception of the human soul as a spotless bride, wedded to her bridegroom, God. Medieval men appear to have been much less enthusiastic about the idea, and some responded by channeling their religious devotions into the other form of worship promoted by Bernard: the fervent, quasi-sexual adoration of the Virgin Mary.[5]

The language of this veneration, which meshed well with the sentiments expressed by Ovid in respect to male worship of the all-powerful and beloved woman, seems to have been absorbed into the troubadour love songs, with the result that in much of 12th century *romance* literature, we see in the description of the intense devotion of the lover to his lady — often a chaste, impossibly beautiful, and all but unattainable woman — a close approximation of the language of medieval man's eroticized worship of the Mother of God.

Some scholars believe that the love poetry of Moorish Spain was also an influence, but whatever their literary heritage, the troubadour songs of courtly love, chivalry, and *romance* spread rapidly across much of Western Europe during the 12th century. Many of the greatest French poets and troubadours wrote to please the tastes of socially and politically powerful women such as Eleanor of Aquitane (1122–1204), who was queen first of France and then of England, and her daughters and granddaughters. Eleanor was the patroness (and reportedly the lover) of Bernart de Ventadorn, who was renowned as a writer of courtly love poetry. Her daughter Marie was the patroness of the great Chrétien de Troyes, whose poem *The Knight of the Cart* (a tale of courtly, extramarital love sometimes called *Lancelot*) was composed on a plot and a treatment chosen by her. (It has been speculated that Chrétien disliked writing about adulterous love, and that was why he never finished the poem.)[6]

It is of course uncertain exactly what influence the writings of Ovid and Bernard de Clairvaux had on troubadour literature. But what is certain is that the relationship of the male and female lovers in the *romance* genre is a sadomasochistic one, in which the woman is granted all the emotional power, and the man worships her with a single-minded devotion.

Romance never went entirely out of fashion (it was a great influence on Shakespeare, for example), and the extent of the revival in the late 18th century was so great that it launched the Romantic Era. We can see the old medieval themes in many of the most popular works of the 1800's, including Tennyson's *Idylls of the King*, the novels of Sir Walter Scott, and the Wagner operas *Tristan und Isolde* and *Parsifal*, and one of the most important of these themes was that of a longing for something unattainable.

One of the earliest works of the Romantic Era was Goethe's *The Sorrows of Young Werther*, first published in 1774. Following the pattern of a *romance* tale, the story's title character, a sensitive and refined young man, becomes obsessed with the unattainable Charlotte, a woman he idolizes as the paragon of beauty and desirability — the being in whom all feminine virtues are gathered and made perfect. Charlotte is radiant, Charlotte is marvelous, and everything Charlotte says and does is fascinating. What makes the story so amusing, and yet so disturbing in hindsight, is that Charlotte is in no way the goddess that Werther thinks she is. In fact, Charlotte is a thoroughly pedestrian, middle-class nonentity. Werther is a ridiculous figure, seeing his first love with the unfocused eyes of a silly adolescent.

Whether or not Goethe realized it, he was helping to create a model that would be extremely difficult for women to live down. When the women's suffrage movement first began to gain strength and attract real attention, around the middle of the 19th century, the bookshelves of the Western world were sagging beneath the weight of literary works by popular Romantic authors, in which the idolized and "perfect" woman was depicted as a trivial object, rich in beauty and feminine virtues, but lacking any qualities that were admirable in a "manly" sense. These were qualities such as physical strength, intelligence, innovative ability, wit, experience of the world, and learning.[7]

It was a humiliating and impossible situation for women, especially since most were barred from obtaining more than a minimal education at best. Conventional wisdom held it unnecessary for a woman to be educated, because she would never have reason to put it to use. The only proper jobs for a genteel woman were menial ones such as governess, hired companion, or dressmaker.

It was also a difficult situation for authors who worked in the *romance* genre, for those who opposed the growing demands for women's rights accused them of being weak, fatuous, and degenerate. What else could one call an author who used his medium to suggest that the great goal of a man's life should be the single-minded, slavish pursuit of that unworthy creature, woman? As a result, the depiction of women in Romantic literature and art grew more condemning. The new heroine was still young and attractive, but now she was abnormal. Instead of the pretty and ordinary Charlotte, she was the sexless blonde madonna, Micaëla, or else Micaëla's counterpart, the devouring dark-haired whore, Carmen.

Based on the evidence of his first two operas, *Le Villi* (1884) and *Edgar* (1889), the librettos of which were foisted on him, it is clear that Puccini was at a total loss when confronted with the madonna and the whore. He hadn't the faintest idea of what to do with either of these creatures. But with his third opera, *Manon Lescaut*, Puccini gained control over the content of his librettos, and neither one of those characters would ever darken his stage door again. His heroines were *women*. And they made the decisions about their lives.

Puccini drew his heroines in very feminine lines, but he never equated femininity with weakness. His soprano heroines are sisters to the beautiful and domineering lady of the medieval *romance*, and as the composer aged, his heroines became ever more courageous and powerful. Similarly, his tenor heroes, brothers to the *romance's* obedient, tortured suitor, became ever more enslaved by the women they happily worshipped. This is an important point: unlike the distraught male victims of witchy women like Carmen and Dalila, Puccini's men enjoy their subordinate position.

What, then, is this genre called *romance*, and why did it serve Puccini so well? The medieval songs and poems dealt with the subject of erotic love, which was often spoken of in essentially mythological terms as a cruel and powerful god, working his will on young, attractive, upper-class men and women — knights and ladies— who are helpless to resist his harsh commands.

What these characters experience is the sort of ferocious, all-consuming passion that most adolescents would immediately recognize from their own emotionally exhausting experiences with first love. The courtly lovers of *romance* are of course just characters of song, story, and poem, and few people outside of literature would be able to sustain their intense passion for anything approaching the length of time they do. Nor could many people endure the incredible physical ordeals the courtly lovers are often required to go through.

These physical ordeals, like the emotional ordeals, are not simply gratuitous tortures, however. These ordeals, at least in the best of *romance* literature, are ennobling, for their purpose is to transform those who are knights and ladies in name alone, into knights and ladies in deed and spirit. As might be expected, there is often a religious component to the medieval romances, and thus the ordeals represent not only a striving toward the earthly status of *parfait gentile knight* and his lady, but also a striving toward perfection in the sight of God and the Virgin Mary. Subsequent to the medieval period, much of the Christian element was dropped from *romance*—indeed, an intense, near-pagan devotion to unspoiled Nature replaced it at the start of the Romantic Era—but the intense emotionalism was retained, along with the worship of the impossibly beautiful and unattainable woman, and the near-mythological conception of love as a powerful and cruel force, incapable of being resisted.

As Puccini himself frequently remarked, he needed a libretto that excited him emotionally; otherwise, he was unable to compose. He needed to love his characters intensely, especially his heroines. And it was absolutely vital for his characters to feel passionate longing for each other—that *romance*-type longing that can never be satisfied. There are a few occasions in Puccini's operas where the music falls utterly flat, and the reason is almost always that the character in question feels no sexual passion—no longing. In *Tosca*, for example, an otherwise thrilling score is marred by what is sometimes called "Scarpia's Credo." This is one of the dullest arias Puccini ever wrote, and the reason is that while Scarpia does want Tosca, he doesn't *want* Tosca. There's no romantic, sexual passion in the man. The same problem afflicts the tenor's final aria in *La Rondine*.

Based on the operas that Puccini produced, and our awareness of the subjects he considered and rejected, it's clear that only stories containing the classic elements of *romance* were capable of exciting him for the length of time necessary to write a full-length opera.[8] Following is a list of the core elements of the *romance*, all of which helped to shape the literature of the Romantic era, and the characters that inhabit the Romantic World of the Rose Cycle.

Love as a Form of Madness

On the part of the *romance's* knight, love is often experienced as near-insanity. The knight is obsessed by thoughts of his lady, and this causes him to experience physical problems that mirror the symptoms of illness. He grows pale, suffers loss of appetite, and is unable to sleep. He trembles, sighs, groans, and weeps. If this passion is not reciprocated (and sometimes even if it is), he may truly go mad, and even die.

Frequently this passion simply happens. Eyes meet, and the God of Love looses one of his golden shafts. Once in a while, however, Love as Madness is shown as resulting from magic. The best-known example of this is, of course, that of Tristan and Isolde, who unwittingly drank a love potion and became utterly, wretchedly, consumed by love. (In some versions of the story, Tristan does lose his mind over Isolde, and he deteriorates so badly that when his friends at last find him, living in the forest as a naked lunatic, even Isolde cannot recognize him.)

The Knight as Slave, the Lady as Mistress

The love between knight and lady in *romance* mirrors the ideal devotion of a medieval vassal to his liege lord, or of a Christian man to the Virgin Mary. The knight is the humble, willing, obedient servant of his lady, who, as a human woman, is often haughty, demanding, capricious, and even cruel. Her lightest word to the knight is law, and he leaps to obey.

An example of this behavior can be found in a song by the 12th century French troubadour Bernart de Ventadorn, which in part reads, "Good lady, I ask you for nothing but to take me for your servant, for I will serve you as my good lord.... Behold me at your command ... you would not kill me if I gave myself to you..."[9]

The conventions of *romance* only allow the knight to rebel against his lady under two circumstances: he may disobey her if her command runs contrary to his duties as a knight, or if her command is that he cease to woo and/or serve her. An example of the latter sort of rebellion occurs in the German *romance* called *Parzival*, by Wolfram Von Eschenbach, in which a haughty lady loved by the knight Gawan repeatedly tries to drive him away with words of scorn.

"No man," she declares, "ever lugged such stupidity around as you do, wanting to do service for me. O, but you would do well to give it up." Gawan naturally desires this lady's love above all else, and so he answers, "...if I can't win that, then a bitter death must soon be mine. You are destroying your own property, for even if I gained my freedom, you would still have me for your vassal."[10]

It should be obvious why the anti-feminists hated *romance*-based literature, and felt such contempt for those who authored it.

Love Described in Violent Metaphors

With a romantic situation such as that described above between the knight and his lady, the works of *romance* literature often use the terms of combat or destruction to describe what takes place between the two emotionally. The knight willingly calls himself the lady's "captive," and declares that she has "conquered" him and taken him "prisoner."

Love as a Painful but Exquisite Torture

Having avowed himself a conquered prisoner and a slave to his lady, the knight goes on to describe the pangs of love as torture, but a torture he delights in. He is in agony, but the last thing he wants is for the agony to stop. One of the French troubadours of the Provençal region, Le Chatelain de Couci, put it this way in a song: "Lady, I have no torment that is not my joy ... she makes me live in a wild disorder of grief and happiness, and I don't know whether she does this to try me, whether she does it for pleasure, to torture me, to see if the pain makes me give up."[11]

Night as the Refuge of the Lovers

The affair between knight and lady in medieval *romance* is usually illicit, with the lady being either engaged or married (usually, but not always, unhappily). It is for that reason that Night, whose darkness provides a concealing cloak for secret meetings, is a friend to the lovers, while Day, which aids spying eyes, is their enemy. Richard Wagner made great use of this element from the original works on Tristan and Isolde when adapting their story for his opera.

In comprehending the works of Puccini, it is critically important to observe his handling of the seasons of the day. Night and Day mean to his lovers fully what they do to the knight and lady of *romance*— and much, much more. Puccini loved the night. It intoxicated him and stimulated him mentally, and so he did most of his composing at night. The effect on human life of moonrise and sunrise is THE critical feature of the Romantic World of the Rose Cycle, and will be discussed in detail in the next section and in following chapters.

Specialized Songs: the Dawn Song, the Dusk Song, the Spring Song

With night serving as the refuge of the courtly lovers, there came into being among the lyrics of the Provençal troubadours a category of song that treated of their fear of morning. This is the Dawn Song.

The Dawn Song, called *aubade* in Provence, and *alba* in Italy, became very popular in the Western European prose literature that descended from *romance*, and a beautiful example from the late 1500's can be found in Act 3 of Shakespeare's *Romeo and Juliet*, in the scene which finds the young couple's wedding night drawing to a close. Romeo has been banished, and must flee Verona or be arrested, but his bride tries to convince him to stay a few more minutes by assuring him that night is not yet over.

"Wilt thou be gone?" Juliet begins. "It is not yet near day. It was the nightingale, and not the lark, that pierced the fearful hollow of thine ear." At length she admits that indeed, "...more light and light it grows," and Romeo sadly concludes the song with, "...More light and light, more dark and dark our woes!"

Within Puccini's Rose Cycle, things either terrible or wonderful happen *because* of the rising or setting of the sun, but he is understated about this, and on only two occasions does a character announce at the top of his lungs that sunrise is an important moment. The first of these utterances comes from a distant female voice, heard near the end of *La Rondine*'s Act 2. The voice sings a melancholy song, extremely meaningful in the context of the Rose Cycle, that concludes as follows: "Will you tell me who you are? I am the dawn, born to put to flight the magic of the night moon. Do not trust in love."

The second prominent Dawn Song belongs to Calaf, of *Turandot*. This is, of course, "Nessun dorma": No one sleeps. But "Nessun dorma," is a Dawn Song with a twist to it. As I shall later show, *Turandot* was meant to be the concluding chapter of the Rose Cycle. Puccini intended to finish his cycle by bringing his pair of lovers out of the world of *romance*, with its domineering lady and submissive knight, and into a new world where the two would be equal partners. So it is that in "Nessun dorma" Calaf, who wishes to make his love for Turandot a sanctioned, rather than an illicit love — a thing of Day, rather than of Night — looks forward with glad anticipation to dawn, rather than mourning the passing of darkness. If no one in Peking has discovered his name by dawn, Turandot must marry him, and the reign of Night will end. Calaf therefore waits eagerly for the sun to rise, singing, "All'alba, vincerò!": At dawn, I will win!

An apparent conflict regarding dawn seems to be visible in the closing moments of *La Fanciulla del West*, which ends at sunrise. With the lovers united at last — a first in Puccini — this should be a scene of unrestrained joy, yet it is one of the most grief-stricken moments in all of his works. Sunrise had previously always meant death to Puccini's romantic lovers, and at the close of *Fanciulla* neither he nor they seemed to have any sincere desire to step into the hateful world of Day.

The characters of the Rose Cycle love their world of *romance*, and so many of their most passionate arias are some form of Dusk Song. This is Puccini's corollary to the Dawn Song, and it expresses an intense love of and longing for night. Tosca's "Non la sospiri la nostra casetta," in which she sings to her lover Cavaradossi of the passion that awaits them that night in the starry darkness, is a Dusk Song, as is the love duet that ends Act 1 of *Madama Butterfly*.

Several of the men's Dusk Songs are backward looking, for they are sung by characters who are preparing to die, or who have lost their love, and are remembering the rapturous love they once experienced in the night. Cavaradossi's "E lucevan le stelle" is one of these, as is the achingly beautiful "Resta vicino a me," sung by Michele in *Il Tabarro*.

Another category of troubadour song is the Spring Song, in which knight and lady look forward to the coming of springtime, which, since it is the season of rebirth, is associated with a renewal of love. This is the core sentiment of the Spring Song — the anticipation of a rebirth of love — and in Puccini we tend to find it in arias sung by, or duets initiated by, the sopranos. An obvious example is the Flower Duet of *Madama Butterfly*. An exception is the *Turandot* Spring Song, "Là, sui monti dell'est," which is first sung by a chorus of boys. This song expresses the longing for Turandot to come down from her place on high, and the hope that April will blossom. Whether that will happen is the crux of the opera, thus Puccini employed the Spring Song as the most important and most frequently recurring piece of music in the *Turandot* score.

The Knight's Trial

This is the last major element of the traditional *romance*, and lacking it a story containing all the other elements runs a serious risk of being labeled a "cheap romance."

The love affair of knight and lady usually drives the plot of a courtly romance, but as I noted above, in the best of these tales the love affair is not there for itself alone. Rather, it provides a reason for the knight to undergo a quest, or some sort of trial — one that will call on all his abilities as a knight and an adherent to the laws of chivalry.

What we generally see in the medieval stories is a young man knighted on the strength of his potential. He starts out, therefore, a knight in name only, and it remains for him to prove himself a knight in fact. For example, in the Middle English story *King Horn*, the title character is knighted as a young man, and immediately afterward his lady asks him to marry her. Horn's response is classic: "With spear I shall first ride, and my knighthood prove, ere I thee begin to woo."[12]

What is it that the *romance* knight must do during his Trial? He must show courage and loyalty. He must defend good and battle evil. He must aid the weak, and if his defeated enemy begs mercy he must grant it. He must obey his lord and his lady, unless their commands run contrary to his duties as a knight. It does not matter whether the knight wins any particular combat. What matters is that he exert himself to the limits of his abilities, for if he does that he will realize within himself the ideal of knighthood. In other words, it does not matter whether he wins or loses, but how he plays the game.

"Cheap romance" is the sort of label a number of critics have not hesitated to apply to the operas of the Rose Cycle, and yet Puccini gave his tenor character something like a Trial in every one of them. The thing is, he gave an even more taxing Trial to his soprano character. As I said earlier, far from being the pathetic waifs they are so often characterized as, Puccini's Rose Cycle heroines are the actual heroes of their operas. They are utterly feminine, but extremely powerful. They are emotionally stronger than their lovers, and I repeat: if there are any serious decisions to be made, any vengeance to be taken, or any rescuing to be done, it is they who will do these things. Anyone who has read a modern romance novel, in which stories the heroine is always the most important character and the actual hero, should easily recognize the close kinship between the romance novel and the librettos of Puccini.

That Puccini chose the *romance* genre in which to work suggests that when it came to drama he was far more interested in and musically inspired by strong female characters than by strong male characters. So it was that even in *Turandot*, where he gave a major and quite traditional Trial to Calaf in an attempt to end the Rose Cycle with an equality between the sexes, he couldn't resist giving an even more impressive Trial to the secondary soprano, Liu, whose strength, courage, and nobility during her Trial far outshine that of Calaf during his.

Calaf's Trial is a truly demanding one in every way except the directly physical. He must have the courage to attempt the deadly Contest of the Riddles, and the wit to answer those riddles. He must then show knightly courtesy and bravery by offering Princess Turandot a second chance to win, and so risks his life where a lesser man would simply have demanded his prize. Calaf must then maintain his resolve to have Turandot to wife, in the face of fabulous bribes and terrifying threats. The only thing he does not do is to face a direct physical challenge.

Fascinatingly, the physical challenge is faced by the slave girl Liu, a character created by Puccini. Her Trial is much shorter than Calaf's, lasting only a few minutes, but the selflessness and bravery it reveals, and the violence with which it ends, thoroughly overshadow the efforts of Calaf, whose goal appears to be nothing more than the attainment of a personal desire. Calaf is a man and a prince, and so we expect brave deeds from him. Liu is a young girl and a slave, and so when she does brave deeds we are doubly impressed, especially since her deeds truly are greater than those of the prince.

The end result of Liu's Trial is that she succeeds in her attempt to protect the lives of Calaf and his father, at the cost of her own. There is no further effort one could have asked of her. A young girl and a slave, she has achieved the ideal of knighthood. Could one have asked more of Calaf than he gave? Absolutely. But we should remember that Puccini did not finish working with Calaf. The composer died before finishing *Turandot*, and his work ended with the death of Liu.

These elements from the realm of medieval *romance* contribute greatly to the Rose Cycle, but if they were all there were we would not have a cycle but rather a collection of similar but unrelated operas. That is, of course, what Puccini's operas have always been thought to be.

Two things bind Puccini's works into a cycle. The first is the strange physical setting—a Romantic World in which all the operas are placed. This is a world with some unusual types of people and some very odd laws. It is a world that, despite extreme differences of time and place across the various operas, is both amazingly consistent and utterly unique to Puccini.

The second thing that binds the works together is a continuing, and rather shocking, story—one with a beginning, middle, and an end—that runs beneath the operas' obvious, surface plots. Both of these subjects are explored in the next chapter.

2

The World of the Rose Cycle

The story line of the Rose Cycle is set in a parallel world. I call this realm the Romantic World of Giacomo Puccini. This Romantic World has a lot in common with the real world, but it also has some non-realistic features. The characters of Puccini's World know and understand these features, but just as you and I rarely spend much time discussing, say, the existence of the law of gravity, the characters of the Rose Cycle rarely talk much about the laws of their world. They simply accept them. Before we start examining this parallel world, with its unusual people and its odd laws, we should briefly go over where Puccini's various operas fit into the Rose Cycle.

The Operas of the Rose Cycle

Puccini's first two operas were *Le Villi* and *Edgar*. Their librettos were written by Ferdinando Fontana, a young Milanese poet and journalist who was introduced to Puccini by the latter's friend and former teacher, Amilcare Ponchielli, the composer of *La Gioconda*.

Fontana seems to have had a very good opinion of his own writing skills, and although there has been disagreement among scholars as to his willingness to make changes in his librettos,[1] Puccini at this stage of his career had little power to make demands of his librettist. Unlike Puccini, Fontana had the typical attitude of a 19th century man towards women, at least when it came to opera librettos, and thus both *Le Villi* and especially *Edgar* suffer terribly from madonna/whore syndrome.

The heroine of *Le Villi* is Anna, who begins as a chaste madonna. Because of her lover's unfaithfulness, however, she dies of grief and is transformed into a vengeful ghost-being called, in Italian, a Vila. The whore of the story is a vile courtesan who is spoken of, but who does not appear on stage. The hero is Roberto, who falls into the clutches of the whore, and so betrays his madonna. The vile whore who leads Roberto to ruin is of course the independent and sexually liberated woman who so fascinated and disgusted men like Fontana.

Puccini had no conception, at least dramatically, of either a "madonna" or a "whore." His heroines are young, beautiful, passionate, and sexual beings. To him, sex was life affirming, and the very idea of despising or punishing his unmarried female characters for engaging in it would have been ludicrous to him. The concept of chasteness as a positive characteristic of women seems to have been alien to his mind.[2]

Turandot, for example, is a horrifying being *because* she rejects sex. It is what makes her *death* affirming. It is Calaf's duty to awaken sexual desire in her, which will transform her into a normal person. Angelica, in the one-act *Suor Angelica*, has been forced into a convent as a consequence of having borne an illegitimate child, and Puccini clearly considers this a monstrous and cruel injustice. Unlike Verdi, who in several of his operas depicts a retreat into religious life as a way of finding as much peace as life is capable of offering, Puccini always represents churches and religion as useless at best, and torture at worst.

Le Villi could with the greatest of ease have been Chapter One of the Rose Cycle, for it contains the (eventually) strong, sadistic soprano character and her (eventually) weak, masochistic lover, but Fontana didn't share Puccini's tastes in drama, and so there are numerous other elements in the libretto (most of them clustered in the first act) that kept that from happening. Puccini was fortunate, however, that the second act does feature the sadomasochistic *romance*-inspired couple he needed in order to be inspired musically. The second half of *Le Villi* has some exciting music and reveals a composer of great promise, and it serves as a marvelous introduction to the cycle.

Edgar, on the other hand, belongs entirely to the madonna/whore school of librettos. Though it was based on an overwrought and incredibly convoluted story/poem by Alfred de Musset,[3] critics often cite Bizet's *Carmen* as a possible influence. Perhaps the success of *Carmen* did aid in Fontana's decision to use Musset's story, for both works feature a devouring gypsy temptress and an angelic girl-next-door, who compete for the attentions—indeed, the very soul—of the male lead.

Edgar and his two adoring women turned out to be stick figures, with whom Puccini could do little. Perhaps the amorous Tigrana (the Carmen-like, sexually liberated woman) might have fueled his imagination, if it hadn't been for the fact that almost every time her lover Edgar speaks to her it is with the loathing and disgust that decent, Victorian-era men naturally felt toward beautiful women who dragged them into bed and forced them to have incredible sex.[4]

Puccini soon came to detest *Edgar*, although he was kind and generous in his comments about Fontana, declaring openly that the "blunder" of this opera was more his fault than that of his friend.[5] *Edgar* bears no relationship to the operas of the Rose Cycle, and it's worth noting that in contrast to the music of *Le Villi*, much of *Edgar*'s score sounds uninspired and effortful. (There are some exceptions, however, including the funeral music for the title character, which opens Act Three, and the lovely soprano aria, "Addio, mio dolce amor," which follows the funeral music.)

Those operas that belong to the Rose Cycle proper are all the other full-length works Puccini wrote, plus the one-act *Suor Angelica*. As for the other two operas of *Il Trittico*, *Il Tabarro* is in essence a cycle-related short story (a horror story), while *Gianni Schicchi*, which was inspired by an anecdote in Dante's *Inferno*, is an anomaly, bearing no relationship to any other work Puccini wrote. Only in this one short work, steeped as it is in the gleeful, malicious humor of the Italian *Commedia dell'arte*, was Puccini able to find inspiration in a libretto that didn't focus on a situation rooted in the sadomasochistic world of female-oriented *romance*.

This, then, is how Puccini's operas can be classified in the system I have called the Rose Cycle. *Edgar* and *Gianni Schicchi* are completely outside the cycle. *Le Villi* is an introductory work. *Il Tabarro* is a related short story. The remaining seven, full-length operas, and the one-act *Suor Angelica*, form the cycle itself. With this in mind, we can start examining the parallel world in which the cycle is set.

The Laws and People of the Parallel World

Law #1: Night = Life, Day = Death

The first thing one should be aware of when trying to grasp how the Rose Cycle works is the association of night with life, and day with death. Says *Tosca*'s Angelotti, "I fear the sun!" And he has good reason.

Notwithstanding the powerful influence of medieval *romance*, much of Western literature sees in the close of day a metaphor for the end of life. The lines from Dylan Thomas, "Do not go gentle into that good night. Rage, rage against the dying of the light," pretty well sum up this approach, which is obviously completely at odds with Romeo's "...more light and light it grows.... More dark and dark our woes."

Puccini's World is that of illicit *romance*-type lovers such as Tristan and Isolde, and so within the Rose Cycle, life begins to stir not with the rising of the sun, but with the rising of the moon.

Of the nine operas that fall within the scope of the Rose Cycle, eight open at sunset, with full night coming on as the act progresses toward a love scene, or a vision of love. Because of second- and third-act requirements, it was necessary for *Tosca* to open at day, but shortly into the first act Tosca tempts her lover with an intoxicating vision of a night of love at his villa, beneath a full moon. This aria of Tosca's, "Non la sospiri la nostra casetta," is a Dusk Song, meant to fill the audience with the spirit of Night, causing us to forget the unpleasant fact that technically speaking, it is day.

The soprano and tenor characters of the Rose Cycle live and love almost entirely in the night. Very rarely one of them will express a longing for the sun, but on the occasions this happens it is for a calculated reason. The fact is that dawn brings death in Puccini's World, either physical or romantic, just as it brings death to the illicit lovers of medieval *romance*. What actually causes his characters to die, however, is something unique to Puccini. In essence, they're killed by the waning of the moon. As I noted earlier, Puccini was only one of many *fin de siècle* artists who associated women with objects from the world of nature, and the image of woman-as-moon goddess was a common one. But if one examines Puccini's post–*Edgar* operas, it is evident the Puccinian moon has unusual powers.

Puccini's World is ruled by his soprano heroines, and beginning with the first chapter of the Rose Cycle proper, *Manon Lescaut*, the composer repeatedly links his heroines' beauty and power to the beauty and power of the moon, giving great significance to those moments when the moon first rises, and when its rays physically touch the heroine.

In this world, dawn does not bring death to the heroine and her lover for the reason it does in the traditional medieval romances; i.e., that spying enemies are able, in the light of day, to observe the lovers' forbidden meetings and then denounce the couple to the lady's husband. Rather, dawn brings death to Puccini's lovers because dawn is the moment when the moon, and therefore the heroine, loses her power. Observe that:

Mimi dies when a ray of sunlight steals through the window of the Bohemians' garret and strikes her face. Cavaradossi and Tosca die at dawn. (*Tosca*'s first act was set at day out of necessity, so the final act could take place at the fatal hour of sunrise.) Madama Butterfly dies at dawn. Suor Angelica dies when the moon disappears behind a cloud. Liu dies at dawn. For Dick Johnson and Calaf, dawn will prove their hour of greatest peril. In *Turandot*, the Prince of Persia cannot be executed until the moon has risen, for it is at that moment the princess gains her killing power: a power she will lose at sunrise.

THE WAKING DREAM. There is a line in the libretto of *Manon Lescaut*, sung by the chorus early in the first act, in which sunset is referred to as "...the hour of waking dreams, when hope struggles with melancholy" (*l'ora delle fantasie che fra le spemi lottano e le malinconie*). This is the single most important line in the Rose Cycle, and so I will repeat it: Sunset is ... *the hour of waking dreams, when hope struggles with melancholy.*

In numerous personal letters, Puccini described himself as chronically depressed, and extremely fearful of the passage of time and the approach of death.[6] These feelings are everywhere evident in the operas of the Rose Cycle, and they account for the "waking dreams" of the characters and, in the music, the intense sadness that is mixed with an almost equally intense joy. So, what is the "waking dream"? And what is the nature of the "hope," that struggles with melancholy?

The Italian word I have translated as "waking dreams" is *fantasie*, which is obviously cognate with the English "fantasies." I have used the other term because in English, the word fantasy can carry a note of scorn that does not hold for the Italian. In Italian, "fantasies" are imaginings, or fancies; that is, products of the imagination — things that are not definitely true, but could perhaps be true. Beginning with *Manon Lescaut*, Puccini's young lovers will regularly refer to their *fantasie*, or, more often, their *sogno* — their dream.

The "waking dream," which begins at the hour the Italians call *prima séra* (literally, "first evening"), is an attempt by these characters — young people who love life and one another passionately, and dread the loss of both — to use the powerful emotions engendered by love to persuade themselves they can escape death. The waking dream is a period of hope, during which Puccini's lovers attempt to persuade themselves that through love, they can make the night last forever.

The first time we see this attempt is in Act One of *Manon Lescaut*, when, shortly after moonrise, Des Grieux begs Manon, whom he has just met and has fallen madly in love with, to make this moment "eternal and infinite." Following them, the enraptured Rodolfo of *La Bohème* will see in Mimi, who stands before him haloed in the silvery light of a full moon, "...the dream that I would dream forever." And as Madama Butterfly stands under the star-studded sky on her wedding night, she sings, "I am like the little goddess of the moon," and she vows that she is Pinkerton's for life. One by one the characters of the Rose Cycle vow eternal love, in a night which they always hope might last forever.

This sort of declaration is of course not unique to Puccini. Characters in opera are prone to extravagant utterances about how their love will never die. But there is something unique in Puccini, and that is the intense focus on night, and the palpable fear that prompts the declarations of never-dying love. As *La Rondine*'s Magda will say to her newfound lover, when dawn brings to a close their life-altering night at the Bullier's dance hall, "This is my dream, do you understand? But I tremble and weep."

La Rondine and *Turandot*, the final two full-length chapters of the cycle, contain the most pointed statements Puccini made regarding the meaning of sunset and sunrise. It was with the first chapter, *Manon Lescaut*, that we learned sunset was "...the hour of waking dreams, when hope struggles with melancholy." Here is what *La Rondine* has to say about sunset and sunrise, in a song sung by a distant voice, heard by the frightened heroine: "In the uncertain light of morning you appeared to me.... Will you tell me who you are? I am the dawn that was born to put to flight the magic of the night moon. Do not trust in love!"

Turandot has the final word on this truth of Puccini's Romantic World, and it comes in the form of the first of the Princess's three riddles. On pain of death Turandot demands that Calaf name the thing she describes thus:

"In the dark flies an iridescent phantom. It soars and spreads its wings over gloomy, infinite humanity. All the world invokes it, and all the world implores it. **But the phantom vanishes at dawn, to be reborn in every heart. And every night it is born, and every day it dies.**" This phantom, Calaf answers, is *La Speranza*: Hope. And Turandot agrees: "Yes, hope, which always deludes." The waking dream, in other words, is a vain hope — a delusion. Night has, therefore, two meanings in the parallel world of the Rose Cycle. First, it is a magical place in which love blossoms and the moon reigns and lends her beauty and power to the soprano heroine. Second, it is a short, fixed span identified with the short, fixed span of human life.

Law #2: Wealth and Power Debar One from Love

The next important feature of Puccini's World is the extremely hostile relationship between love and wealth. These two are mutually exclusive in this world, for here wealth is poisonous and corrupting, and love is denied to anyone who lusts after it.

Puccini did not draw this element from medieval *romance*, which has little to say on the subject of money. But a scorn for money was very much in keeping with the spirit of 18th and 19th century Romanticism, and in light of Puccini's intense love of Richard Wagner's music and his operas, it is worth pointing out a parallel with Wagner's Ring Cycle.

In Wagner, it is Alberich's choice of gold and power over love that begins and drives almost the entire plot of the cycle. In Puccini, that same choice of gold over love is made in *Le Villi*, and it continues as a theme in every subsequent full-length opera, forming much of the basis of the plots of *La Fanciulla del West*, *La Rondine*, *Suor Angelica*, and *Turandot*.

In the earlier Puccini works, this element seems a bit perfunctory. It seems like something tossed in as an expected part of a Romantic-type work. In the 1800's, young, passionate, artistic, nature-loving people weren't supposed to care about money. (Which was convenient, because such people usually didn't have any money.)

But beginning with *La Fanciulla del West*, one can sense this element becoming truly important to Puccini. One can see a deliberate opposing of gold and love in this opera — not just in respect to the main characters of Minnie, Jack Rance, and Dick Johnson, but also in respect to the chorus of gold miners, all of whom have left their homes and families in favor of a search for gold, and suffer intense loneliness as a result.

The importance to the plot of the choice between gold and love steadily increases in the final works of the Rose Cycle. And because of the consistent use of this element, right from the beginning, in *Le Villi*, Alberich's Choice takes its place as one of those "laws" that have a hold in the parallel world in which Puccini's characters live. Whether by accident or design, Puccini never allows this law to be violated. His characters have their choice: gold and/or power, or love. They cannot have both.

The People of Puccini's World

As for the characters who inhabit the world of the Rose Cycle, they come in four basic types.

The Alberichs

The first character type is the person who, with full knowledge of the soul-destroying consequences, has committed himself to gold and/or power. Because these people have chosen as Alberich did, I've found it a convenient shorthand to refer to them as "Alberichs." These characters are of course always wealthy and/or powerful. They are mature, and sometimes elderly. Until the final two chapters of the Rose Cycle, all of the Alberichs are men. The last two Alberichs are the Princess Aunt of *Suor Angelica*, and the Princess Turandot, and fittingly in this female-dominated world they are by far the most cold-hearted and horrifying of the lot.

Notable among the earlier Alberichs are Geronte, Lescaut, Alcindoro, Scarpia, Pinkerton, Yamadori, Jack Rance, and Rambaldo. Even if menacing, a few of these men are pitiable, for although none has any intention of giving up his gold, a few of them remember love and continue to long for it.

Whether motivated by poisoned love, like Jack Rance, or sheer lust and hatred, like Scarpia, a male Alberich knows no way of obtaining the woman he desires other than by buying or forcing her. The last in this miserable line is *La Rondine*'s Rambaldo, who is explicitly emotionally dead. There is no love remaining in Rambaldo, who is a banker, and no lust, yet even he seeks the company of the soprano heroine.

The Vacillators

Hovering about the Alberichs are the "Vacillators." These are the characters who have succumbed to the temptation of gold, but who decide to renounce it because they cannot bear the loss of love. Vacillators include Manon, Musetta, Dick Johnson, and Magda.

The Artists

The third major character type is the "Artist." These tend to be young men (although there are a few women), who are filled with strength, hope, and *joie de vivre*. Puccini loved the Artists, who live for art and love, and who despise gold and those who have forsworn love for its sake. It is extremely important to observe that throughout the entire Rose Cycle, not one Artist among all the painters, poets, musicians, singers, and dancers, is ever, *ever*, paid in money for producing art. The Artists include *Manon*'s Madrigal Singer and Dancing Master, the four Bohemians, Mimi, Tosca, Cavaradossi, Butterfly, and Prunier.[7]

By nature the Vacillators belong to the community of Artists, and their tragedy lies in their having fallen under the spell of gold, and so having turned away from their own kind. As Act One of *La Rondine* opens, we observe that Magda is a Vacillator. Young and beautiful, the pampered mistress of the banker Rambaldo, she has everything she could desire, except love. The envy of her friends, she is miserably unhappy. But then something happens. A handsome, penniless, and very innocent young man appears, and Magda decides to leave Rambaldo and his wealth for him. The young man cannot be told about her past, however. He cannot be told that she had ever lusted after gold. He would quite rightly despise her for that. So Magda decides to deceive him. She says nothing about ever having been associated with gold, and she pretends to belong to the fourth and last major category of characters who people Puccini's World. Magda pretends to be that woman whom I call, "The Lady of the Rose."

The Lady of the Rose

The Rose Cycle is named for The Lady of the Rose, whose character type is comprised of those soprano heroines who have wholeheartedly chosen love, never wavering, never tempted by gold. Puccini used flowers, especially red roses, to symbolize this character's moral purity, and her faith in undying love. Those who, unlike Magda, hold this title rightfully, are Mimi, Tosca, Butterfly, Minnie, and Angelica.

Flowers are of no more than clichéd importance in *Le Villi* and *Edgar*, in both of which operas the soprano heroine makes her entrance holding and singing about a spray of flowers. Flowers have even less importance in *Manon Lescaut*, although it's worth noting that Manon's luxury-loving nature would scarcely have allowed her to be associated with them in a Puccinian way, even if they had by that time begun to figure as an important element in his world. With *La Bohème*, however, the red rose emerges as the personal symbol of the heroine.

Mimi's first aria, "Mi chiamano Mimì," serves as the beginning of the full identification of the heroine with flowers in general and roses in particular. Mimi embroiders flowers, so not only is she the first Lady of the Rose, she also has Artist stature, equal to the poet Rodolfo. He himself declares this when he introduces her to his friends at the Café Momus: "This is Mimi, gay flower girl. Her presence completes our gracious company. Because ... because I am the poet; she is poetry. From my mind blossom songs, from her hands blossom flowers, and from exultant spirits blossoms love."

Clearly Mimi is employed as an embroiderer; it's how she makes her living in the real world of the opera's surface plot. Significantly, though, she doesn't *say* that. She says she makes lilies and roses as her special pleasure, which is the same special pleasure she receives from the fragrance of the blossoming rose that she keeps in a vase in her room, and from the "rose" colored bonnet Rodolfo buys for her.

Again, many *fin de siècle* artists were fond of portraying women with — or even *as*— flowers. One such painting, from 1903, is the "Rosa Mystica," by Edgard Maxence [8]— a faux-religious watercolor that depicts a hollow-eyed young woman crowned with white roses, shoulder-deep in a sea of white roses, her hands together (apparently *bound* together) in prayer. Nothing is missing (there's even a sliver of moon) in this portrayal of chaste, mindless, passive, feminine beauty. Nothing, that is, except the white handkerchief on which this dully-staring and apparently tubercular creature will probably need to cough blood any moment now.

The *fin de siècle* image of woman-as-flower was in part a legacy of the Romantics' worship of Nature, but it also seems to have been part of the vicious backlash against the women's suffrage movement that had begun in Europe around the time of the Enlightenment, and had gained strength with the French Revolution. As the 19th century wore on, women's demands for social justice — for the right to control property, to publish books, to divorce, to enter the professions, to take part in public life — grew louder. And the louder their demands, the more fiercely they were opposed by certain powerful members of the ruling class (including, oddly enough, Britain's Queen Victoria). Artists joined in the debate, and whether voluntarily or under pressure, quite a few came down on the side of male supremacy.[9]

Flowers are beautiful, innocent, and pleasure-giving, but they are delicate, weak and lacking in intelligence, so they need to be protected and cared for by those stronger than themselves. The same was obviously true, said scores of pictorial artists, of women. This was not, however, what Puccini was saying in his own association of women with flowers. Puccini's use of the image combines a sincere, personal love of nature and its beauties with the core sentiment of the medieval *romance's* Spring Song. Every time he summons the image of the rose—in connection with Mimi, Tosca, Butterfly, Minnie, Magda, and Angelica—his purpose is the representation of their hope for renewal. The rose is a part of his characters' struggle against death. The rose represents undying love.

This use of the rose as a symbol of rebirth did not originate with Puccini, or even with the medieval *romance*. In legends and folk tales that span much of the globe, the rose has been a resurrection symbol for millennia.[10]

In our own time, the best known work that uses the rose as a symbol of the rebirth of love is undoubtedly the play *The Rose Tattoo*, by Tennessee Williams. The main character is Serafina Delle Rose (Serafina of the roses), mother of Rosa, and widow of Rosario, who wore oil of roses in his hair and bore the tattoo of a red rose on his chest. Serafina mourns the death of her husband for three years, and keeps his cremated ashes—"the ashes of the rose," she calls them—in an urn, so she can still have him near her. She is almost as dead as her husband, until the day when another man comes to her, bearing the rose tattoo on his chest, and love and Serafina are reborn.

It can sometimes be difficult, in Puccini's operas, to distinguish between his own, deliberate use of flower symbolism, and clichéd images which he simply picked up, ready-made, from his source material. It was not he, for example, who gave Tosca the given name of Floria, which is a version of the Latin word for flower. She came to Puccini already christened by Victorien Sardou. It was also Sardou who decided that in Act One of his play, Tosca would make the 19th century heroine's standard entry-with-flowers, and Puccini uses this same entry in his opera. But Puccini takes Tosca deeper into the garden, amongst the roses.

Flowers are mentioned in Tosca's most important arias, "Non la sospiri la nostra casetta," and "Vissi d'arte." Tosca's hands, her lover says, "...were made for gathering roses." And almost the final words Tosca speaks to her doomed lover, whom she believes she is about to rescue and bring to a place of safety and love, are, "Who suffers any more on this earth? Do you smell the scent of the roses?" This is the sentiment of the Spring Song—the message is that of rebirth, and undying love.

Like the opera singer Tosca, Madama Butterfly is also an Artist, who as a geisha sang and danced in exchange for sustenance (not money). Her opera is drenched in flowers, which by this time have overtaken the actual production of art as a means of identifying the state of a Puccini character's morals. It is less important for us to know that Butterfly used to sing and dance than it is to know that she is "...una ghirlanda di fiori freschi"—a garland of fresh flowers.

In anticipation of her husband's return after his three-year absence, Butterfly inserts a red poppy in her hair as a symbol of the rebirth of their love. This flower is a delicate one, suiting Butterfly better than the hearty rose, but as Butterfly and her maid strip the garden and scatter flowers throughout the house, roses are given the place of honor, decking the threshold over which Pinkerton is expected to step.

Understanding the shift in focus from art to flowers, we can with confidence identify *La Fanciulla del West*'s Minnie as her opera's Lady of the Rose. She does not sing or dance, paint or write poetry, but in the depths of winter as she awaits the arrival at her cabin of Dick Johnson, whom she loves, she searches among her possessions for a cluster of red paper roses, which she tucks in her hair. The paper roses symbolize spring, and Minnie's hopes for love.

Beginning with *La Bohème*, and ending with *Suor Angelica*, Puccini's characters reveal their innermost natures to us by the way in which they express themselves on the subject of flowers. Any character who expresses reverence for flowers is instantly revealed as good.

One might attempt to argue that Pinkerton must therefore be a fine fellow, since he so often refers to Butterfly as a flower. In the long ensemble that begins with Goro's announcement of the wedding guests, and ends with the ceremonial bow of Butterfly before Pinkerton and Sharpless, Pinkerton repeatedly, delightedly, speaks of Butterfly as a flower. But his final line in the ensemble is, "And in my faith I have plucked it!"

This is not the language of reverence; it is the language of greedy destruction. Throughout the Rose Cycle, there is only one other comparable reference to the picking of flowers. That is in Act One of *Manon Lescaut*, when the student Edmund comments disapprovingly on the elderly Geronte's lustful plans for Manon.[11]

All other scenes or mentions of flower-picking, including Butterfly's stripping of her garden, a miner's offer of a handful of wildflowers to Minnie, Minnie's recollection of the spray of jasmine given to her by Dick Johnson, Magda's picking of roses in the last act of *La Rondine*, and Angelica's gathering of flowers from which she will prepare a suicide potion, are reverent in tone. What matters in the Romantic World of Puccini is not just that one speaks of flowers, but also his attitude toward them.

With *La Fanciulla del West*, the rose moves beyond symbol and attains the status of totem. With every mention of flowers it is suggested to us that the characters actually know, on a conscious level, what flowers signify in this parallel world. Let's examine the most important use of flowers in this opera, which is as a means of linking Dick Johnson and Minnie. This linking is done three times, once in each act. (The playwright David Belasco contributed the first two linkings; the third was Puccini's.)

The first linking actually begins before the opera starts. Minnie had been returning home to the mining camp of Cloudy Mountain after a trip to Monterey. Attracted to this beautiful stranger, Johnson approached her stagecoach, and by way of introduction he gave her a spray of jasmine blossoms. Minnie happily recalls this moment in Act One, when she and Johnson meet again, months after her trip.

In itself, this first linking is much like the standard entry-with-flowers of *Le Villi*, *Edgar*, and even *Tosca*. The Act Two linking, however, has real significance. Unbeknownst to Minnie, something terrible happened to Johnson just after he gave her that spray of jasmine. (David Belasco elaborated greatly on the encounter between Johnson and Minnie in the novelization he did subsequent to the opera, writing a long and exciting section to precede the one used as the opening of both the play and the opera.) What happened to Johnson was that he reached out his hand for Alberich's gold, and lost his right to love. Act Two takes place in Minnie's cabin, and in anticipation of Johnson's visit Minnie tucks her red paper roses in her hair. Johnson does not tell Minnie he became a bandit after he met her on the road from Monterey. He knows he is now unworthy of the love of The Lady of the Rose, and yet he wants it. He tries to embrace her, and some instinct seems to warn Minnie something is wrong, for she seeks protection in her roses. "Oh, my roses!" she cries. "You'll crush them!" Johnson's response is, "Why don't you take them off?"

On the surface, this is funny. It puts one in mind of a wolf bending over a sweet young thing and asking her if she wouldn't like to slip into something more comfortable. But that holds true only in the surface story set in the real world. In the parallel world of the Rose Cycle, there is nothing even faintly amusing about this exchange. Unlike Pinkerton, Dick Johnson does not throw the language of flowers around carelessly. A Vacillator, he lives in Puccini's Romantic World, and he knows full well what flowers mean. He does not utter that word while he is unworthy to do so. It was not he who spoke of the spray of jasmine in Act One, it was Minnie. This tells us that despite being an actual criminal, he is less steeped in sin than Pinkerton was, and is capable of reforming. But not just yet.

Here in Minnie's cabin, Johnson wants her kiss, and he knows the roses stand between them. That is why he asks Minnie to remove them. It is rather like a vampire asking his potential victim to take off her necklace of garlic. In Belasco's play, Minnie takes off the paper roses and puts them down. In Puccini, however, the stage directions have her put them inside a box and close the lid. It is at that point, when the roses are out of sight, that Minnie succumbs to Dick Johnson's urging, and kisses him.

Eventually Johnson repents completely. Wanting Minnie's love above all else, he renounces gold. But the miners of Cloudy Mountain catch him, and decide to hang him for his past crimes. About to face the noose, Puccini's Dick Johnson, at last worthy to do so, finally utters the word "flower." In the third and final linking, contributed by Puccini, Johnson sings his aria, "Ch'ella mi creda," calling out to Minnie as "...the only flower of my life."

It could be argued by one who does not believe in my Lady of the Rose, that so far all the flower imagery in Puccini has been trivial and coincidental; that Puccini picked most of the incidents up from the stories on which his librettos were based, and meant no more by them than any other artist of his time in associating female characters with beautiful objects from the natural world. But that argument falls to pieces in the face of the next opera, *La Rondine*, the libretto of which had no antecedent play or story.

In this third to last opera of the cycle, the Vacillator Magda, having sung for her well-heeled friends an Artist's song (about a poor girl who rejects the advances of a king, and who dreams of the love of a poor student), is rewarded by the poet Prunier with the highest tribute he knows. In the hush that follows the song, he ceremoniously strews red roses at her feet. Again we see the sentiment of the Spring Song, and this time it is doubled. First is it expressed by Magda through the song (the poor girl dreams of the birth of love), then it is expressed symbolically, via the strewing of the red roses at Magda's feet.

In contrast to Prunier's tribute, Magda's wealthy patron Rambaldo rewards her with an expensive pearl necklace. This would be a monstrous insult if Magda did not deserve it, as one who has chosen gold over love. Even so, this pointed, public reminder of what she has done shames her. The gift embarrasses her deeply.

And so it is that Magda, repenting of her choice, leaves behind her the pearl necklace her Alberich gave her. Changing her fashionable dress for one a working-class girl would wear, and tucking one of her tribute roses in her hair, she hurries through the night to meet the innocent Ruggero at a dancehall called Bullier's, the flower-filled gathering place of the Artists and Students. She assures herself she can pass—that no one will see through the rose to what she really is. Perhaps the Artists will believe she still is what she once was: The Lady of the Rose. Perhaps she can find her way back to the place where love blooms.

The next opera in which the rose appears as a symbol of the hope for rebirth is *Suor Angelica*, which like *La Rondine* had no antecedent work. Angelica is more tightly linked with flowers than any previous heroine, for she spends her life in the convent caring for them, and she understands their properties. Roses are mentioned three times in this short opera. The first is when one of the nuns is punished for having concealed two red roses in her sleeves during chapel. The second is the mention of a recently deceased nun, whose name was Bianca Rosa — White Rose — and who quite likely has a rosebush planted on her grave.[12] The third mention of roses relates to a nun who was stung by wasps while adjusting the roses on a trellis.

Angelica refers to people's wishes and desires as "the flowers of the living," and assures the other nuns they do not bloom in the realm of the dead, since there are no unfulfilled desires there. Angelica's flowers are renowned for their ability to soothe pain, and so when she learns her small son has died, and she decides to commit suicide, she goes to her flowers for help. She calls on them as her friends, and reminds them of how she has always cared for them. She knows they will repay her now, and soothe her pain.

Puccini's final opera, and the one that closes the cycle, is *Turandot*. The Princess Turandot has no interest in love, and so she does not carry the rose — the soprano character's personal symbol. But flowers still exist. They are confined to the royal garden, and that is where Calaf spends what could be the last night of his life — dreaming of Turandot, and of his hope that love might blossom in her heart. Flowers appear in the opera in one other, highly significant way. In the opening of the final scene, the stage directions describe the white exterior of the palace, "...on which the rosy lights of dawn are kindled like flowers." Puccini's final opera ends, in other words, with a depiction of red roses.

The Continuing Story of the Rose Cycle

At the close of the last chapter, I stated that these eight of Puccini's operas form a cycle because they contain a continuing story. What we have so far appears to be a Romantic World that is unique and consistent enough to unify the operas, despite their varying geographies and eras. We have a recurring set of four character types, and several constant themes: the longing for Night, which brings life and love; the fear of Day, which brings death; the antipathy of gold and love; and the increasing importance of the moon and flower symbolism. But what is that continuing story that I claim was introduced in *Le Villi*, begun in earnest in *Manon Lescaut*, and decisively ended in *Turandot*?

It is the story of the soprano heroine — the domineering lady of medieval *romance*— and how her uncontrollable and ever-growing urge to subjugate and victimize her lover leads to such excesses that at long last he rebels against her and the Romantic World of Night. At last he rises to his feet, and sets out to destroy the parallel world.

In *Manon Lescaut*, the hero, having already called himself "dirt in dirt," Manon's "slave and victim," makes an appalling spectacle of himself before the entire town of Le Havre, groveling on his knees in the dirt, kissing the hand of the transport ship's captain, and begging to be put to the most menial work possible, all for the sake of Manon. In *La Bohème*, the hero, unable to work unless his muse is near him, and racked by memories of her, sits home alone, stroking his lover's bonnet and thinking sad thoughts of her, while she is reportedly out on the town with another man. In *Tosca*, the heroine shoves her lover aside and becomes the indisputable hero of the story, knifing the dreaded Scarpia to death before flying to the attempted rescue of her man. He, in contrast, spends the entire second and third acts as a bound, tortured, helpless prisoner, and when she comes to rescue him, she finds him weeping. In *Madama Butterfly*, the heroine revenges herself on the weakling man who betrayed her by saddling him with the crushing guilt of her violent suicide, carefully arranging things so he will find her at the precise moment of ultimate horror. In so doing she ensures that he, who had so lightly forgotten her, will never spend another moment free of torturing thoughts of her. In *La Fanciulla del West*, the heroine enslaves her lover, turning him into a piece of property that serves as a gambling wager, and repeatedly exulting, "He's mine!" Subsequently captured by the miners, he is handed as property from one man to the next, then he listens in silence, his arms bound, while the miners and Minnie argue over who owns him. In *La Rondine*, the heroine's urges begin to turn sick, and she forces her lover into the role of child. She deceives him at every turn, lying to him about her past and even her name, and ultimately decides the course of his life for him while addressing him as though she were his mother and he was her "dear little son." In *Suor Angelica*, the tenor character has shrunk into nothingness, and he whom the heroine loves actually IS her son.

As the curtain finally rises on *Turandot*, we see the soprano character has gone mad with power. With no new and exquisite way remaining for her to subjugate and humiliate the tenor character, she has decided to murder him. The rose has ceased to exist as a symbol, for the Princess Turandot scorns love. She does have an awe-inspiring beauty and power, however, and the result is that the Romantic World of Night is now dominated by the presence of a huge, cold, dead-white moon.

Whether or not Puccini had admitted to himself that death was approaching him and *Turandot* would be his final opera, it is beyond question that the subject of that opera is the end of the Romantic World that had stumbled into existence in *Le Villi*, and then firmly established itself in *Manon Lescaut*. Through the efforts of Calaf, the only male hero of the Rose Cycle, Puccini planned to accomplish the complete destruction of the Romantic World of Night, now moon-haunted, and ruled by a murderous heroine who gladly made Alberich's Choice of power over love. To replace that Romantic World, which he had dearly loved but which had run its course, Puccini planned a new world — filled with sunlight and peopled by a hero and a heroine whose love would be fully sanctioned, and who would live and love each other as equals.

But this was not to be. *Turandot* was suffering massive plot problems in the final scenes when Puccini sought treatment for throat cancer, and tragically, he died from complications of that treatment, leaving his opera uncompleted. The core of these plot problems has never been identified before. Critics have spoken of the cruel nature of the princess, who cannot logically be converted into a person whom the audience likes, and of Calaf's relatively unfeeling treatment of his father and of the slave girl Liu, who loves him. But in truth these are not very difficult problems, and the libretto could easily have been adjusted to eliminate them if Puccini had not been facing a far more severe problem with the libretto, that was clouding his vision.

The real problem with the libretto of *Turandot* is quite obvious, and Puccini himself hinted at it in a letter he wrote on September 13, 1921. This letter was addressed to Renato Simoni, the theater critic and playwright who may have suggested the subject of Turandot to him, and who was co-writing the libretto. In part the letter reads as follows:

> I am sad and discouraged. I think of *Turandot*. It is because of *Turandot* that I feel like a lost soul. That second act! I cannot find a way out.... Should we do what is done in *Parsifal*, with a change of scenery in the third act, finding ourselves in a Chinese Holy Grail? Full of pink flowers and full of love?[13]

What went wrong in *Turandot* is the same thing that went wrong in *La Rondine*, turning the finale of *La Rondine* into one of the most bizarre sights ever witnessed on an opera stage. I am referring, in both operas, to the massive amount of material Puccini had shoehorned into their librettos, after having in desperation lifted this material bodily from the libretto of Richard Wagner's *Parsifal*.

3

The Dramatic Influences of Wagner and the Conclusion of the Rose Cycle

It should be obvious why Puccini had such difficulty finding suitable subjects for his operas. The only thing that appealed to him was the specialized material of medieval-style *romance*, stocked with moon, flowers, night, and passionate love between a young, beautiful, and powerful heroine and her happily subservient lover.[1]

If one reads Puccini's librettos carefully, giving special attention to the stage directions, he'll realize the works have real dramatic depth. The physical and psychological actions are filled with fine detail, much of which Puccini surely knew would not be understood by the audience, assuming they even noticed it.

An example of this is the silent attempt by Rodolfo, near the close of *La Bohème*, to suspend Musetta's cloak across the garret window. The stage directions are lengthy and precise as to how Rodolfo goes about trying to beat the deadly sunlight back from Mimi's face, but his actions, which are now always cut in performance, must be mystifying to anyone who has not studied Puccini closely.

Puccini urgently needed to be excited by his plot. In the fall of 1920, he wrote a letter to Renato Simoni, expressing a fear that *Turandot* would never be finished. "When the fever abates," he wrote, "it ends by disappearing altogether, and without fever there is no creation; because emotional art is a kind of malady, an exceptional state of mind, an over excitation of every fiber, of every atom of one's being, and so on ad aeternum."[2]

The fine and sometimes strange-seeming details of Puccini's stage directions surely helped to keep that fever burning. It may well be that these elements mattered to Puccini solely because of their effect on his state of mind while composing, and that he was unconcerned about whether his audiences ever fully grasped them.

The influence of Richard Wagner on Puccini has been frequently remarked on. Puccini esteemed Wagner's music greatly, once declaring of the score of *Tristan und Isolde* that compared to it, "...the rest of us are mandolin players."[3] It is well known that *Parsifal*—based on another great medieval tale in the *romance* style—was Puccini's favorite opera. Friends told of how he would sit for hours at his piano, playing from the score of Wagner's final work.[4] Whenever Puccini's artistic fever cooled, he felt the urge to open a Wagner score, especially *Tristan*.

One writer on Puccini has remarked that a perceived similarity to *Parsifal* in the prelude of *Le Villi* seemed strange, for in his words, Puccini was "the least Wagnerian of composers."[5] In one sense that is true, for as a thoroughly German composer Wagner was focused on the orchestra, while Puccini followed the Italian tradition of opera in giving preeminence to the voice.

But in another sense, that statement could not be more wrong. Puccini was clearly influenced by Wagner's innovations with harmony and orchestration, as well as his technique of "endless melody." Several of Puccini's musical themes seem to have been built on motifs from *Tristan*, and he made his own, quite beautiful attempt at a version of a Tristan-like endless melody when composing *La Fanciulla del West*.

Puccini also admired some of Wagner's compositional ideas. The musical substance of *Manon Lescaut*'s Act Two dancing lesson and love duet, for example, were likely modeled on Wagner's use, in *Tristan*, of music to relate the idea of sexual intercourse. The *Manon* love duet clearly depicts in music a sexual act complete with buildup, explosive orgasm, and rapturous afterglow, while the dancing lesson, in which the elderly Geronte partners the teenage Manon, just as clearly depicts an old man's attempt at intercourse that ends in humiliating failure, when Geronte loses his musical erection.

But Puccini was particularly drawn to *Tristan und Isolde* because the libretto featured that one subject that never failed to excite him: the romance of a pair of illicit lovers who live rapturously in the Night, and fear the coming of Day. Both composers displayed, in their operas, a real obsession with death. The difference is that Wagner's characters believe there is some glorious metaphysical payoff in dying, while to Puccini, dead meant dead.

La Fanciulla del West is often pointed to as a libretto that contains numerous borrowings from a wide variety of Wagner's works, but if so, the borrower was the playwright David Belasco, not Puccini. Every one of Puccini's alleged Wagnerisms was in the play before the composer ever saw it, except perhaps the last act manhunt, which Puccini invented and which might have been inspired by the *Parsifal* scene of Kundry's wild approach on horseback.[6] It is only with Puccini's next work, *La Rondine*, that we see him indisputably beginning to borrow directly from one of Wagner's librettos. *La Rondine*'s Magda and Ruggero are the first characters Puccini modeled on characters from Wagner, and following them are Liu, Calaf, and Turandot. All five of these characters are Puccini's versions of Parsifal and Kundry.

The libretto of *Suor Angelica* also evidences major borrowing from *Parsifal*, but the character absorbed into that opera was neither Parsifal nor Kundry, but rather Amfortas, who committed a sexual transgression and longed for death to deliver him from his endless, agonizing punishment.

It is tempting to speculate about whether Puccini, while composing *La Fanciulla del West*, in any way connected Minnie Falconer's redemption of Dick Johnson with the actions of Parsifal, but there can be no question that in his subsequent opera, Puccini was not only identifying his main characters with ones from *Parsifal*, he was actually, and disastrously, attempting to incorporate into his libretto several major scenes from that opera.[7]

And yet, strangely enough, since the moment *La Rondine* appeared critics have been sneering at it as *La Traviata*–lite. They point to Puccini's fragile Paris courtesan, who leaves her wealthy protector for an ardent and penniless young man, then gives him up when his respectable family calls, and they shout "Verdi!" They have been shouting the wrong name. Also shouting the wrong name are those who, having observed *La Rondine*'s comic maid who makes an attempt to go on the stage, and who goes to a party dressed in clothes she filched from her mistress, have called out "Strauss!"

As obvious as these borrowings are, I believe that in Puccini's mind they were irrelevant. He probably dismissed the criticisms as untrue, because he wasn't thinking about Verdi and Strauss, he was thinking about Wagner, and about his own earlier operas.

Puccini was sensitive to accusations that he repeated himself, and yet there is a great deal of recycling in *La Rondine*. Numerous incidents appear to have been brought in from *Manon Lescaut* and *La Bohème*, and there is even a small but significant bit from *Le Villi*. What with *Parsifal* in its pages as well, *La Rondine* must be the strangest amalgam in all of opera. Because *La Rondine* is not a well-known work, I will briefly relate the plot before pointing out the material from *Parsifal* and detailing how this opera advances the story of the Rose Cycle, which it does in a fascinating and shocking way.

Synopsis of *La Rondine*

Act One of *La Rondine* (The Swallow) opens at sunset, in the Paris home of Magda, the lovely young mistress of Rambaldo, a wealthy and cold-hearted banker. Present are three male and three female friends, the poet Prunier, and Magda's maid Lisette (who is having a clandestine affair with Prunier).

When Prunier is unable to think of an ending for his new song, "Chi il bel sogno di Doretta" (Who can explain Doretta's beautiful dream?), Magda invents and sings a romantic conclusion to it. Prunier rewards her with a tribute of roses strewn at her feet, and Rambaldo gives her a pearl necklace, which seems to embarrass and distress her.

Magda recalls a romantic night long ago, when she went to a nightspot called Bullier's, where she met and danced with an ardent young man. The boy bought her a glass of beer, and recklessly gave the rest of his tiny all to the waiter in an extravagant tip. The brief encounter ended with Magda inexplicably running away. She never saw the boy again. Now she is Rambaldo's melancholy mistress.

A visitor now arrives: a very young man, come to see Rambaldo with a letter of introduction from his father. This is Ruggero, who is soon established as an utter naïf—simple, artless, and virginal. (Ruggero does not see Magda in this scene.) The guests suggest various places where a newcomer to Paris might go on his first night in town, and their unanimous choice is Bullier's.

After her guests leave, Magda thinks things over. Night has fallen. She goes to her room, then emerges wearing one of Lisette's dresses. She takes one of her tribute roses from its vase, and tucks it in her hair. She is going to Bullier's; back to the place where love once bloomed for her. But can she pass? Will anyone see through the rose, to what she really is? Before leaving, Magda studies her face in a mirror. "But really," she assures herself. "Who would recognize me?"

Act Two is set at Bullier's. Young people swarm through the dance hall, celebrating the night with wine, love, and revels. Flower sellers are everywhere, crying, "Fresh flowers! Fresh flowers! Violets! Beautiful roses!" Ruggero sits alone at a table. A group of pretty girls are intrigued, and they flirt with him. This annoys Ruggero, and he refuses to speak in response to their demands that he tell them his name. Finally the girls leave, and Magda appears at the top of the stairs. Sighting this stranger, a group of young men try to flirt with her. When Magda refuses them, seemingly shy and confused, they demand to know whom she is meeting. Her eyes light on Ruggero, and the young men lead her to his table, then go off laughing. Ruggero is confused. Magda apologizes, and offers to leave, but this display of shyness wins him over. They dance, then he orders two beers. Delighted by the re-enactment, Magda asks him to tip the waiter the same amount as her first young man, but she does not explain why. Magda offers Ruggero a toast: "To your many loves!" He is indignant, and vows that if he were ever to love it would be "...only once, and for all my life!" He asks Magda her name, and she lies to him, calling herself Paulette. Now Prunier and Lisette enter and join them, not revealing Magda's identity to Ruggero. The two couples rejoice in their love, and the young men and women of Bullier's shower the four lovers with flowers. Now Rambaldo arrives, and Prunier hurries the oblivious Ruggero out of sight. Magda tells Rambaldo all is over between them, and with dignity he leaves. It is dawn, and the exhausted revelers have gone home. Bullier's is a depressing sight, with overturned wine glasses, disordered tables, and dropped and crushed flowers. Ruggero reenters, and in his youthful innocence he seems like a ray of hope. "Shall we go?" he suggests gently. The couple exit into the dawn, filled with love and, on Magda's part, intense fear that this beautiful dream — Doretta's beautiful dream — will not last.

The final act begins at late afternoon. Magda and Ruggero are living together on the Côte d'Azur. The lovers are having tea on a terrace a short distance from the sea, which is visible. The mood is narcotic, and "the air is saturated with the scent of flowers." Swallows are flying in the distant sky. Says Magda, "Our love was born amid the flowers." Answers Ruggero, "My very life is amid the flowers." Magda runs to gather roses, and "gracefully throws rose petals on Ruggero." The two are besotted with flowers and with one another. We might be in the land of the lotus-eaters.

The mood changes when Ruggero tells Magda he has a secret: he has written to his parents to ask for money to pay their many debts. Magda is dismayed, but he only laughs, saying, "Let's go begging: 'Who will open their doors to two impoverished lovers?'" This distresses Magda even more, but then Ruggero tells her the rest of his secret: he also wrote his parents for permission to marry her. Magda is stunned. Ruggero paints a picture of married life at his parents' home, where their love will find "the sacred protection of my mother against all anguish and away from all pain!" And perhaps one day there will "...sweetly appear the tiny hand of a little child."

The young man goes to see if an answer to his letter has arrived. Magda is filled with terror. Should she tell him who and what she is, or should she keep silent? (Ruggero never speaks her name during this act, but he clearly still believes her to be Paulette, who wears clothes suitable for a servant girl.)

After an interlude with Prunier and Lisette, in which the poet tries to convince Magda to return to Rambaldo, Ruggero excitedly returns, waving a letter he urges Magda to read. When he says it is from his mother, Magda "staggers, dreadfully pale." She takes the letter and reads it aloud. Mother expresses a wish that the woman who has touched her son's heart "...be blessed, if she be sent by the Lord." Mother speaks of the chosen bride as the future "...mother of your children, for it is motherhood that renders love sacred." The letter concludes with, "Give her my kiss." Ruggero moves to kiss Magda's brow, saying, "My mother's kiss!" But Magda pulls back quickly, crying, "No! I cannot receive it!" The young man is baffled. Magda cries, "I must not deceive you! I was contaminated before I came to you! Triumphantly I passed between shame and gold! I cannot deceive you!" (Note that Puccini is not accusing Magda of any sexual transgressions. Her "shame" lies in her having chosen gold over love — Rambaldo over the young man at Bullier's.)

Ruggero shouts, "Who are you? What have you done? Don't tell me more! What deception?" He is in agony, but Magda tells him, "Your mother is calling you today, and I must leave you because I love you and will not be your ruin! Remember that the sacrifice I offer in this hour I make for your sake." Ruggero begs her not to go, but Magda says, "Let me speak to you as a mother to her own dear little son." She "gently caresses his hair," and finishes with, "You return to your serene house; and I to my [swallow's] flight and my pain. Say nothing more. Let this pain be mine!" Ruggero "throws himself down, sobbing," and as the curtain drops Magda sadly exits amid the first evening shadows.

La Rondine: A Rose Cycle Perspective

There is obviously a great deal to be wondered at in this astoundingly Oedipal story, the Italian libretto of which was written by Giuseppe Adami, based on an original German libretto written for Puccini's use and revised at will by Adami, in accordance with instructions by the composer. The text of the German libretto has not survived. Adami translated it into Italian, and he and Puccini then spent over a year thrashing it into shape.

Before we take up the subject of the scenes Puccini borrowed from *Parsifal*, let's have a look at what is happening in *La Rondine* in respect to the Rose Cycle story.

La Rondine opens at sunset, so at first it seems all is well. Darkness falls, and there is the great scene of the Night of Love, set in a place filled with ardent young people and flowers. Sunrise comes: the time of great peril. A distant voice warns Magda of the danger of dawn. "Do not trust in love," warns the voice, and Magda "trembles and weeps." The lovers in *La Fanciulla del West* were able to survive daybreak, yet all were weeping at their exit, which had the flavor of death. Will the lovers of *La Rondine* do any better?

The final act is set at late afternoon, and the lovers are outside, under the sun. This seems disorienting and even distressing, for the last time we encountered broad daylight was in Act Two of *Madama Butterfly*, when vicious rumors were being spread about Butterfly's son, and Sharpless came to tell her Pinkerton had forgotten her. How is it the *Rondine* lovers seem to be prospering in this horrible daylight? We who have been following the Rose Cycle need an explanation. A scoffer might attempt to argue from a utilitarian point of view, declaring it means Puccini had used up sunset and night in the previous two acts, and thus decided to use some other part of the clock in the final scene. But that argument doesn't hold up.

We will observe that Magda has made an attempt to move out of Night, where illicit love thrives, and into Day, where sanctified love thrives. This cannot of course succeed, and in fact the Côte d'Azur is not a place of sanctified love (that place is Ruggero's mother's house), it is a hiding place. This is what Prunier has come to tell Magda. This is what he means when he says, "Sooner or later you will have to abandon an illusion that you think is real."

Ruggero is not an Artist—a passionate young man of Night, with its frenzied, illicit, moonstruck love. Ruggero is a boy of Day, who wants to marry Magda and move in with his mother and have a baby. (Or at least, find one under a cabbage leaf.)

This division in *La Rondine* between Night and Day is the original, classic division from medieval *romance* tales like that of Tristan and Isolde. It is the division of illicit love that hides in the night from spying eyes, from married love that welcomes the light of day. We had largely forgotten in Puccini that that was the original purpose of the divide between Night and Day, because Puccini had so strongly associated Day with physical death, and Night with the only kind of love that existed.

Despite the somewhat justified criticism that he repeated himself, Puccini made sure he was moving forward in every opera—not only in terms of compositional style, but also in his plots. This included moving forward in the dynamic of the male/female relationship. In *Fanciulla*, Puccini began to explore the possibility of his lovers moving out of Night and into Day. That is why Minnie and Dick Johnson are able to survive the coming of dawn, and why that survival is at the same time filled with such grief. Despite his need to move the lovers into a new phase of their relationship, Puccini clearly didn't *like* Day. The sanctified, married love that thrives in Day appears to have thoroughly bored him.

The *Rondine* character who speaks for Puccini is Prunier, whom Puccini described in a letter to Adami as "more or less the philosopher of the piece." He went on in this letter (undated, but perhaps written in early 1916) to suggest that in Act Three Prunier take Magda aside for a few words regarding her having run away from Night with the innocent Ruggero. In this letter, Puccini suggested that Prunier take Magda aside for a moment and tell her, "'My dear, I know that he wants to marry you, and that is impossible. You were not born to live cooped up in Montauban.' And with that he begins to mock at the old woman and the house and the kind of life they represent."[8]

We should be aware that absolutely no suggestion is being made that Magda, a sexually independent woman, is "unclean," and thus "not good enough" for the thoroughly middle-class Ruggero. Magda's self-accusation referred to her association with gold, which debars one from love in Puccini's World, and Prunier declares that she and Ruggero cannot marry because they are opposites— Night and Day opposites. In the final version of the libretto, Prunier says to Magda, "...this is not the life for you, with its trivial renunciations and nostalgia, with the vision of an honest home in which to bury your love, like the tomb!"

Against his own deep-rooted feelings on the subject, Puccini would continue, in *Turandot*, his effort — begun in *La Fanciulla del West* and more firmly attempted in *La Rondine*— to move his lovers out of Night and into Day, with a sanctified, married, boring love.

The cycle is edging toward its conclusion. Throughout Act One of *La Rondine* we see that the rose has lost some ground since *La Fanciulla del West*. It has slipped from the status of totem, and is back to being a symbol of the rebirth of love. But this meaning is still understood by the characters, which is why Prunier rewards Magda's partial composition and singing of the song of Doretta by strewing red roses at her feet. It is also why (or rather, it is *partially* why) the flower vendors of Bullier's are selling roses, and why the pavilion at the Côte d'Azur is wound about with climbing roses, which Magda picks and scatters on Ruggero.

Rambaldo is the opera's Alberich, and he is more dead inside than any other of Puccini's gold-contaminated characters. Witness the following passage from Act One, which takes place just after Prunier and Magda have finished singing "Doretta's beautiful dream." In respect to love, Prunier states that in everyone's soul there is a romantic devil stronger than anyone.

> RAMBALDO: "No! My devil is asleep!"
> YVETTE: "What a shame! Why?"
> RAMBALDO: "I arm myself with holy water and defeat him. Would you like to see it?"
>   (He takes from his pocket a jewel case containing a pearl necklace and gives it
>   to Magda.) "There!"

In Puccini's World, Rambaldo's offer of jewelry is an insult to Magda, but a deserved one, for she is a Vacillator who rejected an impoverished, and thus ideal, young lover in favor of the middle-aged Rambaldo's gold. In giving her the necklace, what Rambaldo is essentially saying is, "The poet may have given you an Artist's tribute for your song, my dear, but we two know what you really are. Here's your payment." Magda quickly gets rid of the humiliating object, handing the pearl necklace to her friends without looking at it. The friends admire it eagerly, but the stage directions tell the actors to examine it *not* with an eye to its beauty, but rather to its cost. It's obviously all but impossible for the actors to convey this to the audience, but it was important to Puccini to know that his characters were doing it. Notice too a possible parallel with Wagner's *Rheingold*, in which the Rhine Maidens love their gold not for its value as riches, but rather for its beauty. It would be interesting to know whether it was significant to Puccini that Rambaldo's necklace is of pearls, which come from beneath the water.

Near the end of the party, Magda is seen holding the necklace once more. The soprano is directed to twirl it around carelessly in her hand, then drop it on a table and never look at it again. Having treated the Alberich's gift of jewelry as worthless, it is clear that Magda the Vacillator is ripe for repentance.

It is also clear that Rambaldo the banker is in worse shape morally than Jack Rance of *Fanciulla*. The sheriff still longed for the heroine's love, but in Rambaldo the love of gold has resulted in "soul death." He desires Magda, but there is no passion remaining in him. Not even lust. This makes Magda's association with him particularly terrible.

In addition to being the opera's philosopher, Prunier is its Artist, and for the first time since *Tosca* we have a practicing, professional artist in the role. And yet Prunier comes off as a distasteful character. Not because he is having an affair with the maid Lisette (whom he hopes to promote to Artist stature by launching her on a singing career), but because he appears to play a shabby part by trying, in the final act, to convince Magda to return to Rambaldo.

To a degree Prunier has prostituted himself, but less so than Magda. While he moves willingly in the society of the Alberichs in exchange for a good meal and some amusing company, he has one foot planted firmly in the world of Art. Prunier does not take money for his art. He did not display any interest in the pearl necklace, and he understood what it represented. The woman he has chosen to love is a servant. And he conceived of Doretta, who rejected the advances of a king and dreamed of the coming of a poor student, who would love her as no rich man could.

After the strewing of the roses, Prunier has another moment of glory in the Bullier's scene, when Rambaldo comes to confront Magda. Prunier goes to meet the banker, who silently extends his hand. According to the stage direction, Prunier takes Rambaldo's hand in his own, and looks at the banker's ring. "Oh!" he exclaims. "What a big emerald!" This offends Rambaldo, who brusquely says, "Leave me alone, please!" It is obvious why Rambaldo is offended. In the parallel world of the Rose Cycle, there is no better way of declaring a man unworthy of a beautiful young woman than by remarking on his possession of wealth. As Rambaldo is on his way to see Magda, Prunier might just as well have stared at the banker's nose and said, "Oh! What a big wart!"

It's easy to misinterpret the role played by Prunier in the final act, in which he comes to the pavilion where Magda and Ruggero are living. In part he has come to return Lisette, whose singing career did not work out. But he has also come to speak to Magda on behalf of Rambaldo, who wants his beautiful mistress back.

At first glance it might appear that the values of the Rose Cycle Artist had completely broken down, for here is a poet trying to convince a lovely young woman to return to the man who deliberately put his romantic devil to sleep. But what is actually happening is that Prunier is telling Magda her love is passionate and sexual in nature, and she therefore belongs in the Night, not in the Day with a boy like Ruggero, who wants marriage, a home, and children.

Even if this were not the case, Magda would still have the problem of her theft of the identity of The Lady of the Rose. She is still a Vacillator who has not confessed to and paid for her crime against the community of Artists. And when she returns to the Night, exiting "amid the first evening shadows," she is not returning to passionate, illicit love, but rather to her soul-dead Alberich.

These inconsistencies simply point out why *La Rondine* did not achieve success. It is confused in several ways, and the story of the Vacillator who longed to live in respectable Day did not interest Puccini musically.

Images of *Parsifal* in *La Rondine*

It is at last time to speak of *La Rondine*'s Ruggero, who is neither Alberich, Artist, nor Vacillator. He is a nice young fellow of Day, so what is he doing in a leading male role in the Rose Cycle? Ruggero is in fact Parsifal the innocent, and playing opposite him is Magda, who is Kundry, the initiating woman who possesses all the knowledge the young man lacks. (Caveat: In order to follow the remainder of this chapter, familiarity with the plot of Wagner's *Parsifal* is essential.)

The flower-filled sites of Bullier's and the Côte d'Azur are Puccini's version of Klingsor's garden of the Flower Maidens. From the rise of the curtain on Act Two, through the conclusion of the opera, Puccini will be incorporating into *La Rondine* the *Parsifal* scenes of Parsifal's encounter with the Flower Maidens, the Initiating Kiss of Kundry, and the Redemption of the Sinner.

Now, earlier in this chapter I stated it was the heroines of Puccini's last two full-length operas who were modeled on the character of Parsifal, yet here I am saying that in *La Rondine* it is Ruggero who enacts the role of Parsifal. To clarify what is admittedly a confusing situation, initially Ruggero and Magda respectively enact the roles of Parsifal and Kundry — the innocent boy and the beautiful temptress who leads him into sin. A few minutes before the final curtain drop, however, Puccini has his two characters switch roles. Magda thus takes on the task of redeeming Ruggero from the sin into which she has drawn him.

To set the stage, at the beginning of Wagner's opera, Parsifal arrives at a place called Montsalvat. In Puccini, Ruggero arrives from a place called Montauban. Parsifal, who on arrival speaks of his mother, is the "guileless fool." Ruggero, who on arrival speaks of his father, is incredibly naïve, and is deceived by almost everyone he meets.

The first words spoken in the Bullier's scene are "Fresh flowers! Fresh flowers!" The stage directions describe "a great profusion of flowers in vases on the tables in the hall and in the loges." With flowers sitting unattended in vases on every table it is unlikely anyone would expend money buying them, yet, "flower girls mingle with the crowd," crying out violets and roses.

We are in Klingsor's garden, and soon we are shown Puccini's version of Parsifal's encounter with the Flower Maidens. Ruggero sits at a table, alone and silent. Beautiful girls swarm around the virginal young man, whose heart has never known what Wagner called "the tormenting flame of love." In the original garden of Klingsor, Parsifal does not know his name, and here Ruggero refuses to give his name to the chattering maidens who try to pique his interest.

As in Wagner, Puccini's maidens grow more demanding, chiding Ruggero for his coldness. Half angrily, with a gesture of irritation (Wagner's stage direction), Parsifal and Ruggero drive off their respective maidens. "We give [Parsifal] up for lost!" cry Wagner's Flower Maidens, and those of Puccini leave Ruggero, laughing, "He scorns our beds!"

Now Kundry enters the flower-filled garden. She is the one destined to awaken the tormenting flame of love in the heart of Parsifal the innocent. Magda descends the staircase and goes to the table where Ruggero is seated. Soon he will, for the first time in his life, fall passionately in love. This ends the Puccini scene of Parsifal's encounter with the Flower Maidens and his introduction to Kundry.

In the final minutes of the last act of *La Rondine*, we see a confused and effortful reworking of the *Parsifal* scenes of the Initiating Kiss of Kundry, and the Redemption of the Sinner. It is at this point that Magda and Ruggero switch roles, with her becoming Parsifal the redeemer, and him becoming Kundry, who is in need of purification.

To set the stage again, back in Klingsor's garden, as Kundry begins her temptation of the virgin Parsifal, she speaks to him of his mother. When she has done so, it is time for her to bestow the Mother's kiss that will, in a horrifying, incest-laden manner, awaken the sexual urge of Parsifal. Wagner's Kundry kisses Parsifal, having said, "She who once gave you life and being, to subdue death and folly sends you this day, as a last token of a mother's blessing, the first kiss of love."

Moving to Puccini's pavilion at the Côte d'Azur, Magda proceeds to read the letter from Ruggero's mother, who has written, "May she [the chosen bride] be blessed ... give her my kiss!" Ruggero draws Magda to him, saying, "Here is my mother's kiss!" As the bestower of the Mother's kiss, Ruggero has become Kundry; as the receiver of the kiss, Magda has become Parsifal. To be perfectly accurate, both Magda and Ruggero now have aspects of both Parsifal and Kundry at the same time.

Wagner's Parsifal and Puccini's Magda both draw back in terror from the Mother's kiss. Parsifal flings himself on his knees, crying out to God to know how he, a sinner, can be purged of his guilt. Magda (as Kundry) realizes she has drawn Ruggero (Parsifal) into sin, and she decides that she herself will purge the young man's guilt. She will redeem him!

"I cannot be your ruin!" she tells Ruggero (Parsifal). "Your mother is calling you today, and I must leave you because I love you and will not be your ruin! Remember that the sacrifice I offer in this hour I make for your sake. Say nothing more. Let this pain be mine."

Having brought salvation to the guileless fool whom she initiated into love and sin, Magda-Kundry-Parsifal exits to follow a path of suffering, while Ruggero-Parsifal-Kundry sinks slowly to the ground.

In commenting on *La Rondine*, critics have lamented the "weakness" of the tenor role. Puccini of course made Ruggero weak deliberately, compounding him out of his own standard, masochistic hero, and the guileless fool that is Parsifal.

That Wagner's Kundry awakened Parsifal's sexual urge by invoking his mother was extremely unfortunate for the development of Magda and Ruggero, for the very unbalanced power relationship between an all-knowing mother and the son whose maturity she has deliberately delayed (as Parsifal's mother did) fit quite perfectly into the sequence of highly sadomasochistic *romance* relationships Puccini had created, and resulted in a *La Rondine* couple whose sexual partnership is decidedly unsavory.

Having seen the tremendous amount of *Parsifal* material that is contained in the last two thirds of *La Rondine*, we should look back at Act One, where we will see something interesting in the scene of the pearl necklace, given by Rambaldo to Magda.

Magda has just finished singing "Doretta's beautiful dream," and Prunier has stated that in everyone's soul there is a romantic devil who is stronger than anyone. The following exchange then takes place:

> RAMBALDO: "No! My devil is asleep!"
> YVETTE: "What a shame! Why?"
> RAMBALDO: "I arm myself with holy water and defeat him. Would you like to see it?"
>   (He takes from his pocket a jewel case containing a pearl necklace and gives it to Magda.) "There!"

Rambaldo is Wagner's Klingsor, who castrated himself to destroy his sexual urge and then became a magician.

Images of *Parsifal* in *Suor Angelica*

The degradation of the tenor character having apparently reached its apogee in the enslavement of Dick Johnson and the infantilization of Ruggero, there would seem to be no further humiliation and torment that Puccini's domineering heroine could subject her lover to. What on earth will she do to the poor fellow in *Suor Angelica*?

Puccini sidestepped the issue in *Suor Angelica*. If the soprano treated her beloved like her child in *La Rondine*, he actually IS her child in *Suor Angelica*. There is nothing unseemly about this— nothing in *Suor Angelica* suggests any emotions other than those of a mother toward her son — but having followed the cycle this far we cannot fail to observe how perfectly the dynamic of the heroine and her beloved in *Suor Angelica* follows that of *La Rondine*. The father of Angelica's child is never mentioned. For all we know there was a virgin birth. The child is Angelica's beloved — there is no other.

So what is the material in *Suor Angelica* I claim was borrowed from *Parsifal*? In fact it is astonishing how much overlap there is between *Suor Angelica* and *Parsifal*. A number of these overlaps are probably coincidences, but several of them surely cannot be other than deliberate borrowings by Puccini.

To begin with, two of the major scenes of *Parsifal* take place in the hall of the Grail Knights. Theirs is an all-male, monastic society. *Suor Angelica* is set in a convent, which of course houses an all-female society of nuns. This can easily be dismissed as a coincidence, and indeed, Mosco Carner declared Puccini was doing a mirror-image of the all-male society in Massenet's *Le Jongleur de Notre-Dame*.[9]

Early in *Suor Angelica*, one of the nuns joyfully points out the order's fountain, which has a jet of water that spills into a basin on the ground. She has seen that the rays of the setting sun are about to strike the water. This is an annual event at the convent, lasting three nights. When the light strikes the water, it turns it the color of gold. In *Parsifal*, the great act of devotion that takes place in the Grail Hall is the uncovering of the Holy Grail, a crystal chalice housed in a golden shrine. When the chalice is uncovered, a dazzling ray of light shines down from above, striking the chalice and turning it a brilliant red. This, I think, is not a coincidence.

Also not a coincidence is that *Angelica*'s event of the golden water, described as "a shining sign of the goodness of God," takes place once a year, and lasts three days. We are told it is springtime — the month of May. To be precise, it is *quindena*, a Catholic feast day that falls 15 days after Easter. In other words, the story takes place on a day of celebration, the date of which is determined by the phase of the moon. (Easter falls on the first Sunday after the first full moon that occurs after the spring equinox.) Puccini has set his opera on his own version of Good Friday, which is the day on which the last act of *Parsifal* is set. He moved the date of his three-day celebration of the event of the golden water to *quindena* because in his opera, the chief deity is not the male God, but rather the Virgin Mary. In *Parsifal*, it is God who sends the ray of light that strikes the Holy Grail, causing Amfortas' father to exclaim, "How brightly our Lord greets us this day," and in *Suor Angelica* the nuns declare it is the beautiful smile of our Lady that comes with that ray.

Angelica could easily be likened to Parsifal's mother, whose name was Heart's Sorrow, and who died of grief after her son left her. I think it more likely that Angelica was modeled on Amfortas, who committed a sexual sin, and was sentenced by God to an unbearably long and tormenting punishment. Both Angelica and Amfortas had something forcibly taken from them — Angelica lost her son, and Amfortas lost the Grail Spear — and these losses both resulted in a torturing pain that will not stop until the lost thing is recovered.

What really proves the borrowing from *Parsifal*, however, is the scene in *Suor Angelica* that takes place between Angelica and her coldly cruel Aunt, who forced the girl into the convent and has never allowed her to see or hear from any of her family, including her little son. This scene, in which Angelica describes her terrible longing for her son, and her Aunt insists on never-ending repentance, is surely drawn from *Parsifal*'s first scene in the Grail Hall.

In that scene, Amfortas describes his searing pain — a pain that no repentance can ever still. He gives a long cry, twice, begging God for "Erbarmen! Erbarmen!" The word means, "Mercy! Mercy!" and Amfortas' cry is drawn out: "Erbaaaaaaaaaarmen! Erbaaaaaaaaaarmen!" In *Angelica*, the Aunt describes how she engages in a mystical communion with Angelica's dead mother, and how when the trance passes, she has only one word to say to Angelica: "Espiare! Espiare!" The word means, "Atone! Atone!" and the Aunt's cry is pitched and drawn out almost exactly like that of Amfortas: "Espiaaaaaaaaare! Espiaaaaaaaaare!" It appears that to Puccini, Angelica's cruel Aunt, who arranged and enforces the girl's long punishment, is God — the same God (except this one is female) who, in *Parsifal*, has arranged and enforces the long punishment of Amfortas. The Grail knight cries, "Mercy!" and the unpitying answer in Puccini is, "Atone!"

But with *Suor Angelica* done, and the beloved reduced to an actual child, what next? Puccini seems compelled to keep strengthening his heroine. In each successive full-length opera she must dominate the male in some new and more exquisite manner. But she must love him as well, while at the same time now playing the powerful role of redeemer. How can these three violently conflicting urges all be satisfied once more?

Images of *Parsifal* in *Turandot* and the Conclusion of the Rose Cycle

In turning at last to *Turandot*, we should first examine the relationship of Calaf's father Timur and the slave girl Liu, which has been completely misunderstood in the past, and which is the key to the conclusion of the Rose Cycle.

Liu describes herself as, "Nothing — a slave," yet between her and the blind, elderly Timur it is she who is all-powerful and he who is helpless. It does not matter that the girl's actions toward Timur are loving and deferential. What matters is that she saved him from death, "dried his tears" (his words), acts as his eyes, provides his food, and leads him wherever she decides he should go.

She calls herself a slave, but what is he? What is he, who was once a king, and who is now utterly dependent on a young, female slave? It is almost as though they were mother and child, in a continuation of the couple from *La Rondine*.

With those three conflicting urges to satisfy in his heroine—the urge to dominate, to love, and to redeem—what Puccini elected to do in *Turandot* was to split his standard soprano and tenor characters in two, resulting in two couples, both with dominating females and males in great peril.

The character of Liu contains all the sweet and gentle aspects of the previous heroines, so she will love and redeem. Turandot contains the killer instinct of the heroines whose power has been steadily growing since *Manon Lescaut*, so she will dominate. All the love Puccini's heroine normally feels for her lover has been allotted to Liu, while Turandot feels nothing but the urge to murder him.

What the two women share is something that a Puccini heroine cannot exist without, and that is the desire to totally direct the course of the tenor character's life—to dominate him completely. Recall Manon, who in the final moments of her life, as her despairing lover threatened suicide, told him, "with her last breath, imperiously": "I don't want that."

Liu's speeches are all pleading, yet in her final scene she shows the same single-minded determination to control the tenor character's life as the previous heroines did. When the Princess demands that Liu reveal the name of the Unknown Prince, the girl refuses, for it is her intention that Calaf will win Turandot for his own. It is irrelevant that this is also what Calaf wants. What matters is the exhibition of the heroine's control over the tenor character's life.

And Calaf's life is indeed in Liu's hands. If she reveals his name, he dies. If she doesn't, he lives and gets Turandot. And notice how skillfully Puccini snatched the task of winning Turandot away from Calaf and gave it to Liu! It simply went too much against his natural inclinations to utilize a male in the dramatic role of hero.

Liu knows what she wants for the tenor, and she means to have it, even at the cost of her own life. She has taken the role of redeemer much further than Minnie and Magda did. It will not satisfy Liu merely to rescue or renounce; she must be martyred, and so achieve true hero status.

As for the two males, the character of Timur has been given all the helpless love and dependency seen in the previous male leads, while Calaf has all the standard youth and ardor. He also has something never before seen in a Puccini hero, and that is the determination to throw off the shackles that have fit so comfortably on all his predecessors (and on Timur), and move out of the moonlit Night forever, and into the golden light of Day, dragging the woman he desires with him by main force, since she refuses to go with him voluntarily.

When Liu dies, just as the sun is rising, Timur follows her body as it is carried to the graveyard, vowing to rest beside her "in the night that has no morning." This very moment—the moment when the last soprano heroine dies at dawn and she and the man who loves her go to a realm of endless Night—marks the end of the Romantic World of Giacomo Puccini, built on the yearnings of medieval *romance* lovers like Tristan and Isolde. Puccini and his would-be hero Calaf must now usher in their new world, or the cycle will end not with chaos, but with a void.

Princess Turandot cannot conceive of a relationship between male and female that does not consist of one as the slave of the other. It is almost as though all through the Rose Cycle the soprano and tenor characters truly have been the same two people, only with different names, and playing a sadomasochistic game that grew increasingly rough, and now has spiraled totally out of control.

Looking at it from that perspective, it seems as though Turandot remembers the way she treated Dick Johnson and Ruggero, and fears the consequences, should Calaf gain power over her. That would be the reason why, when Calaf successfully answers the final riddle, Turandot turns to her father in a panic, crying, "You cannot give me to him, a slave dying of shame!"

The use in *Turandot* of the *Parsifal* scenes of Parsifal's encounter with the Flower Maidens and the Initiating Kiss is foreshadowed in Act Two by the emperor's ministers, Ping, Pang, and Pong. Just prior to the Contest of the Riddles, the three sing in hopeful anticipation, "Everything in the garden whispers, and the golden campanulas tinkle.... Words of love they breathe.... The dew shimmers on the flowers. Glory, glory to the beautiful unclad body that now knows the mystery it was ignorant of."

Calaf successfully answers the riddles, and then, like the knight of chivalry he is, he nobly gives Turandot a second chance to win. If the Princess can discover his name before dawn, he will submit his head to the Executioner's sword. Throughout the night in which no one sleeps, the people of Peking try desperately to learn the Unknown Prince's name, while he reposes in the royal garden, surrounded by flowers.

The young man's reverie is interrupted by the arrival of the three ministers into the garden. They parade before him a bevy of beautiful girls—the Flower Maidens—who are all for him if only he will give up his quest. (Parsifal's quest was of course the recovery of the spear that was lost by the Grail community when Amfortas succumbed to Kundry's sexual temptation.)

When the beautiful Maidens fail to move Calaf, the ministers offer riches and then power if only he will turn his back on love. (It's Alberich's Choice again.) This too fails to tempt the Prince. The ministers turn frantic, but moments later the soldiers come in with Liu and Timur in custody, and the scene of Liu's torture and suicide takes place.

The most difficult part of Puccini's struggle with the libretto of *Turandot* was the subsequent scene. His Princess had such a cruel nature that by the time of his death Puccini, despite having worked on the opera for years, had been unable to think of a satisfactory way in which she could be shown to have reformed, especially in light of Liu's suicide and Timur's consequent grief. Puccini touched on this problem in numerous letters, including the one to Renato Simoni that I quoted a part of in the previous chapter. Recall his comments regarding the need to "...reach the final scene in which love explodes.... Should we do what is done in *Parsifal*...?"

Puccini did do what was done in *Parsifal*, not just in respect to the scene with the Flower Maidens, but also those of the Initiating Kiss and the Redemption of the Sinner. Only this time, the latter two scenes are reversed, with the Redemption taking place before the Kiss.

And just as in *La Rondine*, the Redemption is carried out by the soprano heroine. Liu is the redeemer, and the redeemed is Turandot. In his difficult struggle to promote the tenor character to the role of hero, co-equal to the heroine, Puccini ironically (and in truth, predictably) only succeeded in erasing him from the picture completely. Now, only the two sopranos matter. As they face off against each other, the divided halves of one woman, the impotent Calaf, according to the stage directions, stands to one side, his arms restrained by Turandot's guards, and his feet tied together.

Liu has told the Princess that it is love that gives her heart the courage to withstand torture, and she continues as follows:

> "Such a love, secret and undeclared,
> such a great thing that these tortures
> are sweet to me
> Because I offer them to my **Lord**.
> Because, by being silent, I give to him,
> I give to him your love.
> I give you to him, Princess,
> and I lose all! And I lose all!
> Even the impossible hope!
> Bind me! Torture me!
> Give me torments and spasms!
> Ah! As the supreme offer of my love!"

In these lines, which could have been written by one of the Provençal poets whose knights longed to be tortured for love, or to suffer martyrdom for the sake of their Lady, we hear the words, not of the redeemer, but rather of the Redeemer, who has chosen to die in agony for the unforgivable sins of another. Liu is not giving Turandot to her *signore*, Calaf; she is giving Turandot to her **Signore**, God. By means of Liu's martyrdom, Turandot achieves a divine forgiveness, just as Kundry did when Parsifal baptized her. But we still need "the final scene in which love explodes...."

Puccini did not live to complete *Turandot*. On November 29, 1924, he died of heart failure following an excruciating treatment for the throat cancer that had been tormenting him for years. Composer Franco Alfano was enlisted to compose the final two scenes, with the aid of dozens of pages of notes that Puccini had left among his papers.[10] We can see the effect of one of these notes in the melting of the heart of Turandot—a melting that is brought about by Calaf's kiss, which awakens the tormenting flame of love in the heart of the virgin Princess. This kiss is the Initiating Kiss of Kundry.

That this has not been understood has been a great problem in the appreciation of the final scenes of *Turandot*. Some critics, not understanding what the Kiss had meant to Puccini, have mistakenly concluded he intended to say that all that was necessary for the man-hating Turandot to become a "real woman" was for a real man to grab her and give her a good, uh, "kiss."

Puccini of course meant nothing of the sort. In his doomed attempt to merge parts of *Parsifal* with his own libretto, it seemed possible that he might be able to do what Wagner had done: successfully rehabilitate his spellbindingly beautiful woman who had sinned beyond forgiveness.

But that was not possible, since no one in the audience would understand that Turandot had been granted a religious forgiveness. She appears simply to be deciding that life with Calaf would be nice, and from now on she'll be good. As she has not undergone such intense suffering as Kundry endured, nor even asked for forgiveness, the audience cannot accept that she should not only be forgiven, but should prosper as well.

Yet we must not overlook the fact that the final scenes of *Turandot* are not Puccini's work. They are Franco Alfano's work. Puccini hoped to create a new world for his heroine and his hero, but as fate would have it, he only lived long enough to destroy the old one.

As far as the work of Giacomo Puccini is concerned, his Rose Cycle — so strange, so personal, so beautiful — ends at the point where Arturo Toscanini halted the world premiere performance of *Turandot*. That is, it ends with the death of the heroine at dawn, and the promise of the man who had loved her to follow her and rest beside her forever, in the Night that knows no end. The Rose Cycle ends with the fulfillment of the waking dream of endless love in endless night, and perhaps that's for the best.

PART TWO

4

Le Villi

Libretto by Ferdinando Fontana
First performed at the Teatro dal Verme, Milan, May 31, 1884

Musically, *Le Villi* is a journeyman work, composed on a libretto by a writer with severe limitations. But it is also a fascinating opera, combining as it does Puccini's unalloyed delight in a sexually powerful female character, with Fontana's intense misogyny.

In Act One, the heroine conforms to Fontana's vision of the "good girl." Anna is gentle, passive, and utterly sex-less. Not surprisingly, the action is dull and cliché-ridden. Act Two, however, finds the good girl transformed into a Victorian gentleman's nightmare, and the result is electric.

The legend of the Villi is best known to music-lovers through the 19th century ballet *Giselle, ou les Wilis*, by Adolphe Adam. The singular is "Vila," and the word means "perish." To the Slavs who created the myth, a Vila is a young woman who died before her wedding day, was a suicide, or died unbaptized. She appears at night, and lures men to their death by inviting them to her grave.

In Fontana's version, the Villi are young women — that is, virgins — who have been betrayed by their lovers, and have died of grief and been transformed into vengeful ghost-maidens who spend their nights dancing frenetically in the woods. In the dark of night, deep in the forest, they wait in a sort of wolf pack for their faithless lovers to pass by. When one of the betrayers is spotted, the fiendish maidens pounce on the terrified man and force him to dance with them until he dies of exhaustion. One does not have to be Dr. Freud to suspect that a male fear of sexual inadequacy may lie behind this version.

One might be tempted to interpret the legend of the Villi as one that grants great power to women, for the Villi are young, beautiful, and able to revenge themselves on their masculine betrayers. We should not be deceived, however. There was a great vogue for such stories in the Europe of the 1800's: stories of female mythological creatures, and of women who took the form of animals or monsters (vampires were a favorite, and led to the "vamps" of the silent film era), and savagely preyed on decent men. At least in part these stories of young, beautiful, and evil women who can kill strong men surely reflected a 19th century sense of unease as to the awful things that might happen to society if those agitating women were able to gain a measure of power.

Along with the flower-girls, the moon-maidens, the cat-women, etc., the catalog of *fin de siècle* art is chock full of representations of madly dancing women. Some writers of the era offered a sober opinion that women liked and were good at dancing because, like savages and little children, also renowned for their pleasure in dancing, women had small and inferior brains. Those who are weak of mind, the theory went, make up for it by a focus on the body.[1]

Even a cursory examination of the libretto of *Le Villi* shows an attitude of utter revulsion towards women, whom Fontana represents in three ways: as the sexless madonna, the vile whore, and the evil witch. The men, interestingly, he depicts as either completely ineffectual (Guglielmo, the father), or as putty in the hands of feminine evil (Roberto, the putative hero).

Roberto and Anna, who are engaged, have the sort of romantic relationship one might expect from a "decent" young couple of the time. That is, they are essentially brother and sister. During the first act Roberto and Anna exhibit no sexual interest whatsoever in one another, so Puccini had nothing on which to build one of those explosive first-act finales he would become so famous for. But even though the music of Act One is not "exciting," attentive listening reveals a 17-jewel brain at work. All through the first act, Puccini is skillfully laying the groundwork, largely through rhythm, for a marvelous intermezzo and concluding act.

Subsequent to the first act, Roberto betrays his Anna by succumbing to the wiles of the *cortigiana vil*— the vile courtesan who lives in the big city where Roberto has traveled to collect an inheritance. The brokenhearted Anna dies of grief, turns into a Vila, and so gains an urge to dance madly in the woods at night and murder Roberto.

For his part, Roberto has been sucked dry by the evil, big city whore, and he fearfully returns to his simple woodland home. Reduced to rags; cold, frightened, and guilt-ridden; he clearly cannot wait to take his punishment from the vengeful ghost of Anna.

This sadomasochistic setup is just what Puccini needed to prime his musical pump. Act One contains what purports to be a love duet between Anna and Roberto, but the REAL love duet comes in Act Two, when Anna-the-Vila confronts Roberto over his betrayal, and the terrified Roberto realizes that Anna is going to kill him. This passionate duet, built on the music of Anna's grief as she pined away, climaxes on the duo's ecstatic singing of the drawn-out word *morrir*: DIE. This love duet is a tiny Liebestod!

There is a clear difference between Fontana's and Puccini's mutual fascination with the sexually independent woman. Fontana represents sex as filthy, with the courtesan having "lured Roberto to the obscene orgy." (This does indeed sound just like Giulio Ricordi's letter to Puccini, berating him over his affair with Corinna. See footnote 2, Chapter Two.) Puccini, on the other hand, is blissfully unaware of any such things as "filth" and "obscenity."

To Puccini — and I am speaking in terms of the stage, since I have no opinion whatsoever about the composer's personal life — sadomasochism is a game that greatly increases sexual excitement. And as it happens, his characters prefer having the woman in control, rather than the man. Puccini doesn't think Anna-the-Vila is a monster. He thinks she's wonderful. Throughout the Rose Cycle, his heroes are devoured by attractive, sexually powerful women — just as Samson, Don Jose, and countless other 19th century opera heroes are devoured — but Puccini thinks this is marvelous and exciting.

The powerful women and submissive men of his Rose Cycle are *having fun*. Compared to the neurotic characters created by Fontana and his ilk — the repressed men, the chaste little girls, and the sharp-toothed sluts— Puccini's passionate and devoted romantic couples seem, until we near the end of the cycle, pretty well-adjusted, if a bit kinky.

What keeps *Le Villi* from being Chapter One in Puccini's Rose Cycle is of course the first act, which is thoroughly anti–Puccinian in its rejection of sex. There is also a bit of a problem in Act Two, in the overt hostility of Anna-the-Vila towards Roberto.

In the coming works, Puccini will several times tease his audience with the idea of the heroine killing her lover, but until *Turandot* this is only a part of the erotic game. *Turandot* returns the couple to the action of *Le Villi*, with the fierce Turandot's declared intention to murder Calaf, and thus a perfect dramatic circle is described in Puccini's operatic cycle.

With its use of so many of the elements of Puccini's Romantic World — Alberich's Choice between gold and love, the association of the heroine with flowers and the moon, and a dominant/submissive relationship that explodes into passion at night — *Le Villi* is a promising introduction to the Rose Cycle.

The short, graceful, and lightly scored prelude to *Le Villi* is formed from several pieces that will be prominent in the body of the opera. We first hear, in its sketchy, introductory form, music that refers to Roberto's assurance to his worried fiancée, that she should, "Doubt God, but never doubt my love." Succeeding this is the "A" section of the choral prayer that will launch Roberto on his trip to the city, where he will indeed forget Anna.

Next we hear that portion of the prayer music that will recur in the remorseful Roberto's Act Two aria, "O sommo Iddio," in which he prays for one last moment of happiness before death. The "A" section of the choral prayer returns, followed by a reiteration of Roberto's "Doubt God" phrase.

The conclusion begins with a shimmering, redemptive-sounding repetition of "O sommo Iddio," and ends with the sounding of three soft notes that appear to be a gentle version of the three hammering notes that will conclude the opera. Puccini was extremely fond of "bracketing" both large and small sections of his operas in this way. It was one of his most workmanlike techniques, and one of the most satisfying.

The prelude, then, is entirely about Roberto — his promise, his departure, his failure and subsequent remorse — and it appears to grant him a forgiveness that he will not receive within the opera itself.

The action begins with Italian opera's traditional *coro d'introduzione* — the chorus of introduction. A happy group of mountaineers is gathered around a festive table in the middle of a forest clearing, clinking glasses, shouting *Eviva!* and preparing to provide exposition to the audience.

We are deep in Germany's Black Forest. At right is the humble dwelling of old Guglielmo Wulf, father of Anna. At left is a path that soon loses itself in the woods. At back is a small bridge that spans a hollow. It is late afternoon in spring, and everything is green and blooming. Garlands of flowers are hung all about.

The table is laden with bottles, glasses, and plates of food. Seated at its head are Guglielmo, Anna, and Roberto. Nearby stand a few musicians. The young couple's engagement is being celebrated, along with Roberto's imminent trip to the city of Mainz. Roberto is dressed for travel, and his suitcase sits on a chair.

After a few shouts of *Eviva!* and a congratulations to the betrothed couple, the exposition begins. To some light and cheerful accompaniment, the mountaineers explain that "the old woman of Mainz" made Roberto her heir. The treasures she hoarded up were many indeed, and although Roberto will go to the city a poor man, he will return a rich one and marry his beloved. It's Alberich's Choice!

The choice between gold and love will be one of the hallmarks of a Puccini libretto, and here it is in the first five minutes of his first opera! Roberto's bag is packed — he has succumbed to the lure of gold, and as a result he will lose his love. It would be terribly interesting to know whether Puccini was consciously aware of this element that would become an iron law of his Romantic World, but whether by design or by chance, an iron law it will be. A Puccini character can have gold, or love, but not both.

Notice, too, what the misogynistic Fontana has done. It is "the old woman of Mainz" who enticed Roberto to leave his home and his love. She hoarded up "treasure," and for some mysterious reason named the young man her heir. Some synopses of *Le Villi* state that the old woman is a relative of Roberto's, but that's not what the libretto says. The mountaineers call her simply *la vecchia di Magonza*: the old woman of Mainz.

There is a distinct suggestion of the witch in this treasure-hoarding old woman, and it is tempting to speculate on a connection between her and the *young* woman of Mainz; that is, the "vile courtesan" who will ruin Roberto and take all of the treasure. Could the old woman and the courtesan be in league? Could they (horrors!) be the *same person*? Wild speculation aside, it is a simple fact that two women, one old and one young, are to be the agents of the innocent young man's moral ruin, at which point he will return home to be killed by a third woman: his vengeful sweetheart. The poor Victorian-era male. Everywhere he looked there was a devouring female lying in wait! To round off the exposition, the chorus reprises their opening shouts of *Eviva!* A brief fanfare is then heard.

Le Villi is what's called an "old-fashioned number opera," which means there are no smooth transitions from one passage to another. Either there is a brief silence between numbers, or else there is an obvious seam, tacking the two blocks of music together. With *Manon Lescaut*, Puccini would demonstrate his mastery of the art of smooth transition, but here in *Le Villi* he evidences no interest in it. The fanfare, tacking the introductory chorus to the next number, is a very obvious seam.

That next number is the *Gira!* waltz, which is graceful, elegant, and startling in several ways. To begin with, German peasants would certainly not be waltzing. Musicians at this sort of gathering would likely play a traditional German folk dance for couples, like the Ländler. As the party got warmed up they would probably play a courtship dance like the energetic Schuhplattler. But Puccini was not interested in sounding authentically German in this opera, and he had a good reason for structuring this number as a waltz.

The waltz is in minor mode, and there is a strong pulse on the first beat of each triplet. What with the strange words sung by the dancers, this seems an oddly feverish piece of music for an engagement party. *Gira! Gira! Gira!* the dancers sing. "Turn! Turn! Turn! Jump! Turn! Jump! The music throbs in delirium, the dance propels us on!"

Both Fontana and Puccini are foreshadowing the Villi's dance of death. The dancers' cries of "Jump!" and "Turn!" will be repeated by the ghost-maidens, during their pursuit of the guilty Roberto, and the talk of "delirium" and of how "the dance propels us on" refers both to the maidens and their prey. Admittedly, this is an awkward bit of irony, since the words are so inappropriate in this initial appearance.

As for Puccini, he chose a waltz rhythm for this first dance because he is setting up the metric pattern that will dominate the entire score. Anna's upcoming *romanza* is another waltz, and the triplet is heavily featured in the music of the Intermezzo that describes her sad pining away and shows her funeral cortege. The culmination of all this triple-time music is the wild dance of the Villi, which is a tarantella. Puccini did not simply launch one rhythm and mechanically stick with it to the end, he is using rhythm to accomplish foreshadowings, and create opportunities for reminiscence. Although the *Gira!* waltz really does not fit in this opening scene, either in word or in tone, one has to admire what Puccini was attempting, and acknowledge how well the triplet pattern works in the subsequent scenes.

With the first section of the *Gira!* waltz done, the music changes character via a shift out of the minor. A faintly comical horn introduces the B section of the waltz, which is a lovely, pirouetting dance. The reason for the shift, and for the comical horn, is that the young people are inviting Anna's elderly father to join in the dancing. The old fellow agrees, and with a gallant gesture he invites one of the young girls to partner him. Skillfully they whirl about, to the applause of Guglielmo's friends.

Guglielmo now dances off with his partner, and the waltz returns to its original character. *Gira! Gira! Gira!* cry the dancers, and they too dance off, Anna and Roberto included. The last of the partygoers clear the stage, to the accompaniment of a lightly scored version of Guglielmo's dance. A sad wisp of this carefree dance music will recur in Act Two, revealing the regretful state of mind that causes Roberto to sing his anguished aria, "Torna ai felici dì" (My thoughts return to those happy days).

Anna had been on stage at curtain rise, but she is granted a diva's entrance now. She steps onto the empty stage, a cluster of forget-me-nots in hand. Although the association of his heroine with flowers would eventually grow as important to Puccini as an opening at sundown, in this first opera the flowers seem little more than a clichéd element of 19th century theater: Enter chaste heroine, with flowers. And yet the forget-me-nots do have a purpose, for Anna intends to sing her entrance aria to them, then tuck them into Roberto's suitcase where (she hopes) they will help him to forget her not.

There is a moment of silence as the soprano prepares for her aria. The heroine is indeed chaste in appearance, and being that this story is fueled by repressed sexual urges—Roberto is *lured* to the orgy by the vile courtesan; he is *forced* to dance with Anna and the Villi until he dies of exhaustion—it would be best not only to admit this, but to play it up when staging the work.

Anna should appear in Act One in very demure dress, her hair modest and restrained, and her makeup minimal. In Act Two she should appear as Fontana's nightmare/fantasy of the sexually devouring female—the human black widow spider—with an alluring costume, her hair loose and wild, her face heavily made up, her fingernails long and painted. In other words, the chaste maiden should throw off her clever disguise and reveal the vile courtesan whom Fontana knew was there all the time.

The few measures of introduction to Anna's *romanza* have a strangely chilly sound. Played mostly by woodwinds, and featuring a spare little two-note figure that alternates between rising and falling, it foreshadows that wintery music that opens Act Two of *La Bohème*, set in the dark, snowy morning at the Paris gate.

Anna's song, "Se come voi piccina," "If I were tiny" (like you, pretty flowers), is another waltz, and while it is pretty it is also rather lifeless—something for a china doll rather than a woman with blood in her veins. The problem for Puccini was that Anna feels no sexual passion. She sings to her flowers, wishing she were tiny like them, so she could always stay close to her love.

Strings and high woodwinds are again featured (the brass is saved for the Intermezzo, where it is employed in the "hunting" music of the Villi), and although the song has a sweet and old-fashioned sound, there is perhaps something just a little creepy in the closing words. Anna tells the flowers that they, luckier than she, will follow her love over hill and dale, whispering, "Forget me not!" And then she begins to hide the little bouquet in Roberto's suitcase.

It's a pretty thought—Roberto opening the bag in Mainz, and finding this token from his sweetheart—but if one is looking for sub-surface meaning he could find some in the fact that Anna is speaking to the flowers, hiding them in Roberto's luggage, and urging them to do something in respect to him. This is, after all, a *legend*—a story about young women who turn into supernatural creatures and savagely revenge themselves on faithless lovers. What with our already-existing suspicions about "the old woman of Mainz," it's worth considering whether there isn't something faintly threatening about the idea of the forget-me-nots secretly following Roberto all the way to Mainz.

To one who thinks this may be reading too much into a pretty little *romanza*, observe what happens next. While Anna is putting the flowers into the suitcase, the orchestra gives out some overwrought music (another unskillful transition), and Roberto enters and comes up behind Anna, and says, "Ah, I've caught you!" Case closed.

Roberto takes the flowers from the startled girl, kisses them, and places them inside the suitcase. He thanks Anna, but says he would prefer a smile from her. She shakes her head sadly, and we hear a faint reiteration of "forget me not."

Roberto assures Anna he'll be back in a few days, but Anna has had a prescient dream. She dreamed she was dying as she waited for him, and though awake now, she is convinced she will never see him again. The young man dismisses Anna's fears, and urges her to think instead of the happy days that lie ahead for them. "But do you really love me?" asks Anna worriedly.

Scarcely noticeable as it lightly carries this conversational *parlando* is the music of the upcoming love duet. Playing love duet music during pre-duet conversation is a signature technique of Puccini's, and he probably did it for both practical and dramatic reasons. The practical reason is that he is acquainting the ears of first-time listeners with the melody of a tune that is meant to be a highlight of the opera, so it will go over better when played in earnest. The dramatic reason relates to the organic nature of the score. The love duet music first sounds, unobtrusively, while the couple is talking of this and that. The music tells us their feelings for one another are growing, so when love finally explodes and the duet is played in earnest, it seems believable, being the culmination of a process.

The love duet of Anna and Roberto—"Tu dell'infanzia mia"—is notable both for what is said, and what is not said. The young man addresses his sweetheart as "my cherub," and in his opening solo section he reminds Anna that she, who "in my childhood shared joys and caresses," taught him the sweetness of life via her own sweetness and virtue.

Is it any wonder Roberto is such easy prey for the courtesan of Mainz? To Fontana, nice young men didn't speak of erotic passion to nice young women, so poor Puccini was handed the task of writing a love duet for a pair who will probably seal their upcoming goodbyes with a handshake.

Roberto goes on to allude to the all-important gold-versus-love dichotomy, reminding Anna that when he was poor, she promised to prize his love "above any rich man's." In other words, Anna was also offered Alberich's Choice, at least in theory, and she chose love over gold. The young man concludes his solo section with a dangerous suggestion; that is, that Anna should "Doubt God, but never doubt my love." So hubristic and impious is this that the audience is encouraged, even in advance of Roberto's betrayal of Anna, to conclude he will have to be punished.

Anna believes him, though. In her solo section she employs his same music, and prays that his sweet words will comfort her grief during the dark hours of waiting. She will, she says, repeat his words to herself again and again, and now she quotes them: "Doubt God, but never doubt my love." That she is quoting his words is significant. Fontana does not have Anna say, "I will doubt God." She only quotes Roberto, so the sin of impiety does not touch her. The two sing together for a few lines so as to close the piece as a duet, and they conclude with a calm, placid, passionless declaration of "I love you!" This, from the composer who would write the orgasmic love duet of Manon and Des Grieux!

Although there is no church in sight, a bell now tolls for the Angelus. It sounds four times, is briefly silent, then sounds four times more. Puccini uses tolling bells in almost every one of his operas, and they almost always signify imminent disaster or death. One could argue that is their meaning here, although in fact they are the transitional element leading us to Italian opera's traditional *Preghiera*.

Before hearing the Prayer, though, we should note that the mountaineers urge Roberto to hurry and be on his way "before the sun's merry ray has disappeared." A suggestion of stealthy footsteps is heard from the strings, perhaps referring to the Villi, or perhaps to forest dangers in general.

Question: Who sets out for a long trip, on foot, through a forest, at sundown? This is a decidedly strange time for Roberto to leave the village. And considering the environment of the story — Act One is relatively happy, set in spring; Act Two is scary, set in winter — it seems as though Act One should be in full daylight. Act Two is, after all, in the darkest night, with a full moon shining. Why, then, does Act One close at sundown?

Despite Puccini's love for a sundown opening for his operas, a different consideration seems to be at work here. Roberto is heading off to disaster, and after the act ends the next thing we will hear is the story of Anna's grief and death, and the next thing we will see is her funeral cortege. Following that will be this same clearing on a winter's night. The setting sun at the close of Act One seems meant to lead us into the gloom of the Intermezzo and the second act.

The mountaineers' calls to Roberto to hurry strike fear into Anna's heart, and Roberto says to her, "Anna, courage!" Limply, she answers that she fears she will die. This looks like a setup for a "logical reminiscence" at the end of the opera, when the terrified Roberto pleads with Anna-the-Vila, "Anna, pity!" while fearing HE will die.

The men of the chorus offer to see Roberto to the forest's edge, but he first asks Guglielmo to give him a blessing for the journey. Anna's father, now acting as communal Father, invites everyone to gather around, and they kneel for the choral prayer.

We hear music from the prelude as Guglielmo begins the A section. His vocal line is very simple. A solo clarinet is briefly heard during this section, but most of the accompaniment is soft, sustained chords, with the orchestra, especially the flute, doing a remarkably good impersonation of a church organ. Guglielmo asks the angel of God to take their prayer to the throne of the Lord.

The B section is led off by Anna, who is then joined by a few other voices, part-singing the second verse. The violin is featured here, and hope is expressed that the road will be propitious for every pilgrim, and that no dream of love will suffer disillusionment. (The latter hope of course is for Anna, and the former is for Roberto.)

Repeating the B section's words, Guglielmo uses new music for the C section. This is the music that will recur in Roberto's anguished "O sommo Iddio." The recurrence will be bitter, for the road was not propitious after all. Using this music, Roberto will then mournfully sing, "This is the end of my road." Despite this being a "number" opera, Puccini is intent on accomplishing unity, and so beginning with the *Gira!* waltz, words, rhythm, and melody are all being directed down a carefully laid out path, the goal of which is the confrontation between the relentless spirit of Anna and the guilt-stricken Roberto, and the Villi's wild dance of death.

Those who sang the preceding sections begin the reprise of the A section. Soon the full chorus joins in, singing behind them. The voices weave in and out, creating a tapestry of sound, in great contrast to the simplicity of the initial solo by the bass voice. The orchestra swells, with voices and music building to a great climax. The voices of Roberto and Anna are clearly discernible as a couple, and they are balanced by the deep voice of Guglielmo.

This is a lovely piece of choral writing, very like Puccini's other great choral prayer, that concludes *La Fanciulla del West*. The conclusion of the *Fanciulla* prayer, however, is much better than the conclusion of this one. Here, after a soft, peaceful reiteration of the music from Roberto's "never doubt my love," there is a brief pause. The orchestra then blares some excited sounds, and Roberto shouts, "Father, Anna, goodbye!" The rest of the cast respond, "Goodbye, Roberto, goodbye!" with Anna's soprano knifing through the mass of male voices.

As Roberto starts confidently down the forest path, the orchestra, trying desperately to sound heroic, first bellows the music of "You, who in my childhood shared joys and caresses," followed by Anna's "Forget me not," then "May the road be propitious!" and finishes up with some meant-to-be-impressive flourishes. The final tableau is a pretty picture of Roberto and his friends standing by the bridge, waving at the others.

To this point in the opera, Puccini has undoubtedly had a difficult time fitting music to the bland material, but with the start of the Intermezzo one can stop feeling sorry for him, because he is now very much in his element. From here on the opera will be filled with grief, terror, anger, sexual passion, and that sense of *muoio disperato*—"I die despairing"—that *Tosca*'s Cavaradossi put a name to, and that lurks within the breasts of all of Puccini's masochistic heroes. Except for the grief of Anna's father (which, because it is not sexual in nature, does not really move Puccini), the remainder of the story inspires the composer to some very good, and very exciting music, as well as to some excellent techniques, both musical and dramatic.

Part 1 of the Intermezzo is called "The Abandonment." Without orchestral accompaniment, a narrator declaims an eight-line poem telling of how the siren of Mainz, who "bewitched both young and old," lured Roberto to "the obscene orgy," where he forgot his love.

Note Fontana's conflicted, tangled perspective on this matter. The sexual woman has an almost super-human power that gives her the ability to drag even the most powerful men down into the gutter against their will. Not only are men helpless against this creature (who seems as non-human as the Villi), they are both guiltless and guilty at the same time.

They are guiltless because no man can successfully fight against a siren. (Even the great Odysseus had to have his crew tie him to the mast while they, their ears stuffed with beeswax, sailed their ship past the rocks where the deadly sirens sang their bewitching song.) And they are guilty because they know perfectly well, pretend though they might to the contrary, that they long for an uninhibited sexual relationship with a beautiful woman. Roberto is guilty, and he will have to be punished for having given in to his immoral lust. Or is he actually innocent, and Anna-the-Vila will kill him because all women, even the most chaste-seeming, are bent on luring men to their ruin?

Puccini, thank goodness, had no share in this neurotic mental conflict, and if the siren of Mainz had slunk onto his stage he wouldn't have had the faintest idea what to do with her; just as he had no idea what to do with the evil siren Tigrana (!), with whom Fontana burdened him in *Edgar*.

The narrator goes on to describe how Anna waited in anguish for Roberto to return, and how when winter came, "she closed her eyes in eternal sleep." The music that describes Anna's sad vigil begins softly, with strings, harp, and high woodwinds. The main rhythmic figure of "The Abandonment" is a climbing, winding triplet: three climbing notes, then a falling back by one step to begin the next three climbing notes. After a few moments, we hear women's voices chanting a *requiesce* for Anna. "Like a lily cut down," they sing, "in the coffin she lies. Like moonlight is the whiteness of her face. O pure virgin, rest in peace."

Again we have an association of the heroine with flowers, and now begins her association with the moon. Fontana's image is one that will recur in Puccini only with his final opera, *Turandot*. The image is that of a pure, bloodless virgin, who gains a killing power beneath the white light of a cold moon. Between *Le Villi* and *Turandot*, Puccini's inclination is for the moon to be the source of a warm and silvery light that grants the heroine beauty, strength, and passionate love.

Note too Fontana's description of Anna as a "pure virgin." In this version of the legend, those who become Villi are young women who were on the verge of becoming wives, but whose hopes were dashed by faithless lovers. Legend frequently grants virgins special powers; for example, the power to tame the unicorn. Even among real people, virgin status has been believed by some to confer special powers, as with Joan of Arc, the Maid of Orleans. Even England's Queen Elizabeth I had a special aura about her (which she carefully promoted), granted by her status as the Virgin Queen.

In a sense, to be a virgin is to be non-female — to have evaded the woman's "natural" role of wife and mother. Think of Miss Havisham in Dickens' *Great Expectations*. She is Dickens' version of a Vila, for she is a woman for whom time stopped when her lover jilted her at the altar, and who devoted the rest of her life to revenge on men. In truth, the antifeminists should have approved of the Villi, for like Miss Havisham these young women are acting out of anger at having been denied their natural, subordinate role of helpmeet and mother. At any rate, it is their spotless virginity that grants the Villi their power to kill men.

The music of "The Abandonment" grows more passionate, and the tempo accelerates. We are hearing a description of the longing in Anna's heart as she waited in vain for Roberto. Soon the curtain rises, and through a scrim we see Anna's funeral cortege, which emerges from Guglielmo's house. The music grows calm again as the *requiesce* is repeated by the singers.

That we have heard nothing like a funeral march is owing to the fact that Puccini intends to repeat this music during Anna-the-Vila's confrontation with Roberto. Puccini is not interested in Anna's burial; he is interested in her emotions during the vigil. When the confrontation takes place, Anna will first remind Roberto, with his own music, of how he swore eternal love, and urged her to doubt God, but not him. Then she will use the "Abandonment" music to describe the grief she felt as she waited for him, and how, with all hope gone, "...you made me die." This confrontation is the opera's actual love duet — the miniature Liebestod.

The curtain falls, and the narrator begins Part 2 of the Intermezzo, called "The Witches' Sabbath." The narrator recites another poem, this one sixteen lines, relating the legend of the Villi: a story that strikes terror in all faithless lovers. If one of these betrayers should be so unfortunate as to meet with the Villi during their nightly dance, the maidens laugh, and dance furiously with him until he dies of exhaustion.

Having gone through all of his inheritance, Roberto has been cast aside by the siren of Mainz, and, says the narrator, he has come home. He is in rags, and knowing the legend of the Villi he is trembling not only with cold, but with fear. Already he has reached the middle of the dark forest.

The curtain rises again, now revealing the clearing in winter. The trees that had been green and blooming are leafless, and laden with snow. The black sky is studded with stars, and the moon shines bright. Wills-o'-the-wisp enter from all sides and float above the scene, then the Villi come out to dance.

Their music is a tarantella, which is a fast dance for couples in triple time. Puccini could not have selected a more perfect style of music for the vengeful ghost-maidens who dance men to death, for the tarantella was once believed to be a cure for tarantism, which is a nervous affliction that manifests itself in hysteria and an uncontrollable urge to dance.

In the tarantella, the couples form a circle and dance clockwise until the music changes to a faster tempo. At that point they reverse direction, dancing faster. This pattern continues, with the couples changing direction each time the music accelerates, until it is impossible to keep to the beat. The tarantella suggests frenzy, compulsion, and eventual collapse from exhaustion, which is why Puccini chose it for his Dance of Death.

Puccini began the triplet pattern in the *Gira!* waltz (during which the dancers sang prophetically of how "the music throbs in delirium, the dance propels us on"), continued it in Anna's *romanza* to her flowers, intensified it in the winding, climbing triplets of "The Abandonment," and now brings the pattern to its wildest expression in the tarantella of "The Witches' Sabbath."

The Villi's dance is also a hunt for the betraying lover, and Puccini divides his orchestra to simulate the hunt. Different sections of the orchestra trade off short parts of the music, and at different volumes, and the impression given is of a quarry dashing here, there, back, forth, in a mad attempt to outrun pursuers. The brass comes out in full force, calling to the hunters.

We hear a hunting horn baying in pursuit, then pure dance music. The Villi will later chant *tra-di-tor*—betrayer—and we hear now the distinctive triplet pattern that will carry that accusation. Also heard are the orchestral cries of "Jump! Turn! Jump!" that first appeared in the *Gira!* waltz. The impression here is of a band of pursuers (maenads come to mind) whipping themselves into a frenzy, pausing to dance, then returning to the pursuit. The prey is caught, tugged back and forth and whirled in circles, then released, only to be pursued and caught again. An emphatic, pounding conclusion to the Intermezzo describes the kill, and the curtain drops.

Act Two begins with a mournful, dragging death march played by the horns. Guglielmo, sunk in grief, comes outside his home for his *scena ed aria*. The horns seem like a sad reminiscence of the one that invited him to dance at his daughter's engagement party.

As I already pointed out, there are several parallels between *Le Villi* and *Turandot*. Both have a heroine who is openly determined to kill the tenor lover. Both show her at her full, killing strength at night, beneath a huge, white moon. Another parallel occurs now, in Guglielmo's opening *recitative*, in which we hear words that we might have expected to hear from Timur, after the death of Liu. "No!" cries Guglielmo. "It is impossible that your guilt should not be punished.... What horrible offences did we ever inflict on you, that you should kill that angel and sadden my last days with such anguish?"

During his aria, "Anima santa della figlia mia" (O blessed soul of my daughter), Guglielmo expresses hope that the legend of the Villi is true, so Anna might be avenged. In other words, he gives the audience permission for them to enjoy Anna's transformation. The music of this aria is not terribly interesting, but its conclusion is notable for a little run up and down the scale by solo flute, overlapping Guglielmo's final line. Perhaps Puccini meant to suggest the ghostly voice of Anna, trying to comfort her father.

Guglielmo goes into the house, and the music of the Villi returns. We hear their eager voices from off stage, calling to one another and to Anna, for they have spotted Roberto, who has entered and is now walking onto the bridge. The betrayer approaches, and gleefully the maidens urge the damned soul to hurry on. (Roberto senses the presence of something that means him harm, but at this point he cannot actually see the Villi.)

Roberto now has a long solo scene, in which he enthusiastically indulges himself in a *muoio disperato*—"I die despairing." Almost all of the Rose Cycle heroes have what we may as well term a "masochism aria," and this is Roberto's. The young man is a pitiful sight; clad in rags and trembling with cold and fear. But those familiar with Puccini will realize that both he and Roberto are enjoying these sensations. Roberto has come back because like the knight of a medieval *romance*, he enjoys being made to suffer by his lady. Roberto wants to be punished by Anna; but he will stretch it out as long as possible, for a pleasure delayed is a pleasure enhanced. Roberto pauses on the bridge and looks toward Guglielmo's little dwelling. "Here is her house," he declaims in a monotone. It has been a horrid night already, and strange voices have been pursuing him. He tries to laugh off the legend of the Villi, but their music recurs, attacking his words and giving them the lie.

Descending from the bridge, Roberto continues to assure himself it is remorse alone that pursues him, not the Villi. He terms this remorse a *vipera dal veleno infernal*—a "viper of the poison infernal"—and Puccini directs him to trumpet the word "infernal," so that it is high, loud, and sustained.

This is another of the composer's favorite techniques: having his tenor characters express their guilt, humiliation, fear, and despair, at the top of their lungs and during their most impressive arias. During these masochism arias, the heroes essentially strip themselves naked and demand that the entire world behold their shame. Puccini never wrote a single aria of this sort for one of his heroines, so one can only marvel that so many critics have declared that Puccini loved to "torture" his "frail heroines." Even in the agonized "Sola, perduta, abbandonata" the sobbing Manon Lescaut finally summons a steely strength, and masters the terror that prompted her outburst. Puccini's tenor characters do not master their fear—*they revel in it.*

A sad little recollection of Guglielmo's dance music is now heard, telling us what is in Roberto's mind, then he begins his aria, "Torna ai felici dì." His sad thoughts have returned to those happy days, when May laughed with flowers, and love bloomed for him. But then, he continues, everything was darkened by lugubrious mysteries. (What Fontana meant by this strange expression is also a mystery.) The sad dance music is repeated, and Roberto concludes with another loud, high, sustained cry of despair and fear, as he trumpets the fact that his heart now contains nothing but sadness and terror.

He regards the door of the cottage nervously. "Perhaps she still lives," he says, without much hope. But as he walks toward the house, the climbing, winding triplets of "The

Abandonment" reveal the truth. Roberto decides to knock on the cottage door, but as he raises his hand, some mysterious force seems to stop him. He cries out in horror that a terrible shudder ran through him, and that although he tried, he could not lift his hand to the door. Again and again he repeats these words, and suddenly the voices of the Villi are heard, again urging the damned soul to hurry on.

Apparently spent, the young man kneels for his prayer aria, "O sommo Iddio" (O great God), which employs the music of the C section of Act One's choral prayer. When sending Roberto off on his journey, all had prayed the road would be propitious for him. Now, Roberto admits his road has come to an end, and he prays for forgiveness, and with that a single moment of happiness before death.

But there will be no forgiveness. With every turn and twist he makes—trying to laugh off the legend of the Villi, trying to knock on the door, trying to pray—the Villi head him off. They again urge the damned soul to hurry on, and Roberto jumps to his feet, cursing the day he left this place. He also curses the beauty of the vile courtesan, his voice a trumpet on the word "beauty." "Be cursed forever!" he cries. "Be cursed!" Though addressing the siren, he is in fact speaking of himself. It is he who is cursed forever.

There is a long pause while Roberto stands in helpless confusion. The orchestra refuses to assist him, noodling a few noncommittal bars in the lower woodwinds before the bassoon gleefully plays the opening bars of the tarantella.

"Hurry! Hurry! Hurry!" demand the Villi, then suddenly we hear Roberto's name, called from off stage. "Heaven!" he gasps. His name is called again, more insistently. "Her voice!" says Roberto. "She's not dead!" It is indeed Anna's voice, but no longer is it the gentle coo of a warm, living girl. It's as hard and brittle as ice.

Anna-the-Vila appears on the bridge and directs her fierce gaze toward the frightened man. No longer is she Love, she says. She is Vendetta! Roberto gasps, and falls again to his knees as Anna descends from the bridge and approaches him.

The gentle music of her sad suffering during "The Abandonment" is heard, and in a droning chant Anna asks Roberto whether he remembers what he told her in the month of flowers. In case he has forgotten, she repeats the words with which he silenced her fears—word for word, and with same music, note for note: "You, who in my childhood shared joys and caresses.... Doubt God, but never doubt my love." She must have repeated his words again and again as she waited through the long months of spring, summer, and autumn, until winter came and she waited no more.

Their Liebestod begins with Anna's accusation of, "I loved you; you betrayed me. I waited, and you never came." The music is from "The Abandonment," and with her voice now rich and ardent, Anna tells her lover of the tremendous pain caused by suffering in silence; of how, "with all hope gone from my heart, you made me die."

Roberto makes no effort to fight back musically. He doesn't try to break Anna's rhythm, nor does he try to top her by altering the key, as Calaf will do to Turandot during "In questa Reggia." Instead, he submits to Anna completely, joining his voice to hers in the duet, agreeing with her words, and singing her music. The only difference is that she looks back at her past suffering, while he looks forward (with barely concealed desire) to his own suffering:

> But what a tremendous pain
> It is to suffer in silence/I will have to suffer
> With all hope gone from my heart/With remorse in my heart
> You made me die/I feel I will die.

This is the cruel, imperious lady and submissive knight of *romance*. Love is a painful but exquisite torture to him, and the last thing in the world he wants is for the torture to stop. The duet becomes truly fiery, the music reaching upwards in an unmistakable expression of passionate sexual desire via Anna's signature triplets—those climbing, winding triplets. Tenderly the pair repeat their final lines, their voices twined in a loving caress until they join together in an exultant, orgasmic utterance of the final word of the duet: "die!"

Soft notes from the horn serve as the transitional phrase. As though some outside force were working on him, compelling him to this, Roberto begins to approach Anna, whose arms are open to embrace him. For a moment he is seen to struggle against this force, and it actually appears that he might break the spell and run. But the outside force—no, it is the *inside* force—is stronger, and he rushes to Anna's enfolding arms.

From off stage the (male) voices of the Spirits are heard, warning to the music of "The Abandonment" that no mercy will be granted the betrayer. The Villi join in, agreeing that he who in life was deaf to love will find no forgiveness in death.

The tarantella resumes, and as the terrified Roberto breaks away from Anna and runs for the refuge of Guglielmo's house, he at last sees the Villi. "Turn! Jump! Turn!" the savage maidens shout, descending on him from all sides. He lurches in a new direction, only to run straight into Anna, who seizes him and leads him triumphantly in the Villi's mad, whirling dance of death. "Turn! Jump! Turn!" Utterly helpless, the exhausted Roberto assumes his favorite position—on his knees—and begs for his life. "Anna, mercy!" he pleads. But there will be no mercy. "You're mine!" she cries, and it is left to the director to devise the most satisfactory way of dispatching Roberto before Anna-the-Vila disappears. After some final, exultant shouts of "Hosannah! Hosanna!" from the Spirits and the Villi (obviously meant to capitalize—in triple time—on the heroine's name), the orchestra sounds three thunderous chords as the final curtain drops.

5

Manon Lescaut

Libretto by Leoncavallo, Praga, Oliva, Giacosa, Illica, and Ricordi,
after the *Romance* by the Abbé Prévost
First performed at the Teatro Regio, Turin, February 1, 1893

After the utter debacle of *Edgar*, Puccini determined he would never again accept a libretto that did not appeal to him emotionally. He had no doubts about his talents as a composer. All he needed was a juicy story, and he could not fail. The story of Manon might have been tailor-made for Puccini, for Prévost's book was thoroughly *romantic* in substance. The Chevalier Des Grieux's love for Manon is pure "Love as Madness," and no matter how Manon tortures him, he remains her willing "slave and victim."

Puccini was proved right about what sort of fuel was necessary to feed his artistic fire, for *Manon Lescaut* was a tremendous hit. The relationship of Manon and Des Grieux — a sadomasochistic love between a bewitching and strong-willed woman and an enraptured and weak man — would prove the pattern for all of the subsequent full-length operas of the Rose Cycle.

The curtain rises on the 29th bar of a lively orchestral prelude, the music of which will be heard on numerous occasions throughout the first act, underpinning dialogue and serving as transitional music. The setting is a French town called Amiens. We see a large square, with an avenue to the right. At left is an inn with a covered walk, under which are tables and chairs. An outside staircase leads to the upper story of the inn. We can tell even without the cheerful music that good things await the people who are strolling Puccini's avenue and inn yard. For one thing, the setting is outdoors, and the inn suggests the likelihood of wine. But let's pause at the moment of curtain rise to ask ourselves that all-important question: "What time is it?"

Sundown is fast approaching, and the avenue and inn yard are host to students, citizens, and soldiers. Some stroll, others talk, some sit at the tables, drinking and playing cards. Many opera composers summon crowds by declaring a public holiday. Others use break-time at the factory, or a religious event. Puccini wants no such artificial means. By instinct his people gather at sundown, which is the gateway to Night. As the sun fades in Puccini's World, life begins to quicken.

The leader of the students is Edmund, and he utters the first words heard in the Rose Cycle proper: a madrigal verse the composer directs him to sing in a style "between the comic and the sentimental." The mixture of opposite emotions—comedy with sentiment, joy with sadness, hope with melancholy — is perhaps the most personal feature of Puccini's art. We might label this the Puccini Mixture, and we will see and hear it everywhere. It is in the music, the lyrics, and the action of all of his post–*Edgar* operas.

The madrigal has a mood quite different from that of the cheery prelude. It has a narcotic sound appropriate to its subject, the Night. If Puccini had been planning this series of operas I call the Rose Cycle, he could not have inaugurated it more perfectly than by means of the opening madrigal of *Manon Lescaut.*

Edmund hails the night, approaching with its cortege of zephyrs and stars, and dear to poets and lovers. The song is interrupted by the mocking laughter of the students, who jeer that night is also dear to thieves and drunkards. (Note the mixture of high and low: of poets and lovers with thieves and drunkards.)

There is something primitive and even savage about the students. They are not really people; they are the embodiment of Youth. Don't be deceived by their talk of kisses, sighs, and caresses; they are not interested in love, but in the brief, riotous pleasures of the senses.

Edmund takes no offence at the interruption of his song, and catching sight of a group of pretty shop girls, he begins another madrigal, addressed to them. The students join him as he sings, "Youth is our name, and Hope is our goddess...." The word "hope" is a loaded one in Puccini. The shop girls will respond to the bittersweet madrigal, which ends with a request that they yield up their hearts, with a song of their own, also speaking of hope. The girls sing, "A wave of perfume fills the air, the swallows fly to their nests ... and the sun dies! And this is the hour of waking dreams, in which hope struggles with melancholy." I addressed this line in Chapter 2, calling it the most important line in the entire cycle, in that it introduces the concept of the "waking dream" of a life and a love that will never die.

"Hope" is what one does at sundown, when the waking dream begins. It can be difficult at first to grasp how much the night means to Puccini's young people, for not only are we accustomed to associating night with death, Puccini to some degree encourages our misunderstanding via such lines as the one from the shop girls: "...and the sun dies!"

That Puccini associates day, rather than night, with death is revealed again and again throughout the cycle, but it's addressed most openly in *Turandot*, during the Contest of the Riddles. The first riddle is as follows:

> In the dark night flies a rainbow-hued phantom.
> It soars and spreads its wings above the gloomy, infinite human crowd.
> The whole world invokes it, and the whole world implores it.
> But the phantom disappears at dawn, to be reborn in every heart.
> And every night it is born anew, and every day it dies.

The phantom of Turandot's first riddle is *La Speranza*: Hope.

The impression offered by the shop girls' line in *Manon* is that their sense of melancholy stems from a sadness at the disappearance of the sun. In fact, it stems from their awareness that all too soon the sun will return, and that rainbow-hued phantom called Hope will die again.

Des Grieux enters, and the students greet him. Edmund invites him to join with them and "...laugh and let your cares be vanquished by giddy adventures." Though also a student, Des Grieux is different from the others. He returned their greeting, but he showed no inclination to join them, and when stopped by Edmund he does not speak in response to the invitation. Des Grieux is of a higher social class than the others. His title is Chevalier, which gives him the same knightly rank as a hero of a medieval *romance.*

Again Edmund is not offended. He guesses Des Grieux must already be occupied, consumed by love for some unattainable lady. (Note the classic element of *romance*: the knight in love with a lady who is unattainable, ensuring that his passion cannot be satisfied and will torture him beautifully forever.)

Des Grieux scoffs, saying he knows nothing of love, that tragedy — or rather, that comedy. (Again, the Puccini Mixture.) Puccini is working with the character of Des Grieux as taken straight from Prévost's story.[1] In the book, Des Grieux is 17 (he's about 19 in the opera), and has been studying for a religious life. At this point his heart has never once been touched by love, and he is destined to love only once, and forever.

Not being of Des Grieux's class, Edmund and the students refuse to believe the Chevalier's denial. It is unnatural for Youth not to be on fire with passion, so they insist he must be in a bad mood as a result of a love affair gone sour. "By Bacchus," they declare, "you're angry over a jilting, friend."

Bacchus was the wine and fertility god of the ancient Greeks and Romans. No doubt these university students would be steeped in classical literature, and inclined to refer to it in their conversation, but the reference to Bacchus also bolsters the idea that the students are a primitive group, devoted not to romantic love but to wine and revels. The nature of the love that Des Grieux will feel for Manon is Bacchic: an uncontrollable, frenzied, religiously-oriented sexual passion.

And yet Des Grieux is not a follower of Bacchus like his friends, he is a true knight of chivalry, and so he feels not just sexual passion, but rather Love as Madness, as in the medieval *romances*. And he can feel this love for only one woman, ever. As yet he knows nothing of this, for he has not yet seen Manon. But the frenzy lies within him, ready and waiting to be born. All unknowingly Des Grieux reveals this in his aria, "Tra voi, belle," a song he uses to needle the shop girls, whose pretty faces mean nothing to him.

The A section of this serenade is placid, gently rocking in its rhythm, and the young man addresses the girls with what seems like gallantry as he asks them if there is, among them, a rosy-lipped girl who waits for him. There is a change in the B section, however, when — unknowingly — he speaks of Manon. The tenor's voice adopts a hypnotic rhythm, and a tone of mystery aided by a subtle part for the oboe.

"Reveal to me my destiny," sings Des Grieux, "and the divine, ardent face that I shall fall in love with, that I may see and adore her eternally!" Hearing this, the students burst into mocking laughter. It was mockery on Des Grieux's part too, yet without knowing it he is also completely sincere. Des Grieux spoke of "destiny," which is another loaded word in Puccini. It always has positive, mystical connotations.

"Tra voi, belle" is an aria in the old-fashioned ABA form, and in using that Puccini was employing a style appropriate to an operatic character of the era in which this story is set: the early 1700's. The song concludes, therefore, with a repetition of the opening section. Using the same words, music, and sentiment with which he began, Des Grieux banteringly asks the shop girls if there is one among them who waits for him.

The girls had at first been flattered by the song, but by its end they have realized they were being teased, and they go off angrily. Edmund and the students, on the other hand, are immensely pleased by the song, which seems to have shown that like them, Des Grieux does not take love seriously.

At this moment, the coach from Arras, carrying Manon, is nearing the square. The coach has not yet been seen or heard, but something excites the orchestra and the chorus, which sings, "Dancing, drinking, folly, the cortege of voluptuous desire now passes through the streets, and the night will reign. Shining and impetuous, a radiant poem: all conquering — all are conquered by her light and her frenzy!"

The sun has set. Manon and the moon have come. A cornet plays the part of the postillion's horn, and music from the prelude shifts attention to the coach that now wheels into the square and stops before the inn. Edmund and the others look on with interest as first Lescaut (Manon's brother) descends, then the elderly Geronte, who gallantly assists Manon. Gazing with admiration at the lovely Manon (who is 16 in Prévost, but 18 here), Edmund and the students hungrily wonder, "Who would not give that beautiful little lady the genteel salute of welcome?"

A moment earlier, as they were observing the coach door opening, the crowd said, "They're getting out, let's look!" In Italian, the words "let's look" are the two-syllable word "vediam." This is sung on a descending second, and that is Manon's personal musical motif. As Lescaut and Geronte deal with the innkeeper, Des Grieux looks at Manon in amazement and gasps, "God, how beautiful she is!" And all the while the orchestra cries, via the descending second, "Ma-non! Ma-non! Ma-non!"

Geronte informs the innkeeper he will be staying the night. Lescaut and Geronte go to look over the rooms, and Manon sits down to wait. The coach pulls out, and everyone goes about his business. Everyone except Edmund, that is, who watches as Des Grieux approaches Manon.

In Prévost, Des Grieux would, much later in life, look back in amazement at his boldness in addressing Manon. "I have," he would say, "marveled a thousand times since, thinking on it, whence came of a sudden such boldness and ease in expressing myself; but if it were not Love's way to work miracles, they would never have made him a god." This is, of course, the Love as a God sentiment of *romance*.

Des Grieux asks the girl her name. (Laying the groundwork for the tenor's upcoming aria, "Donna non vidi mai," the music of this conversational exchange is a gentle, understated version of that aria, in a lower key.) "Manon Lescaut, I am called," is the girl's response. The two notes on which she sings her first name are her descending-second motif, and it is fitting for this self-absorbed girl that her motif is her own name. We will hear her musical name many times during the course of the opera, thus the thought of Manon will fill the world for us, just as it will fill the world for Des Grieux.

Des Grieux confesses to Manon that he feels himself drawn to her by some strange fascination, and he begs to know when she will be leaving. That fatal hour of her departure is of course Dawn, and her destination is a convent. (To Verdi, convents are places of refuge for women who have suffered enough from the cruelties of the world. To Puccini, they are places where women are punished for enjoying life too much.) This seems terribly wrong to Des Grieux, who asks what fate it is that makes war on her — a girl who has April flowering in her face. Edmund slyly draws the students' attention to Des Grieux, deep in conversation with the beautiful stranger.

Manon answers Des Grieux's question, saying that the fate he refers to is her father's wishes. Using Puccini's language of Night, the young man passionately rejects this: "Upon your destiny shines another star!" Manon picks up the Night language, saying mournfully that her star is setting. With the setting of stars comes dawn, which is death, which is Manon's departure for the convent.

Needing time to think, Des Grieux asks Manon to come back later, so they two can conspire against her fate, and win. She asks his name; it is Renato Des Grieux. Manon's brother calls, and she hastens to answer him obediently. Des Grieux pleads with her again to come back later, and she agrees to return when it has grown darker.

Real passion fills Des Grieux's voice in "Donna non vidi mai" (I never saw a woman such as this). Having heard the melody before, if only half-consciously, we can better appreciate it now. The second line of the aria is, "To tell her: I love you, awakens my soul to a new life." It is possible this line is an allusion to Dante's *Vita nuova*, the greatest of Italian medieval *romance* works. Des Grieux would know that book, and surely at least one amongst the numerous librettists who worked on *Manon* would have known it.[2]

"Manon Lescaut, I am called," repeats the young man reverently, and the two-note motif of Manon's name is further impressed on us. Des Grieux calls her utterance "a gentle whisper," and begs "..deh! non cessar! deh! non cessar!" This line means, "Oh! Don't stop! Oh! Don't stop!" The listener should fix in his mind the eight notes on which this line is sung, and the words that go with them, for in Act Two the music will be used to form a new and critically important melody. If, at that time, the listener can recall this music and the words associated with it — Oh! Don't stop! — he will realize that Puccini must have been laughing hysterically when he conceived of the reappearance of the music. His aria concluded, Des Grieux stands in an ecstasy. Edmund and the students approach, and mockingly comment on what they have seen. Angered by the laughter, the young man stalks off without replying.

The students return to flirting with the shop girls in a series of exchanges filled with the Puccini Mixture of opposites: "...who wins and who loses ... who weeps and who laughs ... sweethearts faithful for an hour." Lescaut and Geronte walk down the staircase, busy in conversation, and the spying Edmund watches intently. The two men stroll the square, and with feigned casualness Geronte asks after Manon. Is it true the dear girl will be taking the veil? That Geronte already has plans for the dear girl is evident, for his question was preceded by a few bars of sneaky-sounding music: the theme of Geronte's Plot. Lescaut's lack of enthusiasm for the "convent" idea is obvious, and so Geronte is encouraged to pursue the subject.

Evidently the conversation between Geronte and Lescaut during the coach ride was brief, for Geronte neither introduced himself nor described his business. He does so now, revealing that he is Geronte de Ravoir, the king's Treasurer General. The delighted Lescaut proceeds to dangle his sister before the rich old man. "Think of it," says Lescaut regretfully. "Only 18 years old! So many dreams and hopes...."

Geronte lunges at the bait, inviting Lescaut and his sister to dinner so they two can console her. Lescaut accepts, and offers to buy the old man a drink. Geronte excuses himself with the explanation that he must give the innkeeper some orders. He has to see about a coach and horses, so he can steal Manon away!

It is now full night, and waiters bring lamps and candles out to the tables where the students are drinking and playing noisily at cards. A skillful gambler, Lescaut approaches the tables, and when he reports an error by one of the players he is invited to join the game. Soon his attention is completely absorbed.

Addressing the obsequious innkeeper, Geronte orders a carriage and fast horses to be stationed behind the inn in one hour. A man and a young girl will come for the carriage, then they'll be off to Paris, like the wind! With this, the sneaky theme of Geronte's Plot is heard.

The old man reminds the innkeeper that silence is golden, and seeing an opening the innkeeper answers, "I love gold." Satisfied he is dealing with a man who can be bought, Geronte hands over a purse, then exits with the innkeeper, who is to show him a back way out.

Edmund watches them go, and muses on what he has heard. He alludes to the myth of Pluto, the god of the underworld, who ravished away the lovely Proserpine while she was picking flowers. It is Geronte's age and wealth that have set Edmund against him. Age and Wealth have no place at Love's table. It is unnatural for Geronte to be thinking of sighs and kisses.

Des Grieux enters, absorbed in thoughts of Manon. Edmund informs him of what is about to happen, using a flower metaphor that continues his comparison of Manon to Proserpine: "That flower which only now smelled so sweet, will soon be uprooted, poor flower, so soon it will wither!" The music of Geronte's Plot is heard as Edmund tells the astonished Des Grieux that an old man is about to carry off his girl.

Des Grieux begs Edmund to help him, and Edmund agrees. He takes charge immediately, and goes to the table where Lescaut is absorbed in the cards. He whispers to a few of the students, and based on the action that follows he must be saying, "Keep the soldier busy. Get him drunk."

Edmund exits to see what he can do about the carriage. The card game ends, and Lescaut drinks with the students. To the opening strains of "Donna non vidi mai," Manon appears at the top of the stairs, looks about, sees Des Grieux, and comes to him. Considering her later behavior, her opening line is ironically funny: "Do you see? I am faithful to my word."

We saw in Des Grieux's description of April flowering in Manon's face, and in Edmund's likening of her to Proserpine, the stirrings of the Flower symbolism that will be of such importance in the subsequent operas. It stirs again when Des Grieux counters Manon's comment that she ought not to have come back, by saying that such grave words "...are not suited to the charming youth that decks your face with flowers."

Manon's response, beginning with the words "Eppur lieta" (I was happy), moves her conversation with Des Grieux into a new phase. As the two alternate passages, their voices double a highly insinuating melody that features instruments we will come to identify with Manon: the flute, oboe, and clarinet.

The girl sadly describes a lost happiness: a youth of laughter and dancing. Des Grieux answers her as he habitually will, using the language of courtly romance. "**Submit** your sweet lips and your heart to this new **enchantment**.... Love will **conquer** sadness...."

The duet is interrupted by a shout from Lescaut. With the cry of, "No more wine? Is the barrel empty?" Puccini effects a skillful transition that shows the strides he has made since *Le Villi*, with its awkward fanfares and chiming bells that tacked one number to another. Hearing Lescaut's shout, Manon and Des Grieux draw back, and the young man changes the subject from love, to Geronte's Plot. That theme sounds as Des Grieux informs the stunned Manon the old man plans to kidnap her. Before she can recover, Edmund rushes in and tells Des Grieux the coach is in place, and they should go at once.

Manon resists, but Des Grieux implores. He at last convinces Manon to leave with him, and Edmund throws his cloak about Des Grieux to conceal the fact that it is not Geronte rushing toward the coach. The lovers run behind the inn, accompanied in their dash for Paris by a bit of melody from their love duet. The melody had carried the words, "Make this moment of a day eternal and infinite ... ah, my very breath ... oh, my infinite spirit."

No sooner have they vanished then Geronte enters. The old man observes Lescaut, involved in another card game, and he gives a sigh of satisfaction. His Plot music sounds as he gloats, "Now is the moment to seduce the little sister, with ardor. The sergeant is intent on the game! Let him remain!"

It is a bit of mockery at the old man that the libretto requires him to ask the innkeeper whether supper is ready. It is a given that an elderly man seeking the love of a young girl is a fool, and when the old fellow shows an interest in food he is doubly ridiculous. This mockery is emphasized musically, for as the carriage rolls away the postillion's horn is sounded at the very moment Geronte inquires about supper.

Pleased by the innkeeper's answer, Geronte orders him to "...inform the young lady that...." But Edmund interrupts, and making a mocking bow he points toward the road to Paris and informs his Excellency the girl has gone off with a student. Geronte looks where Edmund is pointing, then runs to the table where Lescaut is still engrossed in his cards. "They've carried her off!" bellows Geronte. "Who?" asks Lescaut, not looking up. "Your sister!" shouts Geronte. Cursing, Lescaut runs out of the portico. The frightened innkeeper runs off, and the students gather around Edmund, who explains with gestures what he has been up to.

"Let's follow them!" urges Geronte frantically. "It's a student. Let's follow them, follow them, follow them!" Thoroughly frustrated, the old man throws his hat down. Lescaut calmly studies the students, who have assumed an air of indifference. Lescaut decides pursuit is useless. They have no horses ready. And yet all is not lost. Tact is required, and the soldier rises to the occasion.

"I see," he says to Geronte pleasantly, "Manon's charms and grace have awakened in you the affection of a father." Grasping for the shreds of his dignity, the old man agrees that is entirely the situation. All finesse, Lescaut ventures to offer some advice. They have not lost Manon. She has merely gone to Paris.

A reprise of "Tra voi, belle" begins, this time with Lescaut as the solo voice, backed by Edmund and the students, whose fresh young voices mock Geronte with lines based on Aesop's fable of the fox and the grapes. That Lescaut sings to this music, and in concert with the students, seems to show us that despite being older than they are, Lescaut is kin to the students, with teeth as sharp as theirs.

This reprise of "Tra voi, belle" is more insinuating than Des Grieux's playful version, with a more rocking rhythm. The baritone sings a great quantity of 16th notes, and this plays delightfully against the voices of the students, whose tenors sing falsetto, and all of whom favor quarter- and eighth-notes.

In the first A section, Lescaut soothes Geronte with the assurance that a student's purse is always light. His sister doesn't care for poverty, and will gladly throw over her student and accept a palace in his place. The B section as originally sung by Des Grieux was his unwitting vision of Manon, whose divine and ardent face he would adore eternally. The words were a vision of frenzied, passionate love. The words put to this section by Lescaut are a perfect opposite—an expression of rationality: "You will be the father of an excellent daughter, and I, sir, will complete the family. Clearly, calm is required ... philosophy." As with Des Grieux, the students erupt in laughter at the conclusion of this section.

With his repeat of the A, Lescaut picks up Geronte's hat and returns it to him. In the morning they two will after the lovers. But now, to supper! Lescaut takes the old man's arm and ushers him into the inn, still talking at him soothingly. The students' ending raspberry to Geronte is, "To the old fox, the fresh and velvet-skinned grape will ever be sour!" At their final burst of laughter, Lescaut rushes out and glares menacingly, and the students disperse, still laughing.

Act Two begins with an elegant and mysterious melody played by solo flute, backed by harp and strings. What strikes one on the rising of the curtain is the complete artificiality of this indoor scene, in an immense contrast with the natural, outdoor setting of Act One.

We see a room in Geronte's Paris home, where Manon is now installed. No matter where the eye lights, all is glittering and false. There are no scenes in Puccini in which wealth is shown even in a neutral light, and as soon as we see Manon, we realize the terrible effect wealth has had on her. Having grown tired of poverty, she has betrayed Des Grieux and prostituted herself out of greed for gold.

The woman in this glittering room is not the sweet, artless girl of Act One. Manon is now a Vacillator — one of those citizens of Puccini's World who have reached out for gold, and lost their right to love. Manon now has all the gold she could ever want, but the only love she has is that of her Alberich, Geronte. And that love is withered and gray.

Swathed in a hairdresser's cape, Manon looks right at home in this sumptuously decorated room. She sits at her toilette table, looking in the mirror at her elaborate wig. Her eye spots a rebellious curl, and she snaps an order at the Hairdresser who dances attendance on her. A flute trills softly and a triangle shimmers as the Hairdresser leaps for the curling iron, and deftly adjusts the curl.

Satisfied with her wig, Manon studies her face. She demands powder, and the Hairdresser expertly attends to her cheeks with a puff. More orders follow, and the man applies pencil to the eyebrows, dabs on a bit of cream, and sprays a wave of perfume.

Lescaut enters, and bids his sister good morning. Notice what time it is. It is Day, which is the time that it must be while we are indoors, and in the midst of such disgusting wealth. Manon is no longer the obedient little sister, so she ignores her brother's greeting. Instead she calls for rouge and pomade. Driving home the message that it is day, Lescaut comments that Manon seems a little angry this morning. She denies it, and Lescaut lets the subject go.

But he clearly enjoys needling his sister, thus he looks around the room and mischievously asks where Geronte is. Manon again ignores him, and calls for a beauty patch. The Hairdresser offers a box containing a variety of patches, and Manon rummages amongst them, unable to decide which shape to choose.

Lescaut makes suggestions: the Impudent One? The Rogue! The Coquette! Manon decides on two. The Killer will highlight one eye, while the Tempter will draw attention to her lips. The Hairdresser applies the two patches, then removes the cape from Manon. The lackey bows to Manon, then exits.

Lescaut looks at his sister and exclaims admiringly, "You are splendid and shining!" This sounds like the cry of the chorus as the coach approached the inn yard: "Shining and impetuous, a radiant poem ... all are conquered by her light...."

This seems not to be a coincidence, for Lescaut begins to speak of the inn, where Manon impetuously ran off with her student. He never lost hope, says Lescaut, and soon found Manon in a little cottage, where she had Des Grieux's ardent kisses, but no money. Naturally, he adds, she abandoned that humble abode for a palace of gold.

This last line will linger in Manon's mind, and she will use its music in a moment in her aria, "In quelle trine morbide," in which she looks back with longing on that humble abode. Geronte too will use the music of this line when, betrayed in turn by Manon, he reminds her of the many proofs of his love, one of them being the palace of gold.

At first feigning indifference, Manon finally admits to her teasing brother that she longs for news of Des Grieux, whom she abandoned without a farewell or a kiss. She looks around the golden room, and begins "In quelle trine morbide" (In those delicate laces).

The song expresses Manon's longing for Des Grieux and the happiness she knew in their little cottage. It seems that all of her life is destined to be spent in looking back on a time of happiness now lost, for the feelings she expresses are much like those of "Eppur lieta."

In his book *Puccini*, Carner refers to Puccini's habit — a "foible" he calls it — of having one of his characters express a desire to live in a small house, "preferably in the country," where he or she believes that life would be ideal.[3] As examples, he cites *Manon*, *Tosca*, *Fanciulla*, and *La Rondine*, all of which operas contain characters who want to leave the place in which they currently live, in favor of a smaller home far away. He should have added *Butterfly*, *Il Tabarro*, *Suor Angelica*, and *Turandot*.

This longing for the little house is not a "foible," and there is more to it than the gooey romantic thought that Carner suggested. The regret expressed by Manon, for the little cottage where she was happy with her beloved, is the first sounding of a theme that grows increasingly strong, and increasingly sad, in the subsequent operas. What is being expressed is a desire to escape — to go some place far away, leaving troubles behind. Here in *Manon* the concept of the little home that is someplace that is *not here*, seems unremarkable, but by the time of *La Fanciulla del West*, the expression of the longing for *là lontano* — the place that is *far away*, where people love you, and there are no troubles — is so strong it seems it simply must be a personal expression of Puccini's.

Perhaps the most significant line of "In quelle trine morbide" is the one that concludes the first section, which describes Manon's current life. Manon has spoken of "...a cold, deadly silence, a coldness that freezes," and she concludes the passage with, "And I, who had gotten used to a voluptuous caress of burning lips and passionate arms ... now have ... an entirely different thing." This line is laying the groundwork for something quite extraordinary; that is, a musical depiction of the feeble embraces of Geronte.

Any number of composers have written music descriptive of sexual intercourse, but in the time during which Puccini was composing *Manon*, the only such composition most people were aware of was the Act Two love duet of Wagner's *Tristan und Isolde* (which has been jokingly called the world's longest act of coitus interruptus). In Act Two of *Manon*, Puccini depicts in music not only a completed act of sexual intercourse, between Manon and Des Grieux, but also an abject failure due to loss of erection (Manon and Geronte). The line quoted above from "In quelle trine morbide" sets the stage for that musical failure, which takes place during Manon's dancing lesson. Before the dancing lesson failure, however, Puccini gives us another and much stronger hint about poor Geronte's lack of vigor by means of the Madrigal that will be sung in a few minutes.

Having concluded "In quelle trine morbide" on a note of intense longing for the little house where she had briefly lived with Des Grieux, Manon listens with interest as her brother, who has been watching her with unease, tells her he has been in contact with the young man. The musical interval of Manon's name is sounded again and again as Lescaut describes Des Grieux's demands to know where the girl is, giving the impression of her name being urgently called from high and low.

Lescaut reveals he has been instructing Des Grieux in the art of gambling, having convinced him that if he is to have Manon he must have gold. (This is an important subject in Prévost's book, but it's an awkwardness in the libretto, since no more is heard about Des

Grieux gambling. Puccini needed for there to be some explanation as to why Lescaut was in contact with Des Grieux.) Manon's brother has also been instructing her lover in the art of cheating, which is accomplished via elaborately ruffled shirt cuffs, capable of concealing a multitude of sins. Lescaut and his sister engage in a duet in which Manon pines for the burning kisses of Des Grieux, and Lescaut chuckles at the thought of how the young man will fleece one and all.

Manon's gaze falls on her reflection in the mirror above her toilette table. Her passion for Des Grieux is forgotten, and the artificial music of the opening returns as she admires herself and fishes for compliments from her brother. Is she not perfection in her gown, her wig, and her figure? Indeed, she is perfection. And now, the marvelous scene of the Madrigal begins.

It is sometimes the case in Puccini's World that those who have thrown in their lot with the Alberichs are as hostile as the latter are to Art. As the Madrigal Singer and his (actually her, for this is a *travesti* role) musicians enter and take their positions, Lescaut insults them. "Who are these mugs?" he asks his sister. "Charlatans or tradesmen?" Visibly bored, Manon sits down on the sofa. They are musicians, she tells her brother. With a sneer she adds, "Geronte composes madrigals."

At first it might seem that Puccini was careless about the distinction between those who are Artists and those who are Alberichs, but that is not so. Puccini identified Geronte as the composer of the Madrigal for one reason only, and that is that the Madrigal further reveals Geronte's lack of sexual vigor, first hinted at in "In quelle trine morbide."

Sung by a mezzo-soprano backed by woodwinds and strings, the Madrigal is quite pretty. As an example of passion, however, it is feeble in the extreme. The lyrics describe Manon as a mountain-wandering nymph, and Geronte as her shepherd lad swain, expiring at her feet. The lad plays on his pipes, weeping, and praying that the lovely shepherdess will have pity on him. And surely she will, for — the song concludes — Manon "...to that sweet, piping plea has never said 'No.'" The "piping plea" of course refers to the childishly high voice of a very old man.

Puccini may have gotten the idea for this wicked song while writing the upcoming love duet for Manon and Des Grieux. It probably amused him to consider what a love duet between Manon and Geronte would sound like. What resulted was a love song in which Manon, bored stiff, takes no part, and Geronte's part is delivered by proxy. Being that the Madrigal Singer is played by a mezzo, Geronte's role is essentially performed by a eunuch!!

But the joke does not end here. Puccini continues his merciless skewering of Geronte via the dancing lesson that immediately follows the Madrigal. With that song now finished, the irritated Manon gives her brother a purse and tells him to pay the group off.

Even in this first opera of the Rose Cycle, Puccini does not allow an Artist character to take money for his art. Although he was mocking Geronte during the Madrigal, he was not mocking the Singer and his group, and he does not allow them to be tainted by gold. Lescaut cries, "What! Insult the Arts?" He pockets the purse and says grandly to the musicians, "I dismiss you in the name of Glory!"

It's funny to watch him evade paying the musicians, but beneath the comedy Puccini was serious. His Artists are beings of the world of Nature, and they produce their art as naturally, and for the same reason, as plants produce flowers. Neither takes gold in exchange for the beauty they create.

The Madrigal group having exited, a string quartet enters. Through the French windows at back, we see friends of Geronte arriving, and Geronte greeting them. Manon has no more use for the quartet than she did for the singers. Gesturing at the newcomers, she tells her brother, "Madrigals! Dancing! And then music! They're all beautiful! But they bore me." She goes to meet Geronte, who enters with the Dancing Master to begin Manon's lesson in the minuet. Lescaut, who has been growing uneasy over his sister's discontent, remarks to himself that a bored woman is something to fear. He ponders what to do.

The string quartet begins tuning up, and in an inspired touch, Puccini has Lescaut conceive his plan during the tuning-up music. "Let's go for Des Grieux!" he decides. "It's up to the master to direct events!" This delightful passage suggests, via the tuning up sounds being made by the quartet, that a show will soon take place, with Lescaut acting as conductor.

The Dancing Master has been receiving instructions from Geronte, and during that time the old man's friends were fawning over their patron's mistress. As will be made painfully clear, these "friends" are nothing but hangers on, who flatter and dance attendance in exchange for the morsels that drop from Geronte's plate.

The Dancing Master offers his hand to Manon. He too is an Artist, and if one pays attention to the Lesson scene he will surely feel sorry for him. Dancing is a serious matter to the Dancing Master, but the world in which he teaches is populated with Alberichs, who respect neither him nor his art. Manon is less than perfect in her rhythm, but Geronte and his friends praise her expertise. Impatiently, the Dancing Master urges his pupil to ignore the onlookers' flattery, for dancing is a serious thing.

The lesson continues, with Manon looking through her lorgnette at her admirers, who gush over her beauty and skill. Increasingly impatient, the Dancing Master calls for a partner for Manon. It is here that Puccini will administer the *coup de grâce* to poor Geronte, who leaps to his feet.

Geronte and Manon begin to dance, and as they do the onlookers make a subtle and dirty joke at their expense. "Bravo!" they cry. "What a pair! Hurrah for the fortunate lovers! See! Mercury and Venus.... Here joy with love and riches is most happily united."

Mercury and Venus are both Roman deities, but they have nothing to do with one another in Roman myth. The only situation in which Mercury and Venus are found together is in a now outdated medical treatment. Up until 1910, mercury was used as a treatment for venereal disease. There was a saying at the time: "A night in the arms of Venus leads to a lifetime with Mercury." Geronte's friends have in essence declared that Manon (Venus) is a prostitute, and that Geronte (Mercury) has paid for her favors and gotten himself a dose of syphilis to boot.

And now the dancing turns to a merciless representation of sexual intercourse between Manon and Geronte. The music rises higher and higher as the young girl and the old man minuet, and the excited voices of the onlookers provide enthusiastic encouragement, essentially shouting, "Go! Go! Go!" Higher and higher rises the music until suddenly, something goes wrong. The encouraging voices go silent as the watchers realize what is happening, and the music cuts out — all except the strings, which give a thin, agonized cry and then begin to fall, down, down, down, ending in a spiraling collapse that concludes with a mournful droop. Alas, the poor old fellow couldn't keep it up. Given the music, there is no way to end the dance except with the tired and dizzy Geronte humiliatingly collapsed into a chair.

Using the same classical/romantic verbiage as Geronte's Madrigal, Manon turns to the old man and in her most coquettish manner sings him a pretty cantata about a faithful little shepherdess who longs and sighs for him. As Geronte gapes at her adoringly, she finishes with a brilliant high C. Coming as it does on the heels of Geronte's musical loss of erection, the listener is invited to speculate on what Manon's solo high C might represent.

Geronte's friends have declared Manon to be the miracle of love, but now the old fellow notes that the day is advancing, and a gay crowd will be strolling the avenue. The friends note how quickly time flies. Poignantly, Geronte answers, "That is something I know from experience." Clearly, Geronte loves Manon, and he now takes affectionate leave of her so she can put the finishing touches on her toilette before joining him in the glittering world of Society. He kisses her hand, promising to call for a sedan chair.

With Geronte gone, Manon picks up a hand mirror and looks at herself with satisfaction. She puts on her cloak, and as she does she hears a sound behind her. An ominous thrumming is heard in the timpani, but Manon hears only that someone has come in. Thinking it is a servant, she asks whether the sedan chair is ready. She turns, and in shock sees a wild-eyed Des Grieux.

Manon rushes to her beloved and, astonishingly, is taken aback at his stern look and reproving, "Ah, Manon!" She makes no attempt to justify herself; she is far too instinctively clever for that. Instead, she begins her attempt to get around Des Grieux by crying out despairingly that he no longer loves her.

The music of the scene that follows—the scene of recrimination and forgiveness—will recur during the Intermezzo that precedes Act Three, and again during the early part of Act Four, when Manon is facing death. It is worth the listener's while to fix this music, and the words associated with it, in his mind, for the recurrences are extremely moving.

As Manon cries that Des Grieux no longer loves her, he is already feeling her fatal pull. Desperately he shouts at her to be silent—"Taci! Taci!"—for she is breaking his heart. This piece of melody recurs in Act Four when Manon has fainted from thirst and exhaustion and Des Grieux is begging her to speak to him. The recurrence is masterful, for what is more natural at such a moment than for Des Grieux to think back on a time when he shouted at Manon to be silent, and to realize that now he would give anything in the world if only she would speak, no matter what she said.

Revealing she does not understand Des Grieux at all, Manon now asks his forgiveness, saying, "Don't you see? I'm rich." She gestures at the room, telling him this feast of gold is for him. Des Grieux is sickened by her words, and seeing this, Manon changes her tack. She kneels at her lover's feet, pleading for forgiveness, and in her most seductive manner she coos, "Perhaps, compared to the Manon of before, I am less pleasing and beautiful?"

Des Grieux cries, "O, temptress! Here again the same spell that once bewitched me!" It is hopeless for him to continue resisting. Triumphant, Manon rises and embraces him, telling him to yield to her. "I can fight no longer," admits Des Grieux, "I am conquered." This concludes the scene of recrimination and forgiveness, and the love duet begins.

The love duet is built on Des Grieux's Act One aria, "Donna non vidi mai"—"I never saw a woman such as this." The first line of the aria is clearly audible in the duet, and is heard in the exchange, "Oh! Come! Put your arms around Manon who loves you," and "I cannot resist, o temptress." As the duet proceeds, the music of the earlier aria continues; first, that of "...simile a questa" (such as this), and then that of "...susurro gentile" (gentle whisper).

As is the dance of Manon and Geronte, this duet is a musical representation of sexual intercourse. This time, however, the conclusion is volcanic. Once more the music rises higher and higher as the level of excitement grows. As the climax nears we hear its approach sung by Des Grieux, and when the climax is reached the lovers will sing together, ecstatically.

The approach of climax is given out in Des Grieux's line, "Nell' occhio tuo profondo..." (In the depths of your eyes...), the music of which is a slight variation on the concluding line of "Donna non vidi mai." Manon sings a line in response, then the two reach their musical orgasm, singing together on that same, slightly altered, line from the aria. The original words to this last line from Des Grieux's aria are, "Deh! non cessar! Deh! non cessar!": Oh! Don't stop! Oh! Don't stop!

In case we missed it, Puccini gives the audience a last chance to figure out what the love duet represents by following it up with a dreamy little interlude, which clearly describes afterglow. As the harp ripples, the lovers utter endearments. "Manon," murmurs Des Grieux, "you bring me near to death." This utterance refers not to real death, but to what the French call *le petit mort*—the "little death" that is orgasm.

The love duet has been badly misinterpreted, with one critic remarking in a puzzled manner on the "incongruously martial" sound of the music of orgasm.[4] Puccini treated this passage with some humor during the duet (and we can only imagine how he must have laughed to himself in theaters, as audiences wildly applauded the climax), but that's only natural. Young lovers are a bit ridiculous.

But throughout the rest of the opera this piece of music—"Deh! non cessar!/Nell' occhio tuo profondo"—is treated very seriously. We'll hear it next at the conclusion of the Intermezzo, where it shimmers and glows like a hopeful star in a dark sky. We'll hear it again, shouted triumphantly from the brass when Des Grieux gains permission to join Manon in exile. No matter how it is played—humorously, hopefully, joyfully, sadly—it always represents undying love. Oh, may it never cease.

Manon and Des Grieux are still enjoying afterglow when they receive a sudden shock. The door opens, and in walks Geronte, who had grown impatient waiting for his beloved and has come to see what is keeping her. Manon utters a scream, and if this seems an overreaction we should realize that in essence Geronte has walked in on these two in bed, immediately after they've finished making love.

Appalled, Geronte takes refuge in irony and a studied courtesy, "apologizing" for having arrived at an awkward moment, and observing that Des Grieux appears to have forgotten how one ought to conduct himself in another man's home. The old man is actually terribly hurt, for he loves Manon. He reminds her of the many proofs he has given her of his love, and we hear a fragment of music from Lescaut's earlier aria, in which he commented on Manon's having abandoned Des Grieux for a palace. Also noticeable in the reproach is the music of Geronte's Plot.

A better person than Manon would have admitted that Geronte was right, and apologized for hurting him, but instead she responds with a cruel jibe that engenders in him a bitter anger and a thirst for revenge. She picks up her hand mirror and shows the old man his reflection, sneering, "Love? Look at yourself! And then look at us!" Alas, Age has no place at Love's table. Deeply offended, Geronte leaves, but not before uttering a menacing promise that they three will meet again—and soon!

The foolish Manon is overjoyed at Geronte's departure, aware only that she and her handsome lover are alone in her beautiful, golden room. "Ha! Ha!" she laughs, and the orchestra laughs with her, joyously singing her name: "Ma-non! Ma-non! Ma-non!"

Grimly, Des Grieux tells Manon they must leave this old man's house at once, and only now does it occur to her that having broken with Geronte, she will not be able to continue living at his expense. The orchestra describes her sorrow as, crestfallen, she looks around, saying, "What a pity. All these splendors, all these treasures. Alas! We must leave!"

The Des Grieux of Prévost had by this time great experience with Manon, and it is from his experience that Puccini's young man is filled with despair at her mournful cry. He knows Manon loves only him, but he also knows that the very thought of poverty is enough to send her running to a wealthy man's arms.

Des Grieux begins the lesser of his two Masochism Arias. "Ah, Manon," he begins, and the tempo is slow and dragging, as though he were trying to walk while burdened with a crushing weight. Sadly he says she is always the same — loving, but ready at any moment to be dazzled by the gilded life. While he himself, "dirt in dirt," her "slave and victim," has dishonored and sold himself for her sake. In a tone of utter despair, he concludes with a question for his cruel mistress: "In the dark future, tell me, what will you make of me?" Humbly, Manon begs his forgiveness, and promises to be faithful and good.

The door bursts open, and the orchestra chatters with excitement as Lescaut rushes in. It is clear that a catastrophe has taken place. The frightened couple demand to know what has happened, and a rapid trio ensues as they trade lines with Manon's brother, who gasps out the news that Geronte has denounced Manon to the authorities. Having been reported as an immoral woman, she is subject to arrest and exile from France!

Lescaut urges the two to run, for soldiers are on their way. Des Grieux would be happy to comply, but Manon cannot bear to leave empty-handed. Frantically she begins snatching up jewels, while her lover pleads with her to run. Lescaut spares a moment to sorrow over the loss of Geronte's strongbox, but he too warns Manon she must go at once. Her response is, "It would be imprudent to leave this gold, oh, my treasure!"

Almost mad with frustration, Des Grieux briefly stops the wild trio with the bravura cry, "You must bring only your heart with you! I would salvage only your love!" Her Vacillator's heart poisoned by gold, Manon ignores him.

Soldiers are surrounding the house, and seconds remain in which Manon might yet escape. But still she cannot bring herself to leave her golden room. Terror vies with hilarity as Manon runs back and forth, unable to decide which way to go or what to do, and Des Grieux wrings his hands in helpless anguish.

At last Lescaut pushes the two into an alcove that leads to the outside, and follows them. But it is too late, and almost at once Manon runs back into the room, screaming in fear of the pursuing soldiers. Lescaut follows, and then Des Grieux, determined to protect his beloved. Hard on their heels are a sergeant and two constables, and now the back door is thrown open and a triumphant Geronte enters with more soldiers. The terrified Manon drops her cloak, and her jewels and other treasures go skittering across the floor. Geronte laughs mockingly, and despite Manon's fright and Des Grieux's anguish the sight is indeed rather funny. It is the last moment of humor in the opera.

The furious Des Grieux draws his sword and prepares to rush his enemies, but he is stopped by Lescaut, who prudently warns him, "If they arrest you, Cavalier, who will save Manon?" At a sign from Geronte, the sergeant and two of his men lay hands on Manon and drag her away. The desperate Des Grieux tries to follow, but is held back by Lescaut. The curtain drops to Des Grieux's agonized cry of, "Ah, Manon! Ah, my Manon!" It is as though his heart has been torn in two, and one half taken away.

The Intermezzo that precedes Act Three replays much of the music of Act Two's "recrimination and forgiveness" scene, in which Des Grieux confronted Manon but soon was vanquished by her beauty and her pleading. Before that music begins, however, we hear several bars from an instrumental work Puccini had composed as an elegy on the death of Duke Amedeo of Savoy, a member of the Italian royal family.

The piece is called "Crisantemi," meaning "Chrysanthemums." In Latin culture, the chrysanthemum is the flower associated with funerals and remembrance rites. During the remainder of the opera, the music of "Crisantemi" will serve as the theme of Manon's Death.

After the introductory bars from "Crisantemi," the replay of the "recrimination and forgiveness" music begins. It starts with the music to which Des Grieux had cried, "Be silent, be silent, you're breaking my heart!" It continues with the next line, Manon's, "I want your forgiveness. Don't you see? I'm rich."

It is difficult to recognize the music of the Intermezzo without having heard the opera several times, and there is an opportunity here for the kind of effective visual picture that Puccini always strived for — a mimed scene — that would help the audience understand the music.

Just before the Intermezzo begins, a spotlight could highlight one side of the stage. As I imagine it, we see the prison at Le Havre, where Act Three will be set, and Manon is there, alone in a cell. The music begins, and on the other side of the stage we will be shown what Manon is thinking, which thoughts reflect the scene of recrimination and forgiveness being replayed in the music.

The spotlight on Manon would go down, and come up on a shadow box. Manon is there in silhouette, dressed as she was in Act Two. Des Grieux enters, also in silhouette, and with expressive gestures the two shadow figures act out what is taking place in the music. Des Grieux wrings his hands, Manon kneels and implores. At last he forgives her, and she rises.

The last bars of the Intermezzo employ the music to which the love duet climaxed: "Deh! non cessar!/Nell' occhio tuo profondo"; that is, the theme of Des Grieux's undying love for Manon. As this music sounds, shimmering with a warm hopefulness after the sweet sadness of the preceding melody, the figures in the shadow box embrace, then fade away as the light on them goes down. At the same time, the spotlight comes up on Manon, who stands alone in prison, her face in her hands as she weeps in regret for what she so carelessly threw away.

When the curtain rises on Act Three, a square near the harbor is revealed. At left is a military barracks. It is here the prisoners are kept, awaiting transportation to the French colony in America. It is here Manon lies, after a long journey from Paris on foot and in chains. Des Grieux and Lescaut have followed her, hoping to rescue her before she is forced onto the transport ship.

Dawn is approaching, the most perilous moment on the clock of the Romantic World. As the scene progresses, the stage gradually lightens with rising of the sun. Des Grieux and Lescaut enter, and to mournful music from the horns the tenor sings of the endless, cruel anxiety that has tortured him since Manon's arrest. The technique is one of Puccini's favorites: the orchestra carries the melody, while the voice chants above it in a near monotone. The effect is hypnotic, and haunting. Lescaut urges patience. He has bribed the guard who will take the next watch. When the man comes on duty, he will walk away so Des Grieux can go to the barred window and speak to Manon. Lescaut, who has reckless friends, will go meet them and start the escape attempt.

The guard changes. Lescaut's man signals to him, then leaves. Lescaut goes to the window and summons his sister, who has received word of his plan. Manon appears to the opening measures of "Donna non vidi mai"—I never saw a woman such as this! Manon is in a miserable state after the long journey from Paris, but there is no irony in the recurrence of the music. To Des Grieux, Manon is always Manon, the incomparable beauty, and heart of his heart.

The unhappy girl reaches through the bars, and Des Grieux seizes her hands and kisses them fervently. Lescaut exits to lead his friends in the escape attempt. The lovers whisper endearments, but are interrupted by the entrance of a Lamplighter, snuffing out the lamps in the square. The fearful lovers are silent as the Lamplighter crosses the stage, singing a melancholy song, the subject of which will be taken up again in *La Rondine*. It is the story of a girl named Kate, who was approached by a king who wished to seduce her. But Kate had no lust for gold, and so she answered, "Why do you tempt the heart of a maid? The Lord made me beautiful for a husband." The Lamplighter exits.

"It is dawn," whispers Des Grieux. He urges Manon to go to the prison gate, where Lescaut and his men will meet her. Manon is afraid, and she tells Des Grieux she senses something, a fatal threat. "Crisantemi," the music of Manon's Death, steals in, and singing to it Des Grieux begs Manon to try to escape.

He begs so piteously that Manon, now singing to her own Death music, agrees. She withdraws from the barred window, and the music of "Deh! non cessar/Nell' occhio tuo profondo"—Des Grieux's undying love—sounds in the orchestra. Perhaps this music now also represents her undying love for Des Grieux.

A shot rings out, and Lescaut runs in, shouting that the rescue attempt has failed. He urges Des Grieux to run, and Manon calls from the window, adding her pleas to those of her brother. "If you love me," she cries, "in the name of God, fly!" Des Grieux is dragged away by Lescaut, and the stage fills with excited townspeople who have heard the shot and the shouting of the soldiers.

As the townsfolk mill about, a drum roll is heard. The doors to the barracks swing wide, and a troop of soldiers marches out, a sergeant at their head. They guard twelve women convicts, including the wretched Manon. The captain of the transport ship enters with some of his men, ready to take the prisoners on board.

Reading from a list, the sergeant first calls the name of Rosetta. As their names are called, the women cross the stage and the captain notes them in a book. With the exception of Manon, who is third, and a girl called Ninon, who is next to last and who covers her face with her hands, the women appear unconcerned. Perhaps they are simply trying to maintain some dignity before the townspeople, who laugh and comment as freely as if they were looking at cattle in a marketplace. In the rhythmic laughter of the chorus, we hear an echo of the laughter of the students from Act One.

Lescaut has not abandoned hope, and as the roll call continues he tries to stir up a riot amongst the townspeople by telling them that Manon and the poor young man approaching her are married. On their wedding day, he declares, the girl was abducted by a rich old man who enjoyed her for a day and then cast her aside. Her unhappy bridegroom, he says, "searches and finds his ravished wife again," degraded and in chains. Sympathizing with the young couple, the crowd begins to grow angry.

Des Grieux appears, and as Manon passes by he approaches and takes her hand. Manon is at her best when things are at their worst, and now she cries, but she also begs Des Grieux to forgive her and to go back to his father's home and forget her. This is the beginning of Manon's Trial, which will continue through the opera's end, and during which she will demonstrate her courage in the face of death. Des Grieux rails, "In my soul there is only hatred, only hatred, of men and of God!"

The music of the Embarkation Aria begins, and the sergeant orders the women into single file. Seeing Manon and Des Grieux together, he grabs her and shoves her toward the other women. That is the last straw for Des Grieux. Out of his mind with rage he seizes Manon and shields her from the sergeant with his body.

In sympathy with the young man who is only trying to defend his ravished wife, the crowd shout to Des Grieux to have courage, and they move toward the sergeant threateningly. Suddenly the ship captain steps forward, and the people fall back respectfully.

Des Grieux had been shouting defiance, but when he sees the captain he too has the wind taken out of his sails. He lets go of Manon and cries, "No! No! I am mad!" (This is one of four times that Des Grieux is described as "insane" in respect to Manon.)

What Des Grieux wants, next to Manon's release, is to be allowed to go with her on the transport ship, and in Prévost, nothing could be more casual than the method through which he accomplished this. As he subsequently relates to a friend, "...I had no difficulty in being taken on board ship. In those days they cast about on all sides for young folk willing to join the colony of their own accord. My passage and my keep were offered me gratis."

Obviously there isn't a particle of drama in this, and Puccini would have to come up with something more interesting with which to conclude his third act. On August 5, 1892, Giulio Ricordi wrote the composer a letter, suggesting the following scenario:

How about this: Manon marches slowly with the others while Des Grieux begs her: "I have obtained the permission"; then, half crying, half speaking, "Manon, Manon, I will follow you!" Manon turns, she falls to her knees, she lifts her arms to heaven in a gesture of joy and gratitude. Des Grieux runs toward Manon, and the curtain falls.[5]

If possible this is even less interesting than Prévost, and Puccini naturally rejected it. What he settled on, however — the Embarkation Aria — is an absolutely incredible display of masochistic groveling by the tenor character.

Having already described himself as Manon's "slave and victim"—"dirt in dirt"— the Chevalier Des Grieux falls to his knees before the captain of the transport ship, and before the startled eyes of the entire town of Le Havre he begins to beg wildly. (Note that while Ricordi wanted Manon on her knees, Puccini preferred that posture for Des Grieux. Recall too that he dropped *Le Villi*'s Roberto to his knees three times. Puccini will put the tenor on his knees again and again — in *Butterfly*, *Fanciulla*, *La Rondine*, *Il Tabarro*, and *Turandot*.)

"Look at me," cries Des Grieux. "I'm insane, look at me, how I weep and implore.... How I weep, see, how I beg for pity! Hear me! Accept me as a cabin boy or for more menial work, and I'll come gladly! Accept me! Ah! See, how I weep and implore. Take my blood ... my life! I implore you, I beg your pity! Ah! Pity! I won't be ungrateful!"

When the amused captain condescends to accept his service, smilingly saying, "Come on, cabin boy, get busy!" Des Grieux, who had been regarding the man with "a terrible anxiety," gives a cry of joy and kisses the captain's hand. Manon expresses her own joy, the lovers embrace, and as the orchestra triumphantly thunders the theme of Undying Love, Lescaut shakes his head and slowly exits, never to see his sister again.

One might be excused for thinking that after this astounding scene, Puccini would find no greater means of humiliating his tenor character.[6] But in truth Des Grieux is psychologically primitive. A true knight of medieval *romance*, his passion for Manon is pure, unadulterated Love as Madness. There is no future in a character with such a mindset, and Puccini would abandon such obvious use of the Love as Madness technique until *Turandot*, where it would resurface — with an important difference — in Calaf.

The final act is set in America, in the burning desert bordering New Orleans. As the curtain rises, sunset is approaching. *Manon* is unique in Puccini, in bringing death to one of the lovers at night. In the Romantic World, the time from moonrise to sunrise generally represents the natural lifespan for the young lovers. Their stories begin as the sun is fading, and thus they are born at sundown. Soon the moon rises, and the Night of Love ensues. As night progresses, the lovers live passionately, and try desperately to hold on to the waking dream of endless love in endless night. But they age as the night grows old, and when the moon is killed by the sun, death comes for Mimi, Cavaradossi, Tosca, Butterfly, and Liu.

One might argue that Puccini set Manon's death at sundown out of convention — the close of day equals the close of life — but this seems very unlikely. Even in this first opera of the cycle, he has identified Manon with the moon, and romantic love with night, and he has identified a loveless and mismatched relationship based on gold with day. Night is beautiful to Puccini; Day is hateful.

The only sensible reason for Puccini to have set Manon's death at sundown was as a way of showing that Manon truly has repented of her lust for gold, and has returned to being what she was in Act One — a *romance* character who belongs to Night. Having Manon die at the precise time of night at which she first appeared in the opera, and outside, under a dark sky studded with stars, Puccini is telling us that what she was when we first met her, she is again, and will be forever. As she herself tells us, she will never see the sun again. This is not cause for sorrow, but rather for rejoicing.

The opening music of the last act is built on "Crisantemi," the theme of Manon's Death. As the curtain rises to reveal the exhausted couple, the orchestra sounds Manon's personal motif, in a sad cry of, "Ah, Ma-non. Ah, Ma-non."

Puccini was unable to incorporate into his libretto the section of Prévost's book that told of the adventures of Manon and Des Grieux at the French colony in Louisiana. On their arrival in America, the couple found that unmarried women were assigned to single men by the colony's governor. They assured the governor they were married, and he accepted this. So did the governor's nephew, although reluctantly, for he was overwhelmed by Manon's beauty, and wanted her badly.

The colony turned out to be a good place, and Manon and Des Grieux grew so happy with their new life they decided to go legitimate. They confessed they were not married, and asked for permission to be. Instantly the governor's nephew demanded that Manon be given to him. Des Grieux refused, and killed the young man in a sword fight. The couple then fled the colony, and so it is that they are now where we find them — in this terrible desert on the outskirts of New Orleans, where they are in great danger of dying of exposure.[7]

Manon's Death is sounded as Des Grieux urges his beloved to lean on him. A circle that was opened in Act One now closes as Manon echoes a plaintive cry from the chorus at Amiens: "The breeze wanders over the plain, and the day is dying." She falls, and confesses she can go no farther.

Fearfully, Des Grieux asks whether she is suffering, and for a moment Manon loses her courage. "Horribly," she admits. But when she sees how much this distresses him she says that all she needs is a short rest. Manon has been greedy and foolish, but she is redeemed by her immense courage in terrible circumstances, and her resolve not to break down in front of Des Grieux. We see in Manon the bravery and strength of will that will characterize all the heroines who will follow her. She achieves the *romance* ideal of knighthood.

Utterly spent, Manon faints. Des Grieux calls her anxiously, and as he does the music shifts to that of the Act Two "recrimination and forgiveness" scene. The unconscious Manon has not answered, and Des Grieux cries, "See, it is I who weep and implore.... Ah! Manon! Answer me! You're silent!?" The musical recurrence is dramatically perfect, for the melody to which Des Grieux has been singing had originally accompanied his "Be silent! Be silent! You're breaking my heart!" Now, with death approaching his adored Manon, he thinks back in anguish to that time when he angrily told Manon to be silent, and with his heart breaking he prays that she might speak to him now.

Manon regains consciousness, and the music of recrimination and forgiveness continues as she begs her lover for help against the thirst that is killing her. She, who once implored him to look upon the feast of gold and forgive her, now asks whether it is he who is imploring her, and she asks him for water with which to sustain her life.

Des Grieux would give all of his blood for Manon, but as he looks desperately in all directions, the music of Manon's Death returns. "And nothing! Nothing!" he cries in agony. He calls out to the God "...to whom even as a child I directed my prayers." But the prayer will not be answered. Manon tells Des Grieux that only he can help her. He must leave her, and go look for help.

In spite of her optimistic words, the orchestra continues to sound Manon's Death as Des Grieux lays her gently on the ground and tries to decide what to do. When Manon's Death gives way to the shimmering theme of Undying Love, a sudden resolve comes over Des Grieux, and he leaves.

Manon's great aria, "Sola, perduta, abbandonata," is sometimes criticized on the grounds that Manon is not alone, nor lost, nor abandoned, but rather is faithfully attended by a devoted man whom she has caused a great deal of anguish and trouble. I think, however, that what Puccini was attempting to do via this aria was to show us Manon's inner strength. Sung at her moment of greatest physical weakness, it is an aria of hurricane force.

Oboes and flutes—the seductive woodwind instruments that express the idea of Manon—twine together in a sad but insinuating melody as she gives way to utter despair. But even so, she will not go down without a fight. Manon raises herself up, and cries out against the approach of death.

She has a vision, a memory of the life she and Des Grieux had hoped to make for themselves in this land. Alas, in spite of her sincere repentance, her beauty stirred up new trouble in the form of the governor's nephew. His death haunts Manon, and it is that of which she is thinking as she cries, "...my hateful past rises up again ... it is stained with blood."[8]

Manon calls on the tomb as a haven of peace. But no Puccini character really believes this. The aria ends with the agonized cry, "No! I don't want to die! Beloved, help me!" Des Grieux returns, and Manon embraces him fiercely. Having regained control of herself, Manon spends her final minutes telling her beloved how much he means to her. Fire imagery appears as Des Grieux refers to her as his "flame of eternal love," and Manon answers that "the flame is going out."

Manon's Death resumes in the orchestra as Des Grieux feels a chill invading his lover's face. Singing to her own Death music, Manon begs for a kiss, and in despair Des Grieux cries, "Without you I am lost! I will follow you!" She refuses his vow of suicide, commanding him, says Puccini, "with her last breath, imperiously," "I don't want that." There is no question but that the Chevalier will obey his lady's order.

She bids him a last farewell, saying, "I shall not see the sun again." The impression is of loss, of a terrible sinking into blackness, but in fact her acknowledgement that the sun will never touch her again is cause for rejoicing in Puccini's World. It is the waking dream that now comforts Manon. Like Tristan and Isolde, Manon believes she has attained the never-ending Night, in which love lasts forever.

"My faults will be carried away by oblivion," she sings, and the music is one of the dainty minuets of Act Two, now played in the manner of a dirge.[9] Her voice faltering, she speaks her last: "...but my love, does not die." With his incomparable lady gone, the Chevalier Des Grieux, "insane with grief," falls unconscious across her body. The orchestra cries, "Ah! Ma-non! Ah! Ma-non!" and the curtain drops.

6

La Bohème

Libretto by Giacosa and Illica, based on *Vie de Bohème*, by Henry Mürger
First performed at the Teatro Regio, Turin, February 1, 1896

La Bohème's theme is the brevity of life. There are four scenes in the opera, and in sequence they encompass dusk, night, dawn, and daylight; thus the story of the love of Rodolfo and Mimi is figuratively portrayed as taking place in a single day. Puccini uses fire as a symbolic element — as a metaphor for life. Both are ardent and beautiful; both terribly brief. Rodolfo and Marcello introduce the image almost immediately, when in Act One they compare love to a hearth, "...that consumes much, and too quickly. Where man is the fuel and woman the andiron. The one reduced to ashes as the other watches." At this point the image is a conventional one from *romance*, involving Man putting his emotional all into a romantic relationship, only to find that Woman is heartless. The image undergoes a change, however, when fire is physically introduced via the burning of Rodolfo's manuscript in an attempt to gain some heat in the frigid garret. This scene is taken from the source book, Henry Mürger's *Vie de Bohème*, and it's instructive to compare the original with Puccini.[1]

Mürger's character, Rodolphe, is not burning the only existing copy of his play. Rodolphe has revised the play many times, thus he can afford to burn some of the earlier drafts so his hands will be warm enough to wield his poet's pen. Mürger makes a few quips that verbally confuse the burning of the manuscript with a performance of the play.

For instance, he observes that the second act was burning "amid much applause." (Rodolphe, still cold, is beating his hands together.) When the young man is able to write only two lines of his poem during the burning of the third act, he mutters, "I always thought that act was too short." Mürger describes the dénouement as flaming up in the stove, coinciding with a spurt in the poet's inspiration. After the manuscript finishes burning and the poem is simultaneously completed, Rodolphe shoves the remaining manuscripts under his bed. With a final, deliberate confusion of manuscript burning and play performance, the young man comments, "It won't go beyond a second night."

Puccini concentrates on the play as a depiction of human life. As Marcello and Colline comment on the drama/fire, they use the same sort of quips Mürger did, but with a difference, in that scenes from human life are described as flashing by with terrible swiftness. The story is brilliant, the boys concede, but it doesn't last long. A flame dies in the stove, and Rodolfo says an ardent scene of love died with it. A page crackles. "There were kisses there," says Marcello. All too quickly the fire burns itself out. It was, Colline sadly observes, "...a useless and fragile drama."

Mürger's scene ends cheerfully, with the fire finishing at exactly the right moment: with the completion of the poem. In Puccini, the boys pause as the last flame dies, and there is silence as they gaze with regret at the now lifeless stove, cooling just as a newly lifeless body cools.

Puccini's scene is so simple, yet so brilliant. A wonderful example of the Puccini Mixture of opposites, its subtly melancholy lines are scarcely noticeable amidst a scene of youthful fun. How beautifully the words mesh with Puccini's music, with its own unique mixture of joy and sorrow. How effortlessly it sets up Rodolfo's upcoming relationship with Mimi, which will flash by with such fearful swiftness that it will seem all its joy and sorrow was experienced in a single day. How perfectly the words and music of this sunset scene express the concept of "...the hour of waking dreams, when hope struggles with melancholy."

Fire next appears in connection with Mimi, who knocks at Rodolfo's door because her candle has gone out. The candle's fragile flame represents Mimi's life force, already flickering dangerously as tuberculosis races through her young body. In response to Mimi's request for help, Rodolfo relights her candle with his own, but again it goes out. He tries once more, but his own candle is extinguished by the wind that blows through the hallway of the chilly apartment building.

This scene parallels one in Mürger, between characters named Francine and Jacques, but Mürger lacks the pathos of Puccini. The original finds the cheerful Francine singing as she climbs six flights to her apartment. It's a nuisance that her candle was blown out by the wind, and noticing a light under her neighbor's door, she knocks.

Jacques' apartment is filled with smoke. In contrast to Francine, Jacques had been depressed, and in such moods he chose to smoke tobacco sprinkled with laudanum. It is the smoke that makes Francine faint when the door is opened, and like Puccini's Mimi, she drops her candle and key. The next moments are much like those in the opera: the sprinkling of water on the girl's face, the hasty departure, the return for a light for the candle, the extinguishing of both candles by the wind, the search for the key, the touching hands, the shining moon. It is only later the reader learns Francine is consumptive. In Puccini, our immediate awareness of Mimi's illness is what suggests the connection between the flickering candle flame and her own faltering life force. It is also terribly cold in Puccini, which is not the case in Mürger.

In modern productions of *Bohème*, the original stage directions regarding the final extinguishing of the two candles by the wind are often ignored, and the tenor and even the soprano are instructed to blow out their candles deliberately, so as to show they wish to give Mimi an excuse to stay. A deliberate blowing-out of the candles destroys Puccini's metaphor of Fire as the life force, which is expressed for the last time in the final act.

In that act, Mimi has returned to the garret to die in the company of Rodolfo and the other Bohemians. Musetta is warming cordial over a spirit lamp. Moments after Mimi's death, which at first goes unnoticed by the friends, Musetta realizes the flame of the lamp is flickering. She calls Marcello's attention to it, and asks him for something with which to protect it. This appears to be a reenactment of the scene from Act One, when Mimi asked Rodolfo for help in keeping her candle flame lit.

Without an understanding of the Fire metaphor, Musetta's final request of Marcello seems like filler. With an understanding, her appeal for help recalls to us the short-lived drama/fire, and Mimi's fragile-flamed candle. Moments later the Bohemians realize their friend is dead, her warm and beautiful flame too soon extinguished.

In my comment above, regarding the first appearance of the Fire metaphor, I noted the use by Marcello and Rodolfo of the submissive knight/cruel lady language of *romance*.

There is in *La Bohème* a small but significant change in the sadomasochistic dynamic from that of *Manon Lescaut*.

Des Grieux and Manon were a classic *romance* couple, with the devoted male struck down by Love as Madness. In *Bohème*, Puccini added something to Rodolfo's psyche to increase his suffering: the guilt of a man unable to provide for his desperately ill lover. Of course, we saw guilt on the part of Des Grieux in the last act of *Manon*. He too was unable to provide for his lover, who was dying of exposure. But it was entirely Manon's fault they were in their extreme situation. In *Bohème*, it can be no one's fault but Rodolfo's that he is poor, and cannot buy warmth and food and medical care for Mimi. We should note as well how skillfully and intently Puccini humiliates Rodolfo during the final scene. Not for him the simple terror of *Le Villi*'s Roberto, or the masochistic groveling of Des Grieux at Le Havre. Rodolfo is shamed to the very core of his being.

The young man has nothing to pawn, to pay for a doctor and medicine. It is Musetta and Marcello who fetch those things. Even Colline has a coat he can sell. Rodolfo can't provide Mimi with the muff she longs for, either. It is Musetta who gives Mimi the muff, and in a moment of terrible shame for Rodolfo, when Mimi asks whether it was a gift from him Musetta quickly answers that it was. Mimi then lovingly reproaches Rodolfo for having spent so much money on her, and he weeps bitter tears of humiliation. "Such a cold little hand," Rodolfo said when he first met Mimi. "Let me warm it for you." To his lasting shame, he never was able to do that.

La Bohème opens with one of the most pulse-quickening of introductions. A mere 39 bars, and we are in the bare and freezing Paris garret that is home to the painter Marcello, and his friend, the poet Rodolfo. Sundown is fast approaching. In *Manon*, Puccini-type Artists appeared in the persons of the Madrigal Singer and the Dancing Master. Manon was a Vacillator, with one foot in the world of Night, where she was natural, artless, and filled with love, and the other in Day, where she was artificial, studied, and cold. Geronte was the Alberich: aged, gold-poisoned, and barred from the joys of love. There was no Lady of the Rose. Here, in the second opera of the cycle, we see as either main or supporting characters all four of the types I have identified as belonging to Puccini's Romantic World.

The four Bohemians are Artists, who live for art and love and despise gold. They live in the night, and as close to outdoors as possible, since their garret apartment serves at best to keep the snow from falling on their meager possessions. Musetta is the Vacillator, who for a while indulges herself in the gold of her Alberich, the wealthy old Alcindoro. Mimi is the first of the cycle's sopranos who are unreservedly devoted to love, and whom Puccini strongly associated with flowers. Mimi is the first Lady of the Rose.

As the curtain rises on Act One, Marcello is at work on a painting of "The Passage of the Red Sea," and finding it hard going with hands as cold as his. Rodolfo, who ought to be at work on an article he owes a publication called "Castor," is looking out the window that slopes across one side of the room, and envying the people whose chimneys are spewing smoke into the gray sky of this Christmas Eve.

Puccini works more with personal musical themes in this opera than he did in *Manon*. In her opera, only Manon herself had a motif, and it was simply the interval of the descending second, which seemed to speak her name. Here, every one of the main characters has his own melodic theme, although these are never developed and their use can be confusing.

The opera's introduction serves as the theme of the Bohemians in general, but it does double duty as Marcello's theme. The reason is that Puccini decided to assign as each person's theme, the music to which he or she first enters or sings (or, in Musetta's case, is described by someone else). Marcello speaks first, so he gets the Bohemians' Theme. The music of the gray skies of Paris, to which Rodolfo first sings, will be his theme, and so on for all of the other characters.

Marcello complains that his hands are as cold as if he had been holding them in "that ice-house that is Musetta's heart!" Once again we are in the realm of *romance*, with a happily tormented gentleman the victim of a cruel lady. Moving from ice to fire, Marcello and Rodolfo describe love as a stove in which man is burned to ashes while woman looks on unmoved.

There isn't a stick of firewood in the apartment, which aside from art supplies and manuscripts contains little more than necessities. The young men simply must get some heat going, so Marcello suggests burning one of the chairs. But Rodolfo has a better idea, and grandly declares, "Let thought burst into flame!"

Marcello guesses this means he should burn his painting, but that was not Rodolfo's plan. His idea is to burn the manuscript of his play. Rodolfo gives the first act to Marcello and tells him to tear it up. Rodolfo touches off the torn pieces of his work, and as the young men bask in the heat, harp and strings give us the leaping flames and voluptuous warmth that so delight the shivering friends.

This musical description of fire is something new for Puccini. With *Bohème*, Puccini's orchestra gains an ability to paint pictures and depict extra-musical sounds. From now on this will be a favorite technique, and the attentive listener will be able to hear in his scores such sounds as twittering robins, buzzing wasps, dripping blood, and the final beats of a dying girl's heart.

Now the third member of the Bohemians enters: Colline the philosopher, who has been trying to raise money by pawning some of his books. The music to which he enters is his personal theme, which will recur in Act Four. A Puccini Artist like his friends, Colline knows the most appropriate way of raising money is by barter. But to his disgust, all the pawnshops were closed in honor of Christmas Eve. Without a doubt, he declares, this pawnshop closure is a sign the Apocalypse is near. But now Colline sees a sight that is even more strange: a fire in his friends' stove. Informed that Rodolfo's play is being given "to the flames," he declares the work to be brilliant. Alas, though, it doesn't last long. The harp reveals the winking out of the blaze.

The second act follows the first into the stove, and the second burst of flame is described via a dazzling passage in the brass. "A page crackles," observes Colline, as the orchestra twinkles with harp, bells, and triangle, and in a tiny musical gem, Marcello declares "there were kisses there."

It is no accident that the music of Rodolfo's second act is the most beautiful and brilliant piece of the drama/fire. Life's second act is young adulthood, filled with vigor, freedom, dreams, and love. Act Two of the opera literally parallels the musical description of Act Two of the drama/fire, beginning with a dazzling passage in the brass. There will be kisses for Marcello there, as well.

By now we should have developed a sensitivity to Puccini's mixture of emotional opposites. When we see a scene of gaiety, we should expect notes of sadness. The final three acts of Rodolfo's play are fed to the stove all at once, suggesting the increasing speed with which time seems to pass as we age, and the three young men sing cheerfully of "beauty vanishing in happy flames."

The fire almost out, Colline condemns the "inept, futile drama," and Marcello signals a musical pause by reporting that the fire "crackles, withers, dies." The harp describes the fire's death, and for a moment there is silence as the boys look sadly at the lifeless stove. The mood is swiftly lightened, however, when Marcello and Colline shout "Down with the author!" finishing off the game of having watched a performance of Rodolfo's play.

Another of Puccini's now-expert transitions takes place as the apartment door bursts open and two delivery boys, accompanied by Schaunard's Theme, enter, staggering under loads of firewood, wine, cigars, and food. The astonished friends exclaim over the great feast destiny has provided them with, and as the delivery boys exit, the final member of the quartet comes in. Triumphantly, Schaunard the musician tosses some silver coins into the air, and the others scramble for them and for the provisions.

Schaunard has a story to recount of how he came by all this bounty, but to his annoyance the others are too busy getting the food and wine onto the table and starting up the stove again to pay attention to his story of the Englishman, the parrot, and the infatuated maid. He arrives at the end of his tale, and realizes his friends haven't heard a word. (The sun is setting now, and with the room darkening Marcello lights two candles and places them on the table.)

Has Schaunard violated the Code of the Artists and accepted money for Art — in this case, playing music? No, he has not. Schaunard thought he was being engaged to give piano lessons, but to his surprise the Englishman pointed to a parrot on another floor of his building and said, "You will play until that bird dies." (A muted trumpet describes the parrot's squawks.)

The parrot was a loud, obnoxious bird belonging to a loud, obnoxious actress, and for some time the Englishman had been losing his battle to get some peace and quiet. Realizing the actress must sleep during the day, he hired Schaunard to play scales all day long, until either the actress conceded defeat, or the bird died. Three days of playing scales can hardly be described as music-making, and so Schaunard's acceptance of silver (after having killed the bird with parsley) leaves him unblemished as an Artist.

Seeing his friends have laid the table, Schaunard stops them as they are about to fall on the food. This food, he declares, was bought as insurance against the dark, insecure future. The music grows briefly tender. Puccini's young men know about hunger, but they are too young in bohemian life for it to have become the terrible, gnawing enemy that it will. At this point they are simply hungry with the healthy appetites of Youth.

It is the custom, Schaunard reminds them, to dine out on Christmas Eve. He suggests they save the food for later, and go to the Latin Quarter for dinner, to the Café Momus. As he describes the Quarter, filled with pretty girls and their student beaux, the "Latin Quarter" music of Act Two carries his words.

A pre-dinner toast is about to be drunk when a knock is heard. Marcello asks who it is, and when he hears the answer — Benoit — the orchestra reacts with mock horror. "The landlord!" cries Marcello. Owing him rent for the last quarter, it isn't good to meet him when they're broke. But it's even worse to meet him when they're flush. "There's nobody here!" shouts Colline.

But Benoit persists, so Schaunard opens the door. The landlord enters, and proffers a bill for the past due rent. Marcello is the quickest thinking of the boys, and with a show of hospitality he offers Benoit a chair. The old man is suspicious, but as Schaunard plays along and seats him, Marcello offers a glass of wine, which is readily accepted. All seems cordial as they drink one another's health, but then Benoit returns to the point of his visit: the rent!

Marcello refills the landlord's glass. Another toast is drunk, but again Benoit returns to the point. Marcello displays Schaunard's coins, and as Benoit looks at them greedily, Rodolfo and Schaunard softly ask their friend whether he's lost his mind. Colline looks on and says nothing.

Having satisfied the old fellow's eyes, and again refilled his glass, Marcello begins a friendly conversation. He asks the decrepit coot how old he is, and catching Marcello's drift Rodolfo interjects, "Oh, about our age." There's that Mixture again. Rodolfo's line is funny and tragic at once, for while there is of course a tremendous difference in their ages, did not the drama/fire just demonstrate how quickly life flashes by? Only yesterday the shriveled Benoit was a lad, and what he is today, the Bohemians will be tomorrow. As Benoit assures them he is much older than they, Marcello persists in believing there is little difference. Why, didn't he see Benoit with a pretty young girl at the Bal Mabille a few days ago?[2]

At first reluctant to talk about his exploits, Benoit falls victim to the wine and the flattery and begins to hold forth about his taste in women. Benoit dislikes truly fat women, but he also warns the boys against women who are downright lean. Thin women are nothing but trouble, he declares.

In Mürger, Benoit begins making some really vulgar remarks, and so when, in respect to those troublesome thin women, he happens to mention his wife, it's not entirely a joke that the boys react with exclamations of outrage. (To Puccini, Benoit's real offence is his age and his devotion to money. He is a minor Alberich.)

The friends demand that this wretch leave their virtuous home at once before he pollutes it any further with his lewd principles. Frightened, confused, and more than a little tipsy, Benoit finds himself thrust out of the room. Everyone laughs as Marcello slams the door and declares, "I've paid the rent!"

Momus is calling, and Schaunard urges his friends to each take their share of his coins. No one thanks him or expresses surprise, for these are Artists, and what belongs to one belongs to all. A mirror is handed to the bearded Colline, and Marcello urges him, now that he's rich, to visit a barber. (Puccini specified in the stage directions that the mirror is cracked.)

Cheerfully, Colline agrees, and the boys head for the door. All except Rodolfo, who needs to finish that article for "Castor." His friends promise to wait for him on the street, and they start down the rickety staircase. There is no light, and Marcello warns the others to hold onto the rail. There is a crash and a shout from Colline, and Rodolfo calls down, "Colline, are you dead?" With pitch-black humor, Puccini has him answer, "Not yet."

Rodolfo had assured the others he would only need five minutes, but after sitting at his desk for a moment he throws down his pen in disgust. (Mindful of thrift, he has blown out one of the two candles Marcello lit.) Rodolfo tells himself he is not in the mood to write, but his real problem is lack of inspiration. He is in need of a muse, and fortunately, one is approaching his door this very moment.

To Henry Mürger, chronicler of bohemian life, men were artists and writers and thinkers, while women were muses. His women characters sing, or model, or do some minor acting, which, being merely an imitation of life, is not something requiring real talent. (This was the general view of the acting profession in the 19th century.) Mürger's women are good at making clothes, but that is simply to follow a pattern somebody else created. The women of *Vie de Bohème* are merely girlfriends, and the greatest skill one of them can have is a skill for making coffee.

There are repeated flashes of undisguised contempt towards women in Mürger, who despite his "bohemian" tales appears to have been pretty conservative. While his male characters are uniformly well educated and honorable, several of the girlfriends, including Mimi, are barely literate, and they sometimes exhibit a sort of low cunning, that serves as the female version of intelligence.[3]

Puccini had no agenda except the making of good theatre. But in making good theatre he clearly felt it necessary to alter the power relationships he found in his source material, tipping the balance of power in favor of the women (eventually, overwhelmingly in their favor). The dominant characters in *La Bohème* are Mimi and Musetta; the weak characters are their adoring men, Rodolfo and Marcello. In Puccini, Mimi fulfils the role of muse for Rodolfo, inspiring his aria, "Che gelida manina," with the mere touch of her hand. But her skill as an embroiderer of flowers gives her, in the composer's eyes, the same rank of Artist held by the male Bohemians.

While Rodolfo was seeing his friends off, a solo violin supported him with Rodolfo's Theme. Now, a soft knock is heard at the door, and as the orchestra gently sounds Mimi's Theme via the opening measures of "Mi chiamano Mimì" (They call me Mimi), the voice of a young woman is heard.

Here is the first use of what will become one of Puccini's favorite devices: the introduction of a character via the offstage voice. Puccini began introducing his characters one by one in *Le Villi*, but the introductions were crude and stagy. We can see evidence in *Manon* of how hard he had been thinking about the problem, for not only does he give the audience time to get to know one character before bringing on another, he also has the chorus announce the arrival of the title character.

Here in *Bohème* he has hit on the best device of all. The offstage voice directs our attention to that spot on the stage where the singer will make her entrance, and inspires curiosity about the author of the voice. Rodolfo is as curious as the audience regarding the woman on the other side of his door, who says her candle has gone out. The poet hastens to open the door and invite her in. Mimi demurs, but when he persists she enters, coughing painfully. This frightens Rodolfo, and Mimi's Theme halts.

He asks whether she is ill, and she blames her shortness of breath on the steepness of the staircase. (In an age without elevators, the higher the floor, the poorer the tenant. The Bohemians live on the top floor, and not just because it provides the best light for Marcello's painting.) Worn out, Mimi faints, and her candle and apartment key fall to the floor. Rodolfo catches her, and places her in a chair. He hurries to fetch water, and as he sprinkles it in her face, the plinking of violins over flute describes the drops of water hitting the girl.

Mimi recovers somewhat, and Rodolfo helps her to a chair near the warm stove, and fetches her a glass of wine. It is fortunate Mimi arrived in the wake of Schaunard's bounty, and with Rodolfo here alone she might be excused for assuming he is fairly well off. This is of course not true, and in the last scene, when Mimi is dying, Puccini will see to it Rodolfo is stripped bare of any such pretensions, in a radical departure from Mürger.

Rodolfo looks at Mimi's pretty face admiringly as she sips the wine, but a moment later she stands and, assuring him she is better, asks him to light her candle so she can go. Reluctantly he complies, but no sooner has Mimi gone than she is back again, having realized she dropped her key. There is a breeze in the hallway, and as Mimi stands at the door her candle goes out again. Rodolfo moves to relight her candle a second time, with the only one that remains burning in his apartment, but he is caught in the same breeze. Instead of succeeding in helping her, he loses his own flame.

It is full night now, and pitch dark in the apartment. It's time for the Night of Love. Apologizing for being a bother, Mimi asks Rodolfo to help her search for the key. The two get down on the floor and feel about. Rodolfo finds the key, and silently pockets it. Mimi suspects, but when he denies having found the key she continues, as he does, to feel about on the floor. A moment later, his hand touches hers. Startled, Mimi gets to her feet.

The opera's first aria begins: Rodolfo's "Che gelida manina." Rodolfo has found his muse in Mimi, but his inspiration is fired not by the muse's kiss, but rather by contact with her hand. It is the touch of Mimi's hand that touches off this aria, and indeed the first words of Rodolfo's song are, "Such a cold little hand. Let me warm it for you."

"It is the night of the full moon," he sings, and on the word "night" the flute, which has been silent for 50 bars, begins an anticipation of the loveliness of the rising moon. The flute serves as the offstage voice of the moon, piquing our interest in her. This will be a gentler moon than Manon's. There is no frenzy in it. Yet Mimi's moon is no less powerful. In a few minutes Rodolfo will see Mimi haloed in the silvery light of her moon, and love will conquer him, and take him prisoner.

Puccini continues the technique he used in *Manon*, of having the orchestra acquaint the audience with a "big tune" before playing it in full force. The music of the introduction to "Che gelida manina" will be repeated in full voice when Mimi and Rodolfo exit arm in arm, to close the first act.

Rhetorically Rodolfo asks, "Who am I?" He is a poet, and so he writes. And the way he lives is— he lives. He freely admits his poverty, and significantly he makes no claim that someday he'll be successful and well off. A Puccini Artist would never dream of saying such a thing, for that would be the death of his Art, and of his hopes for love. Rodolfo produces rhymes and hymns to love because it is his nature to do so, just as it is the nature of a flowering plant to produce blossoms. One doesn't ask a plant how it lives. It just lives.

During "Che gelida manina," Rodolfo experiences the beginning of the waking dream. Having told Mimi he indulges himself like a great lord on rhymes and hymns to love, he goes on to speak of dreams, delusions, and castles in air. He had thought those things were his treasures, but now he has seen Mimi and touched her hand, he realizes the dreams he had treasured are as nothing compared to her. A crescendo begins as he says those treasures "have been replaced with..." and the crescendo peaks with an optional high C for the tenor on the words "...la speranza." Hope.

It is Hope: the word that animates the waking dream; the word associated with moonrise; the word that will answer the first of Turandot's riddles. Here, it receives the greatest emphasis of any word so far in the opera: a sustained *fortissimo*, on that optional high C.

The aria's end is almost conversational, terminating with a plea that Mimi tell her own story. She does so in "Mi chiamano Mimì," which is built on her entrance music. Mimi describes herself as a maker of artificial flowers, and although she obviously earns her living as an embroiderer, she doesn't SAY that. What she says is that making lilies and roses is her special pleasure. It is the same special pleasure that she gets from the rose she keeps in a vase in her room; or rather, the pleasure of the living rose is greater, for it carries a delicate fragrance. Mimi is the first in a line of six sopranos who will fill the role of Puccini's Lady of the Rose: the young and beautiful woman who is entirely devoted to love, and who has a special bond with roses.

The lily and the rose are often paired in Western literature, since the colors are suggestive of white skin and red cheeks or lips.[4] For millennia, roses— perhaps because of their thorns, and a color suggestive of blood — have been used as a resurrection symbol. Puccini uses the rose in just such a way: as a symbol of rebirth. Mimi's aria carries much of the material of a medieval Spring Song, reaching its emotional climax as she sings of her joy at the coming of spring, when the first ray of the April sun belongs to her.

The music to which Mimi tells Rodolfo about her rose is repeated from an earlier section of the aria, in which she had sung of those things that possess for her "...a sweet charm, that speak of love, spring, dreams, illusions, that have the name of poetry." This is the foundation of the waking dream, and being that the music is repeated in connection with Mimi's rose, we may infer that all of these beautiful things— the waking dream itself— may be summed up in the rose. The music recurs at several critical points in the subsequent acts, and we might identify it as the theme of Mimi's Rose.

The love expressed for the sun in this aria is in part a carryover from the form of the Spring Song, which traditionally anticipates a rebirth of love in spring, the season when all things are renewed. But the positive remark Mimi makes about the sun is ultimately revealed as deceptive, and dreadfully ironic.

Sunrise brings death in Puccini, and in *La Bohème* the composer heightens the pathos of Mimi's last-act death by harkening back to her expressed longing for the sun. A cold, gray dawn arrives in Act Three, but the sun itself comes only in Act Four. It is that first ray of the April sun that Mimi had longed for, and it steals through the garret window, touches the girl's face despite Rodolfo's efforts to keep it away, and it kills her.

But now, from down in the street, Rodolfo's friends call to him. When the poet goes to answer, he opens the window, and the glorious light of the full moon suddenly fills the room. Rodolfo does not see this at first, for he is calling to his friends that he is not alone, and they should go on to Momus and get a table. The discerning Marcello observes, "The poet has found his poetry." The chuckling friends leave, and as Rodolfo turns to look at Mimi, he is stunned by the sight of her, bathed in the silvery light of her glorious moon. Rodolfo and Mimi have now entered completely into the waking dream, and for so long as the light of the moon shines on Mimi, her beauty and her strength will endure, along with the dream of a love that will never die.

A passionate duet ensues—"O soave fanciulla" (O lovely girl)— as the enraptured Rodolfo sings of how Mimi has been haloed by the light of the rising moon (which is described by a rippling harp). As did Des Grieux, Rodolfo now sees before him the face that he would adore eternally; or, as he phrases it, "...the dream that I would dream forever."

Puccini has one more innovation with which to charm us, before he closes this enchanting act. Unlike the standard form for a passionate duet, "O soave fanciulla" does not start slow and build to a great climax; rather, it begins with the climax and proceeds to dissolve into song-like conversation regarding what the couple ought to do next. The ardent Rodolfo has one thing on his mind, but the sweetly coquettish Mimi would prefer to be taken to dinner first.

Arm in arm, to the music that opened "Che gelida manina" with the words, "Such a cold little hand. Let me warm it for you," the two exit to join the others, concluding their duet from off stage with an intense yet delicate declaration of love. The night is young, and so are Rodolfo and Mimi. Sunrise is a long way off. Perhaps dawn will never come, and they will indeed find endless love in endless night. We can hope, anyway.

Act Two begins a few minutes later, and it is introduced by a brass fanfare. Much of the music of this act belongs to a single melodic and rhythmic "family," which is why one tune seems to slide so easily into another. The most important members of this family are the fanfare, the "Latin Quarter" music that Schaunard introduced in Act One, and a little melody that will carry Rodolfo's condemnation of Musetta as a flirt who abandoned his friend Marcello.

Just as Schaunard predicted, the Latin Quarter is crowded with girls and students, and with them are street vendors, children and their parents, and an overflow crowd of hungry customers sitting at tables on the chilly sidewalk in front of the Café Momus. Waiters dash about trying to satisfy demands for food and drink, while vendors cry their wares, including — interestingly enough in late December — fresh flowers.

Let's take a moment to recall the music of Rodolfo's drama/fire, Act Two, which began with a brilliant brass fanfare, and then burned with such heat and beauty. The Bohemians are in Act Two of their lives, young adulthood, and we are now in Act Two of their opera. As with the drama/fire, we will soon see an ardent scene of love and kisses, and it will be over sooner than expected. Who is optimistic enough to believe that Act Three will bring greater warmth, or even an equal measure? The essence of Puccini is a desperate clutching with both hands at happiness that will not endure.

The Bohemians are burdened with Schaunard's coins, and although they did not violate the Code of the Artists to get them, money is nevertheless contaminating, and it is best to get rid of it as soon as possible. The friends set about this with dispatch, exchanging the pieces of metal for objects of real worth, such as a pipe and a horn for Schaunard, a coat and a book for Colline, a mysterious parcel for Marcello, and a bonnet for Mimi.

Translations of the libretto often render the bonnet as pink in color, but it's just as correct to describe it as "rose." Asks Mimi of Rodolfo, "Mi sta ben questa cuffieta rosa?" — Does this rose bonnet look well on me? In the two bars of music that come between her question and Rodolfo's warmly affirmative answer, we hear a motif that expresses Mimi's Special Desire. As she will tell the boys in a few minutes, she has wanted such a bonnet for a long time. The motif will recur in the final act, carrying Musetta's decision to get the dying Mimi a muff for her hands since, "it may be the last time the poor girl has a special desire."

As snatches of conversation are given out here and there, it is easy to miss a poignant remark made by Schaunard. He has been watching the crowd, which despite the merry-making of Christmas Eve displays a touch of exhaustion and even sadness, and he says, "Pushing and trampling and running, the crowd hurries to its delights, feeling wild desires — and remaining unsatisfied." Colline shows his friend the book he has bought, and Schaunard seems cheered; perhaps because Colline at least has found something that makes him happy.

Delighted with her bonnet, Mimi pauses to look in a store window, where she sees a coral necklace. She admires it, and Rodolfo jokes that if things work out with his millionaire uncle, he'll buy her a more beautiful one. A desire for jewelry is not appropriate for a Puccini heroine, and in some versions of the libretto an admonishing comment is given via the conversation of a nearby couple, also looking in the window. The woman says, "Oh, stupendous jewels," and the man answers, "Eyes are more beautiful."

Marcello, in the meantime, has been playing the part that Puccini usually reserves for the tenor: the young man with a virgin heart, who vows to love only once, and forever. Standing alone and forlorn in the middle of the street, the baritone addresses a passing girl. Rhetorically he suggests they strike a bargain to buy and to sell. "For a sou," he declares, "I'll sell my virgin heart." Of course, Marcello's heart is not a virgin; it is pledged to the imperious Lady Musetta. If the girl he addressed had shown interest Marcello would have run like a greyhound; however, she only laughs at him, and walks on.

Mimi and Rodolfo are nearing the café, and the poet observes Mimi looking at a group of students. Sweetly, but reprovingly, he asks her whom she is looking at. Mimi asks if he is jealous, and Rodolfo replies, "To a happy man, suspicion is always near." It is night, and in his heart Rodolfo knows day is coming, and when it does his dream of love will end.

The other Bohemians have snagged a sidewalk table. Again, Puccini's "good" characters don't like to be inside buildings, unless they're fairly primitive. Little cottages are all right, as are drafty apartments and cabins. The watchword with buildings is the same as with money: enough for survival, but no more.

Just as Mimi and Rodolfo are reaching Momus, we hear another introduction via the offstage voice. It belongs to Parpignol the toy seller, and in strangely melancholy accents he calls out his wares: "Here are the toys of Parpignol!" This cry transitions the action of the crowded street into an intimate scene amongst the Bohemians, and as though bracketing the scene with a pair of bookends, the identical cry, repeated in a few minutes, will close it.

Puccini makes an event out of Mimi's introduction to Rodolfo's friends. Says Rodolfo, "This is Mimi, gay flower-girl. Her presence completes our gracious company. Because ... because I am the poet, she is poetry itself." His song turns rapturous as he expands on this thought: "From my mind blossom songs, from her hands blossom flowers, and from exultant spirits blossoms love." One may assume from these words—"I do A, she does B, together we do C"—that Puccini considers Mimi as much an artist as Rodolfo.

Marcello, Colline, and Schaunard chuckle at Rodolfo's poetic words, but they take seriously his characterization of Mimi. Puccini allows a woman to be admitted as one of the Bohemians, and the boys induct her with a mixture of humor and solemnity. Speaking in turn, Colline and Schaunard intone the Latin phrases of initiation: *Digna est intrari. Ingrediat si necessit.... Accessit.* (She is worthy. Enter if you must.... I agree.)

Again the offstage voice is heard, as Parpignol repeats his advertisement. The voice is closer now, and as the initial cry opened the scene at the table, the second cry closes it. Colline provides the transition to the next scene, via a bellowing call for salami.

Parpignol makes a brilliant entrance, pushing a barrow decorated with fresh fronds and flowers. Following him is a crowd of excited children, shouting for toys. When the Bohemians place their extravagant dinner order—venison, turkey, wine, lobster, crème caramel—they sound very much like the children, all shouting for their hearts' desires, with no thought to the expense. Perhaps Puccini's point is the same as that made in the scene with Benoit: there is little difference in the ages of man. Childhood, adulthood, decrepit old age.... Scarcely is one aware of having attained one phase before the next has succeeded it.

In a pretty arietta, Mimi shows off the bonnet she had wanted for such a long time. Rodolfo, she declares, was able to read her heart, and thus he is a clever man who understands love. Colline and Schaunard laugh a bit, but Marcello bitterly speaks of the waking dream. He has awakened from his own dream, and knows what lies ahead for the starry-eyed young lovers. Looking at Mimi, for whom it is still the first flush of Night, he says, "Oh beautiful age of illusions and utopias! One believes, hopes, and all seems beautiful."

The music he employs is that of Mimi's affectionate phrase about Rodolfo's cleverness; that is, the music of Young Love. By using Mimi's music, Marcello communicates that he knows that age — he can sing to that tune — but he is no longer that young and naïve. Mimi fears she has offended Marcello, but Rodolfo tells her he is in mourning.

Schaunard and Colline decide to change the subject, so they call for a toast. Supposedly it's a neutral one: "Down with troubles, up with glasses! Let's drink!" But the music of the toast is Mimi's music of Young Love. Marcello attempts to drink to it, but before he can set cup to lips he sees a sight that causes him to break off and shout, "I'll drink some poison!" What he has seen is his adored Musetta, beautiful as a dream, laughing shrilly, and followed by a pompous, prosperous, and very old man: Alcindoro.

Alcindoro is our gold-poisoned Alberich, debarred from Love. Trotting behind the lovely Musetta, Alcindoro puffs, and complains at being forced to run like a laborer. Musetta snaps, "Come, Lulu!" and orders the old man to sit with her at a table near the Bohemians.

In Marcello, Musetta, and Alcindoro, we see something close to the classic triangle of medieval *romance*. Marcello is the anguished knight, eating his heart out over his tormenting, illicit passion for the cruel and imperious lady, Musetta. Alcindoro takes the role of cuckolded husband. Looking at the old man in distaste, Schaunard describes him as "...that ugly thing all in a lather."

Although Puccini uses the scenario of the courtly love triangle, his sentiment is slightly different, for it focuses on wealth and age, which here and in *Manon Lescaut* are so closely tied as to be impossible to untangle. The Bohemians' attitude toward Alcindoro is the same as that of *Manon*'s Edmund toward Geronte; that is, a wealthy old man's desire for a pretty young girl is an affront to Youth, and must be thwarted, but as yet we cannot tell which is the real offence — age, or wealth. That it is wealth and/or power — Alberich's Choice — becomes clear in *Tosca*. After *La Bohème* there will never again be a question about this matter. In Puccini's World, it is *wealth and power* that is corrupting. It is *wealth and power* that debars one from love.

Reluctantly, Alcindoro obeys Musetta's order to sit down. Unlike the vigorous young Artists, who insist on sitting outdoors, the old man cannot bear the discomforts of the natural world. Grumbling, he turns up his collar against the cold. Mimi comments on Musetta's beautiful clothes, and with an Artist's scorn for finery, Rodolfo responds, "The angels go naked." (This is a reference to the art motif of Sacred and Profane Love, in which the contrast between erotic and Platonic love is portrayed via two images of the goddess Venus. The erotic Venus wears rich garments; the spiritual Venus is naked.)

Introducing Musetta's Theme, Marcello describes his lover to Mimi: "Her first name is Musetta. Her last name — Temptation. Her occupation is being a Rose in the wind.[5] Always turning and changing, her lovers and her loves. She's like an owl — a bird of prey. Her regular food is hearts. She eats hearts! And so I have no heart."

Musetta has been watching the Bohemians, and is irked that Marcello won't look at her. Like Manon, she can't bear the thought that a former lover no longer pines for her. Trying to gain Marcello's attention, Musetta smashes a plate, and when that doesn't work she decides to really test her power, to see if she can still make him "yield."

Colline and Schaunard are thoroughly enjoying their food, as well as the floorshow Musetta and Marcello are staging. In a continuation of the connection made in the drama/ fire, between real life and life as a play, Colline and Schaunard agree that "the play is stupendous." Soon Marcello and Musetta will be in each other's arms, experiencing the warm and beautiful kisses that enchanted Marcello when Act Two of Rodolfo's play burned.

Rodolfo reiterates his fear of losing Mimi, saying, "Keep in mind I wouldn't always be forgiving you." Mimi doesn't understand that the clock is ticking on their Act Two, so she asks with genuine puzzlement why he speaks to her so, when she loves him and is entirely his.

Musetta begins her song of temptation, "Quando m'en vo." She praises her own beauty, and assures Marcello he remembers her and suffers, and feels dead inside without her. With an Alberich's antipathy to Art, Alcindoro mutters, "...that scurrilous song moves my bile!"

Marcello writhes in agony, and in an allusion to the story of Odysseus, who had himself tied to the mast of his ship so he could hear the sirens' song without rushing to his destruction, Marcello begs his friends to tie him to his chair. As the song continues he becomes increasingly upset. Finally he tries to leave, but the stage directions declare that he "cannot resist the voice of Musetta." Rodolfo's sympathies are entirely with his friend, and he tells Mimi, who is inclined to pity Musetta, "...Marcello once loved her, but the little flirt abandoned him for a better life." Puccini is planting this melody here so he can set up a wonderful ending to this act.

The melody of "the little flirt abandoned him" carries the meaning of Musetta's playing a dirty trick on a man by leaving him for somebody else, and we will hear this same music at the start of the act's close, when Musetta plays a dirty trick on Alcindoro, whom she will not only leave for another man, but will stick with her friends' enormous dinner tab.

The music of "the little flirt abandoned him" will then merge with an emphatic recurrence of the "Latin Quarter" music, which will be played in connection with the military parade that comes on stage. This gives a flavor of glorious triumph to the doings of the Bohemians, as well as bracketing the entire act with the "Latin Quarter" music.

Colline and Schaunard continue to watch the "play." Colline sees that Marcello is somehow enjoying his agony, and he declares that as pretty as Musetta is, he himself would never be caught in such a situation. Schaunard is certain that Marcello will yield. He knows the world of courtly, sadomasochistic love, and using the language of that world he says that to a pair like that, "The noose is sweet; both to the one who gives it, and the one who receives it."

Musetta has observed that Marcello is vanquished. All she needs to do now is get rid of "the old mummy." She shrieks in pain, yet the sound is one of near-pleasure. Displaying her foot coquettishly, she begs the horrified Alcindoro to tear off her shoe, which supposedly pains her terribly. Alcindoro is sent on his fool's errand of fetching a new pair of shoes, and Musetta rushes to Marcello's arms. Schaunard comments that, "We're at the last scene." It's the last scene of the play starring Marcello and Musetta, the last scene of Act Two in Rodolfo's play, and the last scene of Act Two of Puccini's opera.

But now an unpleasant shock is received when the waiter presents the bill for dinner. In another of those melancholy comments Puccini sprinkles throughout his works, Schaunard looks at the bill being proffered by the waiter, and comments, "So soon?" Yes, the bill always comes due — Act Two always ends — sooner than we had expected.

The boys pass the bill from one to another, dismayed at the total. From a distance a military tattoo is heard, heralding the retreat to the barracks. Searching their pockets, the Bohemians are puzzled at their near-emptiness. What could have happened to Schaunard's trove of coins? (The orchestra answers the question by sounding the Bohemians' Theme.) No one recalls the purchases that were made: the pipe, the horn, the coat, the book, the bonnet, and the mysterious parcel.

Street children begin the concluding music, singing of the coming parade of soldiers. This concluding music takes the melody of "the little flirt abandoned him," combines it with the rhythmically charged "Latin Quarter" music, adds Schaunard's Theme (to remind us that the boys were earlier provided with a "great feast" by destiny), and spices it with a bit of military music to go with the parade. The result is a delightful summing up of ideas in this last two minutes of the act: Christmas Eve in the Latin Quarter, Musetta and her tricks, the military parade, yet another great feast that is about to be paid for by destiny, and the triumph of the Bohemians.[6] Making certain we remember the "little flirt" and her dirty trick, Puccini immediately follows the children's line with Musetta's demand of the waiter, that he give her her bill, and add her friends' bill to it. "The gentleman who was with me will pay," she tells the waiter, to the relief and delight of the boys. Musetta drops the combined bill on Alcindoro's plate, declaring, "...where he was sitting, he'll find my salute." Rodolfo's reproachful music — "the little flirt abandoned him" — comments on Musetta's action, but it isn't reproachful any more.

The Retreat crosses the scene, headed by the drum-major, carrying a glittering baton. The triumph of the Bohemians impresses itself on us in sound and in sight, for the six friends join the end of the procession. Since Musetta can't walk with only one shoe, Marcello and Colline carry her on their shoulders. The crowd happily accede to the suggestion that Musetta is being carried in triumph after some military victory, and with gestures they acclaim her as though she were heroine of the day. Bringing up the rear is Schaunard, blowing loudly on his new horn.

The stage empties as the grand procession moves off, then Alcindoro returns, carrying a pair of shoes. He is a ridiculous and pathetic figure as he looks in vain for Musetta, and even more so when the waiter points out to him the horrendous bill. Shocked at what he owes, and bereft of the lovely girl he had planned to spend his night with, the old man collapses into a chair as the off stage voice of the military band sounds its last strains: "...but the little flirt abandoned him for a better life." Musetta the Vacillator has returned to the community of Artists, where love — and poverty — awaits.

Act Three is set at a tollgate at the Barrière d'Enfer. At left is a tavern, in front of which is Marcello's painting of the Red Sea, now titled, "The Port of Marseilles." Paintings of soldiers, also done by Marcello, decorate the walls on either side of the tavern door.

It is dawn, on a cold day in February. The light is uncertain, and subsequent to the two startlingly loud notes that open the act, flute, harp, and triangle give us a delicately chilly description of lightly falling snow. Customs guards sit around a glowing brazier, trying to warm themselves, and street sweepers and peasants bringing farm products to sell in the city call out to the guards to let them pass. The guards open the gates and collect tolls from the people, who then go their various ways.

As the peasants cry their wares — "Butter and cheese!" "Chickens and eggs!" — they seem like a shadowy image of street vendors of the Latin Quarter of two months ago. Reinforcing that image is the off-stage voice of Musetta, who sings from within the tavern a fragment of her now melancholy waltz. The stage is gradually cleared of people, and when only the sergeant remains, the first bars of "Mi chiamano Mimì" steal in on the strings. Mimi enters, coughing painfully, and asks the sergeant which is the tavern where a painter is working. The sergeant indicates the building where Marcello's picture is hanging.

A waitress emerges from the tavern and Mimi asks her to tell the painter that Mimi is outside, and needs to speak to him. A low thrumming, soft but ominous, is heard in the lower strings and timpani. As Mimi waits anxiously, the bells of the hospice Maria Teresa are heard, tolling matins. In Puccini, tolling bells are almost always associated with disaster. These are no exception, for they are reporting that Day is coming.

While the bells were ringing, the Bohemians' Theme began to sound. Doing double duty as Marcello's Theme, it was announcing his entrance. The cheerful theme seems out of place in this gloomy setting, and so will several other characters' personal themes, when they too recur in this act and the final one. Puccini would later use his themes quite skillfully, but on several occasions in the last half of *Bohème* the recurring personal themes— which say nothing more than, "Here he/she is again!"—contribute jarring notes.

Having hurried out to greet Mimi, Marcello explains that he and Musetta have been living at the tavern for the last month. The owner doesn't charge them for room and board, and in return Musetta gives singing lessons, and Marcello, in addition to having given the man his Red Sea painting, is continuing to paint soldiers on the interior of the tavern. In bartering their art for the necessities of life, the pair have remained true to the Code of the Artists. No money has changed hands.

As Marcello speaks of Musetta, an oboe chimes in with Musetta's Theme. This is the music of Marcello's angry introduction: "Her first name is Musetta ... her last name is Temptation." The theme sounds out of place, for it recalls negative things about Musetta, which don't apply at this time. A moment later, Marcello's Theme is heard, when the young man tells Mimi about his painting, and the theme adds a slightly confusing suggestion of Bohemian fun.

Tearfully Mimi begs Marcello for help. Rodolfo, she says, is consumed by jealousy. Everything makes him suspicious. He rages, telling her to find another lover. What can she say to him? Her unhappiness is dreadful, but the irony delicious. Of all the people she might consult, it is Marcello whose advice she seeks. Her lover is jealous and controlling, and shouts that she is a flirt. How can she get him to stop? Of course Marcello hasn't the faintest idea of how to halt Rodolfo's jealousy, and he foolishly offers his own "carefree" relationship with Musetta as a model. "I take Musetta lightly," he declares, "and she takes me lightly. Song and laughter, that is the flower of unchanging love."

However silly Marcello's advice may be, Mimi has no one else to turn to. Marcello agrees to help her and Rodolfo end their relationship, and he goes to the tavern window and points to where Rodolfo lies sleeping on a bench. Mimi is racked by a fit of coughing, and explains to her worried friend that the emotional upheaval of the night before, when Rodolfo stormed out, left her exhausted.

A bit of Rodolfo's Theme sounds as Marcello observes the poet beginning to stir, and he urges Mimi to go home. Mimi starts to leave, but seeing Rodolfo come out of the tavern, she hides behind a tree, wanting to hear what he says about her. Affecting nonchalance, and singing confidently to his theme, Rodolfo tells Marcello he wants to break with Mimi. Seemingly world-weary, Rodolfo claims to be bored. Marcello accuses his friend of being jealous, crazy, tiresome, and stubborn. Mimi has crept closer, and she whispers that

Marcello's accusations will only make Rodolfo angry. Defending his fits of jealousy, Rodolfo claims Mimi is a flirt. But when Marcello essentially calls him a liar, Rodolfo drops his protective shield of anger and admits the truth: he is afraid.

Rodolfo's Masochism Aria begins with a chant of, "Mimì è tanto malata!" (Mimi is so ill!), and his monotone singing beautifully communicates numbness and despair. As Rodolfo describes Mimi's rapid decline to the shocked Marcello, Mimi comes closer, horrified to hear Rodolfo say she is dying.

Rodolfo blames himself for Mimi's condition: his apartment is squalid, there's no fire, and the freezing wind roars through. The young man is filled with shame, which he sings of at the top of his lungs, climaxing on a high B flat, sung *fortissimo*. Mimi is a hothouse flower, he concludes, but poverty has robbed it of its strength, and love is not enough to restore it to life.

The difference between Mürger's and Puccini's attitudes regarding Mimi's illness is worth remarking. Mürger's Mimi says it's her own fault she's sick — she's been eating bad food, has been unhappy, and has spent too much time modeling in unheated studios. "After all," she sadly tells a friend, "it's my own fault. If I'd stayed peacefully with Rodolphe, I wouldn't have gotten into this state." In other words, Mürger blamed the victim.

Puccini chose to reject any suggestion that Mimi's illness was her own fault. He elected to blame *Rodolfo* for it, even though Mimi was *already sick when she met him!* And the reason for this is, he wants to humiliate Rodolfo. Mimi may be frail; Mimi may be dying; but the person Puccini is torturing here is Rodolfo. The three friends — Marcello, Rodolfo, and Mimi — finish Rodolfo's lament together, and their final words are, respectively, "Mimi," "love," and "death." Mimi's sobbing aggravates her cough, and at last Rodolfo realizes she's there, and has heard everything he said. He urges her to come into the tavern where it's warm, but she recoils from the thought of going into the building, saying she'll suffocate in there. A transition occurs when a laugh is heard from the tavern, rippling above Musetta's Theme. Glad to find a reason to leave the unhappy lovers, Marcello runs into the tavern, determined to teach that flirt not to laugh with other men.

"D'onde lieta uscì," Mimi's song of farewell, is built on the B section of her aria of introduction, "Mi chiamano Mimì." While Mimi contributes a new melody and new words, the orchestra supports her with the old music. The result is something magical. Two bars before Mimi begins singing, the orchestra starts playing, "They call me Mimi..." and with this in our ears, our minds turn back to that moment when we saw her standing in the doorway of Rodolfo's apartment.

The soprano begins with, "Though joyously Mimi came at your call of love" (she enters the apartment), "she returns now, alone, to her lonely nest. She returns once again to making artificial flowers." The voice pauses briefly as the flute plays the passage, "Alone I prepare my suppers. I don't often go to church...." (Here we have a picture of how she will spend her solitary days from now on. She *speaks* of her embroidery work, but the orchestra suggests the other things in her life.) The orchestra then cuts out very briefly, so we are focused on Mimi saying, "Goodbye, without rancor."

The orchestra returns as Mimi sings, "Listen, listen. Gather the few things I've left. In my little chest are locked that band of gold, and my prayer book." The flute sings, "Alone I prepare my suppers. I don't often go to church...." Mimi continues, "Wrap them all in an apron, and I'll send someone to get them."

A solo violin sweetly plays the theme of Mimi's Rose: "A rose sprouts in a vase...."

Puccini at last makes a firm connection between the living rose and Mimi's rose-colored bonnet, when Mimi sings, "Note that under the pillow is my rose bonnet. If you wish, keep it as a remembrance of love. Goodbye, without rancor."

As we go through the remaining operas of the cycle, it will become increasingly difficult to escape the notion that there is some significance in Mimi's offer of her rose-colored bonnet to Rodolfo. More significance, that is, than a simple keepsake, which is what the bonnet is in Mürger. (In his story, the bonnet is not rose, or even pink. It is brown and white striped.) Puccini has tied the bonnet to the rose, which symbolizes undying love.

The aria slides seamlessly into one of Puccini's most breathtaking duets, which becomes a quartet when the quarreling Marcello and Musetta join in. The duet begins with Mimi and Rodolfo trading a series of lines in which they bid farewell to their bitter and sweet memories. Finished with this, they take up the material of a Spring Song; that is, lines in which an unhappy couple express a longing for the rebirth of love, which they couch in terms of a desire for spring to come.

This Spring Song includes typical utterances for the genre—talk of the April sun, of flowers, of birds' nests—then suddenly Mimi adds to the time-honored Spring Song, an incongruous element that is pure Puccini. She speaks of the waking dream, which begins at sunset, and which has nothing whatever to do with the warmth of the April sun. "The evening breeze," Mimi suddenly says, "brings balsam for human suffering." If a love song is to inspire Puccini musically, the characters simply must speak of Night, and its waking dream of endless love.

The duet begins with great delicacy, with soft contributions from upper woodwinds, bassoon, harp, and strings. An insistent little throb from flute and viola adds a pungent note. As the duet proceeds, the cornet joins in, then bass clarinet, oboe, double bass, and English horn, with sound piling up on sound.

The couple say goodbye to all the bitter and sweet memories, then move into the Spring Song via the line, "To be alone in winter, is a thing to die of. Alone!" With this line, a series of crescendos and decrescendos begins, providing that hypnotic, wave-like effect that is signature Puccini. Now trombones and timpani enter, just for a moment, punctuating the tiny space between "Alone!" and the next, balancing line, that introduces the Spring Song material: "But when the spring comes, the sun is our companion."

Musetta and Marcello join in with a full-throated screaming match, complete with smashing crockery. Their argument serves to illustrate the quarrels Mimi and Rodolfo have engaged in, and have just told us of, thus we have a double image of this couple. We see Mimi and Rodolfo fighting and making up—the past and the present—at the same time. The number and depth of mental images Puccini is able to present us with via the combination of music, words, and visual incidents, is really astonishing.

In a strange, Puccinian twist on the Spring Song, Mimi and Rodolfo agree that since it is too sad to be alone in winter, they will stay together until spring, and part then. What we have in this vow to stay together as long as winter lasts is a melancholy awareness of time running out, but it is couched in the terms of the Spring Song. We are sad *now*, even though we are together, because winter is cold and lonely. We will be sad *then*, even though spring is warm and joyous, because we will part. Puccini has brought tremendous melancholy to the Spring Song by having this couple anticipate an event that—renewing and life affirming though it is to everyone else—will bring death to them. It is the Puccini Mixture of joy and sorrow again.

With the couple's agreement to stay together until spring, the level of sound in the quartet begins to decrease. Musetta stalks off angrily, trading insults with Marcello, who walks dolefully back into the tavern. The quartet, now a duet again, fades back into the same delicacy with which it opened, and the lovers walk off arm in arm, vowing to part in the season of flowers.

The final-act curtain rises on the garret of Marcello and Rodolfo. Again we hear the Bohemians' Theme, but its gaiety seems forced. Two months have passed since Mimi and Rodolfo walked off arm in arm. April has come. Marcello is at his easel; Rodolfo at his desk. The two would like to believe they are hard at work. "In a coupé?" asks Marcello with feigned indifference. They've been discussing Musetta, whom Rodolfo recently saw driving by in high style.

To Musetta's Theme Marcello declares himself "really glad" for her prosperity, but Rodolfo doesn't believe him. Saying in an aside that his friend is faking, he continues the practice that began in Act Three, when Marcello stripped away Rodolfo's pretence of unconcern over Mimi. Puccini's men are not ashamed of being emotionally vulnerable, and Rodolfo and Marcello do everything they can to expose one another's weakness and dependency on their women. Striking back at Rodolfo, Marcello lets drop the news that he has seen Mimi. Rodolfo starts, and we hear Mimi's Theme. While Marcello describes how he saw Mimi riding in a carriage, dressed like a queen, Rodolfo feigns indifference. Marcello knows his friend is faking. "He's wasting away," he says to himself.

Obviously we have a narrative leap. In Mürger, Rodolfo and Mimi quarreled more, and Mimi finally left and took up with a young viscount. Mimi soon left the viscount, and tried to make a living doing embroidery and modeling, while fighting a losing battle against tuberculosis. She took nothing with her when she left the viscount, and if Rodolfo only knew it, she hasn't eaten for some time, and has been evicted from her apartment.

For about ten seconds, Rodolfo and Marcello try to work. This act relies heavily on "logical reminiscences," and the music employed here is that of Rodolfo's fruitless attempt to finish his article for "Castor." The attempt is hopeless, and like the bad workman of the proverb the boys blame their tools. With exclamations of disgust, they throw down pen and brush, and give themselves over to expressions of longing for their girls. While Rodolfo sits absorbed in thought, Marcello secretly takes a piece of silk ribbon from his pocket and kisses it

La Bohème is unique among the operas in that it features a Masochism Duet, "O Mimì tu più non torni" (O Mimi, you will never return), the music of which is based on a line of music from "Che gelida manina." The line is "Talor dal mio forziere..." in which the poet told Mimi of how her pretty eyes had robbed him of his dreams, delusions, and castles in air.

Rodolfo begins the duet, which has the lightest accompaniment from the orchestra. He recalls Mimi's beautiful hands, and her snow-white skin. Marcello has put away his piece of ribbon, and is gazing sadly at his painting. He adds his voice to that of Rodolfo, but they are not talking to each other. We are hearing private thoughts. Marcello's emotions cause the instrumental texture to become heavier. He ponders how it can be that despite all his attempts to forget her, all he can paint is the lovely and false face of Musetta.

Rodolfo reiterates the opera's theme of the brevity of life — "Ah, Mimi, my short-lived youth"—and from his desk he withdraws Mimi's rose-colored bonnet. "And you, gay bonnet," he sings, "come to my heart, my heart that is dead, since our love is dead." This is

Rodolfo's final line in the duet, and as he sings it Marcello joins in with, "Meanwhile, Musetta is happy, and my base heart calls her, and waits for her." Rodolfo thrusts the bonnet into his coat, over his heart, then turns to Marcello and asks the time. Marcello shakes off his meditative mood, and answers that it's time for yesterday's dinner.

No sooner has Rodolfo observed that Schaunard hasn't returned than in he comes, accompanied by Colline. Schaunard's Theme comes with them, but the musician's entrance is a far cry from that of the first act, for all he brings this time is four small loaves of bread. Colline has a single herring, salted. The four sit at the table and make an effort to recover the gaiety of Act One. Most of the glasses with which they drank Benoit's health have been either broken or pawned; only one remains. Schaunard pours water into it, and they pass it amongst themselves.

Colline finishes his food quickly and gets up. Colline's Theme is heard (the music of the Apocalypse), and he assumes an air of importance and states, "I'm in a hurry. The king is waiting for me." This theme is developed a bit as the others play along with Colline's claim that he's received an invitation to join the king's cabinet, but soon Schaunard proposes dancing, and a variety of music is heard as each suggests a different dance. They settle on the quadrille, which is performed by Marcello and Rodolfo, but soon a mock sword fight begins, with Colline wielding the fire tongs against Schaunard and his poker.

As the duelists pretend increasing ferocity, they utter a gruesome series of shouts, which are tossed off so quickly, and are so covered by the actors' extreme physical movements and the madly racing music, that we scarcely realize how dreadful this incident is. In a few minutes the boys will be watching Mimi die, and here as they engage in their mock duel Schaunard and Colline shout, "I'll drink your blood." "One of us will be gutted." "Have a stretcher ready!" "Have a graveyard ready!" Rodolfo and Marcello continue their dance while beside them the others play at death. Suddenly the apartment door swings wide, and real death enters.

The distraught Musetta tells the boys that Mimi is outside, and so ill she couldn't climb the stairs. The strings give an agonized cry as Rodolfo and Marcello hurry to bring Mimi in, and the oboe and English horn play a frightened version of Mimi's Theme. Rodolfo and Marcello help Mimi to the bed. Musetta brings the glass of water and gives Mimi a sip.

Rodolfo tells Mimi to rest; she embraces him and asks if he wants her there. "Always, always," answers Rodolfo, and with this he begins the final invocation of the waking dream of endless love. Musetta picks up this thread when she softly describes how the two came here. She heard that Mimi had left the viscount and was "at the end of life." On the word "life," the theme of Mimi's Rose begins, and it continues through the rest of Musetta's speech. Musetta describes how she searched for Mimi, and finally found her stumbling in the street. Mimi said she was dying, and wanted to die with Rodolfo. She asked Musetta to help her get to his apartment.

Mimi's Rose expresses the hope for life and a love that will never die, and now Mimi looks around the wretched room, rises up a little, and embraces Rodolfo, saying, "I'll recover. I'll recover. I feel life here again. No, you'll never leave me." As she sings, Rodolfo doubles her voice, singing of her sweet lips, that speak to him again. At the same time, Schaunard can be seen watching Mimi closely, and Musetta and Marcello have an exchange that shames him. Musetta asks, "What is there in the house? Coffee? Wine?" He admits there is nothing. Only poverty. Standing apart, Schaunard sadly tells Colline that Mimi will be dead in half an hour.

Mimi complains of feeling cold. The hands Rodolfo once found so cold are cold still, and Mimi, wishing she had a muff, asks sadly whether her hands will ever be warm. She coughs, and Rodolfo takes her hands in his, trying, as he did in Act One, to warm her; to lend her some of his own strength.

Although it is April, it is not yet that precise moment in April that Mimi and Rodolfo anticipated in "D'onde lieta uscì." It is not yet spring. We will know when spring has arrived by the entry into the garret of a ray of sunlight, and just as the lovers predicted in their duet, that will be the moment of their parting. When the ray of sunlight strikes Mimi's face, she will die.

It is a remarkable thing Puccini is doing here. He is mixing two major elements of *romance* literature: spring, which symbolizes the rebirth of love; and Day (sunlight), which symbolizes death. That Puccini's art displays an unceasing tug of war between joy and sorrow is expressive of his own deepest feelings; that is, a love of life that was overshadowed by chronic depression and fear of the passage of time.[7]

Mimi greets the rest of the Bohemians. The three young men come to her bedside, and although Rodolfo urges her not to tire herself with speaking, she brushes his concern aside. To Musetta's Theme, Mimi tells Marcello that Musetta is a good person. Marcello takes Musetta's hand and agrees. These are words of farewell, and Schaunard and Colline sadly move away. Schaunard sits at the table and puts his head in his hands. Colline appears deep in thought, pondering what he might do to help.

Having drawn Marcello aside, Musetta takes off her earrings. She tells him to pawn them and buy some cordial (a heart stimulant), and bring a doctor. This pawning of the jewelry was taken from a scene in Mürger, but notice how perfectly it fits into the Romantic World of Puccini. How better can a Vacillator demonstrate her return to the community of Artists than by casting away her jewelry? Somehow Puccini always manages to include in his librettos, elements that uphold, rather than violate, the laws of his World.

Marcello begins to leave, but Musetta stops him and pulls him farther away from Mimi. Flute, oboe, and clarinet sound the motif of Mimi's Special Desire, which we first heard in connection with the bonnet. Musetta has decided to go with Marcello, to get the muff Mimi wants, for it may be the last time the poor girl has a special desire. Colline has come to a decision. As Marcello and Musetta head out the door, Colline picks up his overcoat. The coat song, "Vecchia zimarra," is often characterized in such terms as "dramatically a mistake and musically slight,"[8] but this attitude reflects a misunderstanding of the aria's function.

In Mürger, it is Schaunard who sells a coat. Colline pawns some of his books. These sacrifices are related in a mere three sentences, and there is little pathos to them. In fact, Mürger injects a touch of humor. The passage reads, "Colline, meanwhile, had gone off and sold some books. Had he been offered a price for an arm or a leg, he would have sold it rather than lose one of his beloved volumes; but Schaunard had pointed out that nobody had any use for his arms or legs."

Puccini struggles throughout *La Bohème* with a sense of the futility of life, that flashes by in an instant. But with the selfless gesture of Colline, he imparts a sense of meaningfulness, and even nobility, to the lives of these ordinary and unimportant people. And he does it via a masterful application of the Puccini Mixture of emotional opposites. With "Vecchia zimarra," he gives us a gesture that is of absolutely no practical value, yet of infinite emotional value.

Colline knows that his patched old coat will fetch no more than a few pennies, and that even if this sum were enough to buy something for Mimi, she will be dead within half an hour. Colline loves his coat. He considers it a dear friend. He doesn't sing his aria *about* the coat; he sings it *to* the coat. How easy it would be for him to rationalize keeping this thing he loves so much, knowing that giving it up will serve no practical use. When he comes back with his few coins, these will be deposited on a table, and not used. The money he gets from selling the coat means nothing. Money never does, in Puccini. It's the gesture that matters.

Colline sells his coat because he has decided to share Rodolfo's and Mimi's loss of the things dearest to them. "Vecchia zimarra," Colline's farewell to the thing so precious to him, is dramatically perfect, and perhaps the most heartbreaking yet uplifting moment in the opera. Having no practical effect, the pawning of the coat is an act of pure friendship. The philosopher folds up his dear old coat, then suggests to Schaunard that they put together two acts of pity. He'll go sell his coat, and Schaunard should step outside and give Rodolfo and Mimi some privacy. Deeply moved, Schaunard agrees.

A tender version of Schaunard's Theme sounds as the musician, wanting to spare his friends' feelings, comes up with a plausible excuse to go. He picks up the water bottle, as though he had decided to go out and refill it. Here is another of Puccini's bracketings. When we first heard Schaunard's Theme it was bold and vigorous, played allegro and *fortissimo* by woodwinds and trumpets as he triumphantly brought in his bounty of food, wine, firewood, cigars, and pastry. Now the theme is sounded by the strings, softly and at a moderate pace, as Schaunard, not at all triumphant, leaves the apartment with ... an empty water bottle.

With his departure the orchestra shifts to music from "Che gelida manina"—the music of Mimi's lovely eyes, that stole away what Rodolfo had thought were his treasures, and replaced them with Hope. As this theme sounds, Mimi opens her eyes and looks at Rodolfo. A new theme sounds with the start of Mimi's aria, "Sono andati." "Are they gone?" she asks. "I pretended sleep, because I wanted to be alone with you. There are so many things I must say to you ... or just one thing, but as vast as the sea...."(The music of this aria, through this point, will recur when Rodolfo realizes that Mimi is dead.) "...as the sea, deep and infinite.... You are my love and all my life."

That last clause brackets the aria with the music that opened it: that of Mimi's beautiful eyes. Note too Puccini's characteristic linking of the words "infinite" and "love"—an invocation by Mimi of the waking dream in *words* that coincides with its musical invocation via the theme of Rodolfo's Hope.

The characters now enter completely into Puccini's World as they begin to speak of dawn and dusk. Rodolfo tells Mimi that she is "As beautiful as a dawn." Mimi corrects him, saying, "You meant to say: as beautiful as a sunset." As in *Manon Lescaut*, Puccini only seems to be equating the setting of the sun with death. He seems to have Mimi saying, "My sun is not rising; rather, my sun is setting. I am dying." What he is actually doing is saying that nothing on earth is more beautiful than Mimi, for she is as beautiful as a sunset. Or rather, he is using the Puccini Mixture to say both things at the same time.

Mimi now quotes herself, singing, "They call me Mimi..." which is the music to which, at sunset, she came into the world. Rodolfo continues the reminiscence with the music of Mimi's "little room, that looks out on the roof and the sky." He uses new words, however, saying, "The swallow has returned to the nest, and sings."

The swallow is another resurrection symbol — it disappears in winter and returns in spring. That this was a symbol of significance to Puccini is certain, for he named his next-to-last full length opera *La Rondine* — The Swallow, and the subject is the heroine's attempt to experience a rebirth of love.

Withdrawing Mimi's bonnet from his coat, Rodolfo offers it to her. She exclaims happily, and bows her head so he can put it on her. She rests her head against his chest, and the music of their search for the dropped key is heard, followed by "Che gelida manina," as they reminisce over their first meeting.

But Mimi is seized by her terrible cough, and her head falls back. The orchestra gives a cry of fear, using the same music to which she first entered, coughing, in Act One. (The words spoken at that time were, "Are you ill? No, it's nothing.") Rodolfo cries out, and Schaunard rushes in.

Mimi opens her eyes and tries to reassure them. (Recall Manon, who as death approached her did everything she could to calm her lover's fears. This is Puccini's gentle version of the Knight's Trial. Rodolfo's task is to stand by his lover while she is dying, and he does this well. But Mimi's Trial is greater, and she performs it better. It is, after all, she who is dying, and like Manon, it is she who remains calm during the ordeal, and comforts her distraught lover, rather than the other way around.)

Now Musetta and Marcello return; she with a muff, he with a phial. It is Musetta's Theme that sounds as they enter, probably because it is she who speaks first, asking whether Mimi is sleeping. Marcello has summoned a doctor, and now he places a spirit lamp on the table and lights it. "Who is speaking?" asks Mimi. "I, Musetta," is the answer, and as the orchestra sounds the theme of Mimi's Rose, she offers the dying girl her fur muff. Mimi takes the muff and exclaims over its beauty and softness.

Puccini now does something quite brutal to poor Rodolfo, who is standing beside Mimi and watching her take such pleasure in the muff. For Mimi's next line, Puccini repeats the music of the first line of Rodolfo's "Che gelida manina" — "Such a cold little hand." Rodolfo's next words to Mimi had been, "...se la lasci **riscaldar**" — "...let me **warm** it for you." As the music is repeated now, Mimi sings, "Non più, non più le mani **allividite**" — "No more, no more the hands **frozen**."

This scene is a huge departure from Mürger, who had Rodolphe go out himself, the morning after the dying Mimi came back, and get money to buy food. Puccini's Rodolfo has never been able to do any of the things he wanted to for Mimi — not even to warm her hands. Yes, he gave her a sip of wine and a moment of warmth at the start, and bought her the bonnet, but those things came not from him, but from Schaunard. Now, at last, her poor hands are warm, but it is Musetta who saw to that. And when Mimi looks up and asks Rodolfo whether the muff is a gift from him, Musetta quickly answers, "Yes." The knife is twisted deeper as Mimi sweetly scolds Rodolfo for spending so much money on her. The beautiful rose bonnet is forgotten, and Rodolfo, distraught and humiliated, begins to cry.

"Why are you crying?" asks Mimi tenderly, and as she does, the clarinet and harp begin what is essentially a breath and heart monitor. The clarinet, playing *ppp*, begins seven measures of a sustained B below middle C. This is the sound of Mimi's breathing. The harp begins a resonant "thrum" which we will hear six times. This is Mimi's heartbeat. Somewhere in here (we know this from a stage direction that occurs in a few moments), a ray of sunlight penetrates the garret window, and begins to reach for Mimi's face.

Mimi weakly murmurs over the clarinet and harp, which monitor her ebbing life.

"Here, love" (a "thrum" from the harp), "always with you" (thrum). "The hands" (thrum) "...warm" (thrum) "...and sleep" (thrum). That was the last beat of Mimi's heart, and an eighth-note later the clarinet falls silent as Mimi stops breathing. There is a streak of sunlight on her face. Spring is here. Day has come.

Behind Mimi and the clarinet and harp were the strings, softly playing a passage from "Che gelida manina." It was the music to which Mimi and Rodolfo had exited Act One, into the moonlit night. It seems likely Puccini meant for the words of that moment to be recalled here. As Mimi dies, then, she does so to music that says, "Give me your arm, my little one...." "I obey you, signor!" "Tell me you love me." "I lo..." Mimi dies as the orchestra is speaking the word "love."

Mimi's death is so peaceful that no one in the room notices it. Marcello tells Rodolfo the doctor is on his way. Musetta heats the cordial over the spirit lamp while murmuring a prayer. To the theme of Mimi's Rose she prays, "...don't let the poor girl die."

Another bracketing occurs when Musetta asks Marcello to help her with the spirit lamp, the flame of which is flickering. Obviously there is a breeze in the garret. Marcello shields the flame with a book, and we can no longer see it. This of course parallels Mimi's request for Rodolfo's help with her candle, and it seems also to be a visual representation of Mimi's death — the flame has vanished. Musetta resumes praying, again to the theme of Mimi's Rose.

Schaunard moves toward the bed, and as Rodolfo tells Musetta, "I still hope," the musician sees Mimi is dead. (Recall Turandot's response to Calaf's solving of the first riddle: "Yes, Hope — which always deceives.") Softly, Schaunard tells Marcello Mimi is gone. Marcello goes to look for himself, then falls back, frightened.

Rodolfo moves to the window, for he has noticed that a ray of sunlight crept in and struck Mimi's face. According to the stage directions, "A ray of sun from the window strikes the face of Mimi; Rodolfo moves to repair this. Musetta indicates her cloak. Rodolfo thanks her with a look, takes the cloak, stands on a chair, and studies how best to suspend the cloak across the window."

Colline enters, and he places his few coins on the table for Musetta. Note that he does *not* offer them to Rodolfo. Puccini considers Musetta to be in charge, so when Colline arrives he says, "Musetta — for you," and puts the money down. He then goes to help Rodolfo with the cloak. Everyone seems to understand the importance of getting the sunlight off Mimi's face.

Speaking, rather than singing, Colline asks Rodolfo how Mimi is. Rodolfo indicates the girl. "She's calm." He goes to get the cordial from Musetta, but stops short when he sees the strange expressions on the faces of Marcello and Schaunard. Suddenly frightened, he asks why they are looking at him so. Marcello rushes to his friend, embraces him, and cries, "Courage!" The orchestra begins a reprise of the opening of Mimi's "Sono andati." Rodolfo cries out Mimi's name with utmost despair, and the others assume postures of grief. The curtain slowly drops, and as it does we hear the coda of Colline's "Vecchia zimarra."

Taken together, the passages from the two arias provide this commentary from the orchestra as the opera ends: "Are they gone? I pretended sleep for I wanted to be alone with you. I have so many things to tell you ... or just one thing, but as big as the sea. And now that the happy days have fled, I tell you goodbye, my faithful friend, goodbye, goodbye."[9]

7

Tosca

Libretto by Giacosa and Illica, based on the drama by Victorien Sardou
First performed at the Teatro Costanzi, Rome, January 14, 1900

Tosca is unique in the Rose Cycle in that it opens at morning. The story encompasses one day, and Puccini needed the bulk of it to take place at night, and to conclude with the lovers' deaths at the fatal hour of dawn. That it is full night when the evil Scarpia dies at Tosca's hand is no surprise, for only at night does a Puccini heroine have such power.

Even a casual hearing of the score reveals Puccini has made advances since *Bohème* in respect to recurring music. For the first time, he uses it to reveal characters' thoughts. There are more than a dozen themes of major significance, identifying persons, actions, places, and emotions.[1] The score is overflowing with meaningful recurrences, some of which are employed so subtly they have been misunderstood, and taken for carelessness.

In respect to the Rose Cycle's major character types, *Tosca*'s Alberich is Scarpia, who has forsworn love for power. Cavaradossi is the Artist, and Tosca has a double role as an Artist and The Lady of the Rose. Scarpia is very skillfully drawn, beginning with his entrance into the church of Sant' Andrea. The priests, pupils, and singers of the Chapel are shouting joyfully about the victory of the army over Bonaparte, and about the celebration that will take place that night, when the fearsome Scarpia enters, flanked by several of his policemen. He silences the jubilant crowd in an instant, saying, "Such an uproar in church. A fine respect!" Scarpia likes inspiring fear, and had the group been quiet when he entered he would have snarled that since they were not rejoicing at the army's victory, they must be disloyal.

His next superb move occurs when he makes his presence known to Tosca, who has come to the church to look for her lover, Cavaradossi. Scarpia decides to force the beautiful opera singer to touch him, so he dips his fingers into holy water and extends his hand. This is the only trick that would have worked, and Scarpia thought of it in an instant. There is no way for Tosca to refuse. She must touch Scarpia's hand. With these two moves, Scarpia has been established as lightning-quick in his thoughts, and highly skillful at intimidating and manipulating people. Backed by all the force of the State, he is an extremely dangerous foe. It is the tragedy of Tosca that neither she nor Cavaradossi can appreciate, until too late, how dangerous it is to be in the clutches of the police. Because of their privileged lives and Tosca's influential friends, they think they are safe.

Certain the police can't prove he helped their escaped prisoner, Cavaradossi recklessly laughs at Scarpia's man Spoletta, who, having followed Tosca to the painter's villa, has searched in vain for the well-hidden Angelotti. Cavaradossi doesn't understand the police don't have to prove anything, and in his anger at being laughed at, Spoletta arrests the painter and takes him to the Farnese Palace, where Scarpia and his torture room await.

99

For her part, Tosca does not understand that the only way of keeping Cavaradossi alive is by refusing to give Scarpia the information he wants. Once the police chief learns where Angelotti is hiding, Cavaradossi will be of no further use to him.

Cavaradossi understands this, belatedly. Once he has been arrested, it dawns on him how desperate his situation is. He tries to warn Tosca that if she speaks of what she saw at his villa, her words will kill him. She cannot grasp what he means, and understands only that her lover is being tortured because he will not give up Angelotti. That man is nothing to her, so finally she tells Scarpia where Angelotti is, reasoning that once he has recovered his prisoner, he will release Cavaradossi.

On finding to her horror that Scarpia has no intention of releasing her lover — on the contrary, he now feels free to execute him — Tosca assumes she can bargain with him, or failing that, appeal to the Queen. But Scarpia is an experienced policeman, and in this game of chess he and Tosca are playing, he is always several moves ahead. The only way to defeat Scarpia, Tosca finally realizes, is by knocking the chessboard over, so she stabs him to death. In so doing, she becomes one of the few main characters in Puccini who succeeds in killing another main character — and a woman at that, who kills a man.

Tosca contains everything a chapter in the Rose Cycle must. It has an Alberich, wedded to power and barred from love. It has an Artist and his beautiful Lady of the Rose, both of whom revere flowers, live for the rapturous Night, have a challenging Trial, and die at dawn. It also has a stunning display of sadomasochism between the domineering lady and her submissive lover, that dwarfs anything previously seen in Puccini.

With each succeeding opera, we observe the balance of power between the hero and heroine shifting. We see a progression, in which the leading female characters steadily become stronger, and the leading males become weaker and more dependent on the heroines.

In selecting Sardou's *Tosca*, Puccini chose a work with long and graphic scenes of true sadomasochism, including real, physical torture of the male lead. While the play was successful from the moment of its premiere in 1887, many people at the time thought it disgusting.[2] Bringing *Tosca* into his World not only allowed Puccini to torture his hero more fiercely than ever before, it also allowed him to shift the balance of power between hero and heroine to an unprecedented lopsidedness. Cavaradossi is heroic in Acts One and Two, but beginning with his Act Two entrance he is, and will remain, a bound and tortured prisoner, incapable of defending either himself or Tosca. If the couple is to be saved from Scarpia, it is Tosca who must do it. Tosca must become the hero. And she does.

The lovers start out with a fairly traditional, if illicit, relationship, with her jealous and fearful he might be straying, and him calming the little woman down with a loving paternalism mixed with faint condescension. Some men would be annoyed by Tosca's ceaseless jealousy, but not Cavaradossi. He likes it. "Tosca, my idol," he tells her in Act One, "all things in you please me: the reckless anger, and the spasms of love!" (This is "love as exquisite torture" again.)

We get the impression that these battles, in which she accuses him of infidelity and he at length convinces her of his faithfulness, are an amorous game, in which the two play out a struggle in which she initially resists him, but eventually succumbs to his masterful kisses. Through this repeated conquest, the flame of their passion continues to burn hotly, instead of subsiding to a comfortable, and dull, glow.

Part way into Act Two, however, the relationship undergoes a correction, so Tosca becomes the dominant partner and hero of the opera. With Cavaradossi a tortured prisoner, unable even to speak, it is Tosca who decides whether Angelotti shall be given up; Tosca who bargains for her lover's life; Tosca who picks up a knife and stabs Scarpia to death; and Tosca who hastens to her lover's rescue. The once-masterful Cavaradossi now sits helplessly in prison, torture-wounds throbbing, weeping in despair at his imminent execution. He has just finished his celebrated Masochism Aria, "E lucevan le stelle," and his relief and gratitude — his awe at Tosca's killing power — are palpable.

Cavaradossi's Trial in Act Two is a challenging one: he can stop his torture, if he will give up his friend. Of course he refuses, and so passes this test of strength, courage, and loyalty. But ultimately Cavaradossi fails, for he abandons the struggle. He loses hope, and the last act finds him waiting passively for death as he tearfully recalls his nights of love with Tosca. This is not the behavior of one who has exerted himself to his limits and realized the ideal of knighthood.

Note as well the stage directions for Tosca's entrance in the last act. Cavaradossi has finished his aria, and is sobbing. "Tosca sees Cavaradossi weeping, with head in hands ... she lifts his head." We will see this same mother-and-child display in *La Rondine*, on an even greater scale.

Though Tosca's rescue attempt is foiled by Scarpia's treachery, she nevertheless dies a hero. Rather than allow herself to be arrested, she leaps to her death from the prison wall, a battle cry on her lips. In the surface story, Tosca fails to save her lover because Scarpia deceived her. But in the context of the Rose Cycle, Tosca failed because dawn had come, and her power had waned with the disappearance of the moon. As the final act opens it is still night, but the stage directions note that the uncertain light gradually increases. As Tosca waits for what she believes will be Cavaradossi's mock execution, she fidgets impatiently at the delay and says, "Already the sun rises." Notice too that Tosca is made to urge on her lover's death. When the firing squad assembles she says approvingly that they are getting ready. The squad fires, and Tosca says, "There! Die!" In later operas we'll see this again — teasing hints that suggest Puccini is toying with an idea that tempts him. Right from the beginning, in *Le Villi*, Puccini was attracted to the idea of his heroine killing her lover, and this attraction only grew stronger as he aged.

Tosca opens with three thunderous, savage, unrelated chords: the motif of the ruthless Baron Scarpia, Rome's chief of police. The curtain rises on the interior of the Church of Sant' Andrea della Valle. It is June 17, 1800, and Italy is under invasion by the army of the French, commanded by Napoleon Bonaparte. At right is the chapel of the Attavanti, a family of local aristocrats. At left is a dais, containing an easel with a covered painting, and a basket containing food and wine.

Suddenly, to the accompaniment of an urgent-sounding motif, a man stumbles into the church from a side door. Clad in ragged prison clothing, he is gaunt, exhausted, and terrified. He pauses and looks about fearfully, trying to calm himself. The fugitive is Cesare Angelotti, and he has just escaped from Rome's prison, the Castel Sant'Angelo.

Angelotti had once been a carefree aristocrat, but enemies contrived to have him arrested as a French sympathizer. A book by the Frenchman Voltaire was planted among his possessions, and for this he spent three hellish years in the galleys. Then he was moved to the prison of Sant'Angelo, where he has been for the last year.[3]

His sister, in the meantime, had married into the great Attavanti family, and because of her influence Angelotti's sufferings in prison had been eased. But then Baron Scarpia was transferred to Rome as chief of police. Scarpia made advances to Angelotti's beautiful sister, and when these were repulsed Scarpia arranged to punish her. In a word, Angelotti is to be hanged in three days' time. Hence the escape, and Angelotti's terror.

Determined to save her brother's life, the sister, who is called "the Attavanti," bribed a jailer named Trebelli to help him escape. She also supplied her brother with a ring containing a dose of poison, guaranteeing a swift and painless death if necessary. There will be no help from the rest of the Attavanti clan, for all are Royalists who would turn Angelotti over to the police in an instant. As she cannot give Cesare refuge in her home, the Attavanti has hidden some things in the family chapel, that will help him get out of the city. These include women's clothing, and a scissors and razor.

In Sardou, Angelotti had escaped the previous night. The plan was for the jailer, Trebelli, to come for him during High Mass, when the church would be filled with people, and to conduct him to a carriage that would take him outside Roman territory, where his sister would be waiting. But Mass was celebrated and Trebelli did not appear, and now Angelotti is gripped by fears that the fellow has been arrested and the escape plan revealed. At any moment Scarpia might burst into the church with his men. The one hopeful note is that the prison cannon has not been fired, as it always is when an escape is discovered. And yet, what is Angelotti to do now?

To return to Puccini, who leaves out essentially all this background material, the frightened Angelotti, having just now entered the church, looks about in an attempt to orient himself. With relief he sees the stoup of holy water, a column, and a statue of the Madonna.

"'At the feet of the Madonna,' my sister wrote," he gasps, and we hear a theme that will be associated with Angelotti's loving sister. The fugitive searches for something at the foot of the statue, finds nothing, searches again, makes a gesture of despair, and renews his search. In these moments of vanishing hope, we hear the dreadful, slithering Scarpia chords, then Angelotti gives a cry of joy as he finds that which he has been seeking. "Here is the key!" he cries, almost sobbing with relief. He looks over his shoulder. "And here is the chapel!" He hurriedly unlocks the door to the private chapel, enters, and locks the door behind him.

We now hear a cheery, simple-minded melody that belongs to the fellow who is entering the church. This is the Sacristan—a pious, self-satisfied, dimwitted oaf with a facial tic, whose character is mercilessly described in his music. The Sacristan enters with some paintbrushes in hand. He is always having to wash these dirty brushes, he complains. "Signor Painter," he calls, but then stops with an "Oh?" of surprise when he sees there is no one on the dais. He had thought the Cavalier Cavaradossi had returned to work, but sees from the untouched basket of food that he hasn't.

A bell tolls for the Angelus, and the Sacristan drops to his knees and begins to pray. Cavaradossi enters from a side door. He is young, handsome, and aristocratic-looking, despite his painter's smock. About him is an air of self-confidence, which teeters on the brink of arrogance. Seeing the Sacristan on his knees, he asks what he is doing.

By revealing Cavaradossi's ignorance of a common devotion, the question communicates not only the painter's lack of interest in religion, but also the fact that he doesn't care whether people know this. Cavaradossi is looked on with suspicion in Rome, for although his father was Italian, his mother was French, and the family made their home in France, where they associated with rebels against Church and State. The Sacristan disapproves of Cavaradossi, who never goes to services, or even to confession. The painter mounts the dais and removes the covering from his painting, a representation of Mary Magdalene, whom he has painted with blue eyes and blonde hair. What is this apparent atheist doing in Rome, painting a religious image in a church?

Doing religious art for the Church, at no charge, is a scheme on Cavaradossi's part that keeps him grudgingly welcome in the city. The painter likes Rome no better than she likes him, however he is madly in love with an opera singer, Floria Tosca, who is engaged at the Argentina Theater. When her contract is up she will move on to Venice, where Cavaradossi will gladly follow her. In the meantime, providing the Church with free artwork protects him from the likes of Scarpia.

As Cavaradossi was climbing onto the dais, the Attavanti Theme was heard, revealing that the painter was thinking about the woman who unknowingly served as his model the previous day. Then his thoughts moved on, and we heard a fragment of a theme that will be identified with Tosca, and will soon be incorporated into his aria, "Recondita armonia." This musical depiction of Cavaradossi's thoughts at he approaches and contemplates his painting—first the Attavanti, then Tosca—reveals the feelings that will be put into words in the aria.

The Sacristan's eyes pop when he looks at the painting. He recognizes the face as belonging to a woman who has been praying at the church for the last few days. The Attavanti had come to the church to smuggle in the clothing and other items for her brother. Staying to pray—no doubt partly to avert suspicion, and partly in hopes of gaining divine help for her brother—her beauty caught the eye of the painter.

Scandalized, the Sacristan cries, "Away, Satan, away!" He finds the woman too beautiful. The exclamations of the Sacristan, regarding the disturbing beauty of the woman in the painting, begin a theme that runs throughout the first act. The theme is that of suspicions regarding the loose morals and sexual intrigues of certain women. The subject of the painting was made to be Mary Magdalene so this subject could be easily opened, and so Tosca might seem justified in suspecting the woman who served as model.

Uninterested in the Sacristan's opinions about art, Cavaradossi orders the fellow to hand him his paints. Having done so, the Sacristan turns to washing brushes while Cavaradossi works on his painting, with frequent stops to judge the effects. Suddenly the painter ceases work, and takes a miniature portrait from his pocket. He compares the miniature with the painting, then begins his aria, "Recondita armonia."

"Recondite harmony of diverse beauties!" he muses. He comments that Tosca is dark, and his model blonde. "You have blue eyes.... Tosca has eyes that are black!" This is the first reference to eyes in the opera, but it won't be the last. The opera focuses on watching, spying, and searching, and all three main characters make repeated references to eyes: blue eyes, black eyes, mocking eyes, burning eyes, eyes soft with love and fierce with anger, victorious eyes, languishing eyes, and hunters' eyes. It's likely this fixation on eyes stems from Sardou's having written his play with Sarah Bernhardt in mind, for she was renowned for her compelling eyes.

As the Sacristan continues grumbling, Cavaradossi continues his musing aria. In her mysterious way, he sings, art mingles diverse beauties into one. But in painting this picture, he concludes, his only thought is of Tosca. Obviously we are being informed that we need have no suspicions about Cavaradossi's faithfulness to Tosca. On a deeper level, however, we are also being told about how it is the painting of the Magdalene is so beautiful, and, perhaps, how it is Puccini's operas are so beautiful.

The face in Cavaradossi's painting has been modeled on that of a lovely woman, but the image has been made into Art by his intense feelings for Tosca, who has a very different kind of beauty. The focus of Cavaradossi's musing is the strange way in which the blending of these opposing types of beauty has resulted in the mystery that is Art. The aria seems to express the Puccini Mixture of opposites, in an entirely new and thoughtful way. Previously the composer had expressed his emotional tug of war by writing music that combined gaiety with sadness, or by employing scenes in which his characters are shown having a wonderful time, only to have one say something to the effect of, "This won't last, you know." But in "Recondita armonia," Puccini seems to be acknowledging that this mixture of joy and sadness, as painful as it is to him personally, is what gives his own art its unique and mysterious beauty.

As Cavaradossi resumes painting, the Sacristan attempts to condense a great deal of Sardou's play by muttering about "those dogs of Voltairians" who are enemies of the holy government. The Sacristan serves as the voice of the city, and we can sum up his grumbling as follows: Cavaradossi is not loved by Rome, and if he gets into trouble with the authorities, no one will help him.

Finished with the paintbrushes, the Sacristan makes ready to leave. First, however, he points out the food basket to the painter. It is still full, he notes. Is his Excellency fasting as a penance? "I'm not hungry," says Cavaradossi carelessly. (Originally, he was to have said he had already eaten, but Puccini insisted on changing the line. The composer did not like for his young lovers to show interest in food. Except in the case of the Bohemians, who live hand to mouth, interest in food makes a character seem unromantic, vulgar, and old.) Hoping to claim the contents of the basket later on, the Sacristan puts it aside, then warns the painter to shut the church door after he leaves. Cavaradossi snaps at the pest to go away, and he does.

For a moment Cavaradossi paints in silence. His back is to the Attavanti chapel, where Angelotti, who believes the church is now empty, is unlocking the gate. The painter hears this sound, and cries out that someone is there. To an emphatic sounding of the Angelotti Theme, the escaped prisoner makes as if to hide again. But he realizes he knows that man in the painter's smock. Reaching out in joy Angelotti greets his old friend, and cries that God has sent Cavaradossi to him. (This business of Cavaradossi and Angelotti being old friends is a departure from the play. In Sardou, Angelotti comes forward because, having overheard the Sacristan's jibes, he realizes that the painter has no love for either Church or State.) Puccini's painter stares at this ragged, emaciated man in puzzled amazement, and Angelotti realizes his friend doesn't recognize him. Softly, sadly, he asks whether prison has changed him so much.

Cavaradossi takes a long look, and at last sees his friend. "Angelotti!" he cries, hurrying down from the dais. "The consul of the dead Roman republic!" (This is Illica and Giacosa's attempt at conveying some reason for Angelotti's imprisonment. No more will be heard of the dead Roman republic.)

There is only a moment for Angelotti to report he has just escaped from the Castel Sant'Angelo (the Castle Theme is an important one), and for Cavaradossi to offer help, before the imperious voice of a woman is heard calling. It is Tosca, whom Puccini is introducing via the device of the offstage voice.

"Mario!" Tosca cries, angry at finding the church door locked. Cavaradossi motions for silence, and tells his friend to hide. Tosca is very religious, and would tell her confessor about Angelotti. (In Sardou, she is an ardent Royalist, but Puccini pitched that right out the window.) Calling to Tosca, Cavaradossi hustles the collapsing Angelotti back into the chapel, and gives him the basket of food and wine.

"Mario!" cries Tosca furiously, and the orchestra describes how Cavaradossi composes his features into a smile, and, after opening the door, throws out his arms in welcome. Angry and suspicious, Tosca enters "with a kind of violence." She ignores his open arms— no, she *pushes him away*— and sails into the church, accompanied by an elegant theme played by solo flute and cello, over a lovely string arpeggio, which theme will be incorporated into her Act Two aria, "Vissi d'arte." She also bears an immense bouquet of flowers.

Tosca was supplied with this bouquet by Sardou, whose stage directions may as well have read: Enter (not exactly chaste) heroine, with flowers. Clichéd as this entrance has become, Floria (Flower) Tosca is Puccini's Lady of the Rose. As her great aria tells us, she lives for Art and Love. We will soon see she is also devoted to night and nature, and has a special bond with roses.

Tosca demands to know why the door was locked. Cavaradossi shrugs, and declares the Sacristan wanted it that way. She asks whom he was talking to, and the painter ingenuously says he was talking to her. Having none of this, Tosca snaps, "Where is she?" She is certain another woman was here, for she heard footsteps and a rustle of clothing. (The sounding of the stealthy music to which Angelotti was hustled into the chapel tells us she actually heard him.) Cavaradossi tells her she was imagining things. He attempts to kiss her, and Tosca begins to soften.

Although Tosca is the main character of Sardou's play, the playwright treats his heroine with some condescension. It is well worth looking at the differences between his Tosca and Puccini's. Sardou's Tosca was a "little savage" as a child. "Picked up in the fields by Benedictine monks," she was then taught "to read and to pray." The convent organist discovered she had a voice, and taught her to sing. When Tosca was 16, the composer Cimarosa heard her, and decided to make her into an opera singer. The church fathers objected, and the question was put before the Pope. Tosca sang for him, and the Pope, concluding the human tears her voice would inspire were a kind of prayer, gave his permission for her to leave the convent for a career in theatre.

So far in Sardou, everything has been done *to* Tosca, by men. She hasn't uttered a word about what she wants. This is the history of Sardou's adult Tosca, who is very emotional, very jealous, and not very smart. Puccini has no time for talk about Tosca as a little savage, coming out of the fields and being taught to read and pray. He gives her to us as a woman, fully formed. She still isn't very smart, but then Cavaradossi isn't very smart either. There are two scenes in Puccini, however, that contain great departures from Sardou— scenes in which Tosca is made far stronger, far more heroic, than Sardou's character. The first is the scene of her murder of Scarpia, and the second is her leap from the parapet of Sant'Angelo. These changes are ones we might be able to excuse as simply heightening the excitement of the opera, if it weren't for the fact that Puccini uses the final act to weaken and humiliate Cavaradossi, in another great departure from Sardou.

To return to the opera, Tosca does begin to soften when Cavaradossi tries to kiss her, but she wants him to woo her harder. She gestures toward the statue of the Madonna, and reproves him for trying to kiss her in front of it. To a reiteration of her entrance music (the "Vissi d'arte" melody) she arranges her flowers at the foot of the statue, then kneels and prays. When finished, she crosses herself and rises, and her music shades into an anticipation of her thoughts of the coming night, via a few bars of her upcoming aria, the Dusk Song, "Non la sospiri la nostra casetta."

Uninterested in her devotions, Cavaradossi has returned to his painting. Tosca asks him to stop working, and to listen to her. In other words, Puccini reverses the situation of a moment before, and causes Tosca to woo Cavaradossi. (The reason is that he wants the heroine, rather than the hero, to sing the Dusk Song.)

Tosca tells her lover of her plans for the night. She will be singing, but the program is short. He should wait for her at the stage door, then they will go together to his villa. The Angelotti Theme returns, and the disturbed Cavaradossi says, "Tonight?" We must know from this talk of "tonight" the composer is about to summon up the spirit of Night. It's unfortunate he had to open this act at daytime, and we're inside this building. But at least Tosca can paint us a beautiful picture of Night — of a moon-filled sky that overlooks fields of flowers. And that is what she proceeds to do, in a short passage that acts as a build-up to "Non la sospiri."

Cavaradossi's mind is filled with thoughts of his desperate friend, so he is distracted from Tosca's tempting words. "It's the full moon," she urges, "and the nocturnal fragrance of flowers intoxicates the heart. Aren't you happy?" There is dead silence on stage and in the orchestra while Cavaradossi thinks, and Tosca looks at him with growing amazement. "Very much," he finally answers vaguely. The clarinet makes a dubious comment. "Say it again!" demands Tosca. A bit more firmly, the painter repeats himself.

He does not seem to understand that she was speaking of Night and the natural world — the Romantic World of moon and flowers, the only world in which Puccini's lovers are really alive — and so Tosca makes herself more clear by means of the Dusk Song: "Don't you long for our little house?"

She speaks of being together, listening to the voices of the night in the starlit silences, and finishes, "Flower, O great fields; quiver, sea breezes, in the moon's radiance, ... rain down voluptuousness, vaulted stars! A mad love burns in Tosca!" No Puccini Artist — no knight of *romance*—could resist this call, and Cavaradossi yields. "You have caught me in your snare, my siren..." he cries.

With Tosca's Dusk Song, Puccini launches another of his bracketings — one that doesn't close until the final act. The close is another Dusk Song, Cavaradossi's aria, "E lucevan le stelle" (And the stars were brightly shining), for while Tosca's aria anticipates the Night of Love, Cavaradossi's aria looks back on it.

He promises to come with her tonight, but then, looking toward the chapel, he quickly tells her she must let him work. Being sent away surprises Tosca. Rather lamely, Cavaradossi says "work calls" (but a wisp of "Angelotti" tells what's really on his mind). Irritated, Tosca begins to leave. Before she does, however, her glance falls on the painting her lover has been working on.

Extremely disturbed, she demands to know who that blonde woman is. "The Magdalene," says the painter carelessly. Does Tosca like her? "She's too beautiful!" Tosca snaps. Cavaradossi treats her answer as a joke, chuckling at the compliment he has been paid. Tosca regards him suspiciously. "You laugh?" she asks.

This provoking laughter is an irritating feature in Cavaradossi. Here, it angers Tosca, who tries to remember where she has seen those blue eyes before. Later, Cavaradossi's laughter will so anger Spoletta that he will arrest the painter simply to wipe the smirk off his face. Cavaradossi has no idea what a mistake it can be to make people angry.

Tosca steps onto the dais, looking at the face that troubles her. Then she recognizes it. It's the Attavanti woman. Cheerfully, Cavaradossi compliments her on having figured it out, and the furious Tosca questions him. Does he see her? Do they love each other? It's clear that Tosca is capable of physical violence.

Things have gone too far, so Cavaradossi, who truly loves Tosca, drops his flippant tone and speaks to her seriously. Yes, he did see the Attavanti yesterday, by sheer chance. The woman came to the church to pray, and without being seen by her he drew her likeness for his painting.

"Swear!" demands Tosca feverishly, and he does. She continues to stare at the painting, almost hypnotized by the eyes, which seem to stare back at her. Gently, Cavaradossi urges her down from the dais. Tosca comes down, but her eyes are locked on that face, which she sees as laughing at her with scorn. "Ah!" she whispers. "Those eyes!"

Holding Tosca close, Cavaradossi tenderly begins a song in praise of her dark eyes. This is the love duet, "Qual occhio al mondo." What eyes in all the world, he asks, can compare with the dark, burning eyes of Tosca? Those eyes so soft in love, so fierce in anger, to which his whole being is bound. (Here we see the sentiment of the enslaved knight of *romance*, destined to love only once, and forever. Music from this duet will recur on several occasions, making sometimes-subtle comments on the action.)

This is what both want: the battle, in which Tosca rages and her lover gradually calms her by convincing her of his total devotion. Cavaradossi never grows weary of Tosca's jealousy. He loves the beautiful, celebrated singer, idol of princes, and he loves knowing this desirable woman is wildly jealous of his love. These two look forward to fighting as much as to lovemaking, for it flatters and excites them both. Theirs is a violent passion, and far from being wearisome, their battles are a form of foreplay.

There is no dissolve into a gooey surrender for the heroine, however, for on an amorous level the battling continues, as Tosca bitingly coos such phrases as, "But give her black eyes," and "I torture you relentlessly." For his part, Cavaradossi intersperses words of love with the almost condescending epithet, "my jealous one," and orders that she go now, and leave him to work.

Throughout the first act, Cavaradossi is a proud and masterful man, easily the strongest of Puccini's tenor characters to date. But by the end of the opera Cavaradossi will have been dealt with more brutally, and humbled more completely, than any of his predecessors. And he will go to his death like a sheep to the slaughter.

Tosca extracts a promise from her lover that he will work until evening, and no woman will be allowed in to pray. She offers her cheek, and Cavaradossi smiles. With a touch of mockery, for he finds her piety absurd, he gestures toward the statue. Tosca ignores the mockery, saying the good Madonna won't mind. They kiss, and Tosca moves away. But giving one last, meaningful look at the painting, she adds as her final words, an order: "But give her black eyes!"

She slowly exits, leaving behind the final strains of the love duet, which fade away like a trace of perfume. Cavaradossi shuts the door, then stands for a moment, in love, and troubled. The memory of Angelotti pulls him back to the present, however, and he moves swiftly to open the chapel gate. Angelotti emerges, accompanied by his theme, and the two resume their interrupted greeting. Cavaradossi explains that Tosca is good, but keeps nothing back from her confessor. It was best not to tell her. In response to his friend's questioning, Angelotti reveals that his plan is to either flee the country, or else hide in Rome. "My sister..." he begins.

"The Attavanti?" interrupts Cavaradossi, and we hear her motif, which of course bears a marked resemblance to that of her brother. Angelotti confirms this, explaining that his sister has hidden women's clothing, including a veil and a fan, here in the church. As soon as night falls, he will put them on and slip away. (He of course does not mention the jailer Trebelli, for that fellow was left behind in Sardou's play.)

As Tosca did, Cavaradossi reveals he had thought the Attavanti capable of loose behavior. He had thought, when he saw that young and beautiful woman in church, praying devoutly and behaving cautiously, she had been engaged in some secret love affair. Now he sees it was a sister's love that drove her.

Angelotti declares that she has dared everything to save him from Scarpia, and in speaking that name he summons the policeman's frightful motif, which sounds again as Cavaradossi repeats the name. The Scarpia chords blare forth, but Cavaradossi tops them with ease, belting out heroically, "If it costs me my life, I will save you!"

Here is Cavaradossi's fatal flaw: overconfidence. He does not understand Scarpia isn't just one man, whom another might fight and defeat. Scarpia is backed by all the power of the State, and he could crush Cavaradossi like an insect. It doesn't occur to the painter how easily this happened to Angelotti, who was once a nobleman, as proud and confident as he, but who in an instant found himself thrust into the galleys, and is now a frightened and ragged fugitive. Cavaradossi badly underestimates Scarpia's strength, cunning, and ruthlessness, and this mistake will cost him, his friend, and his beloved Tosca, their lives.

Being an Artist, Cavaradossi should know what a friend Night is, yet he doesn't care for Angelotti's plan of waiting until evening before slipping out of the church. Cavaradossi thinks Angelotti should leave now, and in a classic line, from someone who knows how things work in Puccini's World, Angelotti responds, "I fear the sun!"

Cavaradossi gives Angelotti a key to his villa, and explains how to reach it. (A passage from "Non la sospiri" sounds at this point, describing "the little house.") Angelotti agrees to go, and fetches the dress and the veil his sister left. In his haste, however, he drops the fan, which bears the crest of the Attavanti family on the handle.

Cavaradossi delays his friend for a moment. There is, he says, a well at the villa. If danger presses, Angelotti should go to the well, which was specially constructed by his family a long time ago. There is water at the bottom, but halfway down is a passage that leads to a cave. (The motif of The Well will return in Act Two, when the broken Tosca reveals the hiding place to Scarpia.) No sooner has Cavaradossi divulged the secret of the well than a cannon booms, which sound is immediately followed by the Angelotti Theme. The escape has been discovered.

Cavaradossi insists on accompanying Angelotti to the villa, declaring if they are attacked they will fight. Again we see the painter's fatal overconfidence — his inability to think things through, which is Scarpia's great talent. The thought of fighting on Angelotti's behalf excites him.

During this last passage, the motif of the Sacristan was heard, and far more rapidly than its first utterance. This is a musical warning that the Sacristan is on his way back to the church — is in fact running to the church — and indeed, the moment the two friends exit, the Sacristan bursts in, eager to relate news he feels certain will distress Cavaradossi.[4] The Sacristan is sorry not to find the unbeliever, for in relating upsetting news to him he would have earned an indulgence from the Church.

Suddenly people begin streaming into the building, and the Sacristan tells them his great news: their army, under General Melas, has defeated the forces of Napoleon at Marengo! There will be a celebration tonight, including a gala at the Farnese Palace, featuring a cantata sung by the great Tosca. And here in church, hymns to the Lord!

The Sacristan tries unsuccessfully to shoo the excited choristers into the sacristy to put on their robes. Shouting for joy and running about in circles, "Double pay!" they cry. "Te Deum! Gloria! Long live the king!" (Note how the first cry of joy relates to money.)

But suddenly the crowd is hammered by the three terrifying Scarpia chords, and all turn toward the doorway where the dreaded police chief stands, flanked by several of his men. "Such an uproar in church," he says coldly, his eyes raking the crowd. "A fine respect!" The frightened Sacristan tries to explain the reason for their joy, but Scarpia ignores him. "Prepare for the Te Deum!" he commands, and the subdued choristers slink guiltily into the sacristy to don their robes. The Sacristan tries to slip away with the choristers, but Scarpia stops him with a rough command, and orders his deputy, Spoletta, to search the church for clues.

To a reiteration of the Castle Theme, Scarpia tells the quivering Sacristan that a prisoner escaped from Sant'Angelo, and took refuge here. He demands to be shown the Attavanti chapel. (In Sardou, Scarpia has come to the church because of Trebelli. The jailer was immediately suspected in the escape. He was questioned, and quickly confessed. As for Angelotti's sister, she is beyond Scarpia's reach, for she left the city as previously arranged, and is waiting for her brother outside Roman territory.)

Pointing out the Attavanti chapel to the police chief, the Sacristan is shocked to find it unlocked, and the key there. Pleased, Scarpia enters the chapel only to come out with a sour expression. He had hoped to find Angelotti there. But in his hand he holds the fan the prisoner dropped.

Although Puccini's audience is not informed of it, Scarpia is in deep trouble. Powerful people are looking forward to seeing Angelotti hanged, and they will be very displeased when they find out he has escaped. If Scarpia does not find Angelotti before dawn, the fugitive will have had enough time to flee the city. And if that happens, certain people will see to it Scarpia pays with his life.

There is a moment of near-silence as Scarpia thinks, tapping the fan on one hand. Finally he admits that the cannon shot was a mistake. Perhaps if Angelotti had not been warned, he would still be here. The police chief is cunning and shrewd, and as the Castle Theme thunders he studies the fan. After a moment he notices the device on the handle, worked out in pearls. "The Marchesa Attavanti!" he exclaims.

His eyes flicker to every corner in the church, missing nothing. His gaze comes at last to the dais, and rises to the painting of Mary Magdalene. At first he does not recognize the face, so we hear that portion of "Recondita armonia" which carried the words, "...and you, unknown beauty, crowned with blonde hair!" Here, as on many occasions, the music of *Tosca* reveals a character's thoughts. "Who is this unknown beauty?"

A moment later, Scarpia recognizes the likeness of the Marchesa Attavanti, sister of the escaped prisoner. "Who did that picture?" he demands of the Sacristan, who fearfully names Cavaradossi. The Attavanti Theme sounds, and then, "Him!" exclaims Scarpia. Cavaradossi is well known, for is he not Tosca's lover, and a Voltairean?

Having been told to examine everything, one of Scarpia's men comes forward with the basket that had contained Cavaradossi's unwanted meal. The Sacristan goggles at it.

"Empty?" he gasps. Having excited Scarpia's attention, the Sacristan explains this is the painter's basket, which had been full of food.

Scarpia feels his way carefully. Perhaps, he probes, the painter simply ate his meal. But the Sacristan points out flaws in the theory. The basket had been in the chapel. How could the painter have put it in there when he had no key? And he had said he wasn't hungry. Scarpia has just a moment to work on this—to realize Angelotti must have taken the food—for now Tosca sails into the church, clearly upset. The music to which she enters is Angelotti's Theme, but it is quickly transformed into the melody of the latter part of the love duet. The music seems to be giving us the thoughts of Scarpia, who at first is concentrating on the fugitive, but drops him in favor of Tosca.

What makes this fairly certain is that just when the love duet music replaces that of Angelotti, Scarpia speaks Tosca's name. We can with reasonable certainty identify this recurrence of the love duet melody as including its words, "My jealous one!" "Yes, I feel it.... I torture you relentlessly." What Scarpia is therefore thinking as he watches Tosca enter the church, is that she is a jealous woman, suspicious of her lover, and that he, Scarpia, can play on this. Scarpia mentions Iago, who had a handkerchief with which to inflame a jealous one, while he has a fan.

Scarpia conceals himself behind the column that supports the stoup of holy water. Tosca goes to the dais, looks for Cavaradossi, and, not finding him, goes to search the nave. Frustrated, she returns to the dais and calls Mario's name. The Sacristan approaches, babbling inanely that the painter has vanished. The Sacristan makes his own escape, leaving Tosca badly shaken, and also leaving the church empty, except for Tosca and Scarpia.

Tosca thinks. Mario promised to stay here and work until evening. Why did he lie? "Deceived?" she wonders. "No.... No ... he couldn't betray me!" As she repeats this last phrase the orchestra introduces a compelling, bell-like *ostinato*, doubled by real bells. This hypnotic and beautiful theme circles obsessively, and forms the musical basis of much of the following scene between Tosca and Scarpia.

"He could not betray me!" repeats Tosca, and as she does, Scarpia dips his fingers into the holy water and steps forward, hand outstretched. "Divine Tosca," he purrs. "My hand awaits yours, your little hand, not for gallantry, but for the offering of holy water." As frightful as this action of Scarpia's is, one has to admire the brain that so quickly conceived it. In an instant he hit on the only possible method of forcing Tosca to touch him. The devout Tosca is incapable of refusing to touch this murderous hand, moist with holy water, that reaches out to hers. And so she does touch it, then crosses herself and thanks him. This act of Scarpia's is a small-scale rape, and sets the scene for his full-scale assault on Tosca in Act Two.

Accentuated by the church's own bells, the tolling, eight-note *ostinato* persists and grows as Scarpia continues his oily wooing, flattering Tosca in terms that, if she were paying attention, might remind her of what the Pope said when he sent her off to join the theatre. Hers, says Scarpia, is a noble example, for she draws from heaven a mastery of art so good as to revive faith. But in fact Tosca is paying very little attention, and she only murmurs, "You're too kind."

As people begin to file into the church, anticipating the *Te Deum*, Scarpia continues. He notes how rare devout women are. And here is Tosca, who performs on stage yet comes to church to pray. As actresses were often considered loose women, this sounds like it could be an insult. Suddenly doubled by a blaring horn, the bell-tones of the *ostinato* begin pounding like the blows of a hammer. "What do you mean?" demands Tosca. Scarpia explains himself: "And you are not like certain strumpets who have the face and dress of the Magdalene ... (Scarpia indicates the painting) ... and come here to intrigue in love."

It is telling that Scarpia would refer as he did to the morals of the Magdalene, one of the Church's most revered saints. But Tosca has no interest in defending the saint's reputation. The now-blaring *ostinato* breaks off as, shocked, Tosca seizes on the word "intrigue," and demands proof of the accusation.

Like a gleeful thought Scarpia is trying to suppress, the Castle Theme sounds briefly in the cello and double bass. The police chief shows Tosca the fan, asking whether this is a painter's tool. Tosca grabs the fan, and demands to know where he found it. Scarpia lies, claiming it was found on the dais, and he paints his own picture for the distraught singer — a picture of two furtive lovers who, surprised, left a fan behind in their flight. (We hear a wisp of "Recondita armonia" — the music of the beautiful blonde.)

Examining the fan feverishly, Tosca recognizes the crest of the Attavanti. As Scarpia gloats in an aside, the diva struggles to hold back tears. She indulges in a burst of intense self-pity, mourning that she had come here laden with sorrow to tell Cavaradossi "...tonight the sky will grow dark in vain, for the loving Tosca is a prisoner...."

What a remarkable line. As Scarpia gloats at how his poison is gnawing at Tosca, we can imagine his scorn at her description of herself as a prisoner. What does she know of the sufferings of prisoners? Yet as self-indulgent as Tosca seems, her line has a deeper meaning within the context of the Rose Cycle, that gives it genuine pathos. Night is an infinitely precious time in Puccini's World — it represents the span of human life — and the thought of the sky growing dark in vain — of the Night of Love coming on, and there being *no love* — is actually painful.

The *ostinato* returns as Scarpia addresses Tosca in an avuncular voice. He notes a rebellious tear has wetted her cheek, and asks what distresses her so. "Nothing!" answers Tosca coldly. Scarpia persists, vowing he would give his life to wipe away those tears. So far Tosca has paid almost no attention to Scarpia, and she scarcely heard his last gallantry. She is speaking to herself now, when she mourns that her lover is in another's arms, deriding her. The police chief misses nothing — not a syllable, not a gesture — and he quietly rejoices at the corroding power of his poison.

But now Tosca abandons her attitude of grief, as rage takes its place. "Where are they?" she blazes, to a truly creepy reiteration of the Castle Theme. Oh, if she could but catch them. That traitor! Her beautiful nest is fouled with mud! Tosca turns on the painting in a fury. "You'll not have him tonight!" she cries. "I swear!" (We hear Angelotti's Theme during this passage, with good reason, for when Tosca storms into the villa she will find it is Angelotti, not his sister, who "has Mario tonight.") Pretending to be scandalized at such violent words, Scarpia exclaims, "In church!" Tearfully, Tosca says God will forgive her. He sees how she weeps.

While Cavaradossi's fatal flaw is overconfidence, Tosca's is self-absorption. As much as we admire the loyalty and courage of both, we must admit they are blind. Tosca's whole life is in theatre, where she is the reigning deity. What need has she to fear police? A devout churchgoer is she, and loyal to the crown. Aristocrats vie for her attention, and the queen herself is her friend. True, Rome does not love Mario, but he has done nothing wrong, and so is in no danger.

And those people imprisoned in the Castel Sant'Angelo? No doubt they are there for good reason. If they hadn't done anything wrong, they wouldn't have been arrested. This is what Tosca thinks, thus she is as blind as Cavaradossi, who looks at his trembling, ragged friend, and cannot see he is looking at his future self.

And to be fair, Tosca has no reason to suspect Scarpia is a threat to her or Mario. She knows nothing of an escape from the prison, and Scarpia shrewdly avoids even mentioning Cavaradossi's name. He doesn't need to, for he knows the slightest suspicion is enough to set Tosca off.

In tears, Tosca turns to go, and with a continued pretense of gallantry Scarpia escorts her to the door. As the unhappy woman leaves, we hear a reminiscence of her amorous duet with Cavaradossi. It may simply express her sorrow at the love she believes she has lost, but it could also be a reminiscence of her line, "I am sure of forgiveness, if you look at my grief."

People have continued to stream into the church, which is beginning to fill. Scarpia returns, and makes a sign to Spoletta. We hear a ponderous version of the Angelotti Theme, as Scarpia's mind turns away from Tosca and back to the fugitive. In the background, church bells have begun to toll, signaling the beginning of the *Te Deum*.

"Three men and a carriage," commands Scarpia, beginning the choral passage that concludes the act. He dispatches Spoletta, who is to follow Tosca. Later they will meet at the Farnese Palace, where Scarpia has his headquarters. The deputy hastens after Tosca, and Scarpia begins his great solo.

"Go, Tosca," he commands. "Scarpia nests in your heart." The Cardinal's escort enters, and the Swiss Guard parts the chanting crowd for the procession to the altar. The mighty church organ begins to play, supporting Scarpia's vocal line. Tolling bells provide the bass, and the periodic booming of the celebratory cannon acts as punctuation. And over the huge sound of the chorus, organ, bells, and cannon, is the dark and evil voice of Scarpia, gloating over his impending victory over the lovers—"For the one, a noose; for the other, my arms."

The sound is hypnotic, and like several other of Puccini's finales it rocks the listener as though he were being dragged to and fro by the waves of the sea. The procession has reached the altar, and the chanting draws Scarpia from his reverie. He looks about wonderingly, and making the sign of the cross exclaims, "Tosca, you make me forget God!" He kneels, and enthusiastically joins in the *Te Deum*. But who is being worshipped? Puccini brackets the act by concluding the *Te Deum* with a triumphant *tutta forza* sounding of the Scarpia chords as the curtain drops. When the curtain rises on Act Two, we see Scarpia's room in the Farnese Palace. It is night, and a table is laid for dinner. To one side, a large window looks out over the courtyard.

The opening music consists of a series of three falling triplets, increasingly emphatic, which are succeeded by several familiar themes. This series of falling triplets is a new motif, that will be heard repeatedly during this act. Seemingly an inversion of the three rising tones of the Scarpia chords, they appear to represent the thoughts and resolve of Scarpia in this phase of his effort.

Scarpia is seated at the table, eating, and drinking wine. He is nervous, and the orchestra reveals a series of thoughts via the Castle Theme, Jealous Tosca, and another passage from the love duet. This passage comes from the opening music sung by Cavaradossi alone (his hymn to Tosca's eyes), and here it seems to represent Scarpia's thoughts of Cavaradossi and his relationship with Tosca. (It is irrelevant to Puccini that Scarpia has not "heard that music" before. Certain music represents certain concepts, and Scarpia is thinking of those things, therefore his thoughts are expressed in that music.)

From time to time Scarpia looks at his pocket watch. Angelotti must be recaptured before the city gates close for the night, or he, Scarpia, will be ruined. As yet there has been no word from Spoletta. But Scarpia consoles himself with thoughts of Tosca. Dawn will find Angelotti and Mario dangling from a pair of nooses.

Scarpia rings a bell, summoning Spoletta's underling, Sciarrone. Learning from him that Tosca has not arrived at the palace to sing in the victory celebration, he orders Sciarrone to open the window. An innocent and pretty dance melody, played by a flute supported by viola and harp, floats up from the lower floor. Scarpia orders Sciarrone to wait for Tosca by the palace entrance, and to tell her Scarpia will expect her when the cantata is finished. But he immediately thinks better of this, and writes out a note for the man to give her.

With Sciarrone gone, Scarpia returns to the table and pours himself more wine. To a wisp of the Castle Theme, followed by fleeting reiterations of music from the love duet, he declares that Tosca will come to him, for the love of Mario. "Such is the profound misery of profound love." (There's the Mixture again.)

Observe the number of times Scarpia attends to his appetites during this act. The first thing we see him doing is eating, and time and again he drinks wine, eats, mentions wine, pours wine, eats, offers wine, drinks coffee.... Act Two is about bodies: the physical torture of Cavaradossi, Scarpia's desire to rape Tosca, Scarpia's threat to have Cavaradossi shot, the report of Angelotti's suicide, Tosca's knifing of Scarpia. The drawn-out series of actions involving eating and drinking ties into the focus on flesh.

These actions also contribute to a picture of Scarpia as obsessive and repetitive, which characteristics make him an effective and dangerous interrogator. He doesn't eat and drink nonstop. Rather, he eats; stops and writes a note; drinks wine; stops and talks to somebody; resumes eating.... It's much like an interrogator who casually asks a prisoner a question, seems to drop the subject, repeats the question, goes off in another direction, comes back to the question, and on and on until the prisoner has completely lost track of his answers.

Scarpia now has an *arioso* to sing — Scarpia's Credo, it's sometimes called — but it's not a very good one. The reason is the emotions being expressed were incapable of inspiring Puccini. It's nice to know that Puccini, who wrote such ravishing melodies on the subject of love, was at a loss in expressing horrid thoughts bellowed by a man who prefers rape to "mellifluous consent." For those following the Rose Cycle, however, there is a line worth remarking on in Scarpia's Credo: "I know not how to draw harmony from the guitar or horoscopes from flowers...." Of course he doesn't. Music and flowers belong to the Artists; their beauties do not reveal themselves to those wedded to gold and power. (Yet Puccini can't resist making the orchestra "speak" of these things: a harp arpeggio gives us the strumming guitar, and the flowers burst into bloom via an upwards rush from the clarinet.)

Sciarrone returns, and reports Spoletta's arrival. Scarpia is excited, but when his deputy enters he assumes a casual air. Scarpia is again at his dinner, and he questions Spoletta in a jovial manner, without looking at him. He asks how the hunt went. The nervous Spoletta describes his search of the villa after Tosca's brief visit there: "I sniff! I scratch! I rummage!" Scarpia sees where this is going, and he rises angrily and demands to know about Angelotti. With a gulp, Spoletta admits he did not find the man.

The furious police chief threatens Spoletta with the gallows, but the deputy timidly adds that the painter was there. To a stealthy sounding of the Attavanti Theme, Spoletta reports Cavaradossi had laughed mockingly at the fruitless search, and his attitude was so offensive Spoletta arrested him. This mollifies Scarpia, and as he speaks we become aware of a new and dolorous melody, played by the flute, that we will come to associate with the questioning of Cavaradossi. The Torture Theme is revealing Scarpia's thoughts to us.

The Torture Theme, which expresses not only pain but something that can't be stopped, is followed by the sound of a choral concert, coming through the open window. The cantata has begun, and therefore Tosca must be here. Throughout the following scene, during which Cavaradossi is brought in and put to the initial questioning, the cantata mingles, frighteningly dissonant, with the Torture Theme.

Spoletta reports Cavaradossi is in the antechamber. When Scarpia hears this, the stage directions tell us, he is struck by an idea. He orders the painter brought in, and dispatches Sciarrone to fetch the Executioner, and the Judge who will witness the prisoner's confession. (Probably the "idea" is that he will allow Tosca to hear her lover being tortured.) Scarpia sits at the dinner table, and soon Spoletta brings in Cavaradossi and three Bailiffs, followed by Sciarone, Roberti the Executioner, the Judge, and a Scribe, who will take down the prisoner's words.

Cavaradossi bears himself proudly. "Such violence!" he says disdainfully, determined to show no fear. With studied courtesy Scarpia invites his prisoner to sit. Ignoring this, Cavaradossi demands to know why he has been arrested. But Scarpia cuts him off before he can finish the question, and pointing at a chair, orders him to sit. Cavaradossi refuses.

The dirge-like Torture Theme winds on in the flute, with lower strings contributing a sound like plodding footsteps. Scarpia is not able to finish his first question — "Are you aware that a prisoner...?" — before Tosca's voice is heard in the cantata. This shakes Cavaradossi, who utters an exclamation of dismay. Scarpia pauses on hearing Tosca's voice, then completes his question. Or rather, his statement. Cavaradossi is aware, is he not, that a prisoner escaped from the Castel Sant'Angelo today? Cavaradossi denies it.

Scarpia persists, claiming it was reported that Cavaradossi sheltered the prisoner in the church, and gave him food and clothing. "Lies!" snaps the painter, maintaining his cold disdain. It was also reported, continues Scarpia, that Cavaradossi took the prisoner to his villa. The painter demands to know what proof there is. The police ransacked his home, and found nothing.

"Proof that he is well hidden," says the unruffled Scarpia. With insolence, Cavaradossi repeats that the spies found nothing. Worried about his failure, and still angry at the contempt with which the painter treated him, Spoletta reminds his boss Cavaradossi laughed at their search. Cavaradossi still does not realize, or does not care, how angry his laughter makes people. "I laugh again!" he says proudly. Scarpia cannot let this arrogance pass while his men are present, and rising to his feet, he says in a terrible voice that this is not a place for laughter, but for tears. "Enough!" he barks, and the Torture Theme presses on our ears as the clarinet joins the flute. "Answer me!"

Irritated by the cantata, Scarpia closes the window, abruptly ending the sound of the singing. All pretense of gentility ceases as he demands to know where Angelotti is. Stubbornly, without expressing puzzlement at the prisoner's name, Cavaradossi answers all questions with increasing vehemence, shouting, "I don't know," or "I deny it!"

Scarpia calms himself, and in a paternal tone urges Cavaradossi to think well. After all, a prompt confession will save him great pain. A terrible cry is given out by the cello, anguished and unbearably sad. This is a new theme, the Moan of Pain, and as it finishes, Scarpia adds, "I advise you, tell: Where is Angelotti?"

Again Cavaradossi denies knowledge of the prisoner, and now Tosca, responding to Scarpia's note, enters breathlessly. She is accompanied by Cavaradossi's music of Tosca's Eyes—eyes that are soft with love, and rich with anger. She did not expect to find Mario here, and when she rushes to embrace him he whispers she must be silent about what she saw at his villa, for her words will kill him. She signals her understanding, but she does not understand. She does not understand that Cavaradossi's life is secure only so long as the hiding place of Angelotti remains a secret. She does not understand that the moment Scarpia has Angelotti in his grasp, Mario's life will be forfeit.

"Mario Cavaradossi," Scarpia intones formally, "the Judge awaits your testimony." The full orchestra sounds the terrifying Torture Theme, *fortissimo*, as Scarpia signals to Sciarrone to open the door to the interrogation chamber. Cryptically, he tells Roberti to start with "the usual." As the men go into the torture room, the Moan of Pain is again given out—first in the cello, then the viola. Tosca has not the faintest idea of what is about to happen to Cavaradossi, and when Spoletta closes the door behind him, she makes a gesture of surprise. Scarpia and Tosca remain in the office, while Spoletta takes up a position outside a door at back. Scarpia adopts a friendly and gallant air, replicated in the music, while at the same time he puts Tosca in an inferior position. He tells her not to look so frightened, and gestures to her to sit down.

An experienced actress, Tosca composes her features and sits on the sofa with an air of calm. Coolly she declares she isn't the least frightened. (Tellingly, she sings this to the drooping final bars of the Moan of Pain Theme.) Scarpia moves behind her, and leans on the sofa, and we realize why he tried to make Cavaradossi sit. It wasn't only a matter of forcing his prisoner to obey orders. It's also that with his victims trapped in a seated position, Scarpia is able to unnerve and intimidate them by getting behind them and leaning over them. There is, in this act, a deal of subtle and skillful action noted in Puccini's stage directions, but critics have been so focused on the physical torture of Cavaradossi and the mental torture of Tosca that none have noticed how true to life the actions and relentless questions of Scarpia are. There's no telling who it was—Sardou, Giacosa, Illica, Puccini, or Ricordi—but one or more of these men knew something about interrogation tactics and psychological warfare.

Scarpia asks about the fan. That, says Tosca, with an air of indifference, was simply her foolish jealousy. "The Attavanti was not at the villa?" Still calm, Tosca declares Mario was alone. But Scarpia persists, and in a slightly malicious tone he recalls to her her state of mind when she was at the church. Apparently still calm, Tosca says Mario was alone. Alone! But anger is beginning to bubble in her second, insistent declaration of "alone!" Her nerves are beginning to fray.

Scarpia now takes a chair, places it directly in front of Tosca, and looks her full in the face. "Really?" he asks blandly. The singer's façade of calm begins to crack, and she snaps, "Alone! Yes!" Scarpia is pleased with this display of anger, for it shows Tosca cannot maintain a hold on herself even under mild questioning. Using the standard interrogator's tactic of claiming that whatever one says is proof of guilt, Scarpia declares since she is getting upset, she must fear she will betray herself. (He had similarly told Cavaradossi that Spoletta's inability to find the prisoner at his villa was proof the man was well hidden.)

Calling to Sciarrone, Scarpia asks what the Cavalier has said. "Nothing," is the answer. Scarpia orders him to keep pressing, and Tosca's laughing assurance that this is all quite useless tells us that she, poor innocent, thinks Cavaradossi is being treated as she is— he is simply being asked a few questions. How easy this will be, she thinks. They need only deny everything, and after a while Cavaradossi will be released.

With an ironic smile, Tosca asks if one must lie to please him, and Scarpia, serious now, responds that lies are not necessary, but truth might shorten a painful hour for her lover. There is a marked crescendo and decrescendo in this fierce line, which suggests the application of a torture device, followed by its letting-off. This is the Circle of Iron Theme. Scarpia's words puzzle Tosca, and she asks what it is that going on in that room.

His expression now savage, his voice a shout, Scarpia describes the scene: "Bound hand and foot, your lover has a circle of hooked iron at his temples, and at every denial they spurt blood without mercy!" Tottering to her feet, Tosca cries that it isn't true. With the last word she makes a shocking vocal leap to an extended high C, then plunges almost two octaves, to declaim a denunciation of the circle of iron as the invention of a fiend. She listens with great anxiety, clutching at the back of the sofa. Hearing a long groan from the torture room (carried by the Moan of Pain music), she begs Scarpia to have pity. He declares it is up to her to save Cavaradossi, and she quickly answers, "But stop it! Stop it!"

Scarpia orders Sciarrone to halt the questioning, and to a reiteration of the Moan of Pain he demands the truth. Tosca wants to see Cavaradossi first, and when the police chief refuses she goes to the door and calls. Mario tells her they have stopped hurting him, and she must stay silent. With rallying strength he cries that he scorns pain.

Strengthened by her lover's brave words, Tosca declares she knows nothing. Scarpia offers to resume the torture, but as he walks toward the doorway the suddenly frantic Tosca thrusts herself between him and the door. Again Scarpia demands an answer; again Tosca refuses. It is clear to Scarpia she does have the information he wants. Hers are not the responses of a woman who doesn't know what he is talking about.

A repeated element in the opera is the mocking laugh. It once came from Mario, but he is done laughing. Now it comes from Scarpia. Tosca gasps in amazement at the laugh, and Scarpia sneers that never on the stage was Tosca so tragic as now. Only now does Tosca realize how ruthless he is, and how helpless she is. Her old weapons of beauty, fame, and imperious orders are no use here. If she is to prevail over Scarpia, she will have to find new weapons.

In a transport of ferocity, Scarpia orders Spoletta to open the door of the torture room so Tosca — no, *he* — can hear the cries of agony. The deputy obeys, but what emerges from the room is not a shriek of pain but a shout of defiance! Savagely, Scarpia urges Roberti to greater force, and he demands that Tosca speak. "Where is Angelotti?!"

Tosca's speech becomes distracted, and she begins to sob that she can't take any more. Hearing a terrible cry, she goes to the open door and looks within. Horrified, she begs Mario to let her speak. His voice broken by pain, he refuses. She pleads with him again, and he answers roughly, saying, "Fool, what do you know? What can you say?" (Note the similarity to the torture scene in *Turandot*, when Calaf snaps at Liu, "You know nothing, slave!")

The police chief is angered by Cavaradossi's defiance, and worried it may strengthen Tosca, who is obviously near to confessing. He orders Spoletta to silence the prisoner, and the deputy goes into the torture room. With her man incapacitated, Tosca is now free from having to consider his opinion about what should be done. She is free to make life-and-death decisions not only for herself, but for him. She is free to become the hero of this story.

"What have I ever done to you in my life?" asks Tosca in the dull monotone chant Puccini so frequently employs to communicate utter despair. Tosca falls back on the sofa. She chants that it is she who is being tortured, then she bursts into convulsive sobs. Spoletta kneels, and murmurs a prayer in Latin, which addresses of the Day of Wrath.

Scarpia goes to the door of the torture room, and signals to Roberti to begin anew. The Executioner draws a horrible, inarticulate cry from Cavaradossi. At this unbearable sound, forced from a man who can no longer speak for himself, Tosca decides what must be done for him. The music to which Cavaradossi told his friend about the well in the garden sounds, telling us what is in Tosca's mind. She rises from the sofa, and rapidly, in a voice suffocated with emotion, she says, "In the well ... in the garden...."

"Angelotti is there?" demands Scarpia. "Yes," answers Tosca in a choking voice, and again we hear the music of The Well, where Angelotti was assured he would be safe. Sciarrone reports the victim has fainted, and crying, "Murderer!" Tosca demands to see him. The Well Theme sounds softly, suggesting Tosca has earned this privilege, and Scarpia orders Cavaradossi brought forth. The Torture Theme is heard as the unconscious man is carried in and dumped on the sofa. Tosca rushes toward him, but the horrible sight makes her falter. For a moment she covers her eyes, but then, ashamed of her weakness, she begins to kiss him and weep over him. Sciarrone, Roberti, the Judge, and the Scribe leave. Cavaradossi revives, and as he looks at his beloved, we hear the music of Tosca's Eyes. The couple murmur endearments, and Tosca tells Mario that a just God will punish the man who has made him suffer. She seems certain their ordeal is over.

Not understanding why he has been brought out, Cavaradossi asks whether Tosca talked, and she assures him she did not. Loudly, Scarpia says to his deputy, "In the well, in the garden. Go, Spoletta." Furious, Cavaradossi attempts to rise, and he accuses Tosca of betraying him. Too weak to stand, he falls back. Calling his name, Tosca tries to embrace him, but he pushes her away with a curse. (This looks like a mirror image of Tosca's entrance into the church, when Cavaradossi called to her and tried to embrace her, and *she* pushed *him* away.)

All this has taken but a moment, and now Sciarrone enters, with tremendous news that mercifully changes the subject and brings joy to Cavaradossi. Sciarrone reports that Napoleon won the Battle of Marengo. Melas, whose supposed victory was just celebrated throughout Rome, was in fact utterly routed!

This news puts new life into Cavaradossi, described via a great upwards rush in the strings and upper woodwinds, followed by a full-orchestra sounding, *tutta forza*, of the Attavanti Theme. (As the Attavanti freed an unjustly imprisoned brother from a brutal tyrant, the theme is not out of place here.)

The cruelly tortured Cavaradossi rises to his feet, and with a trumpeting cry of "Victory! Victory!" he spits defiance in the face of tyranny. Still supported by strings and upper woodwinds, which suggest a "people's army" on the march (brass would have given us a statist army), and inspired by his enthusiasm to some high A flats, the flashing-eyed Cavaradossi describes how the spirit of Vengeance has awakened in the land, and how the voice of Freedom will bid this sad world to rejoice. Tyrants will be struck down, he cries, and as for Scarpia: "Your heart trembles, pale butcher!"

Nothing could be more magnificent than Cavaradossi. And yet ... Scarpia smiles sarcastically, and orders Sciarrone and the Bailiffs to take the self-confessed traitor away to be hanged. Tosca, who had been horrified at her lover's outburst, now clutches at him desperately. The policemen tear her from him, and as she struggles to follow them out the door, Scarpia pulls her back, snapping, "Not you!" The music of the heroic people's army drops in volume, slides down the scale, and finally shades into the Castle Theme as Cavaradossi is dragged away to the prison. Scarpia closes the door, and now he and Tosca are alone.

We hear wisps of two familiar themes when Tosca turns to the police chief and pleads, "Save him!" The first is Undying Love, from the latter part of the love duet, which carried Cavaradossi's line, "My life, unquiet lover, I will always tell you 'Floria, I love you!'"

Now the others are gone and business has been taken care of, Scarpia intends to enjoy himself. The second familiar theme is that series of three falling triplets, which at the beginning of the act seemed to describe Scarpia's pondering how he might work things out to his satisfaction. Here, the falling triplets again describe the police chief turning his situation over in his mind, and how he might squeeze the most enjoyment from the remainder of this night. With mock puzzlement he responds to Tosca's plea with, "I? ... You!"

Scarpia moves toward the dinner table, then turns back and smilingly observes, "My poor supper was interrupted." Seeing Tosca by the door, motionless and downcast, he invites her — to the same faux-friendly music he employed after Cavaradossi was taken into the torture room — to sit down so they two may contrive how to save her lover. He polishes a wineglass with his napkin, and invites her to taste some of his Spanish wine.

Tosca won't bite this time, and so she does not — as she did the first time Scarpia began to play with her — reply using the Moan of Pain music. Tosca thinks she knows what he's angling for, so she sits across from him, elbows on the table, and looks at him fixedly. Her voice filled with as much contempt as it can hold, she asks, "How much?" Unperturbed, Scarpia pours wine into the glass, and in mock puzzlement says, "How much??"

"The price!" snaps Tosca. As an Artist, she is certain nothing is more important to this creature than gold. But there's that mocking laugh again, as Scarpia finally throws off all pretense, revealing what he has been after all along, in his aria, "Già. Mi dicon venal" (Indeed. They call me venal). In short, he wants her.

Tosca listens to this aria in silence, until the end, at which point Scarpia moves toward her with arms outstretched. (Note during the aria the motif of Scarpia's Lust, first heard when he tells Tosca he doesn't sell himself to women for "a price of money." It's a blossoming theme, played here by the flute, and it will recur several times, including after the murder, when Tosca is setting the candles by Scarpia's head.)

Shocked, Tosca rises, and with a cry she runs behind the sofa for refuge. Scarpia follows her. Foreshadowing the opera's conclusion, Tosca rushes to the window and threatens to jump. Coldly Scarpia reminds her he holds her Mario's life in pawn. Tosca calls his offer horrible, and suddenly she thinks of appealing to the Queen. She rushes to the door, but already Scarpia knows her thoughts. Playing with her again, he invites her to leave if she wishes. "I'll do you no violence," he says, and Scarpia's Lust sounds in the oboe, clarinet, and harp. He's glad to have gotten her hopes up, so he can have the pleasure of dashing them again. When Tosca joyfully moves to leave, Scarpia utters that mocking laugh, and stays her with a gesture.

"But your hope is a fallacy," he tells her. (Yes, it always deceives.) Her lover would be dead by the time she reached the Queen, and her Highness would pardon a corpse. Overcome with terror, Tosca stops in her tracks, and then, staring at Scarpia, resumes her seat on the sofa. She looks at him for a moment more, then turns away, her features a mask of hatred and disgust. Delighted by her expression, the police chief comments gleefully, "How you hate me!" When she agrees, he adds, "That's how I want you!" He moves toward her again.

Tosca runs from him in horror, saying she hates him. "What does that matter?" asks Scarpia rhetorically, "spasms of hatred or spasms of love...." (Even here the composer manages to work in emotional opposites, and it's remarkable how close Scarpia comes to a sentiment expressed by Cavaradossi in the love duet: "Tosca, my idol, all things in you please me: the reckless anger, and the spasms of love!")

Things seem to have reached an impasse, but suddenly distant drums are heard, which sound stops both people cold. Those drums, says Scarpia brutally, are leading the escort of condemned men to the scaffold. Tosca shudders, and Scarpia asks whether it is her will that her lover has but one hour to live.

Exhausted, Tosca leans on the sofa. Scarpia goes to the table, pours coffee and drinks it, then leans on the table and watches Tosca, who, with immense sadness, begins what is perhaps Puccini's most famous aria, "Vissi d'arte." The song is built on the music to which Tosca entered in Act One, and it is a fascinating mixture of the creed of the Artist in Puccini's World, with the Catholic Tosca's utter bewilderment as to why God has not kept his side of the bargain she thought they had made.

Tosca begins the aria by declaring her lifelong devotion to those things that are sacred in Puccini's World: art and love. She has never harmed a living thing; and she's always helped people in distress. In the next section, which contains the music to which she made her entrance into the church, her arms filled with flowers, she speaks of religion, telling God she has been a faithful believer, and she asks why he repays her this way.

Even here, though, when Tosca details her religious devotions, she still speaks of the world of the Artists: "I gave songs to the stars, in heaven, that they shone more beautifully." The aria concludes with a repetition of that bewildered, sobbing question: why does God repay her like this? Unmoved, Scarpia asks whether she has decided.

What weapons are at hand? None of the familiar ones have worked, and even God has let Tosca down. Desperate, she decides to try a tactic she has never used before in her life. It is utterly repulsive, and nothing but her love for Mario would have caused her to consider it. Bereft of weapons, Tosca kneels at Scarpia's feet and begs for mercy.

This is the greatest abuse to which Puccini puts any of his heroines—Tosca on her knees, pleading for her lover—and it is nothing like the public scenes of humiliation and the full-throated Masochism Arias to which he subjects his tenor heroes. There is no suggestion that Tosca is enjoying herself (which is often the case with the tenor characters in their scenes of humiliation) and in a few minutes she will take full revenge for what she has suffered at Scarpia's hands.

But right now, the smiling police chief gives the screws one more vicious turn, saying that he gives in. Scarpia's Lust punctuates these words, played *forte* by full woodwinds. What Scarpia means is that he does *not* give in, and his terms are precisely as he had stated. Tosca has just enough time to refuse with disgust, before the horrid scene is interrupted by the knock of Spoletta.

To the Angelotti Theme Spoletta breathlessly reports the escapee was found, but took poison when captured. This is no matter to Scarpia, who to the Castle Theme orders the corpse hanged from the gibbet. And as for Cavaradossi...

"God help me," whispers Tosca. The police chief looks toward her. Weeping for shame, she nods, then buries her face in the sofa cushions. She immediately pulls herself together, however, and demands that Cavaradossi be released at once. Scarpia claims that is impossible, for a condemned prisoner can't be seen to have been released. Everyone must believe he is dead. There must be a mock execution. As he tells the waiting Spoletta, it must be done "in the manner of Count Palmieri."

The back-and-forth between Scarpia and Spoletta is so filled with vocal winking and nudging that the audience can hardly fail to observe it. Tosca, however, is excited by the idea of a pretend execution, and falls in with the idea at once. She demands to be allowed to warn Cavaradossi herself, and Scarpia agrees, telling Spoletta to admit her at four o'clock, which as we will see is just as dawn is breaking.

There is another thing Tosca fails to observe during this scene, and that is the appearance of another musical motif: that of the Fully Charged Rifles. This motif takes the form of an ascending second, and it is first heard the moment after Tosca nods her agreement to Scarpia's odious proposal. In the brief vocal silence that precedes Scarpia's command to Spoletta to "Listen," the motif is given out by woodwinds, cello, and double bass.

The ascending second recurs three times during Scarpia's assurance to Tosca that something will have to be done under the table — "...can't give him a **pardon openly** ... must believe the **Cavalier is dead** ... **the order** I give him...." — and when Scarpia begins his orders to Spoletta the motif begins blaring from the trombone and bass trombone — "...I've changed my mind." **Blare!** "The prisoner shall be **shot**." The trombones drop out now, and the motif sinks to a whisper: "...as was done with Count **Palmieri**." "I want to warn him **myself**." "So be it ... at four o'clock." **Whisper**. "Yes. Like Palmieri." The motif of the Fully Charged Rifles will recur for the last time during the four measures of music that precede the rifle volley that kills Cavaradossi.

Spoletta now leaves, and Scarpia turns to Tosca, resuming the lustful expression he put off when his deputy entered. But there is one thing more Tosca wants: a safe-conduct out of Rome for her and Mario. Like a polite host remonstrating with a departing guest, Scarpia asks whether she really wants to leave. "Forever," is the cold answer.

As Scarpia sits at his desk and begins to write, another theme is introduced. Played *andante sostenuto, ppp*, by muted violins and violas, this dark and mournful melody is the theme of The Double Cross. At this moment it expresses Scarpia's intention to double cross Tosca. The theme winds on as the police chief writes out the pass he knows will never be used, and as he writes, Tosca wearily drags herself toward the table where the dinner lies unfinished.

She needs a glass of wine to help her through her ordeal, but as she lifts the glass Scarpia filled for her, she notices the razor-sharp knife by his plate. Tosca realizes there is one weapon yet remaining. It is at this precise moment that the theme of The Double Cross moves into its second section, higher pitched, and *forte*.

Tosca quickly glances at Scarpia, but he is absorbed in writing. Cautiously she picks up the knife and hides it behind her back, then leans on the table, continuing to watch Scarpia. A moment later he folds the paper, and comes toward Tosca with it in his hand.

Here is Puccini's first truly important departure from Sardou. In the Frenchman's play, Tosca tiptoes up behind Scarpia while he is sitting at his desk and — just like a woman — stabs him in the back. Puccini either found this despicable, or not exciting enough, or both, so when his Scarpia comes toward Tosca with open arms, shouting "Tosca, finally you are mine!" the theme of Scarpia's Lust bubbling up in the orchestra, Puccini's magnificent heroine stabs him full in the chest, just as he utters the word "mine." The full orchestra sounds the *fortissimo* knife blow, and the diva cries, "This is the kiss of Tosca!"

Scarpia's voluptuous tone turns into a terrible cry. He staggers, beginning to choke as the blood wells up inside him. He shouts for help, and tries to grab hold of Tosca, who draws back out of his reach. All her terror and rage find release as she mocks the choking man. Scarpia struggles to stand, clutching the sofa and moaning that he is dying, and Tosca sneers, "Is the blood suffocating you?" Tosca exacts every drop of revenge coming to her as she tells him he's been killed by a woman — by her, Tosca, the woman he tortured.

Just as she had begged and pleaded in vain, so does he. Just as her cries for help were mocked, so are his. He makes a final, fruitless effort to stand. Tosca bends over him and looks him in the face, and the final words he hears are, "Die damned! Die, die, die!" Only timpani and muted violas witness the police chief's final exhalation. "He's dead," says Tosca in a chant. "Now I pardon him." But as she says this, the first section of The Double Cross is heard. The orchestra is telling us that although Scarpia is dead, he has laid one trap that is yet unsprung.

The Double Cross continues as Tosca goes to the dinner table, puts down the knife, and washes her bloody fingers with water from a jug. Then she smoothes her hair before a mirror on the wall. Recalling the safe-conduct, she looks for it on Scarpia's desk. Soon she sees it in the dead man's hand, and she pulls the paper out of the clenched fist. Tucking the safe-conduct away in her dress, she contemplates the body. Only the cello sounds as she chants on middle C, "And before him trembled all Rome!"

Scarpia's Lust again bubbles up in the orchestra as Tosca goes to the table, and extinguishes its candles. There is a candle burning on Scarpia's desk, and with it she lights a second candle. She takes them to where the body lies, and places one on either side of the head. Scarpia's Lust gives way to a transformed version of Tosca's Eyes, which are soft in love, and fierce in anger. Once more Tosca looks around, and seeing a crucifix on the wall, she takes it down and, kneeling beside the body, places it on the chest of the dead man. Softly, the Scarpia Chords sound, and the moment they finish, there is a roll of distant drums, reminding us of the march of the condemned men to the scaffold. Tosca rises, and exits with great caution, closing the door behind her as the curtain quickly drops.

Four horns, playing in unison before a lowered curtain, sound the opening of the final act. Their theme is an anticipation of the triumphant music of Tosca and Cavaradossi, who when they sing it believe they are moments away from freedom, but are in fact only moments from death.

The curtain rises to reveal a platform of the Castel Sant'Angelo. At left is a casement, beneath which is a table, a bench, and a stool. On the table are a lantern, a large register book, and writing materials. On one wall is a crucifix, beneath which is a votive lamp. At right is a trap door, which opens onto a small staircase that leads to a platform below. It is still night (three o'clock), but little by little as the act proceeds the darkness is dispelled by the grey light that precedes dawn.

Puccini's clock is rapidly approaching the hour of greatest peril, and in warning of that, he gives us a Dawn Song, "Io de' sospiri," sung by a young shepherd passing by with his flock. We cannot tell to whom the shepherd's sighs are addressed, but the song concludes, "Lamp of gold, I die for you." What can the lamp of gold be, if not the sun?

A Jailer with a lantern climbs the stairs. He sits and waits, half sleeping. During this action bells toll (signaling imminent disaster), and we hear a wisp of Undying Love, as well as the first two of the three Scarpia chords, which faintly remind us of all that has taken place before.

Soon a military picket, led by a Sergeant, climbs the stairs to deliver Cavaradossi. (As the soldiers climb the stairs with their prisoner, the orchestra begins to play the music of Cavaradossi's upcoming aria, "E lucevan le stelle." The melody finishes the instant before the Jailer asks Cavaradossi his name, which suggests it represents Cavaradossi's thoughts. Naturally these are interrupted when he is questioned, but the thoughts will resume and be put into words when he sings the aria. Simultaneous with its foreshadowing of the painter's words, this playing of the melody of the tenor's "big tune" warms up the ears of first time listeners, so they will appreciate the song better when Cavaradossi sings it.) The Jailer examines a paper handed him by the Sergeant, opens the register, and writes as he questions the prisoner, confirming the name of Mario Cavaradossi. He then offers the condemned man the consolation of a priest during the hour remaining to him. The offer is refused.

Puccini's Cavaradossi is not the impossibly calm and composed figure from Sardou's play, who takes the opportunity of this final hour of life to catch up on his sleep. Puccini's man is no longer masterful and heroic. He is only a man; afraid, as anyone would be at such a time, and filled with grief. He does not want to die.

Cavaradossi asks the Jailer to be allowed to write a few lines to a person very dear to him. (A cello plays the theme of Tosca's Eyes, followed by the music of "...in Tosca a mad love burns.") Cavaradossi takes a ring from his finger and offers it to the man as a bribe, if he will give the letter to her, and with this gesture he casts away the sole piece of jewelry he wears. Cavaradossi is an Artist of Puccini's World, and he knows it is not fitting that he die with jewelry on him. And the gesture has a double significance, for even in these desperate circumstances, he does not resort to buying the guard's favor with gold; instead, he obtains it through barter, as Musetta obtained Mimi's cordial by bartering her earrings.

The Jailer hesitates, then takes the ring. He motions to Cavaradossi to sit at the table, and tells him to write. Four cellos play the theme of Undying Love as Cavaradossi begins his letter to Tosca, but soon a flood of memories washes over him, and he can't write any more.

A harp arpeggio signals the start of Cavaradossi's Masochism Aria — the backward-looking Dusk Song, "E lucevan le stelle," which provides the closing bracket to the long section opened by Tosca's forward-looking Dusk Song, "Non la sospiri la nostra casetta." A solo clarinet begins the melody of Cavaradossi's aria, the opening, semi-chanted words of which are classic Puccini: "And the stars shone, and the earth was perfumed...." Amidst sweet kisses and languid caresses, he "freed the beautiful form from its veils." This is a Puccini Artist's conception of the Night of Love, but now Cavaradossi is forced to admit that Night is coming to a close. "I die despairing..." he mourns, in a line contributed by Puccini himself, "...and never have I loved life so much."

Puccini's hero bursts into tears, and covers his face with his hands. But no sooner has he done this than the theme of Undying Love is heard. Tosca, accompanied by Spoletta and the Sergeant, comes up from the stairway. Spoletta calls to the Jailer, and they two and the Sergeant go down to the lower platform. A sentry remains to watch the prisoner.

The orchestra becomes increasingly excited as Tosca rushes to the weeping Cavaradossi and raises his head with both hands. Too overcome with emotion to speak, she shows him the safe-conduct. (The numerous mimed scenes in the opera were surely the result of Sardou's influence.)

Cavaradossi leaps to his feet and reads the paper, and together he and Tosca exultantly read out the words that guarantee their safe-conduct. But then Cavaradossi sees the signature of Scarpia. He gives Tosca a meaningful look, saying this is the first reprieve that man has ever given.

"And the last!" says Tosca, putting the safe-conduct away. She describes what happened — "He wanted your blood or my love" — and the music of Scarpia's "...spasms of love or spasms of hate...." carry her words as she relates how the monster told her of the gallows already raising arms to the sky. Lower strings describe the escort drums Tosca heard leading the condemned men, then Scarpia's Lust is given out one last time in the oboe, clarinet, and harp, as Tosca quotes him — "You're mine!"

But now the theme of The Double Cross sounds, as she tells how she saw the gleaming blade as Scarpia sat at his desk writing. "I plunged that **blade** ..." she cries, on an extended high C, which drops an octave to middle C as she finishes "...into his **heart!**"

Chanting on Tosca's middle C, the awed Cavaradossi gasps, "You, with your own hand killed him?" Continuing the chant, Tosca describes how her hands were stained with Scarpia's blood.

Lovingly taking her hands in his Cavaradossi sings a hymn of praise to them: "O dolci mani" (O sweet hands). Tosca's hands, he says, were destined to good things, and perhaps the most important was "...to gathering roses ..." The Double Cross sounds again as Cavaradossi sings, "You gave death, O victorious hands...."

Tosca is in complete charge now, and pulling her hands out of his, she tells her lover of her escape plan. And as she does, she utters an absolutely shocking line — one we never would have expected from the Lady of the Rose. Assuring Cavaradossi that a carriage is ready, she tells him, "I have already collected gold and jewels." In fact, she has them in her purse, *and she shows them to him!*

This is so extremely unlike Puccini that it demands to be addressed. Never before or since will one of his Artist characters express the slightest interest in "gold and jewels," which are in fact anathema to them. Only the greedy Manon loved them. Why on earth, then, does Tosca interject this line, which even if she were not a "good person" of Puccini's World would seem grossly out of place in this highly emotional situation? The only thing that seems reasonable is that Puccini included it as a sort of explanation as to why these two long-suffering characters will have to die. (Aside, that is, from the fact that it is now dawn, and they have been double-crossed.) Recall Des Grieux, who cried to Manon as she was snatching up Geronte's jewels to leave those things, for he wanted to take only her heart.

Tosca goes on to tell her lover of the comedy they must go through — the soldiers shoot blanks, he falls — then away to the ship that will carry them to freedom. She sings a brief Spring Song, asking, "Do you smell the scent of the roses?" Then she adds, not realizing how frightening these words are, "Does it not seem to you that all things in love are awaiting the sun?" (Indeed they are, for are not all things awaiting death?)

Complete enslavement to his lady is expressed by Cavaradossi in his final aria, "Amaro sol per te." Using words of an ideal devotion of vassal to lord, or a human to his god, Cavaradossi declares the thought of dying was bitter to him only because of Tosca, from whom all joy and desire are born. "And the beauty of the things most wondrous will have voice and color only from you."

Tosca contributes a verse to this song, but there is no talk from her of receiving everything worth having from Cavaradossi. She is too masterful for that now. Her lines are simply a hymn to love, which saved his life, and will be their guide on earth, until they dissolve into oneness at sunset.

Tosca is first to emerge from the reverie this talk of sunset inspires in them. She cautions Cavaradossi to fall at once when the shots are fired, and to be careful not to hurt himself. She, being versed in stage technique, could do it easily.

Another mirror image now occurs, as Cavaradossi interrupts Tosca and asks her to speak to him as she did before, for the sound of her voice is so sweet. The first time we heard this sentiment was during the Act One love duet, when Tosca asked her masterful lover to, "Say it again, the word that consoles ... say it again!" Their roles have been completely reversed — Tosca is the masterful one now, and Cavaradossi the supplicant.

Tosca sings of how their love will spread throughout the world, and then, to the triumphant music played by the four horns at the opening of the act, the two sing in unison, if a bit vaguely, of ecstatic souls, celestial ardor, and the soul's harmonious flight to the ecstasy of love. The sky lightens, and a bell tolls the hour of four. Again the tolling bells signal imminent disaster.

The Jailer comes to Cavaradossi and tells him it is time. Calmly, the prisoner declares he is ready. The lovers chuckle softly as they again go over Cavaradossi's instructions to fall at once as the shots are fired, and to not get up until Tosca calls. There have been so many inappropriate laughs in this opera (in fact, there hasn't been a single appropriate one), and apparently Cavaradossi is engaging in a final one. Tosca urges her lover not to laugh, and he replaces his smile with a grim look.

Followed by Spoletta and the Sergeant, the firing squad comes up the stairs, and their officer arranges them in a line. A strange, winding, and repetitive melody begins as the soldiers emerge onto the platform. Tosca watches the men's assembly and their preparations for the execution to music that suggests eager lightheartedness, and impatience. As unknowing as a sheep, the cheerful Cavaradossi follows the officer, who leads him to a wall opposite where Tosca stands in the casement. Offered a blindfold, the condemned man smilingly refuses.

The many ritual preparations try Tosca's patience. "The sun is already rising," she notes, and she asks with exasperation why they delay shooting. At last the soldiers raise their weapons, and as they do, the ascending-second motif of the Fully Charged Rifles begins to blare, *fortissimo,* played by full orchestra. The officer raises his saber to signal the volley, and Tosca covers her ears. At the same time she signals with her head to Cavaradossi, reminding him to fall at once.

The Fully Charged Rifles, which has sounded three times, stops, and the instant it does the officer lowers his saber. "How handsome my Mario is!" exclaims Tosca happily. The squad fires, and Cavaradossi falls like a stone. Pleased with her lover's realistic fall, Tosca approves, "There! Die!" and she blows him a kiss. "There's an artist," she declares.

To the now-blaring melody to which the firing squad climbed the stairs and went through its preparations, the Sergeant goes to check the body, and Spoletta, who has also gone to the body, holds him back from delivering the traditional *coup de grâce.* The soldiers form a new line, and all, including Spoletta, exit, leaving Tosca and the fallen Mario alone.

The music of the firing squad softens to *piano* and an agitated Tosca, fearing her lover will get up too soon and give everything away, repeatedly whispers to him to stay quiet.

She goes to the top of the stairs and listens. For a moment she thinks the soldiers are returning, but at last she feels certain they have gone. She goes to the parapet and looks over, then runs to Cavaradossi. She urges her lover to get up quickly, but he does not respond. She touches him, and then, disturbed, turns him over, only to find he is dead. Shrieking in horror, she throws herself on the body of her beloved Mario.

The sound of confused voices is heard below, speaking of Scarpia's murder. It is Sciarrone, Spoletta, and some of the soldiers. As Tosca weeps over her lover, a voice says, "The woman is Tosca!" The two men run up the stairs, shouting that Tosca will pay for Scarpia's life. Spoletta tries to seize her, but Tosca shoves him so hard he almost falls through the stairwell. Then she runs to the parapet and, answering the vow that she will pay for Scarpia's life, she shouts, "With mine!"

Tosca leaps over the parapet wall to her death, and as she does she calls out a name. But it is not Mario's name. She does not, as a Verdi heroine would, renounce the cruel world, declaring that in death she and her beloved will find the happiness denied them in life. No. The name Tosca calls as she leaps to her death is that of her enemy: "O Scarpia, before God!" The battle continues.[5]

8

Madama Butterfly

Libretto by Giacosa and Illica, after the play by David Belasco
and the story by John Luther Long
First performed at La Scala, Milan, February 17, 1904

Despite the fact that the tenor character is a bounder — the precise opposite of a *romance hero*—*Madama Butterfly* represents the supreme expression of Puccini's personal *romance* credo. Glorious things await in the remaining chapters of the cycle, but with *La Fanciulla del West* the foundations of Puccini's World will begin to crack as the composer attempts to lead the lovers out of the illicit world of Night and into a world of sanctioned, Day-time love.

There is a unique symbolic element in *Butterfly*: the knife with which Butterfly's father performed *seppuku*— the ritual suicide that wipes out disgrace. For one to whom honor is all, the knife is the friend of last resort, for when honor has been lost, the knife can restore it to him — or her — who has the courage to use it.

It's astounding how completely the character of Puccini's Butterfly has been misunderstood. Conventional wisdom has her the child-bride, so naïve and self-deluding she cannot see what everyone around her can see: her American husband, who has been gone three years without a word, has no intention of coming back. She is the "frail waif," so deeply and pathetically in love she commits suicide because she cannot bear the loss of that love.[1] This is utter nonsense. Butterfly is Japanese to the core, in that she is keenly aware of what others think of her, and is constantly on guard against insults that would damage her reputation. To the Japanese of Puccini's era, damage to the reputation had to be repaired, no matter what the cost.

Butterfly is a teenage girl, and not very worldly, but she is strong and determined. She is her father's daughter, and she absolutely refuses to be treated disrespectfully — by anyone. She does love Lt. Pinkerton, but that's not why she marries him; at least, not in Puccini. She marries for love in Long's story and Belasco's play, but in Puccini she marries because she believes Pinkerton, his god, and his country's laws, will safeguard her honor.[2] It's a great risk Butterfly takes when she marries her naval officer. The stakes are honor and disgrace, life and death. If she is right about Pinkerton, the American god, and the American laws, her honor will always be safe. If she is wrong, the knife will help her.

Puccini has made further advances here in respect to recurring music, which no longer includes labels for objects. We rarely see into anyone's thoughts, and when we do it is in a hazy, impressionistic way. Puccini has learned how to employ recurring music more subtly than in *Tosca*, expanding on his use of the "family of motifs" technique. The Love Duet, for example, is linked by rhythm to the Flower Duet, while the music of Butterfly's mother is linked by melody to that of her son. The most significant of the musical families is the one that encompasses the motifs of the Whirlwind, the Rejection, and Pinkerton's Return, all of which point toward the final tragedy, and are linked via an opening pattern of three rising notes, which describe Pinkerton's climb up the hill. The tragedy, these three linked themes tell us, is caused by Pinkerton's having first climbed the hill to the little house.

There are two Alberich-characters in this opera. One is Prince Yamadori—"the rich Yamadori." By now we know that since Yamadori is rich, his love is poisoned. Yamadori pines for Butterfly, but he has no chance of winning her. Only a fool would put her honor in the hands of a man who has married wife after wife, and divorced them all.

The other Alberich is Pinkerton, of course. Shortly after the opera opens, Butterfly's relatives, who have gathered for the wedding, comment on the groom. The mother declares Pinkerton appears like a king to her, and an aunt agrees he is incredibly rich. These are both terribly ominous signs.

Butterfly is Puccini's most perfect conception of the Lady of the Rose. As a geisha, she sustained herself in her poverty by singing and dancing, thus she is an Artist. When, in Act Two, she considers the terrible possibility that she might, as a cast-off wife, have to return to the life of a geisha, she makes clear what she meant by "sustained." Her art was never for sale. If she were to return to singing and dancing, it would be a matter of barter—an exchange for "bread and clothes."

As the promised bride of Lt. Pinkerton, Butterfly is no longer a geisha at the start of the opera. She is still an Artist, however, whose art includes the fashioning of beautiful compliments. She gives one of these lovely creations to the crass and impatient Pinkerton, who essentially says, "That's nice," and throws it away. Asked if he would like another, he refuses. This is a Puccini Alberich, displaying his contempt for Art. Near the end of the opera, Pinkerton settles any question about his nature, unwittingly offering a final, monstrous insult to Butterfly by trying to give her money.

As in *Tosca*, this story starts with the tenor character the dominant partner in the relationship. But so much is Butterfly the hero of her opera that her lover is pushed off stage after Act One, and not brought back until the closing scene, for a mere couple of minutes. When he does return, it is as a guilt-ridden wreck, able to do nothing more than reveal himself as the gold-poisoned creature he is, sing the requisite Masochism Aria at the top of his lungs, then run away, crying, "I'm vile!"

The ceremony Pinkerton and Butterfly go through in Act One is called a marriage, but that's not what it is. Well-to-do Japanese men of that era typically had mistresses, who were either geishas or prostitutes. These relationships were openly acknowledged, and they involved a contract between the man and the establishment where the woman worked. The contract guaranteed the woman a certain amount of money and a residence separate from the place where she had been employed. When Westerners began to infiltrate the Japanese world during the 1800's, some of them availed themselves of this custom.[3]

This sort of contract is clearly what Pinkerton is signing in Act One, and it is clearly what Yamadori is later suggesting to Butterfly, although for decency's sake the terms of marriage are the only ones used throughout the opera. In Belasco, the length of the "marriage" was actually specified: Pinkerton requested that Goro fix him up with a woman for a three-month period.

Butterfly is the most florally rich of all Puccini's operas. Only *La Rondine* comes near in the sheer quantity of flowers brought on stage and in the symbolic use of the blossoms. The reason these two operas so heavily feature flowers is that both librettos are built around the medieval *romance* conceptions of the birth of romantic love, the hope for a rebirth of that love in springtime, and the blast of winter that follows when the hope is not fulfilled.

Audience attention begins to be specifically drawn to the flowers starting with the Act Two "Flower Duet," which is pure *romance* in its expression of the hope for the rebirth of love in springtime. That this is the actual season in which the act is set was made known via Butterfly's recollection that Pinkerton promised to return to her in the season when the robins make their nests. In joyful anticipation of Pinkerton's expected return, Butterfly and her maid strip the garden of every blossom there. All the flowers are brought inside the house, and roses are given the place of honor, at the threshold over which Pinkerton is to step. Symbolically, the house has been transformed into the garden.

As the final gesture of preparation before the vigil begins, Butterfly fixes a red poppy in her hair. Then she stands to begin her silent waiting, watching for Pinkerton as "...the moon's rays illuminate the exterior of the *shoji*." Throughout the vigil the moon shines her silvery light on Butterfly, who stands before us in her white wedding dress. She is "the little goddess of the moon," and if Pinkerton is ever to return to her it will be now, when she and the moon are at their peak of strength and beauty.

Until we reach *Turandot*, the final chapter in the Rose Cycle, every soprano heroine from now on will place a red flower in her hair as she prepares to meet the man she loves. The red flower is not a stand-in for jewelry; it is a declaration on the part of the Lady of the Rose. It represents her moral purity, and symbolizes her faith in undying love.

Yet love does die, for Pinkerton does not come back to the flower-filled house, where the moon shines bravely through the paper wall, silvering both his mistress and her flowers. As the long night passes and the moon begins to weaken, the blossoms start to wilt. The garden had been stripped of every one of its blooms, and so by dawn, when Pinkerton comes to take his son away, all the flowers are withered.

In the final scene we see a genuinely sinister aspect to Butterfly as the Lady of the Rose, and as a woman who values her honor as much as her father did his. That is, the flowers play a subtle part in Butterfly's revenge. The Japanese code of *giri* required that stains to one's honor be wiped out, and in a timely manner. If suicide was deemed necessary, that act not only restored honor, it might even enhance it. Or it could be that an act of revenge on the detractor would take care of the situation by exactly evening the score.[4] If we accept that Butterfly is a woman to whom honor is all, we will understand she cannot take Pinkerton's betrayal of her and his destruction of her honor (and her flowers) passively.

The tardy Pinkerton finally arrives at dawn, to see about getting his son. At last aware of all that has taken place since he left three years before, he gazes in dismay at the wilted flowers that cover the floor of the little house, and cries, "Oh! The bitter perfume of these flowers is like poison to my heart." There is a faint suggestion that the flowers are working on the tenor character with a conscious deliberateness.

Butterfly's suicide — in Puccini — is absolutely not a matter of her being unable to bear the loss of Pinkerton's love. It is a matter of her adhering to the code of *giri*— of not only clearing the stain on her honor, but also of avenging the insult. When Pinkerton at last proves he is no better than Yamadori, Butterfly's love for him disappears. To believe she will let him off after his having insulted her so deeply, is to completely mistake the character of Puccini's heroine (and to grossly underestimate Puccini's longing to have his heroine kill her lover).

This *volte-face* in Butterfly's feelings toward Pinkerton is quintessential Japanese behavior, for in that world only a fool would continue to harbor good feelings toward someone who had shamed her. Butterfly would have killed Goro for damaging her son's honor. Why should she continue to look kindly on a man who has utterly destroyed her own? Pinkerton's horror-filled cry as to the poisonous action of the flowers on his heart is a foreshadowing of Butterfly's revenge on him.

Told by Suzuki of how Butterfly had waited for him all night, Pinkerton does not have the courage to face the girl. He indulges himself in his celebrated Masochism Aria, "Addio, fiorito asil" (Goodbye, flowery refuge), then he runs away, having vowed that Butterfly's face will haunt him, torturing him forever. In part he is ashamed, but he is also very afraid. In running away, he leaves his new American wife behind to face Butterfly, and when the Japanese girl opens the door of her house and sees a strange woman standing in her barren garden in the fierce light of morning, she has one terrible question for Suzuki. Is Pinkerton alive, or is he not?

Her last chance for life with honor rests in Pinkerton being dead. If he is dead, no one can scorn her for his failure to return. When Suzuki admits he is alive, the stage directions declare, "Butterfly stands as if she had received a mortal blow," then she says the words herself: he isn't coming back. Butterfly absolves the apologetic Kate Pinkerton of any responsibility for what has happened, and wishes her happiness. And she tells her to give a message to her husband. If he wants to have his son, he must come back to the house in half an hour.

This is an extremely important departure from Belasco, in whose play Butterfly asks Kate to tell Pinkerton she wishes him happiness, and also asks her to thank Pinkerton for his kindness to her. (The same thing happens in Long's story; only Butterfly says these things to Sharpless.) Belasco then has Butterfly promise to give the child to Kate if Kate will come back in fifteen minutes. In Puccini, Butterfly wishes *Kate* happiness, she certainly does *not* ask her to thank Pinkerton, and she is clearly planning something for him by insisting that *he* come to the house to get the boy. Butterfly has absolved Kate of responsibility for her death, and she absolves her son. But Pinkerton she does not absolve.

In talking to Kate, Butterfly did not step outside her house, which is now a destroyed garden, and as Kate leaves she closes the door. The daylight is hateful to her, and she orders Suzuki to close the windows to shut it out. (Note the similarity to Rodolfo's behavior in the final scene of *Bohème*.)

She goes to Suzuki's shrine and bows before the statue of the Buddha. Clearly she is rescinding her conversion, and asking forgiveness for having turned to the god of the Christians. After a moment of painful meditation, she takes down her father's knife, kisses the blade, and reads the inscription aloud: "With honor dies he who can no longer live with honor." She goes behind a screen, and just as her father did she performs the ritual of *seppuku*, which restores her honor.

And the moment after she has done this, Pinkerton returns, just as she had arranged for him to do, to be confronted by the sight of her breathing her last, lying amid her dead flowers. Butterfly can die in peace, for the last sight she sees is Pinkerton kneeling before her in submission, just as she had done so many times before him. Finally, at the moment of her death, the balance of power between the heroine and her lover has been corrected. Butterfly has all the power; Pinkerton has none. The frightened Pinkerton had already vowed he would be forever tortured by thoughts of Butterfly's face. What will he do now, after seeing this sight?

Whatever the answer, there is no question but that Butterfly did this to him deliberately, and that he will lie pinned, quivering, beneath her ghostly thumb forever. This is how we remember Pinkerton: kneeling, frozen with horror, the cry of "Butterfly!" echoing in his brain. Essentially he is dead. This is the revenge of Butterfly.

Madama Butterfly opens with an orchestral prelude in the form of a chattering, quasi-fugal piece that describes the busy world of the Japanese in general, and the port of Nagasaki in particular. This music will underscore some of the *parlando* of the first act, and serve as utility music during shifts in attention.

The curtain rises to reveal a charming wood-and-paper house on Higashi Hill, which overlooks Nagasaki and its harbor. This house, complete with terrace and garden, is the sort beloved by Puccini's "good" characters. Light and airy, tiny and completely lacking in luxuries, it barely separates its inhabitants from the world of nature that lies just outside the doorstep.

Goro, the obsequious marriage broker, is busy demonstrating for U.S. Naval Lt. Benjamin Franklin Pinkerton the delightful features of this house he has just leased, the chambers and views of which can be instantly transformed merely by the sliding of rice paper panels. Although Pinkerton is amused by the house, and likes the way it can so easily be rearranged, he is also, in his superior masculine way, dismissive of it as a "frivolous dwelling." Goro contradicts him, saying that it is "strong like a tower, from floor to roof." The lovely, delicate, and strong little house is a metaphor for Butterfly herself, whom Pinkerton underestimates just as he does the house.

The busy music of the prelude gives way to a graceful theme marked by a *pizzicato* figure in the flutes. Goro conducts Pinkerton into the garden, and claps his hands to summon the servants: one woman and two men, who kneel respectfully before Pinkerton. (In observing the numerous times people humbly kneel before the smug Pinkerton, we should be aware Puccini is setting us up for the opera's closing tableau: Pinkerton kneeling in submission before the dying Butterfly.) Butterfly's maid Suzuki is introduced as Miss Light Cloud. The men, who are to be the cook and the butler, are Ray of the Rising Sun, and Exhales Aromas.

The lyricism of Goro's introduction dissolves into a recurrence of the busy music of the prelude. This signals a burst of chatter from Suzuki, who has been deceived by Pinkerton's smile. Her eager conversation (the smile is "a fruit and a flower") quickly bores the ever-impatient Pinkerton, and Goro dismisses the servants. He then looks down the hill to see whether the bride is near.

This anticipation of the soprano character's arrival is a new technique for Puccini. In *Bohème* he began to use the offstage voice to pique our curiosity about the heroine. That was how Mimi made her entrance, and Tosca as well. Puccini has now come to understand that rather than simply springing the heroine on us, he can heighten our interest in his most important character by repeatedly having the onstage characters talk about her, long before she enters.

People look to see whether Butterfly is coming, they talk about how lovely she is, they send someone off to fetch her, they talk some more about how pretty and charming she is, they discuss Pinkerton's plans for her (which worry us). And at last, after all the anticipation, right after Pinkerton has offered a toast to the American woman he hopes to marry one day, we hear the offstage voice of this beautiful Japanese girl, breathtakingly lovely, soaring above a chorus of female voices, it's owner singing of love and unwittingly entering into a dangerous situation. Unlike Mimi and Tosca, who after their entrances had to work to make us care for them, Butterfly has built up tremendous sympathy and liking in the audience before she has set one foot on the stage. The entrance of Butterfly is the most skillful introduction of a character Puccini has done so far in his career.

The bride's relatives will accompany her, Goro explains to Pinkerton — the mother, the grandmother, and numerous cousins. (A bustling and somewhat comical theme in an Oriental vein, introduced by solo bassoon, carries Goro's description of the relatives, suggesting a group of busy, self-important, and ridiculous people bobbing along.) There is also an uncle who is a priest, Goro adds, but he won't come to the ceremony. Pinkerton is amused at the thought of the relatives, and is not offended when Goro leeringly remarks that he and the lovely Butterfly can provide for descendants.

Suddenly, an offstage male voice announces the arrival of the kindly, well meaning, but ineffectual Sharpless, the U.S. Consul. That he is American is obvious from the square, cheerful, hearty theme given out by first violins. This is Sharpless' personal theme, which will recur when he departs this act, and several more times in Act Two.

Sharpless puffs as he reaches the top of the hill, then Goro, after respectfully prostrating himself, hurries to fetch refreshments. Sharpless looks down the hill, impressed at the view. "Nagasaki!" he cries, as the orchestra plays a four-chord passage from the prelude, which seems to speak that word. (Sharpless' vocal line is, unfortunately, uniformly dull, thanks to his complete lack of interest in matters of sexual passion.)

The prelude music returns, but a new arrangement ensures its continued musical interest. Pinkerton cheerfully points out to Sharpless the little house that obeys at his command, and as he describes the convenience of the lease (999 years with a monthly option to cancel), we see the house delights him because both the terms and the sliding panels make for a lack of permanence that suits him perfectly. (They also suit Puccini perfectly, for they express the opposites that always appealed to him.) This lack of permanence also extends, in Pinkerton's mind, to the so-called marriage he is about to enter into.

As the two men enjoy a whiskey, Pinkerton relaxes and reveals his philosophy of life in a lyrical arietta, "Dovunque al mondo," which is introduced by the opening music of The Star-Spangled Banner, played by woodwinds and brass. (These measures from Star-Spangled Banner constitute a personal motif for Pinkerton.) Sharpless soon begins to add Puccini Mixture comments to the song — strange comments, to one who does not understand how a philosophy can make life charming, and at the same time sadden the heart.

To a broad, sweeping theme the lieutenant describes his "Yankee vagabond" creed. Dropping anchor wherever he pleases, he stays until a squall upsets the ship. (We will see a mirror image of this "philosophy of life" song, complete with a reference to "vagabonds" and an image of a storm uprooting oaks (rather than upsetting ships), in Butterfly's arietta, "Nessuno si confessa mai nato in povertà," in which she describes how she became a geisha.)

Pinkerton continues, saying his creed is to take everything he wants, while always remaining ready to move on. And what is it that he wants? It is "...to make his treasure the flowers on every shore." (This is the same language of greedy destruction of flowers that was used in *Manon*, when Edmund disapprovingly commented on Geronte's plan to steal away Manon. Pinkerton will reiterate this sentiment soon, when again having referred to Butterfly as a flower, he gloats, "...and in my faith I have plucked it.")

Pinkerton's arietta concludes with a declaration that he is marrying the Japanese way:

for 999 years, with an option to cancel at any time. He rises and touches his glass to that of Sharpless, and to a reiteration of Star-Spangled Banner (which thus brackets the song) they make a toast: "America forever!"

Sharpless now asks whether the bride is beautiful, and Goro declares her to be, "A garland of fresh flowers. A star with gold rays." Annoyed at this intrusion, which includes the offer of a girl for Sharpless—only 100 yen!—Pinkerton orders Goro to fetch the bride. (That Puccini crafted this section as an opposing image to Butterfly's description of how she became a geisha is made even more certain by the music that precedes and carries Sharpless' question as to the frenzy that seems to have taken Pinkerton. It is the music of the closing line of Butterfly's arietta: "You laugh? Why? It's the way of the world.")

This situation Pinkerton has entered into does seem unwise to Sharpless, and in another lyrical arietta, "Amore o grillo," Pinkerton explains that what attracts him is Butterfly's extraordinary delicacy and grace. He feels compelled to pursue this girl, "even if I should break her wings." Thus it is he who first raises the possibility of injuring Butterfly, and he has decided his own desires outweigh that consideration.

In his stolid way, the Consul warns Pinkerton against hurting a girl who loves and trusts him, but Pinkerton brushes him off with a laugh, and a toast to the day when he will have "a real wedding and a real American wife." Pinkerton will indeed be signing a contract that makes Butterfly his acknowledged mistress. The line is also horribly ironic, given Butterfly's determination to be a real American wife. (The music of Sharpless' warning will recur in an "I told you so," near the end of the opera.)

It's significant that the toast Sharpless proposes is "...to your family, far away." We see in this another faint expression, first heard in *Manon*, of Puccini's own longing for a place of emotional refuge—a place far away, where people love you, and there are no sorrows. Butterfly will express this longing in Act Two, when she promises her son his father "...will carry us far away, far away, to his country...." This longing to be in some idyllic place that is *not here*—a place called *là lontano*—will be expressed with unbearable sadness and intensity in every opera subsequent to this one.

Goro announces the coming of Butterfly and her friends, who are approaching the top of the hill. All eyes turn toward the place where the women are about to appear, pinpointed by the chorus of offstage voices. The music employed by Goro, and taken up by the friends on their opening line (on which they merely sing, "Ah! ah! ah! ah!") is that of Butterfly's upcoming, philosophy of life song: "Nobody ever confesses he was born in poverty ... but the whirlwind uproots the most robust oaks."

Sections from this passage, in which Butterfly will warn of how easily disaster can overtake anyone, will recur repeatedly throughout the opera, for the possibility of ruin haunts her, but it's worth stopping to ask a question; that is, who is a sturdier oak than Pinkerton? And who will be absolutely shocked at the opera's end, to find himself uprooted by a sudden, unexpected whirlwind? We are very used to considering Pinkerton as the "whirlwind" to Butterfly's "oak," but it is indeed possible Puccini believed the reverse was also true, and it is also possible that is why he is employing this music for Butterfly's entrance. It seems just the kind of ironic, double-edged comment he would be likely to make in music.

After this line from the friends, the entrance music shifts to that of the last section of the upcoming love duet, as once again the audience's ears are acquainted with a "big tune" before it is played all out. "So much sky, so much sea," cry the friends. Butterfly's voice soars above those of the friends as she sings her entrance line, "Another step, come now."

"Look," cry the friends. "Look at all the flowers!" Accompanied by solo violin, viola, and cello, Butterfly sings, "Coiling over sea and earth is a joyous breath of spring." She is the happiest girl in the world, for she has come at the call of love. "I am come to the threshold of love ..." she sings (using the music to which Pinkerton will later urge her to "Come, come..."), "...where is gathered the good of those who live and those who die." (This Pucciniesque line was probably picked up from a song fragment in Long's story: "It is life when we meet; it is death when we part.")

The friends wish Butterfly joy, but they caution her, before she crosses that threshold, to turn and look at the sky, the flowers, the sea — all the things so dear to her. This is her last chance to draw back. Butterfly now appears with her friends at the top of the hill. With their brightly colored parasols, they seem like a cluster of gently nodding spring flowers. As this lovely sight comes into view, the music shifts from the love duet to a delicate rendition of an authentic Japanese folk song, played by flute, oboe, harp, and bells.[5]

Seeing Pinkerton, Butterfly orders her friends to kneel with her before him. She intends to be a perfect wife, who will give her husband full respect, and no reason ever to find fault with her. (We shouldn't allow the kneeling to make us think of Butterfly as submissive or weak-willed. It's clear from the way she orders her friends and relatives about she is quite bossy.)

After closing their parasols, the entire party kneels before Pinkerton, and at that moment the delicate folk song concludes. (The song will recur several times, including during the B section of Butterfly's arietta, "Ieri son salita," when she admits to Pinkerton she has converted to his religion; at which point her line, "I follow my destiny," explains the significance of the music. We will also hear the folk song melody when it closes the love duet, and thus the entire act, reinforcing it as the music of Butterfly's determination to commit herself to Pinkerton fully. The last time we will hear it is at the end of the vigil, where, having totally shed its delicate melancholy, it will describe the rising of the sun.)

Butterfly and her friends rise and approach Pinkerton ceremoniously, wishing him good fortune and offering respect. The smiling Pinkerton asks whether the climb was difficult, and Butterfly answers with a pretty compliment: "For a well-bred bride, impatience is more painful." Pinkerton thanks her for the rare compliment, but his tone is "a bit deriding." He has no interest in the delicate art of compliments. Butterfly doesn't notice the sarcasm, and takes his appreciation at face value. Sharpless approaches Butterfly, and (continuing with the music of her "destiny") asks her about herself. Her family was once wealthy, she says, looking to her friends for confirmation. They agree that was how it was.

That Butterfly's following arietta, "Nessuno si confessa mai nato in povertà," is her version of Pinkerton's "Dovunque al mondo" is signaled by her use of the key word "vagabond." Following her assertion that her family was once wealthy, she adds, "...there isn't a vagabond who, to hear him, doesn't come of high ancestry." Pinkerton spoke of the squall that upsets the ship, now Butterfly speaks of the whirlwind that uproots the sturdiest oaks. (She is referring to her father's suicide, which plunged the family into poverty.) The motif of the Whirlwind, like those of the Rejection and Pinkerton's Return, begins with three rising notes, very close together. The concepts are already related to one another dramatically, and Puccini is linking them musically as well, such that by the end of the opera they are essentially fused together.

To Pinkerton, the upsetting storm was cause for moving on to other pleasures, whereas Butterfly and her friends reacted to the uprooting whirlwind by learning how to support themselves. They became geishas, a profession that involves the mastery of many difficult arts, and this work is something Butterfly is in no way ashamed of. (Her asserting this tells us that when she decides to commit *seppuku*, as opposed to returning to being a geisha, it is not because there is anything degrading in that work. Rather, it's the loss of face she would have to acknowledge when returning to her former life.)

Butterfly's speech brings a smile to Sharpless' face, and using the same music to which the Consul questioned Pinkerton after "Dovunque al mondo" she demands, "You laugh? Why? It's the way of the world." (As in *Tosca*, there is little appropriate laughter in this opera. Almost all the smiles and laughs are rather insulting.) With misplaced condescension, Pinkerton tells Sharpless this girl sets him on fire with such doll-like ways.

Sharpless asks about her relatives. She has no sisters, Butterfly answers, only her mother, who is very poor. (In Act Two the music of Butterfly's mother will be incorporated, with tremendous pathos, into the music of her son.) "And your father?" asks Sharpless. The dark motif of the Father's Suicide sounds in woodwinds and trombones as Butterfly brusquely answers, "Dead." Clearly embarrassed, the friends bow their heads and fan themselves rapidly.

Oblivious to his faux pas, Sharpless continues the personal questions. The next one, however, delights Butterfly. He asks her age, and rather coyly, she admits to being 15. (This was marriageable age to the Japanese of this time.) Butterfly says, "I'm old already," but although she laughs her music is melancholy, and to Puccini, such a remark is deadly serious. Indeed, Butterfly has only three years left to live.

Goro announces the arrival of more guests, including the Imperial Commissioner, who brings with him a few bars of the Japanese Imperial Hymn. With the Commissioner is the official from the registry office, and these two men go into the house, where the ceremony is to be performed. Last to arrive are more of Butterfly's friends and relations, who enter to a reiteration of the "ridiculous relatives" music. The Lieutenant stares rudely at Butterfly's relatives, laughing to Sharpless over this farce.

The friends and relatives also comment noisily on Pinkerton. In both Long and Belasco, Butterfly had been pressured by her impoverished relatives to "marry" the rich American, and here the mother, aunt, and some friends declare Pinkerton is handsome and rich, and looks like a king. But the cousin, other relatives, and other friends are filled with jealousy. They say Pinkerton isn't handsome at all, and they look forward to him divorcing Butterfly, whose beauty, they sneer, is already withered. (The word they use is *disfiorì*, which is used in respect to flowers.) Sensing he is losing control, Goro shushes the company.

Sharpless brings a more expansive character to the music as he tells Pinkerton he is lucky to have found "...a flower just in bloom." Pinkerton agrees with the image — Butterfly is indeed a flower, the exotic perfume of which has confused his thoughts. "She is a flower," he declares, "and in faith I've plucked it." The Consul knows the ceremony that is about to take place is no marriage, that it is a joke to Pinkerton, and he cautions his friend to be careful, for it isn't a joke to the girl. Pinkerton doesn't answer. Rather bossily, Butterfly calls her mother and the other guests, and tells them to pay attention. In unison, all bow to Pinkerton and Sharpless. The passage ends as the friends and relatives rise, then scatter in the garden to partake of refreshments.

The music of Butterfly's entrance/the love duet returns as Pinkerton leads Butterfly toward the house. He asks whether she likes the house, but Butterfly changes the subject by showing that her large sleeves are filled with objects she would like to take out. Pinkerton is startled, but when she asks if he minds, he answers that of course he does not.

A glissando in the harp introduces Butterfly's removal of the items. One by one she draws them out and shows them to Pinkerton, while the orchestra plays a delicately sad version of a Japanese tune called "The Cherry Blossom." Butterfly's trousseau consists of some handkerchiefs, a pipe, a sash, a brooch, and a fan, and she gives these things to Suzuki, who puts them inside the house. Butterfly has brought a pot of rouge as well, but evidently Pinkerton disapproves of women painting their faces. When he grunts his disapproval Butterfly throws the pot away.

The next object is a long, narrow case. Pinkerton asks what it is, and in a serious voice Butterfly answers, "Something sacred, and mine." Pinkerton is curious, but when he asks whether it can't be seen, woodwinds and strings give a piercing cry. (This seems to be the source of the Pain motif that is heard in Act Two.) Butterfly says there are too many people present, and she takes the case into the house. Evidently she does not allow anyone else to touch even the case. (We should note too that on this one subject, her family's honor, she doesn't give in to Pinkerton's wishes.)

Goro has been watching, and he approaches Pinkerton. Lower strings give out the Father's Suicide, as Goro softly explains the case was a present from the Emperor to Butterfly's father. (He had been a military officer who, Long tells us, was disgraced by having lost a battle while fighting for the Emperor during the Satsuma Rebellion.) Goro tells Pinkerton the case came with an invitation, and he makes a gesture suggesting *seppuku* — the cutting open of the stomach. Softly Pinkerton asks, "And ... her father?" He obeyed, says Goro.

Goro goes into the house, and to the music of "The Cherry Blossom" Butterfly returns to Pinkerton. She takes a few statuettes from her sleeves and shows them to him. These are the *ottoke*. Pinkerton picks one up. He thinks the *ottoke* are dolls, but when Butterfly, in a voice that aches with melancholy, explains they are the spirits of her ancestors, he puts the statuette down. For this one moment he seems genuine as he offers his respect.

With that sensitive subject broached, Butterfly is emboldened to confide in Pinkerton. Her sad and lovely arietta, "Ieri son salita" (Yesterday I went out), is in two parts: an introductory, almost conversational opening, followed by an outburst of lyricism as she is swept away by her emotions.

In the A section Butterfly tells Pinkerton she went to the Mission the day before. She means to leave behind everything Japanese, and commit herself fully to her husband. Fearfully, she admits she did not tell her uncle, the priest, nor do any of her relatives know. The B section employs the same delicate Japanese folk melody that concluded the entrance of Butterfly and her friends, when they closed their parasols and knelt before Pinkerton. Butterfly sings the melody, which is doubled by unison strings. "I follow my destiny!" cries Butterfly, using one of Puccini's most freighted words.

She intends to go to Pinkerton's church, to kneel beside him, and to pray to his god. Wistfully she expresses a hope that in making him happy, she will be able to forget her people. (In Long's story, it is Pinkerton who cuts Butterfly off from her relatives, for they bore him. In Puccini, Butterfly cuts herself off from her people — even before her uncle confronts her — renouncing the Japanese world as one that will not safeguard her honor.)

Overcome by emotion, Butterfly cries, "My love!" and throws herself into Pinkerton's arms. The Suicide motif sounds on her last word, *fortissimo*, and Butterfly pulls back, as though afraid of being overheard. (There is another version of this line, in which Butterfly, rather than crying, "Amore mio!" cries, "E questi via!" (Away with these!), and throws away the *ottoke*. In conjunction with this line, the Suicide motif is more effective.) The stage directions include no reaction from Pinkerton, but there is little time to notice this, since Goro immediately calls for quiet. The ceremony is about to begin.

Sharpless and the officials are inside the house, where a *shoji* has been slid back, opening the room up to view. Butterfly and Pinkerton go into the house, where he stands, and she kneels beside him. The rest of the wedding party remain in the garden, where they kneel. Japanese bells are heard as the Commissioner recites the words of an exceedingly strange marriage ceremony. He invokes neither church nor state as his authority. There are no vows, and neither the man nor the woman is asked to say anything. Puccini feels obliged to use the word "matrimony," but it is Goro the broker who supervises the signing of the contract by Pinkerton and Butterfly. When the signing is complete, Goro declares "all is done." The two are not pronounced husband and wife, and the stage directions do not include a kiss.

Guests offer their congratulations to Butterfly. The music of this scene is quite mournful, and the first congratulation given to Butterfly is in the form of an insult (or rather, harsh reality). Although the friends bow, they greet her as "Madama Butterfly." Quick to notice lack of respect, Butterfly corrects them. Her name, she says, is Madama B. F. Pinkerton. (Sadly, no one ever grants her this title, including Sharpless, who in Act Two addresses her as Madama Butterfly, using as he does the same mournful music that here carries the friends' use of that name.)

The Sharpless Theme is heard, and it appears that its hearty melody represents not only the Consul, but the arrival and departure of officials in general. All three of these men are preparing to leave. The Commissioner doesn't bother to address Butterfly, but he salutes Pinkerton and offers congratulations. The Registry Officer politely wishes Pinkerton many descendants. "I'll try," responds Pinkerton, presumably with a smirk.

The three officials start down the path, but suddenly Sharpless turns back. The music of his warning against hurting Butterfly recurs as he cautions the Lieutenant to act with discretion. Pinkerton reassures the Consul with a gesture, then waves goodbye. Next on his agenda is getting rid of the family as soon as possible.

Sake is brought out, and Pinkerton offers a rather unsuitable toast — "Hip! hip!" — which transitions the music into the brief but lovely "O Kami!" chorus, in which the guests drink to what Pinkerton calls "the new bonds." He does not offer a toast to his bride, or even acknowledge Butterfly's presence. (Kami are the mysterious, supernatural beings worshipped by practitioners of Shinto.) Harp arpeggios add to this all-too-brief passage in which real congratulations are expressed in Butterfly's general direction.

Placing the lyrical, high-voiced "O Kami!" chorus here was a clever move on Puccini's part, for when its gentle, airy lightness and mood of good will is shattered by the entrance of Butterfly's uncle, the Bonze — strange looking, enraged, and shouting "Cho-cho san!" in his penetrating bass — the contrast is immense. (Note again Puccini's negative portrayal of religion, which here, as in *Suor Angelica*, is shown as a cruel agency that persecutes beautiful young women.)

The Bonze's hands are outstretched menacingly, and as he comes toward Butterfly, shouting her Japanese name and crying, "Abomination!" the frightened guests cluster in a group far away from her. The puzzled and annoyed Pinkerton does not go to protect the girl, so she is left to stand alone and defenseless.

Goro refers to the Bonze, whose cries are punctuated by the booming of an offstage gong, as *un corno al guastafeste*, which means something like "a darned killjoy," and he asks rhetorically, "Who will rid us of bothersome people?" (Being that the Bonze is a priest, it is almost irresistible to consider this an allusion to the famous utterance of England's Henry II, in respect to Thomas à Becket: "Will no one rid me of this meddlesome priest?")

A new motif is heard, just before the Bonze demands to know what Butterfly did at the Mission. This dark and angry motif, often mislabeled the Bonze's Curse, refers on its first appearance to Butterfly's renunciation of her people's religion. It continues to sound through the Bonze's exposure of Butterfly's deed, his demand that the guests leave with him, and his declaration that since Butterfly has rejected them, they reject her.

The motif does not refer to a "curse," but to Butterfly's having staked her all on Pinkerton. Puccini uses the Bonze's outburst, and the motif of Rejection, to fix it in our minds that Butterfly has made an irrevocable choice that may turn out to have been a mistake with horrendous consequences. The motif is born from Butterfly's rejection of her people, not from their rejection of her.

The Bonze moves right next to Butterfly, who covers her face with her hands. Butterfly's mother tries to defend her, but the Bonze pushes her away, threatening her daughter's "ruined soul" with terrible punishment. Pinkerton is tired of this nonsense, and he says impatiently, "Hey, I say: enough, enough!" (Some versions of the libretto have him insert himself between Butterfly and her uncle; others have him continue to stand apart.) The Bonze is stunned that someone has dared to oppose him, but he quickly determines his best move is to unite all of the guests in walking out. He orders everyone to leave, saying, as the Rejection continues to sound, "You have rejected us, and we reject you!" The guests join him in shouting the last words.

It is at this point, after the Bonze has already ordered everyone to leave, that the tardy Pinkerton orders everyone to go. His order sounds impressive, for his voice is penetrating and almost heroic, but in substance it isn't impressive at all. And as he shouts that in his house he will have no "bonzeria," the motif of the Father's Suicide sounds, *fortissimo*, and expanded into a theme.

The guests run for the path that leads down to the city, sweeping with them Butterfly's mother, who tries in vain to go back to her daughter. The Bonze exits. Butterfly has neither moved nor spoken during this whole dreadful scene, and she remains standing with her hands covering her face while Pinkerton goes to the top of the path and looks down. The stage directions tell us he is making sure that all of "those bores" have gone. Gradually the furious voices grow softer, the cries of, "Oh, Cho-cho san! We reject you!" fading as everyone runs down the hill. Butterfly begins to cry. Hearing this, Pinkerton goes to her, raises her head, and takes her hands from her face. He addresses her as "child," which is what she is, and tells her not to let the croaking of frogs make her weep.

From far away the voices are heard again: "Oh, Cho-cho san!" Butterfly covers her ears, but Pinkerton comforts her, saying all of her tribe and all of the Bonzes in Japan aren't worth the weeping of her dear and beautiful eyes. Butterfly smiles at this, "like a child," and says, "Really?" And as she says this, the sun goes down. It is dusk, and thus time for her brief period of happiness to begin.

But as she tells Pinkerton she isn't crying any more, and almost doesn't suffer at her people's rejection, her words are carried by a soft and tender version of the Suicide Theme, now further expanded into a full-fledged and harmonized melody, played by divided strings. This is the last time we will hear the Suicide played openly, without disguise, until it returns shockingly, at the end of the opera, like a forgotten voice from the past. (Attentive listeners may detect it before that in "Che tua madre," when Butterfly first contemplates the possibility of suicide.)

Butterfly bends to kiss Pinkerton's hands, telling the puzzled Lieutenant she had been told that "over there" this was considered a gesture of great respect. (We will hear the music of her "great respect" again, during the Intermezzo.) A low and rapid murmuring is heard from inside the house, followed by a recurrence of some of the busy music of the prelude. It is Suzuki, saying her prayers.[6] The love duet begins as Pinkerton leads Butterfly toward the house. "Night is coming," he says, and Butterfly adds "...and the darkness and the quiet." (It is not night yet — only dusk. Night comes at a very particular moment, which is marked in the stage directions.)

Pinkerton summons the servants, and orders the men to close the panels of the house. Butterfly tells Suzuki to bring her her clothes, and Suzuki opens a case and takes out Butterfly's nightclothes and a comb. After handing these to Butterfly, Suzuki bows to Pinkerton and wishes him good night.

This signals a new phase of the duet. There is a brief pause as Suzuki and Butterfly go into the house. A rising and falling figure is heard in flute, horn, and strings, while oboe and clarinet alternate a narcotic twitter that suggests night sounds. (This rising and falling figure, slightly altered, will recur during Butterfly's "Un bel dì," beginning on the words, "Then the white ship....")

With Suzuki assisting, Butterfly takes off her wedding dress and attires herself all in white. Then she sits on a pillow and combs her hair. Suzuki retires. Butterfly and Pinkerton sing at the same time during much of this section, although they are speaking to themselves. Little by little Pinkerton comes near to Butterfly, as she finishes alone, singing, "Butterfly ... rejected ... rejected and happy." There is another pause, then the duet goes into its next phase.

Pinkerton extends his hands to Butterfly, who is about to come down from the terrace. With real ardor, Pinkerton sings to a new melody, and calls her a child with eyes full of magic. She is all his, he says, and he begins a crescendo as he says she is dressed like a lily. He likes her dark hair, and her white veil.[7]

Butterfly comes down from the terrace, and to one of the most exquisite passages in the score she sings, "I am like the goddess of the moon, the little goddess of the moon, who descends at night from the bridge of heaven." Such a line was certain to inspire Puccini, and his scoring is for woodwinds, harp, and strings, playing a delicate little stepping figure that suggests the goddess' gliding walk down the bridge of heaven. Cunningly, this music is heard just as Butterfly is stepping down from the terrace.

Continuing with the melody of "Child with eyes full of magic," Pinkerton takes the duet into its most rapturous passage yet: one that addresses not lust, but love. This is intensely feminine music, written by an emotional and very masculine man who had a passionate love for that which was romantic in a feminine sense. There is no calculation in Puccini's music. In some of his techniques, yes, for he wrote to have successes, and he knew what would please his audience. But there is no faking the emotions at the core. His ability to combine an Italian and masculine strength with a French-tinged feminine grace, seasoned with his trademark Mixture of joy and sadness, is the key to its compelling nature. He was utterly unique in his enthusiastic, unembarrassed embrace of both masculine and feminine.

Pinkerton wants to elicit from Butterfly a declaration of love. Having heard her liken herself to the moon goddess who descends from heaven, Pinkerton prods her a little, saying, "and fascinates all hearts." She evades him, answering, "...and takes them, and folds them in a white mantle. And she takes them away to the higher realms." (Perhaps these words have significance to Butterfly's death, when, after having waited all night in the moonlight, she wraps the white veil around her wound and then dies. It's a consoling thought: Butterfly folded in a white mantle and wafted away to the higher realms by the moon goddess.)

But Pinkerton wants an expression of open desire. He wants Butterfly to want him as eagerly as he wants her. In a way this is unexpected, for up to now he's been extremely selfish. But to have an ardent love duet, both people must participate (although we should note Pinkerton never once says he loves Butterfly), and the only way to prompt an ardent outburst from this 15-year-old virgin is by having her lover ask for one. Pinkerton's question emboldens Butterfly. She admits the goddess knows those words, but perhaps does not want to say them, "for fear of having to die of them."

But love does not kill, says Pinkerton. A thrilling upwards run in violins and violas is heard, then he finishes, "...but gives life, and smiles with celestial joys, as it does now in your long oval eyes." The moment he has uttered the last word we hear the first three notes of the Suicide Theme, played pizzicato by divided double basses. Butterfly tells him she liked him the moment she saw him, but in the pause that follows we hear the Rejection motif, during which Butterfly makes a movement of fear, then covers her ears as though she can still hear her relatives screaming. She recovers herself, however, and turns toward Pinkerton.

An ardent harp, playing upward and downward runs, accompanies her as she tells Pinkerton why she likes him. He is tall and strong, he laughs openly, and he says things she has never heard. "Now I am happy," she says, and the moment she does, night falls. "Complete night," the stage directions note. "Purest, star-studded sky."

"Love me a little," pleads Butterfly, and she goes on to describe her people as ones who are accustomed to "...a tenderness, barely grazing and yet deep as the sky, as the sea's wave." (Note the extreme opposites: barely grazing with as deep as the sky.)

Pinkerton seems genuinely carried away. With great tenderness he says they named her well, in calling her Butterfly. But this saddens her. The Rejection motif sounds as she says she had been told that across the sea, any butterfly that fell into a man's hands was pierced with a pin and stuck on a board. Her voice is filled with pain during the last words, but Pinkerton smiles at her, telling her that is done so the butterfly won't flee.

He embraces her, saying she is his, and this causes her at last to abandon herself completely. "Yes, for life," she cries, make a vow of faithfulness unto death. (It is here, beginning with measure #133, that the Love Duet, entering its final and most passionate phase, begins the rhythmic pattern that will link it to the Flower Duet. The time signature is 6/8, and the basic, linking rhythm is two triplets followed by two dotted quarter notes.)

Pinkerton urges Butterfly to come to him, to banish her anguish, for the night is calm, and all is asleep. The reprise of Butterfly's entrance music begins as she looks at the inky sky and cries in ecstasy, "Ah, sweet night!" The stars are so many, and so beautiful, and in an exquisite finishing touch to the stage picture, fireflies come out, shining around the lovers, the flowers, and the leaves of the trees.

Again Pinkerton urges Butterfly to come, again tells her she is his, but he does not tell her he loves her, and when he sings these coaxing words it is "with greedy love." As he continues to sing, "Come, come," one is reminded of Don Giovanni, sweet-talking another poor girl to her ruin.

The fireflies seem like staring eyes to Butterfly, but the sky is laughing. As Pinkerton urges her to come she concludes this duet with, "Ah, sweet night! All ecstatic with love, the sky is laughing!" If he's up to it, Pinkerton joins her on an optional high C as they go into the nuptial chamber. Otherwise, he can make do with a high A that comes with the consolation of getting the last words: "You're mine!"

The orchestra takes the couple's final notes and uses them to segue into a recapitulation of the pretty Japanese folk song that concluded Butterfly's entrance, when she knelt before Pinkerton for the first time, and that also formed the B section of her aria about her visit to the Mission, when she told Pinkerton she had cast away everything for his sake. This delicate melody, again featuring Japanese bells and a gong, makes for an aurally perfect conclusion to the love duet, and marks, as it did the previous two times it was heard, Butterfly's complete commitment to Pinkerton. "I follow my destiny," it says, as Butterfly enters the house with Pinkerton.

Act Two begins inside the house. It is three years since Pinkerton sailed away on his great ship. It is late afternoon in spring, and Butterfly is now 18 years old. The curtain is closed during the first eighteen bars of the prelude, which gives us a wintery theme. The *pizzicato* theme is played three times; first by unison flutes, then lower by muted violins, and lastly and lower still by cellos and double bass.

This chilly theme will be heard again; or at least, the first six notes of it will be, but it's unlikely the casual listener will recognize it in its rhythmically altered form. The first six notes of the prelude theme give us the motif of Pinkerton's Return, and its first recurrence is in Butterfly's aria, "Un bel dì," on the words, "(un uomo, un picciol punto) **s'avvia per la collina**"; that is, "(a man, a little dot) **starts up the hill**." We'll hear Pinkerton's Return again when Butterfly tells Kate her husband can have his son if he will, "**in half an hour climb the hill**." The final recurrence of Pinkerton's Return is at the close of the opera, given out by the orchestra in between the lieutenant's three agonized, offstage shouts of "Butterfly!" during which time he is, of course, actually **climbing the hill**.

Here in the prelude, the chilly tone of the motif makes it clear, even to those who don't connect the music to Butterfly's weary hope for Pinkerton's return, that the first act's mood of passionate romance is gone. Oboes and clarinets sound the Rejection motif, then the curtain rises. The panels of the house are shut, so the rooms are in semidarkness. Butterfly is lying on the floor, head in hands. Suzuki is praying before a statue of the Buddha, and from time to time she rings a prayer bell, hoping to attract the attention of the gods. This is the tolling bell that in Puccini always presages disaster.

As in the first act, Suzuki is praying to the brother-and-sister deities, Izanagi and Izanami. The music is a funeral dirge. Suzuki prays Butterfly will "weep no more, nevermore," and this prayer will be granted in that terrible, fairytale manner in which the letter but not the spirit of a wish is observed. After Butterfly dies, she will never weep again. At the end of the prayer, the oboe gives a piercing cry. This is the motif of Butterfly's Pain, and it seems related to the music that described her reaction when Pinkerton asked if he could see the knife.

Having listened in silence to her maid's prayer, Butterfly declares the gods of Japan are lazy and fat. The American god, she says, surely answers prayers much more quickly. It must be he doesn't know they live here. Threading through her declaration about the great American god is the Pain motif, and the motif of the Rejection, which declares her allegiance to this god.

Suzuki has risen and slid open the wall that looks onto the garden. Butterfly asks how far away poverty is. The Pain motif sounds repeatedly, with the intensity of a migraine, as Suzuki looks in a drawer, then goes to Butterfly and shows her the few coins remaining from the money Pinkerton left. "This is all that remains," she says sadly, the Rejection motif overlapping her words and Butterfly's response: "This! Oh, too many expenses!" A loyal wife, she blames herself for having spent too much, though she has made the money last three years.

Suzuki points out that if Pinkerton doesn't come back soon, they'll be in a bad way. With a fierce sounding of the Pain motif, this brings Butterfly to her feet, and firmly she declares he will come back. The maid shakes her head doubtfully. Irked, Butterfly approaches Suzuki and asks her why, if Pinkerton did not plan on coming back, did he arrange for the Consul to pay their rent? The Sharpless Theme sounds, to remind us of that bluff and hearty man.

Why, Butterfly continues, if Pinkerton wasn't coming back, did he supply the house with American-style locks? Suzuki doesn't know. Butterfly proudly gives the reason. Her husband fitted the house with locks to keep mosquitoes, relatives, and sorrows out, and "inside, with jealous safekeeping, his wife: I, Butterfly." On the word "safekeeping," the final music of the love duet began a reprise, but Suzuki halts it when she points out one never hears of a foreign husband coming back. This infuriates Butterfly, and as the Pain motif shrieks she seizes her servant and orders her to be silent, or she will kill her.

Angrily she begins to describe how, on that last morning, she asked him whether he would return, but her voice droops with nostalgic sorrow as she recounts his answer. Having lived with him for so short a time, she never learned his true nature. She thinks his heart was as filled with sorrow as hers, and she misinterpreted his habitual grin as a mask for pain. He smiled, says Butterfly, to hide his sorrow, and he answered, "Oh, Butterfly, tiny little wife, I'll return with the roses in the serene season when the robin makes his nest." (Unable to resist the mention of wildlife, Puccini has the flute, oboe, and violins describe the chirping of the robins.)

Supposedly calm and convinced, she declares Pinkerton will return. Suzuki, however, responds with, "Let's hope so." (Clearly, they are doomed, for in Puccini, hope always deceives. In Belasco, Suzuki had witnessed Pinkerton's "return with the robins" promise, and had recognized it on the spot as a brush-off.)

Butterfly urges her maid to say the words with her. Suzuki dutifully repeats "he will return," then bursts into tears. This lack of faith surprises Butterfly, so she describes—so clearly that Suzuki must see it—how it will be that one fine day, when Pinkerton comes back. As she begins, solo violin and clarinet play "as though from far away," muted violins, play "like a distant murmur," and a harp plays harmonics. Everything about this music suggests unreality, distance, imagination, a dream.

On that *bel dì*—that beautiful day—they will see a thread of smoke rising from the farthest edge of the sea. "And then the ship will appear. Then the white ship enters the port, thundering its salute." Carrying these lines is a reminiscence of the opening of the love duet—the little upward and downward scale pattern that followed Suzuki's "Good night" to Pinkerton. A single stroke on the bass drum delivers the distant thundering of the ship's cannon.

"You see?" says Butterfly. "He has come." But she doesn't run to greet him. She stands and waits; waits at the edge of the hill, for a long time. Flutes, clarinets, and bass clarinet play sustained chords, describing the long and patient wait.

Finally, from among the crowd in the city, a man starts up the hill. (Here, woodwinds play the motif of Pinkerton's Return. The steep climb is difficult, so the motif is played slowly, with a *fermata* on the final, all-important word: hill. If one knows what this motif will have come to signify by the end of the opera — if he can hear during "Un bel dì" Pinkerton's agonized cries of "Butterfly," that will surround the motif at the end of the opera — then Butterfly's slow savoring of it here is sheer agony.)

Muted trumpets, playing *ppp* chords, carry Butterfly's breathless questions: "Who can it be? Who can it be?" And when he has arrived, "What will he say? What will he say?" She remembers the affectionate names he had for her, and as she imagines how he will "call Butterfly from the distance," the music of her description of their last morning, when he said, "Oh Butterfly, tiny little wife ..." recurs.

As in Long's story, Butterfly tells Suzuki that when Pinkerton comes and calls out her name, she will hide for a bit: partly to tease him, and partly so as "not to die at the first meeting." Played *fortissimo*, with great passion, the word "die" marks the climax of the aria, and it launches a reprise of the tune, from the top.

Butterfly's vision of her husband's return includes, in both Long and Belasco, her emerging from her hiding place because he is getting angry, but this is not what Puccini's heroine imagines. She imagines Pinkerton in pain, suffering because he cannot find her, and calling out in his grief those affectionate names he once used, when he used to come. As she speaks the words she would have him speak, Butterfly gives him a voice filled with three years' of fear, and sadness, and longing for her.

In light of this is seems likely we should consider the motive of Puccini's heroine in not running to meet Pinkerton to be different from that of Long's and Belasco's heroine. Theirs is a well-brought-up Japanese woman, who believes only a courtesan runs after a man. Puccini's is a woman who wants to be valued. She came to Pinkerton once before, and no matter how much she wants him, she cannot do it a second time. It is a matter of personal honor. That is, it is not the case that she doesn't run down to him because nice women don't do that, but rather that *he* needs to come to *her*— because she's worth it.

In Butterfly's vision during her aria, Pinkerton is in mental pain as he makes the difficult climb up the hill — a climb she once made for him, and he must now make for her. Pinkerton is grieving because he afraid Butterfly may be lost to him. And she does not relieve his mind until he completes the final step and reaches the summit of the hill. Butterfly is envisioning a rebirth of their love, and the scene is a mirror image of that of the birth of their love, which took place with Butterfly's entrance. When Pinkerton finally arrives at the top of the hill, Butterfly will speak to him. And surely the exchange will go like this: (B) "Was the climb a bit hard?" (P) "For a well-bred groom the impatience is more painful." (B) "A very rare compliment."

The vision over, Butterfly's voice quickly slides from confidence to near-hysteria as she turns to Suzuki, crying, with a *fff* on her final phrase, "All this will happen, I promise you. Keep your fear. I, with unshakable faith, await him." With emotion, Butterfly and Suzuki embrace, then Suzuki exits.

The Sharpless Theme is heard, and the Consul and Goro enter the garden. Goro looks inside, sees Butterfly, and tells Sharpless to go in. A bit of the busy music of the prelude is heard, as well as that of Sharpless' appreciative comment about the view of Nagasaki, then the Consul knocks on the door.

Sharpless sees Butterfly, and calls to her: "Madama Butterfly." His words are carried by the mournful music that accompanied the use of this name by Butterfly's friends, just after the wedding. Butterfly does not see Sharpless, and hearing this insulting name, she says coldly, "Madama Pinkerton. Please." Butterfly turns, and Sharpless' failure to amend his address is almost covered by her exclamation of joy. She claps her hands with happiness, and Suzuki enters and prepares a table with smoking materials, pillows, and a stool.

Evidently Sharpless has not been to see Butterfly since the wedding, for he is surprised she recognizes him. To a rapid sounding of the "dawn's early light" passage of Star-Spangled Banner, Butterfly welcomes her guest to "an American home." At her invitation, Sharpless sinks clumsily onto a pillow by the table. The music takes on a light and cheerful tone as Butterfly, smiling behind her fan at the American's awkwardness, inquires after the health of his relatives. Receiving a short but satisfactory answer, she gestures to Suzuki to prepare a pipe.

Despite his years in Japan, Sharpless is unschooled in correct protocol, and he attempts to get to the point of his visit without first going through the required pleasantries. There is a brief lull in the music as he takes a letter from his pocket and begins, "I have here...." But Butterfly gently interrupts him, and the orchestra begins a pretty melody in a Japanese vein as she opens the topic of the weather. Taking the pipe from Suzuki, she draws on it, then offers it to Sharpless, who refuses with a briefness that borders on rudeness.

The Consul tries again to speak of the letter, but Butterfly asks if he would prefer American cigarettes. Sharpless takes one, stands up, and tries again to get to his point. Butterfly offers him a light for his cigarette. He accepts it, but immediately after lighting the cigarette he puts it down, then sits on the stool and holds out the letter.

"Benjamin Franklin Pinkerton wrote to me," he begins. It is a name to conjure with, yet Butterfly's breeding maintains its hold. Rather than demanding to know where Pinkerton is, she asks after his health. On hearing he is well, she rises and sings with joyful lyricism that she is the happiest woman in Japan.

She now attempts to learn when Pinkerton will be returning, but rather than asking this straight out she approaches the question delicately, from an angle that supports her profession of faith in her husband's word. To the music of "Oh, Butterfly, tiny little wife, I will return with the roses," she explains to Sharpless her husband said he would come back when the robins nested, and she asks when American robins do that. (Again the orchestra helpfully describes the birds' twittering.) Goro is in the garden, and he comes close enough to hear what's being said. As Butterfly explains about Pinkerton's promise, and says the Japanese robins have already nested three times, but perhaps American robins nest less frequently, Goro laughs rudely at her innocence.

Butterfly and Goro have a complicated relationship. He feels superior, for he is older and she is only a woman. But he's afraid of her anger, and he's also hopeful of making more money off her. As soon as Pinkerton left, Goro began to suggest new "husbands" to Butterfly. She has rejected all these offers, insisting she is already married.

The most persistent of the suitors is Prince Yamadori, a wealthy businessman who spends most of his time in New York. He makes frequent, short trips back to Japan, however, and each time he contracts for a new mistress. At this point in Long's story he has not yet seen Butterfly, but is intrigued by Goro's description of her beauty. Long has Butterfly agreeing to what he calls a "look-at meeting," during which she and Yamadori will inspect one another closely, but will speak only to Goro. Butterfly has no intention of contracting with Yamadori, but she has no objection to Goro getting a fee for having arranged the meeting, and in a spirit of mischief she likes the idea of fascinating the importuning prince and then dashing his hopes.

She is also hoping Pinkerton will hear other men are besieging her, and this will make him jealous enough to return. A major reason for Long's having introduced Yamadori is that since he is a Japanese who is acquainted with American ways, he can speak with authority about whether Butterfly's "marriage" would be recognized by the laws of America.

Seeing Goro in her garden, Butterfly orders him to be quiet. He leaves to fetch Yamadori. Butterfly confides to Sharpless that Goro is a bad man, and she begins to describe his attempts to fix her up with other men. Then she remembers her unanswered question. The orchestra chirps again, reminding Sharpless of what the question was. The embarrassed Consul confesses he doesn't know much about birds, then tries to return to the letter.

The audience needs to be prepared for the arrival of Yamadori, so Butterfly interrupts and tells Sharpless of how Goro has been pestering her. "Now he promises treasures for a fool," she says, and the Pain motif sounds twice.

Goro has returned and has heard what Butterfly said. Wanting to justify himself, he points out to Sharpless that Butterfly is poor, her relatives have disowned her, and Yamadori is rich. Beyond the terrace we see Yamadori arriving in a palanquin carried by servants. Butterfly smiles and points her suitor out to Sharpless. We are about to see the "look-at meeting."

Yamadori enters to another authentic Japanese tune, called "My Prince." We heard it first a few moments ago, accompanying Butterfly's polite comment on the weather, probably because in Long, this whole scene is about Yamadori, and Butterfly's regal behavior as she entertains him. Like Puccini's use of the Sharpless Theme for the departure of the Imperial Commissioner and the Registry Official, the earlier use of Yamadori's Theme is a bit inappropriate, but surely forgivable.

Yamadori enters the house. He makes a graceful bow to Butterfly, then greets Sharpless. Two of his servants hand flowers to Suzuki, then withdraw. Goro fetches a stool for Yamadori, and places it between Sharpless and Butterfly, who has resumed her seat. The music with which Butterfly addresses Yamadori has proved quite puzzling to critics. Charles Osborne, for instance, notes that, "Butterfly greets Yamadori in phrases full of a tender yearning, though she is supposed to feel nothing but contempt for him. Is this one of those moments when Puccini merely wrote down the notes that came into his head, without considering whether or not they suited the dramatic situation?"[8] Well, no, this isn't one of those moments. In fact, there are no such moments. Puccini was far too professional to "merely" write down notes that "came into his head."

The purpose of the "tender yearning" in Butterfly's address to Yamadori is given in Long's story, in which Butterfly feels a mixture of emotions during the "look-at meeting." Having been alone for three years, she is pleased that Yamadori, so conscious of his own worth and that of his "august family," is panting after her. She is amused at Goro's eagerness for a commission. She is angry that Yamadori actually smiles at her directly, "as if she were a woman of joy!" And she is hopeful that Pinkerton will hear a rich and important man desires her. With the most graceful movements and the most dazzling smiles she does everything she can to fascinate Yamadori. It amuses her and makes her feel powerful and desirable. Dizzy with longing, Yamadori recklessly promises a castle, a thousand servants, and even "a solemn writing."

These are the reasons for the tender yearning of the music as Puccini's Butterfly mockingly says, "Yamadori, the pain of love has not yet disillusioned you? Will you still cut open your veins if I refuse you my kiss?" Yamadori confides to Sharpless that it is troubling to sigh in vain, and "with charming malice" Butterfly remarks he should be used to it, having taken so many wives already.

To the music of Butterfly's, "Nobody ever confesses he was born in poverty ... but the whirlwind uproots the most robust oaks," Yamadori points out he has divorced all these women; or rather, that divorce has "freed him." "I'm obliged," says Butterfly sarcastically, and the enraptured Yamadori assures her he would swear constancy to her. She knows once his desire was satisfied he would divorce her too, proving the whirlwind to her oak, as he did to all his other women.

The teasing has gone far enough, so Butterfly says seriously that her word is already given. The music of "the whirlwind" continues as Goro and Yamadori tell Sharpless Butterfly thinks she is still married, and Butterfly jumps to her feet and angrily says, "I don't **think** so; I am, **I am**." Goro tells her the law declares a woman is divorced merely by being abandoned, and Butterfly shakes her head. She has turned her back on everything Japanese, and now it is time to collect on that sacrifice. The opening of Star-Spangled Banner swells as she proudly says, "The Japanese law. Not that of my country. The United States."

No one ever takes Butterfly's side, and now Sharpless merely says in an aside, "Oh, the unhappy girl!" The stage directions describe Butterfly as very nervous as, warming to her subject, she says in stabbing accents that certainly in Japan a man obtains a divorce by opening the door and driving out his wife in the curtest way possible, but that's not how things are done in America. There, one must go through a long legal proceeding, before a judge who questions the husband about his motives for wanting to leave his wife. If the answer is merely, "I'm bored," the author of this affront to his wife's dignity is clapped into prison at once. Such is Butterfly's view as to what constitutes justice. Not wishing to discuss the matter any further, she goes to Suzuki and orders her to bring tea.

Another passage of music that has proved puzzling now begins— the *valse lente*. As this accompanies the tea-party scene, during which Butterfly is straining to prove herself as un–Japanese as possible, it seems likely Puccini was trying to make the music support this effort. The *valse lente* is dainty, European drawing room music whose echoing effects and shifting tonal center give a sense of unreality. We'll hear music like this in Act Two of *Fanciulla*, in a similar context; that is, when Minnie is entertaining Dick Johnson, whose manners declare him to be above her in social class. The strange music of both these scenes seems meant to tell us these women are struggling to appear poised, but are pathetically out of their depth.

The three men discuss the matter amongst themselves. Goro confides Pinkerton's ship has already been reported to be on its way in, and the yearning Yamadori fears how Butterfly will react when she sees the Lieutenant again. Sharpless, who grieves over the poor girl's blindness, tells the others Pinkerton doesn't want to see her, and he came here to tell her so. Seeing Butterfly returning with the tea, he breaks off.

Butterfly serves the Consul a cup of tea. She then opens her fan, and laughingly observes how tiresome Goro and Yamadori are. She offers tea to Yamadori, but he refuses, and begins to take his leave. "I still hope," he says (and we know how pointless that is), and Butterfly assures him he's free to do that. Yamadori takes few steps, turns back, and to a gentle version of his entrance music he pleads, "Ah! If you wanted...." The trouble is, retorts Butterfly, that she **doesn't** want.

Yamadori and his servants leave. Suzuki clears away the tea things. Goro exits. A gentle version of the Sharpless Theme is heard, followed by a bit of the music to which he asked Butterfly about herself in Act One. Very respectfully, Sharpless invites Butterfly to sit. He takes Pinkerton's letter from his pocket, and asks Butterfly to read it with him. With great emotion she kisses the letter, assures Sharpless he is the best man in the world, gives him back the letter, and asks him to begin.[9]

The word "begin" launches the "Letter Reading" scene, the opening of which is played *pizzicato* by violins and violas, with periodic help from cellos. (The music of this scene is of course replayed for the "Humming Chorus" during the scene of Butterfly's vigil.) The letter opens with, "Friend, look for that beautiful flower of a girl..." and from this it appears Pinkerton is up to his old tricks. He is using the language of flowers while asking his friend to *dump* the Lady of the Rose. This is utterly intolerable. Pinkerton is really going to have to pay for this. Butterfly hears only the reverent language of flowers. Overjoyed, she interrupts to ask, "Does he really say that?" The Consul says he does, but chides her for interrupting. She promises not to do it again.

"Since that happy time," Sharpless continues, "three years have passed." Butterfly can't restrain herself, and she interjects gratefully, "He too has counted them!" Sharpless ignores this, continuing, "And perhaps Butterfly doesn't remember me anymore." On the word "anymore," a solo violin and viola begin to sing a sweet line over the continued *pizzicato* accompaniment. Butterfly wasn't prepared for this. "Don't remember him?" she asks, and she looks toward Suzuki, saying, "Suzuki, you tell him." The maid nods in confirmation, then exits. So shocked is Butterfly she repeats Pinkerton's words: "Doesn't remember me anymore."

Sharpless resumes his reading. The *pizzicato* accompaniment ceases, and the sweet singing of the strings grows stronger and more passionate as all the violins, violas, and cellos take it up, playing a series of crescendos and diminuendos as Sharpless speaks and Butterfly responds. "If she still loves me," says Sharpless, "if she awaits me...."

Deeply moved, Butterfly takes the letter and kisses it. The Consul is made of strong stuff, for he takes back the letter and continues reading. "...I'm relying on you to carefully prepare her...." Eager and radiant, Butterfly excitedly interjects, "He's returning." But Sharpless finishes the sentence, "...for the blow," and with this word, the music of the Letter Reading concludes. Obviously there is a language barrier, for Butterfly did not understand what "blow" meant. Leaping with joy and clapping her hands, she asks, "When? Quickly! Quickly!"

Poor Sharpless has had enough, and resignedly he puts away the letter. A wisp of the Sharpless Theme is heard, followed by three hopeless little *pizzicato* notes from cello and double bass as Sharpless girds himself for the crushing of Butterfly's hopes. The orchestra is silent now; waiting for him to say something it wants no part of. Sharpless shakes his head angrily and mutters a curse at Pinkerton. Then he looks at Butterfly seriously, and addresses her by that name he knows she hates, but which is the only one she is legally entitled to. "Well, what would you do, Madama Butterfly, if he were never to return?"

A stabbing note, which is surely the fourth note of the Suicide Theme — the most heavily accented one — is given out by timpani and strings, and there is a long pause while Butterfly absorbs this shocking question. She stands motionless, then bows her head. There are two things she could do, she says finally. She could go back to entertaining people by singing, "or else ... better ... die." An ominous little two-note figure, rising and falling in clarinets and bassoon, had revealed the stunned young woman's attempt to decide what she might do, and with her decision — die — the bass clarinet, muted horn, and harp joined in for a funereal moan of the word. Sharpless is distressed and moved by her reaction, although he apparently considers it hyperbole. He takes her hands, and with paternal tenderness tells her it cost him a great deal to undeceive her. He suggests she take Yamadori's offer.

Even more shocked, Butterfly pulls her hands away, for he has essentially told her to take up prostitution. "You, sir," she gasps, "say this to me...! You?" Embarrassed, Sharpless can think of nothing else to suggest. (In both Long and Belasco, he knows perfectly well what he's suggesting, and his words, if not his manner, are offensive. He tells Butterfly that Yamadori's offer presents "a great opportunity for you — for any girl in —" he obviously means "in your circumstances," but rather lamely he finishes "— in Japan.")

The Consul is surprised when the distraught girl claps her hands for Suzuki, and tells her "His Grace" is leaving. As he starts to leave, however, Butterfly regrets what she said, and runs to him, sobbing, and stops him. "Please," she says, "insisting is no use." He admits he was brutal, and Butterfly puts her hand on her heart, saying he has caused her terrible pain. She staggers, but though Sharpless moves to support her, she recovers herself at once. She had been thinking of death, but now another thought has come to replace that. To a strange, dreamy, stepwise passage played by muted horns, Butterfly says, "I thought I would die. But it passes quickly, as the clouds pass over the sea...."

Any sense of dreaminess is dispelled by her forceful cry of "Ah!" which is followed by an octave leap as she resolutely demands, "He has forgotten me?" She runs to the room at left, and as she does the full orchestra begins a triumphant introduction to the glorious theme of The Son Without Equal. This is Butterfly's last card. She had hoped she would not have to play it — that Pinkerton would return for love of her. But since Sharpless has dashed that hope, play it she will, for it is surely unbeatable.

Butterfly returns, carrying her little boy on her shoulder, and the theme of The Son (interspersed with a rapid sounding of the opening of Star-Spangled Banner) carries her proud and confident demand: "And this? And this? Can he also forget this?" The Pain motif sounds as she puts the boy down, holding him tightly to her.

With emotion (if not tact), Sharpless asks if the child is Pinkerton's, and Butterfly points out the blue eyes, the lips, and the golden curls, all of which proclaim the boy the son of a Westerner. The music of The Son underscores these lines, as well as the Consul's question as to whether Pinkerton knows about the boy. Butterfly answers no, then the melody of the final part of the love duet recurs as she says the child was born when Pinkerton was in "that great country of his." (The recurrence of the love duet music suggests the boy was conceived on the wedding night.)

The music of the last piece of this exchange is interesting. The theme of The Son resumes as Butterfly asks Sharpless to write Pinkerton and tell him "a son without equal awaits him!" It switches to Star-Spangled Banner for her proud demand, "And you tell me if he won't hurry over land and sea." Beginning with the final word, sea, we hear a series of repeated triplets, that gives the same weird, echoing effect we heard in the *valse lente*, right after Sharpless confided to the other men that Pinkerton "doesn't want to show himself. I came precisely to undeceive her." In employing this weird, echoing effect at the end of Butterfly's triumphant "...tell me if he won't hurry over land and sea," Puccini is either telling us the young woman's hopes are going to be dashed, or else is giving us a Debussy-like picture of the sea.

Butterfly sits her son down on a pillow and kneels beside him, pretending to talk to him, although her words are meant for Sharpless. She asks the child if he knows what that man had the heart to say, then begins her transformation into a great tragic heroine, via her powerful aria, "Che tua madre."

The Consul had suggested Butterfly take Yamadori's offer of "marriage," but of course that's not what the prince is really offering. He's offering an arrangement that, despite any "solemn writing," will end when he gets tired of Butterfly. "Che tua madre" doesn't address the matter of Yamadori, it addresses returning to the life of a geisha, going about the city in all weather, to earn "bread and clothing." The aria addresses dishonor. Yamadori has no importance in himself; rather, he represents a long series of men, who one after another would, if she were to submit to such shame, "marry" Butterfly for a brief period.

A new theme impresses itself on us as she continues, describing how, "to the pitying people, she'll extend her trembling hand, crying: 'Hear, hear my sad song. Charity for an unhappy mother, be moved to pity!'" This is the music, and these are the implicit words, that will close the opera, as Pinkerton and Sharpless rush in to find the dying woman holding out her trembling hand to her son. (The Suicide motif, slightly altered, is clearly audible in this passage.)

Now Butterfly imagines herself, a cast-off wife, returning in shame to her former life as a geisha, dancing and singing as before. The theme of The Son Without Equal returns, carrying her words, "And the gay, happy song will end in a sob!" She drops to her knees before Sharpless, vowing never to submit to such dishonor, and with the rocketing notes Puccini so frequently ties to this word she cries passionately, "Dead! Dead!" On a high A flat she cries "Ah!" then drops a full octave to finish with a final, sobbing cry of "Dead!" Spent, she falls on the floor beside her son, whom she takes in a tight embrace.

Tears come to Sharpless' eyes. He says he is going, and he asks Butterfly if she forgives him. A tender version of the Sharpless Theme, played by solo clarinet, with contributions from flutes and harp, describes his sincere feelings of sympathy, and Butterfly wordlessly rises and offers him her hand. Deeply moved, he takes it. The young woman tells her son to shake hands. Sharpless admires the boy's hair, kisses him, and asks his name.

Answering as her son, she tells Sharpless, "Today my name is Sorrow. But tell Daddy, writing to him, that the day of his return ..." (and here two horns begin a reprise of "Un bel dì" that ends with the Consul's departure) "...Joy, Joy will be my name."[10] Sharpless promises to tell Pinkerton about his son, and quickly leaves.

There is a pause, then the angry voice of Suzuki is heard. She enters, dragging the struggling Goro. She utters a cry, and as she does the full orchestra plays an excited, *fff* version of the Rejection motif. Clarinet and bassoon reduce the motif to an *ostinato* as Suzuki tells Butterfly she caught Goro spreading slander, saying nobody knows who the child's father is. (Goro does this because, knowing Pinkerton is back, he hopes the rumor will reach the Lieutenant, who will break with Butterfly decisively, freeing her to take Yamadori's offer.) The frightened Goro (using lines imprudently uttered by Yamadori during Long's "look-at meeting") gestures at the boy, and explains that all he said was in America, a child whose father has deserted him is always an outcast.

Note the similarity of this scene to that of the Bonze's threatening of Butterfly in Act One. During that scene, Pinkerton made no move to protect her, and expressed no concern about her being insulted or afraid. Here, the stage directions tell us Butterfly instinctively moves between Goro and her son. When Goro says, "In America, such a child is always an outcast," Butterfly shrieks in fury, runs to the shrine, and seizes her father's knife. Shouting that he is lying, Butterfly stands over the cowering Goro and threatens him with the honor-restoring knife. It's clear Puccini considered this scene to be paired with that of the "Bonze" scene. With Butterfly's last cry of "You're lying!" the Rejection motif sounds again.

The terrified Goro emits a cry that is "loud, desperate, prolonged." Butterfly swears that if he says it again, she will kill him. Frightened, Suzuki picks up the boy and takes him into the room at left. Overcome with disgust, and unwilling to use her father's precious knife on such a toad, Butterfly kicks at Goro and orders him to go away. He flees, and for a few moments she remains standing where she is, as though turned to stone.

First flute and oboe, then clarinet, sound the Rejection motif as Butterfly carefully restores the knife to its place by the shrine. Oboe and violin play transitional phrases, then the opening bars of The Son theme are heard. Alone in the room, Butterfly passionately promises her child, "You'll see your avenger will take us far away, far away, to his country, far away he'll take us...." She sings this last word, "porterà," on an extended high G sharp, and as she holds it, the boom of a cannon is heard. Suzuki enters breathlessly, and the orchestra is silent as she whispers, "The cannon of the harbor!" Could it be ... ?

Softly, slowly, flute, violins, and violas begin the first 16 measures of "Un bel dì," as Butterfly and Suzuki run to the terrace. A warship is coming into the harbor. "White," says Butterfly, her voice tight with hope and fear, "...white ... the American flag with the stars." The ship is turning to anchor, and Butterfly runs for the spyglass Pinkerton left behind. More instruments join in the reprise of "Un bel dì" as, trembling, she puts the glass to her eye, and tells Suzuki to support her hand so she can read the name of the ship. It is the one she has been awaiting for three agonizing years: the *Abraham Lincoln*. The naming of Pinkerton's ship marks the end of the reprise of "Un bel dì," at which point certainty as to its identity has caused the dynamic level to rise to *forte*.

Butterfly gives the spyglass to Suzuki, and goes into the house in great excitement. "They were all lying!" Her love, she tells Suzuki, triumphs at the very moment when all were telling her to despair. Her faith in America and Pinkerton has apparently been rewarded, and the Star-Spangled Banner carries the beginning of her joyful cry, "My love, my faith triumphs completely: he's coming back, and he loves me!" while the conclusion is supported by the music of the final section of the love duet (that is, Butterfly's entrance music), played *fff*.

There is essentially no transition into the Flower Duet, which begins with Butterfly telling Suzuki to shake a branch of the cherry tree so she can bathe herself in flowers. Butterfly sings a very simple melody, doubled by clarinet and horn. (This melody, incidentally, is remarkably similar to the music of a parallel scene in *Fanciulla*, Act Two, where the excited Minnie, getting ready for the arrival of Johnson, asks her maid, "Where have you put my red roses?")

Suzuki tries to calm the almost hysterical Butterfly, and when Butterfly asks how long she thinks they will have to wait for Pinkerton to come, Suzuki opines that it might be longer than the single hour Butterfly suggests. Perhaps it will be two hours, Butterfly concedes. Butterfly decides to strip the garden of flowers, and bring them all inside the house. "Everything," she says, "let everything be full of flowers." As she says this, we hear, three times, the motif of Pinkerton's Return; that is, the music of his climb up the hill. The third time it is played by the double bass, the low rumble of which gives the six-note motif a truly ominous cast.

The Flower Duet is of course an updated version of the troubadour Spring Song. Butterfly orders Suzuki to pick every blossom in the garden and bring them all inside. She knows a rebirth of love occurs in spring, so it must be springtime in the house. "I want all springtime to be fragrant here." Suzuki picks the flowers and hands them to Butterfly, who scatters the petals around the house. (This is something of a departure from Belasco, who in addition to having some flowers brought in, also had the two women excitedly arranging Pinkerton's cigarettes, his slippers, his chair, and his bed. In Puccini's World, only flowers matter. Or rather, only flowers and the moon, which will soon rise, and shine her light on the waiting Butterfly.)

Suzuki helps Butterfly strew the flowers. Roses adorn the threshold over which the man will step, and morning glories garland his seat. "We are sowing April all around," they sing. The melody of the Flower Duet begins to trail away. Sundown is approaching — the hour of waking dreams, when hope struggles with melancholy. Suzuki sets a pair of lamps near the toilette table, where Butterfly seats herself. The final notes of the duet slide into a fragment from the close of the love duet as Butterfly tells Suzuki to come adorn her. She changes her mind, and orders Suzuki to fetch the baby first.

Alone, Butterfly looks at herself in a mirror. The fragment from the love duet lasted only while she was thinking about her preparations, and now that she looks in the mirror, what is on her mind is how she will appear to Pinkerton. She studies herself in silence, while we hear five measures of very unusual music. Two flutes, doubled by a harp playing harmonics, play a strange and equivocal passage punctuated by divided double basses playing a *pizzicato* downward run, in octaves.

In *Tosca*, such a moment would have inspired a logical reminiscence — no doubt a sad version of a theme that had been associated with the character's beauty in happier times. But Puccini has developed beyond such obvious comments. The *Butterfly* orchestra gives a hazy picture of the heroine's thoughts as she looks in the mirror and discovers the toll three years of sadness have taken. And haziness communicates more than clarity would have.

Butterfly isn't as pretty as she was when Pinkerton left; or at least, she thinks she isn't. When Suzuki returns, Butterfly tells her in a sad and lovely passage, scored very simply for violins, viola, and cello, to give her cheeks some color, while she herself puts a touch of rouge on the child's cheeks, so the vigil won't leave him looking pale. (It's interesting, but not significant, that the jar of rouge Pinkerton disapproved of has returned.)

Suzuki tells Butterfly to hold still so she can do her hair. A wisp of the Whirlwind is heard, as Butterfly begins to savor the prospect of her enemies' rage. Smiling at her thought, she tries to imagine what everyone will say when they hear the news. And what about the Bonze uncle? They were all so happy over her trouble. She laughs, and to a recurrence of "My Prince" she adds, "And Yamadori, with his languors!" Her hair finished, Butterfly calls for the obi she wore on her wedding night. This is the showy obi that delayed her, and the music of that portion of the love duet recurs for this passage. Butterfly wants to look as she did that first night, but she adds one touch that is new: a red flower in her hair. It represents springtime, and the rebirth of love.

It is now evening, and with a graceful motion, Butterfly signals to Suzuki, who has finished dressing the child in his own obi, to close the *shoji*. She plans to make three little holes through which they will watch for Pinkerton to come, and they will be "as quiet as mice to wait." The night begins to grow dark as Suzuki closes the *shoji*. Butterfly carries her son to the panel, and with her finger she makes three holes: one at standing level, for her; one at crouching level, for Suzuki, and one at a child's level. She sits the boy on a cushion and motions to him to look out. She and Suzuki take their places, and they too look out. A few moments later, three *pizzicato* notes from the cellos introduce the Humming Chorus, which begins the moment full night sets in.

The Humming Chorus, which reprises the music of the Letter Reading scene, accompanies the vigil during the first part of the night, during which Butterfly calmly waits for Pinkerton. Flutes and muted violins and violas join in the delicate *pizzicato* support of the chorus, which is composed of sopranos and tenors, humming in octaves. From off stage, a solo viola d'amore softly plays.

Soon a solo violin, muted, begins a brief but very sweet song that seems meant to communicate the growing drowsiness of the watchers, for it "surrounds" the falling to sleep of Suzuki and the child. The violin marks the raising of the dynamic level from *piano* to *mf*, and just over four bars after it begins to play, it cuts out for three bars, during which the stage directions have Suzuki and the child fall asleep. The violin resumes playing for three and a half more bars, then it goes silent, after which the tempo returns to speed, but the dynamic level drops to lower than it was before.

The Humming Chorus is a superb piece of mood music, and fascinatingly, the path of the melody seems to echo the latter portions of the Act One love duet. After hearing the opera several times, one may be able to "hear" pieces of the love duet, seemingly running in tandem with the Chorus. Butterfly continues to stand like a statue, looking through the hole in the *shoji*. During the last seven bars of the Chorus, a harp gently plinks and a few remaining instruments softly sigh, while the humming voices slowly rise, and the curtain slowly falls.

The Intermezzo that precedes the second part of Act Two begins while the curtain is still lowered. It opens with a harsh statement of the Whirlwind motif, played *fortissimo* by full orchestra. The motif is played a second time, *piano*, then violins, violas, and cellos remind us of the words that became attached to the theme after Goro and Yamadori told Sharpless that Butterfly still thought she was married. That is, the strings play the music of Butterfly's defensive cry, "I don't THINK so. I am. I AM." Having heard a mere six bars of music, all of it pointing towards disaster, we don't need a raised curtain in order to know what time it is. Dawn must be approaching.

The opening of the Intermezzo gives us an impression of Butterfly's thoughts. Four bars after we hear her insistence that she is legally married to Pinkerton, the orchestra begins a series of four iterations, played by opposing instruments, of that passage near the opening of the Love Duet when Butterfly explained to the surprised Pinkerton why she was kissing his hands: "They told me that over there, among well-bred people, this is the gesture of greatest respect."

It's debatable what this recurrence, played with such equivocal shading by a series of instruments, means. The theme is heard first in the violas, playing *piano*, "with passion." Next comes the cor anglais, playing *pp*, "like an echo." Next is a solo violin, playing *mf*, "sweetly" (followed by *tutti* violins echoing "with passion" the last half of the theme). Last comes a solo oboe, again playing *pp*, "like an echo," the last half of the theme.

The passage must be revelatory of the thoughts of Butterfly, who has stood from dusk to dawn, waiting with growing exhaustion for the man whose coming means the difference between life and death for her. But what are those thoughts? The tone of the passage is vague; no doubt deliberately so. There is an obsessive quality to it; we could almost call it an *ostinato*. Perhaps it reveals Butterfly telling herself, "I gave him my greatest respect, and he will come back." Perhaps it reveals her thinking, "He will come back, because I am worthy of respect." In any case it is revealing a woman who is exerting every ounce of her will in an attempt not to give way to despair.

The conclusion of the "respect" passage ends the introduction to the Intermezzo, which beginning with #2 seems to aspire to being a tone poem. The 18 bars that encompass #2 have a surging, passionate character, but they don't seem to mean anything in particular. With the start of #3, however, we hear a suggestion of the Love Duet, which breaks out in earnest seven bars later. (Three bars into the Love Duet music, we hear the Love Duet become fused with the Flower Duet. If one has not yet marked the rhythmic pattern shared by the two duets, it will be obvious here.)

One bar before #4, the music of "the gesture of greatest respect" begins again, in the violins. The curtain rises on the second bar of #4, thus the music of "respect" (which is picked up by upper woodwinds and violas, and rises higher with every repetition) is what we hear when we first see Butterfly. She is standing just as she was when we saw her last — still as a statue, and looking out through the hole in the *shoji*. Suzuki and the child are asleep. The music of "respect" fades away, and the distant voices of sailors are heard from the harbor. We then hear vague sounds from the ships, followed by the motif of Pinkerton's Return; that is, the passage of "Un bel dì" to which Butterfly sang the words, "(a man, a little dot) **starts up the hill.**"

The final section of the Intermezzo now begins. Introduced by muted horns, it is meant to paint an aural picture of the rising of the sun, and the music employed is a speeded up, *pizzicato* version of the delicate folk song that closed Act One: the music identified with Butterfly's "destiny." With this recurrence, Puccini is revealing the horror of that destiny. Butterfly had thought it was marriage to Pinkerton, and safety, but it fact her destiny is dawn, and death.

The music is filled with what aspires to be tremendous excitement, and there are certainly an awful lot of notes (many of which come in the form of rapid scales), but in truth the Intermezzo is far less interesting than the two Intermezzi of *Le Villi*, no doubt because those addressed subjects that stimulated Puccini's imagination: intense grief, love, and death. Although the *Butterfly* Intermezzo does address those same subjects, it does so in a nonspecific way. It is also an attempt at program music, and it doesn't succeed at that. Puccini had many, many strengths as a composer, but a talent for long passages of extra-musical description was evidently not one of them. Actually, the last thirteen or so bars of the "sunrise" section are rather pretty. They sound like a description of choppy water becoming calm, but what they actually describe is the sky becoming calm after the excitement of the numerous stages of sunrise.

If the music of the "sunrise" section of the Intermezzo is less than gripping, the score's technical directions serve as additional proof of how important the subject of sunrise is in Puccini. Recall that the Love Duet's technical directions marked the stages of blissful Night, giving the precise moments for dusk and full night. (At one point Pinkerton also helpfully observed that, "night is coming.")

Now that hateful Day is near, the Intermezzo's technical directions mark the coming of the sun. The score shows the precise moment when "dawn begins." Following this is "pink dawn," "pale dawn" and finally "the sun shines." Suzuki is the first to speak when the action starts, and her words reveal her as one of the "good people" who live in Puccini's World. Opening her eyes and seeing the terrible thing that has occurred, she exclaims in what can only be utter horror, "The sun already!"

Suzuki calls to her mistress and Butterfly, stirring, says confidently, "He'll come. He'll come, you'll see." She is trapped. There is nothing for her to do except continue to express calm certainty in the nobleness of her husband, who is worthy of the greatest respect, until he has proved he isn't worthy of it. It is either that, or ... something too terrible to contemplate yet. Muted violins, playing in octaves, begin a lullaby version of the theme of The Son Without Equal. The theme carries Suzuki's tender urging that Butterfly go and rest. "When he comes," she says gently, "I'll call you."

Two bars of "sunrise" music follow Suzuki's urge, and they make for an effective transition between her voice and that of Butterfly, who doesn't acknowledge what Suzuki has said, and seems lost in a sad world of her own. Butterfly has picked up her sleeping son, and continuing with the music of The Son Without Equal she sings her child an achingly sweet lullaby as she carries him into the room at left. "Sleep my love," she croons, "sleep on my heart. You are with God, and I'm with my sorrow. For you the rays of the golden stars. My baby, sleep." She sings this verse twice, and during the pause after each verse Suzuki sympathetically sings, "Povera Butterfly!" (Poor Butterfly!)

There is a volume of meaning in the melody of The Son Without Equal. The music to which Butterfly told Sharpless about her mother is identical to it. The words used during that earlier passage, which was a response to a question as to whether Butterfly had any sisters, were, "No, sir. I have my mother. A noble lady. But, without wronging her, very poor also" (povera molto anch'essa). Puccini clearly meant for us to recognize that at this point, which is why Suzuki's sad comment, "Povera Butterfly," is accompanied by the identical music of Butterfly's earlier "very poor also" (povera molto anch'essa).

That the music of Butterfly and her mother is the same as the music of Butterfly and her son, tells us several things. It reminds us Butterfly became estranged from her relatives because of Pinkerton, and must have given birth without her mother by her side. It tells us about the transfer of love from one generation to the next — that Butterfly cares for her son as her mother cared for her. The music also makes us realize Butterfly is now in the same position as her mother was: she has no husband, and has been raising her child alone. Butterfly is "a noble lady. But, without wronging her, very poor also."

Puccini also appears to be laying the groundwork for something. We are being made to cast our minds back toward Act One and to remember Butterfly's mother, and to realize that Butterfly has taken on her mother's role. Soon we will hear the voice of Butterfly's father, in the form of the motif of the Father's Suicide, and we will see that the girl is about to take on her father's role as well.

A tender theme is now given out by the strings, and a soft knock is heard at the door. When Suzuki answers she is startled to see both Sharpless and Pinkerton. Tip-toeing in, both men tell her to be silent, and Pinkerton "solicitously" tells Suzuki not to awaken Butterfly. (In fact, he came at this hour hoping to avoid seeing her — the coward!)

Suzuki tells them of how the poor girl waited all through the night with the child. It didn't occur to Pinkerton she might have known he was back, and Suzuki explains that for the last three years, not a ship has entered the port without Butterfly taking the spyglass and examining its color and flag. "I told you so," says Sharpless, and Suzuki offers to go and fetch Butterfly. "No," says Pinkerton quickly, holding her back. "Not yet." Suzuki gestures at the room, filled with flower petals, and to a bit of music from the Flower Duet she tells him Butterfly did this yesterday evening. "Didn't I tell you?" says Sharpless reproachfully, and Pinkerton, "disturbed," comments, "How sad!"

Hearing a sound in the garden, Suzuki goes to look. She is amazed to see a woman. Repeatedly she demands to know who it is, and Pinkerton, "embarrassed," finally says, "She came with me." Disgusted by such cowardice, Sharpless says deliberately, "She's his wife."

Suzuki is horrified, and she raises her arms to heaven, then drops to her knees with her head touching the ground. For the poor little one, she laments, "the sun has gone out!" Sharpless tries to calm her, explaining they came here at such an early hour to see her, and enlist her aid "in the great trial." (We hear a snippet of the "sunrise" music when Sharpless speaks of the early-morning hour.)

Cellos and double bass play three *pizzicato* notes that hint at the Suicide motif, and Suzuki says hopelessly, "What's the use?" As Sharpless continues to try to persuade her, a trio ensues as Pinkerton, becoming more and more upset, paces about the room and takes in the preparations made on his behalf. Sharpless explains it would be best for the child if Pinkerton's wife were to adopt him, and Suzuki recoils at being told she must ask a mother to ... she can't even name it.

As for Pinkerton, his contribution to the trio is filled with guilt and a touch of fear, as Puccini begins to torture him. "Oh! the bitter fragrance of these flowers — like poison it goes to my heart. Unchanged is the room of our love ... but a chill of death is here. [He sees a picture of himself.] My portrait. Three years have passed, and you've been counting the days and hours."

Sharpless insists on Suzuki going with him to meet Kate Pinkerton. The lieutenant, who is now crying, tells Sharpless he can't stay, and will wait for him along the path. "Didn't I tell you?" the Consul repeats, and Pinkerton, sinking to his lowest point yet, thrusts an envelope filled with money at him. "Give her some comfort," he says, then he sobs, "I'm consumed by remorse." We hear another hint of the Suicide motif.

After repeating his "I told you so," Sharpless, to a reprise of the music to which he first warned Pinkerton, reminds him of how he warned him the girl would take the ceremony seriously. Significantly, he says Butterfly has been "insulted." Pinkerton agrees with everything the older man says, and he sobs, "I'll never find refuge from this torment!" Sharpless urges Pinkerton to go, but before complying he pauses for his Masochism Aria, "Addio, fiorito asil." Pinkerton has finally learned the value of flowers, and with sweet and mournful accents he bids goodbye to the "flowered refuge of happiness and love."

We tend to think of "Addio, fiorito asil" as an aria for Pinkerton, but as soon as he has sung the first verse, which concludes with a sobbing admission that he will "always see her gentle face with atrocious torture," Sharpless joins in. He brings the music of the Flower Duet, which Pinkerton deftly transforms into the related music of the Love Duet.

"I can't stand your wretchedness," cries Pinkerton, to the music to which he had once exulted, "My Butterfly! How well they named you." Puccini's tenors always sing their most heroic notes when exposing their guilt, shame, and misery, thus Pinkerton reaches his vocal climax on the words, "Ah! I'm vile!" which employs a high B flat on the "Ah!" when he sings the line the first time, then a high A flat on the same word, with a *fermata*, when he repeats it.

Filled with that sense of "I die despairing" that gripped Cavaradossi in the final act of *Tosca*, Pinkerton runs away. Passing him are Suzuki and Kate, coming in from the garden. Kate has been urging Suzuki to tell Butterfly she should let her and Pinkerton have the boy. "You'll tell her?" Kate asks, and her question is followed by an ominous little figure in the oboe. Suzuki reluctantly agrees. Kate promises to raise the child as if he were her own.

The distraught Suzuki promises to speak to Butterfly, and now we hear Butterfly calling. Kate retreats to the garden, and Butterfly appears at the half-opened door. Suzuki tries to keep Butterfly from coming out, growing more and more frantic as Butterfly tries to pass her, then Butterfly concludes Pinkerton has come, and means to surprise her.

With a mixture of joy and agitation Butterfly rushes around the room, looking everywhere and crying, "He's here! Where is he hidden?" She finally notices Sharpless, and the sight of him alarms her. By now she has looked in every corner. Clarinets and horns play a subdued passage that fuses the motifs of the Whirlwind and the Rejection, as the frightened girl looks around and says, "He isn't here."

She looks out into the garden, and sees Kate. "That woman?" she says in a dull chant, and the words are followed by two bars of dead silence. "What does she want of me?" No one speaks, but Suzuki begins to cry. This surprises Butterfly, who asks the reason. Sharpless approaches her, and the truth occurs to Butterfly, who shrinks like a frightened child. "No," she pleads, "tell me nothing ... nothing ... or I might fall dead on the spot."

She turns to Suzuki, and asks her not to cry, but to answer with a "yes" or a "no." "Is he alive?" The answer is yes, and Butterfly, "as though she had received a mortal blow: rigid," says, "But he's not coming any more. They have told you!" Suzuki admits he's not coming, ever again. "But he arrived yesterday?" presses Butterfly, determined to know everything. Yes, he arrived yesterday.

Butterfly looks with fascination at Kate, understanding she is Pinkerton's wife, and that she herself is not Madama Pinkerton. She knows intuitively that Pinkerton wants his son, and as she cries, "They want to take everything from me! My son!" horns and violins play a mournful version of The Son Without Equal theme.

Sharpless urges her to make the sacrifice for her son's sake, and as he does the cor anglais plays a reminiscence from Act One: the music of Sharpless' comment about Pinkerton's "vagabond creed," in which the Consul said, "It's an easy gospel, that makes life charming but saddens the heart." Overwhelmed by grief, Butterfly accepts her fate, saying, "I must obey him."

By now, Kate has timidly approached the terrace. We're not meant to dislike her, and she makes a favorable impression as she stands outside the house and asks Butterfly if she can forgive her. A mournful scene ensues as Butterfly absolves Kate, wishing her happiness always. Kate and Sharpless contribute low-voiced comments, and Kate asks the Consul whether Butterfly will give up her son.

Overhearing, Butterfly says she will give the boy to Pinkerton, "if he will come for him. In half an hour, **climb the hill**." The last words are sung to the motif of Pinkerton's Return, which was first heard during "Un bel dì," when Butterfly imagined the day she would see a small figure start to climb the hill. After she sings this line to Kate, silence hangs in the air, and one who recognizes the music will automatically fill in the next words from "Un bel dì": "Who can it be? Who can it be? And when he comes, what will he say? What will he say?"

Suzuki escorts Kate and Sharpless away, and Butterfly falls to the floor, sobbing. Cellos and double basses rapidly repeat the motif of Pinkerton's Return, which moves into the woodwinds as Suzuki returns and tries to comfort Butterfly. After a moment, Butterfly comes to herself. "Seeing that it is broad daylight," she pulls away from Suzuki and says, to a reminiscence of the "sunrise" music of the Intermezzo, "There's too much light outside, and too much spring. Close up." Suzuki closes the *shoji*, shutting out the hateful sunlight.

Tenderly, the oboe plays the theme of The Son, as Butterfly asks where the boy is, and Suzuki answers that he is playing. In an anguished voice Butterfly tells her to go play with him. Knowing what her mistress means to do, Suzuki begins to cry, and says she will stay here. Resolutely, Butterfly commands Suzuki to go. Even so, she has to push Suzuki out the door, and as she does, violins, violas, and cellos recall the music of the American locks that Pinkerton put on the house: "Why, with such care, did he supply the house with locks, if he didn't mean to come back any more?"

There is a lamp in front of the shrine, and Butterfly lights it. She bows before the image of Buddha, rescinding her conversion, and trying to steel herself for what she must do. Then she goes to a cabinet, takes out a white veil, and throws it over the screen. Now she goes to the wall on which the knife-case is hanging, near the image of the Buddha. As she does this, cellos and double basses play the first three notes of the Suicide motif. Played *piano* and *pizzicato*, it is enough to hint at the motif, but no more.

Butterfly takes the lacquered case down, and draws out the knife, the blade of which she kisses religiously, holding it in both hands, by the point and the hilt. As she does this, we hear what can only be the voice of Butterfly's father: the Suicide motif, played "rough" by clarinet, bassoon, and lower strings. It is a shocking, shocking sound — a voice from the distant past. As Butterfly chants the words of the inscription, "With honor dies he who can no longer live with honor," we realize that Butterfly has not only grown into the role of her mother (recall the joint melody of the music of the mother and of the son), she has now grown into the role of her father. The deep, strong voice that utters the Suicide motif is now Butterfly's voice.

Or rather, it reveals what she has become. She is a woman of iron will and tremendous courage. And she does not love Pinkerton any more. The Butterfly of Long and Belasco still loved him, but Puccini's does not. He has destroyed her honor. After agreeing to give up her son in obedience to him, she never mentions him again. More significantly, there is not the faintest whisper of Love Duet music in the finale. This proves to us she does not think of him at all. Her last thoughts, her music will tell us, are of her son.

Butterfly aims the knife at her throat, and as she does, the door at left opens. We see Suzuki's arm, thrusting the little boy into the room. Perhaps the sight of him will cause his mother to relent. The child runs into the room, and Butterfly drops the knife, runs to embrace him, and almost suffocates him with kisses.

Her Farewell aria is in two parts. The first is an arioso-like introduction, that touches off the second part by the uttering of the word "abandonment." In the introduction, Butterfly calls her son "little God! Love, my love, flower of the lily and the rose." (She seems to be passing on to him her own identification with flowers.) She tells her son that what she is doing is for his sake, so he can go beyond the sea without being tortured in his maturity by his mother's abandonment.

The aria section is sung as in a state of exultation, and there is something in it that recalls Butterfly's mournful and beautiful line about her *ottoke*: "They are the spirits of my ancestors." Butterfly sings to her boy to look hard, hard at his mother's face, so a trace of it may linger in his memory. Sobbing, she says goodbye to him, and as she does, cellos and double basses begin a death march. Butterfly takes a last look at her child, and tells him to go play.

She sets him on a mat, facing away from the screen, and gives him his doll and an American flag to wave when his father comes. Even if she couldn't be a "real American wife," surely her son can be a real American boy. Gently she ties a blindfold on him. Then she picks up the knife, closes the door at left, and goes behind the screen.

Her last thoughts are of her boy. The orchestra plays part of the opening of the Farewell, the music that carried the words, "Love, my love, flower of the lily and the...." Before the orchestra can sing the word, the Lady of the Rose pushes the knife blade into her throat. The knife is heard falling to the floor, and the white veil is pulled inside the screen.

Butterfly falls, half outside the screen. The white veil is wrapped around her throat. She drags herself to her son, having just enough strength to embrace him. The orchestra plays an urgent figure, suggestive of running, and from outside the voice of Pinkerton is heard, calling, "Butterfly!" three times. The first and second cries are followed by the motif of Pinkerton's Return, and the last is followed by a passage from Butterfly's "Che tua madre." As Sharpless and Pinkerton rush in, they see Butterfly holding out her arm, making a weak gesture toward the child, just before she dies.

In this passage of "Che tua madre," Butterfly had been describing for Sharpless the shame she would undergo if Pinkerton abandoned her, and in her dying moments as she holds out her arm and gestures toward her son, the orchestra plays the music of, "And, toward the pitying people, she'll hold out her trembling hand, crying, 'Hear, hear my sad song. Charity for an unhappy mother, be moved to pity.'" As Butterfly dies, Pinkerton kneels before her, and Sharpless picks up the child and kisses him, sobbing.

9

La Fanciulla del West

Libretto by Civinini and Zangarini, after David Belasco's play,
The Girl of the Golden West
First performed at the Metropolitan Opera House,
New York, December 10, 1910

Fanciulla is Puccini's most complex work, and unless the listener is familiar with the play on which the libretto is based, or better, the novelization David Belasco published shortly after the opera premiered, it's unlikely he'll fully appreciate how wonderful the opera is. Belasco's tale combines the romance novel with the western, and it has some remarkable features. The story is deeply informed by the sentiments of the greatest of all works of medieval *romance* literature: *Vita nuova*, written by Dante around the year 1290. It's strange to find a work by Dante featured in a story set in the American West, but Belasco really wanted it in there, and he managed to make it fit.

The score of *Fanciulla* is indebted to Wagner's *Tristan und Isolde*, the gimmick of which is the stimulation, during the prelude, of the listener's desire for musical resolution, and the refusal to satisfy that desire until the closing bar of the score. Puccini composed *Fanciulla* along similar lines, for instead of following his usual practice of writing stand-alone arias, he wrote quasi-arias, the closing notes of which either trail off inconclusively, or else flow swiftly into succeeding music. This makes for problems during performance, for the inevitable applause is disruptive to the music and the mood of the drama.

The debt to *Tristan* goes further than this "endless melody" technique, however. There are six major, recurring musical themes in *Fanciulla*, and like the quasi-arias, they too frequently fail to resolve. This opera consequently marks another change for Puccini in respect to recurring music. Through *Butterfly*, recurring music involved the recollection of particular lines, memories, or objects, and recurrences in the final scene tended to be brief. Those final scene recurrences are "logical reminiscences," that remind us of earlier events, reveal dying thoughts, and make a narrative closing comment on the story. With *Fanciulla*, however, starting with the prelude, the way is being pointed toward the last act finale, where the six recurring themes are woven together in a beautiful and deeply moving choral passage that strives for an Italian version of the exaltation and shimmer with which *Tristan* makes its cathartic close.

Puccini continues with his "family of motifs" technique in *Fanciulla*, but the six themes of this opera are broader in scope than those of previous works. Most of them refer to philosophical concepts such as loneliness, brotherhood, and redemption. The love duet of course involves recurring music, but its meaning is more complex than the "I love you, I want you, you are my destiny," of prior love duets.

The word "redemption" raises the issue of *Parsifal*. Minnie is the first of Puccini's redeeming women, and being that the librettos of three subsequent operas contain big sections Puccini borrowed from *Parsifal*, it is tempting to try to identify plot elements in *Fanciulla* that "must" have been inspired by Wagner operas. The only problem is, we have proof they weren't.

For example, in the closing moments of *Fanciulla*, Johnson, having been forgiven of his crimes and released from the hangman's noose, kneels at Minnie's feet, and she proceeds to make a gesture of blessing over his head — "as though she were a bishop," marvels Spike Hughes.[1] What are we to think of this, except it must have been in imitation of the baptism scene near the end of *Parsifal*? A glance at the text of Belasco's play reveals the source of that stage direction, all except the actual gesture of blessing. (In Belasco, Minnie simply prays for Johnson while he kneels beside her.)

One might be tempted to speculate Puccini named his heroine "Minnie" after Frau Minne, which is Isolde's name for the goddess of love, and that he named his hero "Dick" after Richard Wagner himself. Alas, that delicious theory is likewise exploded by a consultation of the play, which finds the main characters already christened by Belasco.[2]

There are some actual lines in the *Fanciulla* libretto that appear to have been inspired by Wagner, such as the ecstatic, climaxing line in the love duet, "How sweet it is to live and die, and never part again," which sounds a lot like Tristan and Isolde under the tree. But that line came from Belasco, and he was referring to a passage in *Vita nuova*.

Writers have tried to draw all sorts of other parallels between incidents in *Fanciulla* and in Wagner's operas, claiming for example that Minnie's fondness for her pinto pony equals Brünnhilde's love for her horse; the passionate embrace of Minnie and Johnson equals the passionate embrace of Sieglinde and Siegmund; the storm blowing through Minnie's cabin equals the storm blowing through the house in *Walküre*; the "impotent rival" of Rance equals the "impotent rival" of Melot; and that Johnson being shot after he kisses Minnie equals Tristan's being stabbed after he kisses Isolde.

What a shame all copies of Belasco's play weren't destroyed in a single catastrophe, so we could believe Puccini responsible for all these Wagnerisms in the *Fanciulla* libretto. Alas, the play is still with us, proving that Belasco wrote every one of those things.[3] One might feel inclined to accuse Belasco of having lifted his material from Wagner, but what does that say about the legions of critics who have declared that *The Girl* was a shameless copy of Bret Harte's *Miggles*? (Or was it Sardou's *Tosca*?) Puccini's fondness for *Parsifal* notwithstanding, *La Fanciulla del West* is about redemption because *The Girl of the Golden West* was about redemption.

The story of the Girl opens six months before the opera does, so we must begin with Belasco. The playwright was closely involved with the world premiere of Puccini's opera, and ten months later, in October 1911, he published his story in the form of a novel, the long and exciting opening of which encompasses a period barely alluded to in the opera and the play: the meeting of Minnie and Ramerrez on the road from Monterey. Whether or not Puccini knew about the material Belasco was planning, it neatly fills in all the empty spaces in the libretto.[4]

The story is set in and around a gold-mining camp in California's Sierra Nevadas. The time is the Gold Rush days of 1849–50. The novelist's curtain rises to show a young blonde woman traveling in a stagecoach from the Mexican town of Monterey to her home on Cloudy Mountain, a tall and beautiful peak that has given its name to the nearby mining camp. The Girl's name is Minnie Falconer, and the seat opposite her is piled with souvenirs of Monterey. Every moment of Minnie's visit was thrilling, especially the great rodeo and bullfight.

A horseman appears, and spurs his steed toward the coach. He wears the elegant garb of a Spanish caballero, and as he draws even with the coach he sweeps off his sombrero and offers Minnie a spray of flowers. "See, señorita," he says gallantly. "A beautiful bunch of syringa." He looks into her eyes, and he adds warmly, "For you."

Minnie can tell by his voice, attire, and manners that this handsome young man has a social advantage over her, but she also realizes she has seen him before. The first time was ten days ago, on this very road, when he had looked into the coach as it was heading toward Monterey. The second time was at the bullfight. He had been one of the most skillful horsemen there, and she had distinctly seen him shooting admiring glances at her as she sat in the stands.

With these memories in mind, she is more friendly than she might have been had a complete stranger presumed on her this way. She thanks him, then adds, "But it strikes me sort of forcible that I've seen you before." With even more enthusiasm she goes on, "My, but that bullfight was just grand. You were fine! I'm right glad to know you, sir."

Although the caballero does not introduce himself, his name is Ramerrez. He is a native Californian (Spanish father, American mother), but he has not met many Americans. For a moment he is misled by Minnie's friendliness, for the respectable Spanish women he knows would refuse to speak to a man to whom they had not been properly introduced. Briefly he suspects Minnie of being a woman of easy virtue, then he reconsiders. In Sacramento, where he has spent much time at school, there are a number of quite respectable ladies whose speech is similarly direct.

Awareness of the dreadful mistake he almost made causes Ramerrez to lose a bit of his self-assurance, and as he gazes at Minnie's lovely, smiling face he realizes there is something unusual about her. She has the look of a woman who could be trusted, and who might make the people around her better, simply by existing among them.[5] So when he speaks to her again, it is with more respect than previously. He asks whether she enjoyed Monterey, and soon confesses that after having seen her at the bullfight he has waited for her on this road every day. By now the stage driver has slowed his horses to a walk.

Flattered at the handsome stranger's interest, Minnie asks him about his family. He lives at a rancho owned by his father. His mother died years ago. It's obvious to Minnie that his mother's death still hurts him, and she offers her sympathy, adding she is an orphan, and has no family.

"But I have my boys," she says cheerfully, referring to the miners of Cloudy Mountain, where she runs a saloon called the Polka. The stranger is about to ask who "the boys" are, but Minnie spies some bushes full of ripe blackberries, and the question dies on his lips as she expresses a wish to pick some of the berries. With one hand the caballero pulls up his horse, and with the other he makes a gesture inviting her to take his arm and alight from the stage.

A sudden feeling of shyness grips Minnie. She doesn't know this man, and while talking to him in a stage is one thing, getting out and going berrying with him is something else. It doesn't seem quite proper, and she is conscious again of the difference between his fine manners and speech, and hers. Reluctantly, but definitely, she refuses, and the stranger's face falls in disappointment.

The driver, having overheard the offer and refusal, tells the caballero he is behind schedule, and whips his horses up a little. The rider keeps pace with the coach, but neither he nor Minnie can think of anything else to say. The silence is beginning to grow uncomfortable when suddenly another horseman is seen on the road ahead.

The stranger tells Minnie this is one of his father's men. Fearing there may be trouble at home, he calls to the man in Spanish, and at the answer he tells Minnie, "It is as I had feared." Minnie is sorry he has had bad news, and when he expresses regret that he has to leave her she responds, "Well, I guess I ain't particularly crazy to have you go neither."

Ramerrez asks if she will think of him sometime. Minnie laughs with pretended carelessness, and answers, "What's the good of my thinkin' of you? I seen you talkin' with them grand Monterey ladies and I guess you won't be thinkin' often of me. Like as not by tomorrow you'll have clean forgot me." But with great intensity the young man assures her, "I shall never forget you."

Minnie doesn't trust such words from a stranger, especially one like this gentleman, and she cries, "I almost think you're makin' fun of me!" He assures her he meant every word, and when he looks into her blue eyes he sees "something which the Girl had not the subtlety to conceal." He asks her to tell him where she lives, and Minnie hesitates for a long moment. Too long, in fact. With his pride smarting the caballero reins in his horse, and in an instant the coach has left him behind.

But Minnie did not hesitate for any reason the stranger could have imagined. There is nothing she would like more than to see him again. But the men of Cloudy Mountain are rough miners, and the thought of how they would react to this elegant gentleman made her wince. She couldn't stand the thought of them laughing at his fine clothes and graceful manners, and so she hesitated, too long.... Faintly she hears the words, "Adios, señorita."

With a cry of vexation Minnie looks back. He is still there, looking toward the coach, a horseman silhouetted against the western sky. Ramerrez watches the stage until a turn of the road hides it from sight. He feels a strong urge to follow it, but he remembers the urgent summons from home, and turns his horse toward the road that leads to the rancho.

It is a journey of hours, through wild country, but at length the two men reach the hacienda. What with the remoteness of the site, the armed guards outside the grounds, and the fierce appearance of the men in the courtyard, the place seems like a fortress. Servants rush to take the young man's horse. The scene changes to the bedroom of Sr. Ramerrez. He is a huge and harsh-looking man, and at this moment he is dying.

Sr. Ramerrez was once wealthy and powerful, but only so long as first the Spanish, and then the Mexicans, were in control of California. When the Americans came, Ramerrez found his influence waning, his lands being taken, and his cattle disappearing. So he began a campaign that ultimately resulted in the loss of his entire fortune. He wooed first one European power, then another, trying to convince them that riches awaited if they would enter California and expel the Americans. But his wooing was in vain. When this hope died, he began a violent campaign to have California declared a republic, but after the shedding of much blood this too came to naught.

As the old man lies on his deathbed, he casts his mind back over these events of the last years, and impatiently awaits the arrival of his son. All his life Sr. Ramerrez has ruled his people with an iron fist, and his son has always been obedient to his commands. When the boy enters, the old man feels a sudden qualm. But just as quickly he realizes such a sensation must be due to the weakness that attends the approach of death, so he stiffens his resolve. "My son," he begins. "You promise to carry out my wishes after I am gone?" "Yes, father," answers the young man. "You know that I will." The old man points to a crucifix hanging over his bed, and tells his son to swear. "I swear it," is the response.

The old man calls for a glass of aguardiente. The fiery liquid revives him, and he launches into a diatribe against the hated Americans. The son implores his father to rest, but the dying man shakes his head. "Do you know who I am?" he demands. "No; you think you do but you don't. There was a time when I had plenty of money. It pleased me greatly to pay all your expenses, to see that you received the best education possible both at home and abroad. Then the gringos came. Little by little these cursed Americanos have taken all that I had from me. But as they have sown, so shall they reap. I have taken my revenge, and you shall take more." He pauses for a moment to catch his breath, then in a terrible voice he cries, "Yes, I have robbed — robbed! For the last three years your father has been a bandit!" The son springs to his feet and cries, "A bandit? You, father, a Ramerrez, a bandit?"

"Ay, a bandit, and outlaw, as you also will be when I am no more, and rob, rob, rob these Americanos. It is my command and — you — have — sworn...." The old man falls back, spent, and as the son gazes at him he realizes that in spite of the absolute obedience of his father's men, not one of whom had dared to whisper a word to him, somehow he had known. Or rather, he had pretended not to know, closing his eyes to the grim faces, and the wounds the men of the rancho sometimes rode home with just as a tale of some new robbery hit Monterey. He had pretended not to know, so he would not have to deal with what now confronts him. "You have sworn..." the old man whispers, and the son bows his head in silence. A moment later and Sr. Ramerrez is at peace. But his son is not at peace, and the reason is perhaps not the reason we might expect.

Young Ramerrez will indeed assume leadership of the outlaw band, and he will try to salve his conscience with the argument that he is being forced to do something he detests out of obedience to his father's dying command. But inside he will know this is a lie. He is not being forced. The truth is, he wants to do it. The thought of leading an outlaw gang, of planning daring robberies and executing them with consummate skill, is thrilling, and he will love every moment of it.

From this time, the son of Sr. Ramerrez and the American woman will be split into two personalities, and they are at war with each other. One of them is Ramerrez, who is Spanish, and this man loves being a bandit king. The other goes by the name of Dick Johnson, who is American, and he is ashamed of being a cheap thief. Ramerrez and Dick Johnson know they cannot live together forever, but little do they realize that one day soon, one of them will bleed to death on the floor of Minnie Falconer's cabin, high on Cloudy Mountain.

And so it was that a road agent began to harry the mining camps of the Sierras. Not a week went by without a gold shipment being intercepted. Unless, that is, it was guarded by native Californians or Mexicans. Such men were never molested by the outlaw and his gang. Only Americans were robbed. And women, even American women, were never given the slightest offense. This unusual behavior on the part of a road agent, coupled with his scrupulous care not to kill anyone, soon earned the outlaw Ramerrez a reputation as one who robbed like a gentleman. Wells Fargo put up a reward of $5,000, and set their best man, Ashby, on his trail.

While this was going on, Minnie had been hoping the handsome caballero would somehow find his way to her Polka saloon, but as days turned into weeks, and weeks into months, hope faded. She didn't forget him, though, and it seemed to those who knew her best that something about her had changed. Jack Rance, the sheriff of Manzanita County, sensed it right away. Her feelings for him seemed to have cooled.

And he was right. Minnie had thought a lot of Rance after he first rode into Cloudy — and indeed, what woman wouldn't have? Rance was six foot one, thin and angular. His hair and moustache were black, and his skin pale and waxen. His eyes were a steely gray, and heavily fringed and arched. His nose was straight, his mouth hard and determined, but just. His lips were thin, his teeth brilliantly white. In addition to being sheriff, Rance was an expert card player, and his hands were soft and white. One might have said they were feminine hands, except the fingers were unusually long.

Rance spoke in a drawl, and he was always impeccably dressed. He wore a beaver hat, a broadcloth suit cut in the fashionable "'Frisco" style, a puffed white shirt, and well-polished boots with high arches and heels. A large diamond ring flashed on one hand, and on his spotless shirt was another, larger diamond, held in place by two gold chains.[6]

Rance thought he cut quite a swath, and for a long time Minnie thought so too. In fact, she believed he was the perfect picture of a "gentleman." Her trip to Monterey had disabused her of that notion, however. The moment she met the caballero, she realized the difference between Jack Rance and a true gentleman.

She didn't tell Rance this, of course. She didn't tell anyone about the man she had met — not even her bartender, Nick, who was the closest thing she had to a friend in Cloudy. And yet Rance could tell her feelings toward him had changed. Everything had been fine until she went on that trip to Monterey, so after thinking it over he concluded she must have met some man there — no doubt some shrimp from Sacramento, he thought savagely.

But what about Ramerrez? Had he, in spite of his promise, clean forgot about Minnie? Well no, he hadn't, but if truth be told he hadn't been entirely, er, celibate either. There was a Mexican settlement some miles away from Cloudy, and in it lived a beautiful woman called Nina Micheltoreña. She had once belonged among the best people of Monterey, but then a certain indiscretion on her part made it essential she leave Monterey for an environment where people were less scrupulous as to matters of personal conduct.

Fortunately for Nina, her looks had not been affected by the unfortunate events in Monterey. She soon became the most popular woman in the settlement, and in a moment of weakness Ramerrez too fell briefly under her spell. He even made the mistake of giving her a photograph of himself, inscribed on the back "with love." It wasn't just Nina's beauty that attracted him, however. Nina had a talent for collecting information about where money could be found, and she quickly became one of Ramerrez' main sources of information about when and where gold shipments would be setting out.

But Ramerrez soon began to regret having taken up with Nina, and after steeling himself for an unpleasant scene, he went to the dance hall where she spent her evenings, paid her several times over what he owed her for her most recent information, and told her they were through.

Knowing Nina for a jealous and violent woman, Ramerrez was shocked at how well she seemed to take it. She tried briefly to change his mind, reminding him he had promised to love her forever, but when he held firm she accepted it. It didn't concern Ramerrez much when she added she would rather give him up to death than to the arms of another woman. But it should have concerned him. Perhaps it might have concerned him, had he seen her, later that night, whispering a few words to Ashby, the Wells Fargo agent.

Ramerrez may have given up his affair with Nina, but he hasn't given up robbery. The last piece of information Nina passed on to him concerned a huge stash of gold at the mining camp of Cloudy Mountain, a place Ramerrez has never visited. Her sources told Nina the gold was being kept at the Polka saloon. So that is Ramerrez' next target: the Polka. Leaving the Mexican camp, he puts on the clothes of an American so he can enter the Americans' camp with less suspicion than a Spaniard would have earned. Then he gathers his men, including his lieutenant, Jose Castro, and they set out for Cloudy Mountain, and their next robbery.

Puccini's opera now begins, with a fiery orchestral prelude of 34 bars, played before a lowered curtain. This is the most muscular and evocative prelude Puccini has yet written, and it tells us we are in for a powerful story of romance and high adventure in the great outdoors. Two themes are given out in the prelude, and the beginning of the first consists of an exhilarating upwards rush in woodwinds and strings. The opera is very concerned with the concept of "up"—of rising up, climbing up, reaching up—and this upwards rush is descriptive of that. The setting is the towering peaks of the Sierras, after all. We're going up, up, up!!

The meaning of the first theme—given out in the first three measures of the prelude—is a bit complex, for we hear it in an uncountable number of settings. Sometimes it is reduced to a melancholy and drooping motif, comprised of four falling notes. In this form it's generally used by the principals in lines of wistful *parlando* or *arioso*. We hear this motif repeatedly during the conversation between Minnie and Johnson during the last part of Act One, but it's also heard in the gloomy Rance's Theme.

At other times this first theme is played just as we hear it in the prelude, incorporated into an extended piece of music. The first time we hear the theme in the body of the opera is during the conversation between Nick and Jack Rance, about why the homesick gold miner Jim Larkens is so unhappy. We hear it near the close of the Bible lesson scene, when Minnie speaks of how there is no one so bad he is incapable of redemption. It is used in Johnson's gorgeous confession aria, "Or son sei mesi." The theme seems to be tied to the idea of the lust for gold. It definitely expresses the idea of someone having taken a wrong turn in life—a turn that has hurt him, and has caused him to be in need of forgiveness and healing.

The second prelude theme is one of the finale themes, and it is filled with anguish. Fans of *Tristan und Isolde* should easily recognize in this Anguish Theme, which begins on bar #7, the motif of the hunting horns of King Marke. The Anguish Theme recurs with astonishing frequency, and always in moments of strong emotion, when Johnson or Minnie express longing for one another, and doubt about whether he or she is good enough for the other. As it expresses intense doubt, the Anguish Theme is, logically, the piece of music most frequently denied resolution to the tonic. The theme finally reaches that resolution in a gloriously cathartic moment that caps the last act finale—a moment that finds the entire cast reaching "Up, up, up, high as the stars!"

The prelude concludes with a bold, brassy, strutting, syncopated theme which serves as the personal theme of the supremely confident outlaw Ramerrez, and within the body of the opera it makes its first appearance in Act One, in one of the most thrilling entrances in all of opera: the arrival of the road agent at the Polka Saloon.

The orchestra is silent for one bar as the curtain rises to reveal the interior of the Polka. Along with the expected card tables and bar, there is a balcony that runs the length of the back wall. A sign under the balcony points the way to an adjoining dance hall. A ladder leans against the balcony, so the bartender can climb up in case of trouble. An empty whiskey keg at the bar serves as a safe. Tacked on a wall is a "Wanted" poster from Wells Fargo, advertising a $5,000 reward for the road agent Ramerrez, or information leading to his capture. There is a large door in the back wall, and near it is a big window. Through these we can see the trees of the valley, and the snow-capped peaks of the distant mountains. Sundown is fast approaching, and the outside light is rapidly fading.

Sitting at a table close to the footlights is Sheriff Jack Rance, whose glowing cigar is a bright spot in the dim light of the saloon. At right, a miner named Jim Larkens, who has not made a strike so far, is sitting glumly on a cask, head in hands. During the opening moments, Larkens stands up and takes a letter from his pocket, and after looking at it sadly goes to the bar for a stamp. After sticking on the stamp and dropping the letter in the mailbox, he sits on the cask again. (Like all the other miners, and Rance as well, Larkens is one whose decision to reach out for gold has cost him dearly. Larkens is a Vacillator, and his grief over the resulting loss of his family marks him as one who is ripe for repentance.) Offstage voices of other miners can be heard shouting greetings and questions as to where to go for the evening ("To the Polka?" "To the Palmetto?"), and a solo oboe begins a gently rocking figure, the Polka Theme, that brings to mind the plodding of a tired horse.

From off stage, a baritone sings the opening line of the first significant melody within the body of the opera: the American folk song, "Echoes From Home." "Là lontano, là lontano, quanto piangera," he sings: "Far away, far away, how she'll weep." The words refer to the singer's mother, and he is imagining her tears of sorrow, should he never return home. Time and again characters will refer to loved ones who are far away, or will express the desire to *go* far away. At the beginning of the opera the words seem straightforward, referring to the lonely miners' longing to be reunited with their families, but as the story progresses, both "Echoes From Home" and the concept of "far away" will begin to take on different meanings. The opening bars of "Echoes" — the music covering the words, "Là lontano, là lontano, quantio piangera," can be heard, only slightly altered, in the Love Duet, carrying the line, "How sweet it is to live and die, and never part again." "Echoes From Home" is the first of the six finale melodies. It signifies Loneliness, and being that it is almost the last music played in the finale, this theme essentially brackets the entire opera.

Nick the bartender now enters and begins to light the lamps. According to Belasco, Nick "...wears 'Frisco trousers, very high-heeled boots, a flashy necktie, a gay velvet vest. He combs his hair over his forehead in a cowlick." The music of the opening scene, in which the dim light of dusk is gradually relieved as one by one Nick lights the lamps, has a strange, dreamy quality, to which the ripples of a harp and the sighing of strings contribute greatly. Some have remarked that it doesn't seem descriptive of a saloon in the old West, and they are right. This music describes, as Puccini's "sundown" music always does, "The hour of waking dreams, when hope struggles with melancholy."

As soon as Nick is finished with the lamps, the door is flung open, and in come Harry, Bello (Handsome), Joe, and others of the miners of Cloudy Mountain. Entering with them is a strong and purposeful piece of utility music in 2/4 that carries the fragmentary conversation as the men vigorously greet one another, and call for whiskey and cigars after their hard day of mining. They could have gone to the bar at the nearby Palmetto, which is attached to a restaurant and rooming house, but the Palmetto's bar is pretty miserable — nothing like the cozy and friendly Polka, which Minnie has aspired to make "a real home for the boys." (A sign proclaiming this sentiment hangs on the wall in Belasco.)

Another notable feature of both the play and the novel is the extremely childlike behavior of the miners, who are always called "boys," and often behave like such. Perhaps Belasco felt it necessary to characterize them in this way so that Rance would provide the only real competition to Johnson as a suitor for Minnie.[7]

A minor theme of *The Girl* is the fluidity of identity in the old West, where no one travels under his right name. Most of the Polka crowd have names that are obvious pseudonyms—Sonora, Trinidad, Handsome, Happy, and so on. "Sid" is short for "The Sidney Duck." Johnson has two identities, and even Minnie Falconer (who is usually called simply "The Girl") isn't sure of her own last name, for her father sometimes called himself "Smith." In part this may be romantic myth-making by Belasco, but it's also a plot device. The lack of concern in Cloudy as to people's real identity allows Minnie to brush off Rance's demand that Johnson identify himself and state his business. At the same time, it seems isolating. The more familiar one is with the opera, the more the pseudonyms seem to contribute to the atmosphere of loneliness.

Continuing with the technique he began in *Butterfly*, Puccini piques our interest about the heroine by having one character after another anticipate her entrance. The first instance is Bello's question of Nick, as to how Minnie is doing today. (She's fine.) A game of faro is suggested, with Sid to act as banker. To a boisterous fragment of melody, Sonora, Trinidad, and several other miners now enter. Sonora greets the downcast Larkens, who answers gloomily. The card game begins.

In a scene created by the librettists, Jack Rance speaks now, asking Nick what the matter is with Larkens. This question is carried by the first prelude theme—the one that seems to be connected with the lust for gold. Continuing with the same music, Nick responds that Larkens is homesick, grieving for the mother who waits for him, far away. Rance knows the laws of Puccini's World, and responds, "What a damned country this Golden West is." Nick understands, and says, "Gold poisons the blood of everyone who looks at it." Rance, who is the gold-poisoned Alberich of this opera, gets up, but before he leaves he piques our interest in the heroine, remarking that Minnie is very late tonight.

Attention shifts to the card game, but soon Nick announces, to several bars of rather mincing dance music, "Into the dance hall, boys. They want to dance." ("They" refers to a group of men from the Ridge, a rival mining camp.) Some of the men gladly exit to the dance hall, but Sonora, addressing his friend Trin, sneers, "Dance? They're crazy. I don't dance with men!" Trin agrees.

Sonora turns to Nick, and in a low voice asks whether Minnie has decided to accept him as a suitor. "Sure!" says Nick confidently. Assured he is Minnie's favorite, Sonora orders cigars for everyone, which pleases the avaricious little bartender greatly. A moment later, Trin approaches Nick and asks the same question Sonora did. Receiving the same answer, Trin happily calls for drinks all around, and Nick gleefully fills the order.

We now hear the offstage voice of Jake Wallace, the camp minstrel. "What will my old folks do," he sings, beginning "Echoes From Home" in earnest, "far away, far away, what will they do? Sad and lonely, my old folks will cry and think that I'll never return." Wallace's voice grows louder as he approaches the saloon. Nick announces him to the miners, and the minstrel enters, singing and accompanying himself on a banjo.[8]

Jake Wallace is quite a sight, at least in Belasco, who describes him thus: "...his face [is] half blackened. He wears a long minstrel's duster over his heavy coat, flapping shoes, and a 'stovepipe' hat. He is the typical camp minstrel." The word "minstrel" is used in the sense of the minstrel show. In other words, Wallace does a blackface act.

The words of "Echoes From Home" affect the miners deeply, and they join Wallace as he sings the remainder of the song. Many Americans seem to find this scene either laughable or nauseating, especially when, at the conclusion of the song, the homesick Larkens is driven into a frenzy of weeping, during which he confesses he can't take mining any longer, and wants to go home. He's sick of the pickaxe and the mine; he wants the plow, and his mother. One has to blame Belasco for the words, for they're all his — all except Larkens' desire for "my mother." In Belasco it was "my folks." Words aside, one has to admire the beauty of the music, and acknowledge how good Puccini was at composing for the chorus.

When Larkens breaks down sobbing, his startled friends ask him what's wrong. He begins his explanation, but halfway through he pauses for a moment. During the pause, the music of the first prelude theme recurs — that of the consequences of succumbing to the lust for gold — and it continues for a moment, carrying Larkens' declaration that he's fed up with mining.

Having finished with his explanation, Larkens resumes weeping. The music of "Echoes From Home" — the Loneliness Theme — thunders forth, and Sonora takes up a collection to send Jim home. Sonora's outstretched hat is soon filled with money, which he offers to Larkens along with a suggestion that he buck up. (Again, money is not inevitably evil in Puccini's World. Being that this money is to be used to get someone home to his family, it isn't contaminating, the way money for luxuries would be.) Larkens takes the money, thanks the boys, and leaves. As he stumbles out of the Polka, tears in his eyes, the miners vocalize the conclusion to "Echoes From Home."

This is a rather remarkable scene. It began with a group expressing shared sadness at being apart from loved ones who are far away. The feeling of sadness intensified as the focus was narrowed to one particular person, then the situation turned partially around so that even though the one person was starting off home so as to reunite with his loved ones, both he and the group ended up expressing even more sadness than when the scene began. Is there no possibility of happiness?

To be fair, the libretto is simply following the play — Belasco's Larkens is also crying as he leaves — and the music has to follow the libretto, but it's hard to avoid the feeling that by the time Puccini was composing this opera, hope was losing its struggle with melancholy. As for The Boys, they liked Larkens and it was a touching moment, but now it's done. The utility music returns as the miners resume gambling.

Bello now catches Sid with a card up his sleeve. Sonora pulls his gun, and the miners start baying for Sid's blood. They want to hang the card cheat, but just as they're deciding to "string him," Sheriff Rance reenters and takes charge. He takes out his handkerchief and delicately unfolds it, carefully flicking it over his boots as he calmly listens to the accusations.

Rance thinks being a gentleman involves such ostentatiously fastidious gestures as flicking specks of dust off polished boots with a snow-white handkerchief. An unworldly young woman like Minnie would naturally be impressed by this pseudo-elegant behavior, until she met a real gentleman — a man with what she terms "style."

As the gloomy Rance's Theme is introduced, the sheriff declares hanging too good for Sid. "What's death?" he asks. "A kick in the dark and good night." The theme is thus associated with the idea of violence and death. On several occasions the conversation between Rance and Minnie will be carried by Rance's Theme, and with this device Puccini ensures that we recoil from the idea of Rance as a suitable partner for Minnie.

Rance demands the two of spades, and taking a pin from Sid's cravat, he pins the card on Sid's coat, right over his heart—"like a flower," says Rance. "This is a token," the sheriff explains. Sid can't play cards again, and (adds Belasco) he can't leave the camp. This seems a puzzling scene. Why doesn't Rance agree to the hanging? What's with the card? Belasco needed Sid alive, for he has work for Sid, and the playing card, to do.

Hoping to be allowed to play cards again, Sid will (in the play, not the opera) go up to Minnie's cabin shortly before Johnson gets there, and will ask her to intercede for him. When she angrily refuses, not wanting anything to do with a card cheat, Sid leaves and goes back down the trail. On his way down, he sees Johnson heading up towards Minnie's cabin. Trying to get back in the good graces of Rance and the miners, he tells them what he saw. It is Sid's report that brings the posse up to Minnie's cabin, where they reveal Johnson's true identity to her.

Near the end of the play, Sid makes his final appearance. By this time Minnie too has cheated at cards, and has realized that at some point everyone is in need of forgiveness. Unable to bring herself to confess her own wrongdoing, she asks the boys if they can forgive Sid, and she unpins the card from his coat.

Tightening up the action, Puccini jettisons almost all of this. He leaves in the business of Rance pinning the card over Sid's heart, but that's the end of him. Sid is never seen again in the opera, and all that remains of his activity from the play is his report to Nick (heard at second hand) that he saw Johnson heading up towards Minnie's cabin.

Some productions of *Fanciulla* dispense with the cheating scene, which is a big mistake on both dramatic and musical grounds. From the standpoint of plot, the threatened hanging of Sid mentally primes us for Johnson's possible execution in the last act. As for music, we need the cheating scene for the introduction of Rance's Theme, where it becomes associated with the subject of death.

The distressed Sid is kicked out of the bar. Rance moves things on by suggesting a game of poker, but before the game can get started, Ashby, the Wells Fargo agent, enters. Ashby's entrance theme, played by oboe, cor anglais, clarinet, and horns, resembles Ramerrez' Theme, but it lacks that sense of fire, youth, and strut that so distinguishes the outlaw's theme. Belasco describes Ashby as a man to remember. He seems nervous and dogged, and his movements and speech are quick. He has short white hair, black eyebrows, and very thin lips. He too wears 'Frisco-style clothing, but his shows the wear and tear of the road. Ashby drinks constantly, but while he is never sober, he is also never drunk. When roused to action, his features are startlingly savage.

Ashby orders a drink, and reminding the audience of the as yet unseen heroine, he asks how the Girl is. (She's fine, thank you.) Ashby has come to Cloudy because of Nina Micheltoreña. Furious at having been given the brush-off by Ramerrez, she approached Ashby, who was sniffing around the Mexican settlement's dance hall in hopes of catching the scent of the road agent. Nina told Ashby she would meet him the following night at Cloudy, at the Palmetto, where in exchange for the $5,000 reward, she would tell him how he could take Ramerrez. (All this takes place only in the novel. In the opera, Ashby has stopped in at the Polka because he happened to be in the neighborhood. He will not learn about Nina's offer until the Pony Express Rider enters and brings him a letter from Nina, requesting a meeting tonight.) Incidentally, Nina's name may be a sort of joke on Belasco's part. Niña means "girl" in Spanish, thus both Minnie and Nina are "the girl."

The Wells Fargo man and the sheriff don't like each other, but they respect certain qualities they have in common. Rance is the one who brings up the subject of the road agent, asking Ashby what news there is of him. "They say he robs you like a fine gentleman," the sheriff notes. This is partly a comment about Ramerrez, and partly a comment about Rance. Everyone has heard about the road agent's strangely courteous behavior, but these reports have excited the sheriff's attention in a personal way, because he likes to think of himself as a gentleman. He will be very upset when the so-called Mr. Johnson arrives and shows him up in front of Minnie. Rance's intense desire to be perceived as a gentleman is what will cause him to accept without question Minnie's apparent winning of the card game in Act Two; that, and his certainty that Minnie is incapable of dishonesty.

Pursuing the subject of the road agent, Rance asks Ashby whether the man is a Spaniard. No one knows, says Ashby, but it is known that his gang consists of Spaniards and Mexicans. The Wells Fargo agent has had three hard months of searching for Ramerrez' gang, and he takes his sleep when he can get it. He asks to be awakened when the Pony Express arrives, then exits to a room at right so he can lie down for a while. Nick now brings a tray of drinks to the table where Rance is sitting with Trin and others who took him up on his offer of a poker game. The drinks—whiskey, hot water, and lemon extract—are from Minnie, Nick reports. Everyone cheers "Our Minnie!" who the sheriff declares will soon be Mrs. Rance.

Aware of how this sounds to Sonora and Trin, Nick shoots each a soothing look. The orchestra begins to prepare for a fight as Sonora tells Rance that Minnie is joking with him. "She makes you look like a Chinaman!" says the miner tauntingly. (Belasco uses this expression to signify one who is easily made a fool of, or who makes a fool of himself.)

Rance has a rule about ignoring a drunk's insults. As the orchestra blares an excited version of the violent Rance's Theme, which threatens death, the angry sheriff stands up. "Boy, it's the whiskey talking," he tells Sonora contemptuously. Sonora's friends try to calm him, but he leaps to his feet and advances threateningly.

The insults begin to fly. Miners who had been in the dance hall now pour into the bar. The enraged Rance reaches for his revolver, and seeing this Sonora quickly pulls his own pistol. Trin grabs Sonora's arm just as he's pulling the trigger. Four pounding notes from timpani and bass drum help to emphasize the shot (two before it, and two after it), and the bullet goes wild.

At this exciting moment the big door of the bar is flung wide, and Minnie herself appears. For a moment she stands in the doorway, all eyes on her, as the full orchestra, playing *fff*, gives out Minnie's Theme, which is the second of the six finale themes. At this moment Minnie's Theme is simply entrance music, but at the end of this act the words, "You have the face of an angel" become attached to it.

According to Belasco, Minnie is attired "in a coarse, blue skirt, and rough, white flannel blouse, cut away and held in place at the throat by a crimson ribbon ... it was not difficult to see why the boys of Cloudy Mountain Camp had a feeling which fell little short of adoration for this sun-browned maid, with the spirit of the mountain in her eyes." Right now, however, Puccini has her eyes snapping with anger at the sound of fighting in her saloon. Minnie strides over to Sonora and snatches the pistol. "What's happened?" she demands. "You again, Sonora?"

This dramatic scene of Minnie's entrance is a big departure from Belasco, who didn't allow the Rance/Sonora argument to reach the point of gunfire. Just as it was approaching that moment, Belasco had Nick notice that the Girl was in the dance hall, and was heading for the bar. He warned everyone she was coming, and urged them to pick up their drinks. The quarrel ended at once, and when Minnie entered a moment later, the Polka was as quiet as a library.

From the moment of her entrance until the arrival of Johnson, Belasco has Minnie acting the part of the businesswoman. She's constantly selling drinks and cigars, issuing orders to Nick, making change, and making sure she gets the best of every financial transaction. Puccini's cutting of all this bustling and sordid mercantile business made a big improvement in the scene.

Minnie scolds the boys for cutting up in her place (although Rance, who fades into the background for a few minutes, isn't a target of her anger). She threatens to stop giving them schooling, and like chastened children the miners plead, "No, Minnie!" Sonora explains these things only happen when she's late, for then they get bored, and, well...

A little scene of tribute presentation ensues. It was inspired by a scene in the play, which Puccini altered and expanded. In the original, Minnie has occasion to give Ashby some change. He returns it to her, telling her to buy herself a ribbon over at the Ridge, compliments of Wells Fargo. Irritated, Sonora throws a stack of silver dollars onto the bar and tells Minnie to buy herself *two* ribbons at the Ridge. He stares at Ashby and says challengingly, "Fawn's **my** color!"

Puccini eschews the one-upmanship, not to mention the vulgar and unseemly use of cash, and has several of the boys offer Minnie things they had been waiting to give her. Significantly, the first present offered, by Joe, is a bunch of wildflowers. "In my country," he says, "there are a lot of these." This is of course a perfect first tribute to the Lady of the Rose. We are well beyond the old cliché of "enter chaste heroine, with flowers," yet Puccini made certain Minnie was associated with flowers as quickly as possible.

The next tribute comes from Sonora, who takes a red ribbon from his pocket, telling Minnie he got this today from a hawker who came to the camp from San Francisco. It's deep red, he points out, like her lips. Last comes Harry, who takes out a silk handkerchief, blue, like Minnie's eyes. Note the Pucciniesque character of the latter gifts. The ribbon and handkerchief are described as being beautiful not because they are made of silk or lace, but because they resemble some natural beauty of Minnie's—her lips and her eyes. Neither of the *Fanciulla* librettists was involved in *Bohème*, yet the sentiment is the same: eyes are more beautiful than the most stupendous jewels.

The gentle, lilting music of the tribute presentation establishes the relationship between Minnie and the good-hearted men of Cloudy Mountain, and we will hear a reminiscence of it near the end of this act, where it suggests Minnie's belief that Johnson is a man of similar good character. Minnie thanks the boys, then Ashby reenters, pours a glass of whiskey, and offers it to Minnie, compliments of Wells Fargo. (Notice how this device of Wells Fargo buying the drink keeps the audience from considering Ashby to be a suitor of Minnie's.) She takes a sip then returns the glass to Ashby. She offers Ashby his choice of a variety of cigars, and in contrast to Belasco's Ashby, who says indifferently, "Any'll do," Puccini's man gallantly answers that it doesn't matter which kind, for each will have been perfumed by the hand that touched it.

Nick suggests Minnie work the room, for her smiles sell drinks. "Wicked talker," she reproves him. As she utters this, and turns to greet the sheriff, we hear Rance's Theme, which Puccini has neatly tied to the reproof. To the uneasy music of Rance's Theme, Minnie bids the sheriff a good evening. He answers politely, but there is clearly some discomfort between them, and neither pursues conversation. Minnie has nothing to say to Rance, and what he has to say to her requires more privacy.

One bit of the business transactions remains from Belasco, and that is Sonora's handing a sack of gold dust to Minnie. Part is to be used to pay his bar tab, and the rest is to be placed into the keg that serves as the camp's bank. This was left in so as to transition the conversation to the subject of the road agent.

Noticing Sonora handing over his dust, Ashby declares it foolish to keep so much gold around when there's a bandit about. And there really is a big stash in the keg. Sonora alone has banked $10,000 worth of dust, and that's only his takings for this month. There is some conflict in Belasco, and it spread to Puccini, regarding the financial condition of the miners. Most of the time the men are made out to be slaving for the benefit of impoverished loved ones, far away, but even in Puccini there is quite enough gold in the keg to be worth Ramerrez' time. Belasco also has some of the miners evading *former* loved ones—Handsome, for example, has at least two wives back East somewhere, and Trin has a *widow* in Sacramento. In Puccini, only the diamond-wearing, gold-poisoned Jack Rance has been up to such tricks.

Puccini always tried to eliminate clutter, but he was also aiming to present a consistent picture of the miners as poor, because in his World, rich people are bad and unworthy of love. His miners are working for money to buy the necessities of life for their far away loved ones, and the irony is that the search for gold has cut them off from those loved ones. As we will see in the mail-reading scene, every day brings the men new and painful proofs of the loss of love.

Minnie now takes a Bible from a drawer at the bar. Sonora, Trin, Harry, Joe, and a few others group around her on benches, and wait, restless and noisy, as she thumbs through the book, looking for her place. A simple but exquisite little theme begins as Minnie looks for her bookmark. Launched by solo flute and a harp playing harmonics, this is another of Puccini's "stepping" themes. For three bars, flute and harp walk gently up the scale, then clarinets join them to repeat the walk. The little theme momentarily dissolves, and Minnie finds her place, at the 51st psalm of David.

The attention of the miners is wandering, and Minnie claps her hands for silence. The little theme resumes, now played by piccolo, flute, harp, and celeste. Minnie asks Harry whether he recalls who David was, and Harry gives an answer that has David killing Goliath with the jawbone of an ass. Trin and the orchestra bray like jackasses, annoying Harry. Minnie laughs at the muddle Harry has made of the story, then prepares to read the psalm's second verse.

Muted strings accompany Minnie as she reads, "Sprinkle me with hyssop and I shall be clean...." Trin interrupts, and artlessly asks what hyssop is. (It's an herb used in purification rites.) Minnie says it's a plant that grows in the East (on which word the triangle gives a little shimmer), and when Joe asks if it doesn't grow around here, Minnie tells him a sprig of it grows in everyone's heart.

She continues reading. "Wash me and I will be white as snow, place within my breast a pure heart, and renew in me an elect spirit." (This is what Minnie's Theme, and the associated words, "You have the face of an angel," refer to: not transitory physical beauty, but the pure heart and elect spirit of one who is without sin.)

Closing the book, Minnie sings to the first prelude theme (which by now clearly represents the taking of a wrong path and the need for healing) as she begins to explain the meaning of the passage. "That means, boys, that nowhere in the world is there a sinner whose way to redemption is barred." To new music she adds, "Let each of you keep within you this supreme truth of ..." and now a section of the Loneliness Theme, "Echoes From Home," begins as she utters the final word "...love."

It's the Puccini Mixture again, for words that should inspire joy are followed by music of intense sadness, that carries a memory of the words, "Far away, far away, how she'll weep." Everyone sits in silent thought, as flute, harp, and celeste, neatly bracketing the scene, take a final walk up the scale.

A charming transition occurs, as upper woodwinds and strings play an excited little passage that heralds Nick's announcement of the Pony Express Rider. "The mail! The mail!" is the happy cry from Trin, Joe, Harry, and Bello. (Unfortunately for them, the mail will prove thoroughly depressing.) A moment later bassoons, solo horn, drum, and strings play horsy-sounding music, which soon fades beneath a "Mail" theme, to which the Rider enters.

In addition to mail, the Rider has some news (in the play). There was a big holdup last night at the Forks! "Ramerrez!" he assures the Polka crowd. He urges everyone to watch out, for he saw a Mexican on the trail. (That was Jose Castro, Ramerrez' right-hand man. The plan is for Jose to allow himself to be captured by the men of Cloudy Mountain, and lead them off on a wild goose chase, leaving the Polka and its gold unprotected, at which point Ramerrez and the others will politely rob the place. Jose will then slip away from his captors and rejoin the gang.)

The mail that's delivered in the play doesn't amount to much — a newspaper for Sonora, and some unspecified letters. Belasco brings the Rider into the play for one reason: so that Ashby can bring up the name of Nina Micheltoreña. In the play, Ashby asks the Rider if he drops mail at the Mexican settlement, and when the Rider says he does, Ashby asks if he knows a girl there named Nina Micheltoreña. Ashby wants to intercept any letters addressed to her. Minnie then makes some deprecating remarks about Nina.

Puccini's biggest change to this scene was in having the Rider deliver depressing letters for Happy, Bello, and Joe. Harry gets a newspaper filled with news of calamities, Sonora gets nothing, and Ashby gets a dispatch, through which he learns for the first time that Nina wants to meet with him at the Palmetto so she can sell out Ramerrez. As in the play, Minnie makes her derisive remark about the local bad girl: "She's a phony Spaniard, native of Cachuca. A siren who uses lampblack to give herself a languid eye. Ask the boys about her!" Trin and Sonora, embarrassed, make gestures of denial.

Ashby describes the contents of the dispatch to Rance, who urges him not to trust Nina. With a wink, Ashby reassures him: "Revenge of a woman in love." Saying he intends to keep the appointment, Ashby exits with Rance.

The mail-reading begins. To a delicate rendition of the "Mail" music, the boys read parts of their letters, and the newspaper, aloud. The music isn't sad and lonely, but all the news is. Happy's parrot misses him. Bello's Katy is getting married. Harry's newspaper is filled with stories of disaster, and he wonders what everyone is doing back home — "Are they all right?"

As for Joe, his letter brings him the worst news of all. His friends urge him, "Bad news? Courage!" Sad and angry, Joe throws his cap on the floor, saying, "And now grandma's gone, too." A final, shimmering version of the "Mail" music accompanies Joe as he goes to the bar and demands whiskey. Minnie gives it to him in silence, and he downs it and exits to the dance hall, followed by all the other miners. (Joe's shout for whiskey can be misinterpreted as a sort of shrugging "Oh, well," on the part of what is actually a deeply distressed man.)

Nick enters, and tells Minnie there's a stranger outside. "Who is it?" asks Minnie, piquing our interest in the offstage person. Nick has never seen him before. "He looks like he's from San Francisco." Not only is this fellow a stranger, he has placed an order for whiskey-and-water. Minnie thinks this a strange concoction, and to a brief reiteration of the Polka Theme, Nick assures her he told the fellow, "at the Polka, we drink our whiskey straight."

Minnie declares the stranger will take his whiskey straight or git. Nick reports the stranger will do neither, and he chuckles in anticipation of what Minnie will do. "For much less than this," Belasco tells us, "...many a man had been disciplined by the Girl." Minnie tells Nick to send the stranger in, and she'll curl his hair for him. Nick exits to the Polka Theme.

During the eight bars of music that follow Minnie's order, she and Rance engage in a small, mimed, contest of wills. Rance pays for a cigar with a twenty dollar gold piece, and Minnie gives him his change. He pushes the change back at her; she looks at it scornfully and pushes it back at him. He picks the money up and drops it into an ash receptacle. Tipping Minnie with the change is a common occurrence at the Polka. It's only Rance's change that Minnie rejects, because she knows his feelings for her are getting out of control.

Four bars into this mimed scene, we hear the now familiar Rance's Theme, the gloomy music of which is immediately followed by Rance's declaration, "I love you, Minnie." With an indifferent smile, Minnie tells him not to talk like that, and like a true Puccini Alberich, who knows only two ways of obtaining the company of the Lady of the Rose, Rance, to a passage of new music, offers Minnie a thousand dollars for a kiss. It's really very sad, because Rance's love, poisoned though it is, is genuine. (Contrary to what's often been written about him, Rance is not a villain, and he bears no relationship to Scarpia. Rance is a pitiable character.)

The dark and lyrical music of this exchange between Rance and Minnie will recur in Act Two, when Rance enters Minnie's cabin, gun in hand, looking for the wounded Dick Johnson. This wasn't a labor saving device; the music recurs because the conversation between Rance and Minnie in that scene is a continuation of the conversation in this scene, driven by Rance's love, disappointment, and jealousy. It doesn't matter that at this point he knows nothing of Johnson, for he knows Minnie's feelings for him have cooled. He knows she met someone new in Monterey.

Naturally, Minnie is insulted at Rance's offer of gold in exchange for love, and she rejects it. Rance urges practical reasons Minnie should accept him: there's too much money coming into the Polka for her to run the place alone. "I'll marry you," he offers.

Minnie has a good rejoinder: "And your wife, what will she say?" At this point we see the first of several notable parallels between *The Girl of the Golden West* and *Madama Butterfly*. The reason Belasco burdened Rance with a wife is that he was trying to establish Minnie as someone who was looking for a man who was different from, and superior to, the ones she knew. (In fact, the novelist makes it clear that a significant factor in the love between Minnie and Johnson, both of whom had lived in very homogeneous communities, is the sheer novelty each represented for the other.)

Belasco has Minnie point out Rance is already married, then has her add that Handsome has two wives and Trin has a "widow" (obviously he sent her false word of his own death). In Minnie's idealistic view, Johnson is completely different from these men, just as Butterfly had an idealistic view of Pinkerton as completely different from the men of Japan.

All the men Minnie knows marry wife after wife, and stay true to no one. Like Butterfly, she is looking for the man who will stay true, and that is precisely what she is talking about in her upcoming aria, "Laggiu nel Soledad." Minnie's requirement of Johnson that he be a man with a virgin heart, who will love only once, and forever, takes on a new angle if we view the *Fanciulla* couple through the lens of *Butterfly*, and we will see several other parallels as we go through the rest of the story, including a really touching scene between Minnie and Johnson near the end, that parallels Butterfly's aria, "Un bel dì."

First, however, Rance gets to sing his only aria, "Minnie, dalla mia casa." There's no source for the lines in Belasco, and undoubtedly Puccini had them written because the baritone had to have at least one solo. The theme of this sad and bitter aria is Alberich's Choice — Rance's devotion to gold.

Minnie gently asks Rance if he is angry with her, and if so, why? Rance throws down his deck of cards, and in a harsh and edgy voice sings "Minnie, dalla mia casa," describing how he left his home beyond the mountains, with no one mourning his departure, and him shedding no tears at leaving. No one has ever loved him, he says, and he has never loved anyone. His heart is that of a gambler: embittered, poisoned. "I set out," he sings, "attracted only by the spell of gold. And this is the only thing that's never deceived me. Now, for your kiss, I'd spend a fortune!" We'll hear a fragment of this aria in Act Two when the anguished Rance, filled with jealousy, pleads with Minnie to tell him she doesn't love Johnson.

Poor Rance, thinking the Lady of the Rose would trade her love for gold. Only a man who never mentions money, and who appears not to have more than enough to cover necessities, has a chance of winning a Puccini heroine's love. Rance's proposition causes Minnie to think back on something, and dreamily she responds in a monotone chant, "Love is something different." Rance has no understanding of what she means, and derisively he snaps, "Poetry!"

"Laggiu nel Soledad" is a quasi-aria built on lines from Belasco. A solo violin has a leading part in Minnie's nostalgic recollection of her childhood, and of the parents whose deep love shaped her view of what relations between husbands and wives should be. As we will later see, Johnson's view of what love should be was shaped by his reading of Dante's *Vita nuova* — a collection of 31 poems on the subject of Dante's consuming love for Beatrice, whom the poet saw as the instrument of his spiritual salvation. Johnson will come to see Minnie in the same way — as not only his beloved but as the instrument of his spiritual (and physical) salvation. The lines that went into "Laggiu nel Soledad" are meant to pave the way for the discussion of *Vita nuova* in Act Two.

Lacking Johnson's education, Minnie phrases her sentiments about love in an artless way. She recalls the cheap room in which she lived as a child. It was a saloon, where Minnie's mother cooked and tended bar, and her father dealt cards. Minnie used to sit under the card table, hoping for dropped coins she could pick up and spend on candy. (Puccini has a "ping" from the triangle represent the dropping of a coin as Minnie recalls this.) In Belasco, Minnie's conclusion is that that life was a little heaven, and she sums things up by telling Rance, "I couldn't share that table an' the Polka with any man — unless there was a heap o' carin' back of it. I couldn't, Jack, I couldn't."

There is such warmth in Puccini's little aria, a recollection of love so different from the cold bitterness of Rance's early life, where no one cared for him, and he cared for no one. The entire orchestra joins in near the end, swelling to *ff* as Minnie sings, "They loved each other so much," and with an ecstatic high C as she tears poor Rance's heart out with her final line, "Ah, I too would like to find a man, and I sure would love him."

Belasco's Rance is angered by Minnie's dream of romantic love, and saddened by it, and in a dejected voice he says the boys were right—"I am a Chinaman." Minnie protests, for she likes Rance and is sorry to hurt him. Although she tries not to raise his hopes he reacts strongly to the gentleness in her voice, saying, "Once when I rode in here it was nothing but Jack, Jack, Jack Rance. By the Eternal, I nearly got you then! ... Then you went on that trip to Sacramento and Monterey, and you were different." He sees the way she starts at this, and jealously adds, "I suppose he's one o' them high-toned Sacramento shrimps! ... Do you think he'd have you?"

Puccini cut this insulting line, tightening the action by having Rance move toward Minnie with a violent gesture, just as she is finishing her song. There's no real conclusion to her aria, for Rance picks up her final note and makes it his as, in a threatening voice, he accuses, "Perhaps, Minnie, you've already found your pearl?"

Rance's last word is still hanging in the air as the doors of the Polka are violently thrown open, and in one of the most effective entrances in all of opera, in strides Dick Johnson—Minnie's "pearl"—accompanied by his strutting motif, saddle over his shoulder, his eyes blazing with anger. "Who's going to 'curl my hair' for me?" he demands. His voice is "incisive and harsh, with scarcely a trace of the musical tones she recollected so well," but Minnie recognizes at once the handsome caballero she left back on the road from Monterey. "Why, howdy do, stranger!" she exclaims joyfully.

There is nothing in the appearance of the half–American Johnson that would suggest he is the road agent for whom Ashby has been searching. When Minnie last saw him, he had been attired like a Spanish gentleman, but now Johnson is dressed—"in the very latest fashion prevailing among the Americans in Sacramento in '49 ... on his head was a soft, brown hat—large, but not nearly the proportions of a sombrero; a plain, rough tweed coat and a waistcoat of a darker tan, which showed a blue flannel shirt beneath it; and his legs were encased in boots topped by dark brown leggings. In a word, his get-up resembled closely the type of American referred to disdainfully by the miner of that time as a Sacramento guy...."

Rance's attention is devoted to taking in Johnson from head to foot, so he misses the joyful tone of Minnie's greeting, and the answering look of recognition as Johnson wheels around at the sound of her voice. Johnson begins to regret the challenging words of his entrance, yet Rance's insolent scrutiny and the Girl's presence make it impossible for him to backtrack. As a compromise, he says tentatively, "I'm the man who wanted water in his whiskey." Nick is eager to see the Girl take the stranger down a peg, but to his astonishment Minnie says to him reprovingly, "Nick, the gentleman takes his whiskey the way he likes it." Thinking the world must have come to an end, the bartender totters off to mix the drink.

The music of Johnson's Act Two confession aria, "Or son sei mesi," begins as Johnson inquires, "The girl of the camp?" With this he condenses a few lines in which the outlaw realizes to his dismay that after months of searching for her, the lovely girl from Monterey has turned up as the proprietor of the very saloon where he is about to ply his vocation. Puccini is acquainting us with another big tune as he gives us this beautiful, low-key rendition of "Or son sei mesi"— a piece of music that, if we only knew it, reveals that this man standing before us is the road agent!

Johnson's ruminations are interrupted by Rance, who has been looking on with knitted brows. The sheriff does not suspect the stranger of being the road agent, but his hostility is evident as he challenges him. Rance brusquely declares no strangers are allowed in the camp. When the newcomer ignores this Rance sneers, "Perhaps you're off the road; men often get mixed up when they're visiting Nina Micheltoreña on the back trail." The sheriff doesn't believe his accusation, but it annoys Minnie, who snaps out a protest. Dropping the music of "Or son sei mesi," Johnson declares he stopped in to rest his horse and to have a game of cards. The cards are Rance's domain, so when the stranger picks up the deck the sheriff had been shuffling he says harshly, "A game? And your name?"

Minnie gives a cynical laugh. When the stranger says his name is Johnson, she laughs again, and banteringly says, "Is what?" When Rance demands to know if that is all there is to his name, Johnson adds he is from Sacramento. Minnie extends her hand and welcomes Johnson of Sacramento. Rance starts, and says to himself, "The Sacramento shrimp, by all that is holy!"

Fuming, Rance moves off to one side. Nick exits. Minnie and Johnson converse in low voices, recalling their first meeting. He gave her a sprig of jasmine; he invited her to pick blackberries. And when she went on her way he said.... Embarrassed and shy, Minnie claims she can't remember. But Johnson knows she does remember. Encouragingly he says, "I said that from then on...."

"...you'd never forget me," finishes Minnie happily. Johnson assures Minnie he hadn't forgotten her, and she sadly tells him she had hoped for a long time he would come to the Polka. He points out he didn't know where she lived, and Minnie, recalling how she had delayed answering him until it was too late, is satisfied.

Unable to stand any more of the whispering, the jealous Rance comes over to the table. Accompanied by Rance's Theme, he knocks Johnson's glass of whiskey and water to the floor. As in his clash with Sonora, Rance vows that no one makes a fool of him, and he demands to know what Johnson's business is here. With a haughty look, Johnson backs up one step and begins to reach for his pistol. Minnie stops him with a gesture, and Johnson smiles and shrugs.

Being ignored infuriates Rance, who for the first time does something contemptible. He goes to the door of the dance hall, and in a loud voice calls that a stranger is here, refusing to explain his business. If one listens carefully, he will hear that the music to which Rance makes this statement comes from Minnie and Johnson's Act Two love duet — the line in which they vow, "I'll never leave you." In other words, while Rance claims his beef with Johnson is the man's refusal to state his business, his anger actually stems from his certainty that Johnson is the man who turned Minnie's heart away from him in Monterey.

The boys swarm in, ready for a fight, but Minnie holds up her hand and declares that she knows Johnson, and vouches for him. (Her having done this greatly adds to her anger in Act Two when she learns Johnson is the road agent. It is terribly embarrassing for her to realize she has vouched for a thief.) The miners want to please Minnie by making her friend feel welcome, and they haven't forgotten their dislike of Rance's ways. As the boys shake hands with the smiling, half-amused Johnson, their actions are accompanied by some warm and friendly music.

Harry makes a gesture towards the dance hall and issues an invitation: "Mr. Johnson, a waltz?" Johnson makes a low bow before Minnie, and requests the honor of this dance. The miners are astonished at this exhibit of "style," and for a moment it seems the sort of reaction Minnie had feared may be about to take place. The boys expect her to take the stranger down a peg, but to their amazement she accepts his invitation.

Puccini makes an interesting departure here from Belasco, in which Minnie declares that she doesn't know how to waltz, but she can polka. Puccini's heroine declares that she has never danced before in her life. When Minnie accepts Johnson's invitation to dance, she is granting him the first of three liberties she has never granted any man before. At the end of this act she will invite Johnson to visit her in her cabin, and in Act Two she will kiss him, and all of these are remarked on with great interest as things she has never done before. This series of three of course reinforces the characterization of Johnson as Minnie's "one and only." (Minnie also saves Johnson from violence three times—once in each act.)

A lilting waltz begins, played first by three clarinets, then by three flutes. There is little input from the orchestra, for Puccini wanted the music to be made by the miners, who sweetly vocalize the waltz with "la-la-la"s. As Rance fumes, Minnie and Johnson dance to the music being made by their friends, and gradually all dance off into the dance hall.

The music of the miners' waltz recurs several times throughout the opera, and it is the third of the six themes that feed into the finale. Puccini uses the waltz in scenes that depict the growing love of Minnie and Johnson, but what is ultimately more important is that it first appears in the scene in which the miners welcome Johnson and extend the hand of friendship, and it last appears when they decide to forgive him and release him from the hangman's noose. Its use in the finale suggests the waltz melody stands less for romantic love than for friendship, so it is the Brotherhood Theme. It is also a member of a family of themes, for it is related to the Aspirations Theme, which is first heard near the end of this act when Minnie relates her desire to rise "Up, up, up, high as the stars."

As soon as the miners finish singing, the music shifts from woodwinds to strings, and begins to take on a darker tone. The sense of "endless melody" and of surging dramatic action is enhanced by the segue into the next scene, for there is no definite point at which the waltz music ends, yet soon it is replaced by music of terrible violence and rage, expressive of the desire to murder.

Some time ago Nick left the saloon, and now he returns. Seeing only Rance, who is sitting at the table at right, he asks where Minnie has gone. Angrily, the sheriff answers that she is in the dance hall, "dancing with that fine-haired dog from Sacramento." From not far away, voices that rapidly grow louder can be heard shouting, "Hang him!" "Kill him!" The friendly waltz can still be heard beneath these savage cries, but now a huge crescendo begins, and the music of Brotherhood is lost as Rance and Nick rush to the door and look out. A 2/4 passage of *allegro feroce* begins, and Ashby and some miners burst into the Polka, shoving Jose Castro before them. A solo trombone adds to the sense of utter brutality as Ashby shouts, "Hang him! Hang him!"

Just as he and Ramerrez had planned, Jose Castro has allowed himself to be captured. Castro is a brave and clever man, as devoted to Ramerrez as he was to his father, but one would never know that from his behavior in this scene. He grovels before the Americans in apparent terror, and when he speaks his voice is a whine.

Ashby too appears quite different from the last time we saw him. "His hat," says Belasco, "was on the back of his head; his coat looked as if he had been engaged in some kind of a struggle; his hair was ruffled and long locks struggled down over his forehead; while his face wore a brutal, savage, pitiless, nasty look." (Evidently Belasco forgot he had introduced Ashby as a man with "closely cropped" hair.)

To his dismay, Castro sees his leader's saddle on the floor of the saloon. "He's been taken!" Castro says to himself, using on the last, almost spoken, word a decrescendo and a downward slide in pitch that proves a habitual and distinctive pattern of his speech. Ashby demands a whiskey from Nick. It's cold outside, and the Wells Fargo man is beginning to feel unpleasantly sober.

Rance grabs Castro's hair and pulls back his head roughly. The sheriff has never seen the Mexican before, but he accuses him of being one of the Ramerrez gang. Sonora, Trin, and Joe come in from the dance hall. In a frightened voice, Castro says he ran away from Ramerrez, whom he hates, and he can put the miners on his track. He swears he isn't lying.

Eager to capture Ramerrez, Rance asks the prisoner if he knows where the hideout is. Castro says it is a mile away in the Madrona Canyon, and if many men come with him, Ramerrez can be taken. "I'll plant my knife in his back," vows Castro, and on the last word we hear a descending, four-note motif that signifies the piercing whistle with which the members of the band signal each other.

Rance is in favor of the idea, probably because Ashby is not. Ashby's hopes of capturing Ramerrez are pinned on his upcoming meeting with Nina. He warns that bad weather is brewing, and upper woodwinds describe the swirl of snow. To Rance's surprise, Sonora and Trin take his part. Rance orders Castro to be tied up, and as snow continues to swirl in the orchestra, Sonora and Trin call to everybody to saddle their horses.

Castro now glances into the dance hall, where, to his relief, he sees his boss dancing with a girl. More miners enter from the dance hall, asking where everyone is going. "After Ramerrez!" shouts Rance. Nick asks, "What about the gold?" Sonora answers that Minnie will guard their treasure. Everyone but Nick exits to saddle the horses.

Castro must attract his boss's attention, so in a loud voice, marked by strongly rolling r's, he demands a drink. "Aguardiente!!" he cries, and woodwinds and brass give the motif of The Whistle. Nick goes to fetch a glass of brandy. Ramerrez quickly comes in from the dance hall. While listening to Castro, he picks up his saddle and pretends to adjust the stirrups.

Everything is going according to plan, says the Mexican softly. Their men are hiding nearby. When the posse has gone, one of the band will whistle. As soon as Ramerrez whistles back, the men will come help him do the job. When enough time has passed, Castro will slip away from the posse, and rejoin the band.

Having made their preparations, Rance and some of the miners reenter, and drag Castro out. Rance is the last to go, and he shoots Johnson a rabid look as he does. Nick wishes the posse good luck, and begins to close the saloon. The first of the prelude themes is heard, apparently describing the lust for gold. Nick eyes Johnson suspiciously, puts out the lamp on the faro table, then exits to extinguish the lights in the dance hall.

Over a soft *ostinato* in the strings, a solo oboe plays a slow version of the waltz melody — the music of love and Brotherhood — as Johnson goes to the window and looks at the departing posse. It seems odd, and almost funny, to be observing these preparations for his own capture. He turns back to the saloon, which is silent now, and strangely depressing. Johnson thinks with distaste of why he came here. He walks slowly around the empty room, and when he notices the whiskey keg, which is clearly the bank he had intended to rob, he makes "a gesture of contempt," and moves to pick up his saddle. Puccini makes it clear

Johnson has decided to go on his way without robbing the Polka, and has also decided not to pursue a relationship with Minnie, who deserves better than a thief.

Minnie has been saying goodnight to the boys from the Ridge. She enters the saloon, and as the music of the waltz continues she asks Johnson if he has stayed behind to keep her company and help her guard the place. Perturbed, he answers, "If you like." Johnson frequently says things that are prompted by his guilty awareness that as a thief, he isn't good enough for Minnie, and she interprets these remarks as meaning that as a poorly educated woman, she isn't good enough for him. In the play, Johnson now says it seems strange to have found her at the Polka. What he means is, "here at this place I had intended to rob," but Minnie assumes he means "here in a saloon," and she flushes. These mutual feelings of "I'm not good enough for you" will eventually give way to the realization by both that everyone is flawed, and all must strive to be better. As Minnie will phrase it, we all need to reach "...up, up, up, high as the stars."

Puccini has Johnson tell Minnie that it is strange to find her here, "where anyone can enter to drink ... or rob...." Minnie has lived in saloons since she was a child, and knows how to take care of herself. She assures Johnson she'd be able to deal with any man who came in. "Even if he wanted to rob you of nothing more than a kiss?" Jealousy caused him to ask the question, and he's glad to hear Minnie say that although men have tried, she still has her first kiss to give.

With growing interest, Johnson asks whether she lives here at the Polka. Minnie has gone to the bar, and is cashing in the night's receipts. She tells him she lives in a little cabin on the mountain. This news makes a deep impression on Belasco's Johnson, for earlier that day, as he rode toward Cloudy Mountain, he actually saw Minnie's cabin, from which a faint light was shining. He could tell that whoever lived there must love the mountains, "for no mere digger of gold would think of erecting a habitation in view of those strange, vast, and silent heights."

There was a coil of smoke coming from the cabin's chimney, and the sight of it all but hypnotized him. Beside him, Jose Castro sat impatient and wondering as Ramerrez watched the smoke, conscious of a strange sense of a connection between himself, the cabin, and its inhabitant. And now he recalls that, "Only a few hours back he had stood on the precipice which looked towards it, and had felt a vague, indefinable something, had heard a voice speak to him out of the vastness which he now believed to have been her spirit calling to him." We will realize later, in Act Two, that it is the love of Dante for Beatrice, as expressed in *Vita nuova*, that underpins the belief of first Johnson, and then Minnie, that there is a mystical bond between them.

For the first time, real love is heard in Johnson's voice as he warmly says, "You deserve better than this." These words don't communicate what he means, but at least Minnie is not offended by them. She tells him she is happy, that this is enough for her. A beautiful little theme, which we will hear repeatedly in Act Two, is given out by flutes and oboes as she tells him, "I live there alone, but without fear."

Having finished totaling the receipts, Minnie puts the money in a cigar box, which she deposits in the keg with the miners' gold. With a long and earnest look at Johnson she tells him she feels she can trust him. She danced with him tonight because, as she puts it, "I seen from the first you was the real article." Johnson isn't sure what she means, so she explains. "Before I went on that trip to Monterey, I thought Rance here was the genuine thing in a gent — but the minute I kind o' glanced over you on the road I — I seen he wasn't."

Embarrassed at having revealed so much, she offers Johnson a whiskey, which he refuses. (He considers it impolite to drink in the presence of a lady.)

Puzzled, Minnie asks, "Look here, you ain't one of them exhorters from the Missionaries' Camp, are you?" With a smile Johnson denies this, and Minnie declares she has decided he must be either awful good, or awful bad; that is, he is either "...so good that you're a teetotaler, or so bad that you're tired of life and whiskey." Johnson's response is that he isn't sure himself who he is, but he has loved life, and loves it still. He says that she loves it too, but hasn't lived long enough to see right into the things of the world. Minnie thinks this is quite a joke, and in response Johnson touches on a theme that will become important during the subsequent love scenes, all of which are infused with the spirit of *Vita nuova*. Johnson says, "I mean, life for all it's worth, to the uttermost, to the last drop in the cup, so that it atones for what's gone before, or may come after."

Belasco wishes to focus on the aspirations of mankind as a whole, and so a moment later Minnie declares, "Now, I take it, that what we're all put on earth for — every one of us — is to rise ourselves up in the world — to reach out." Johnson agrees with this fervently, saying, "If only one knew how to reach out for something one hardly dares even hope for. Why, it's like trying to catch the star shining just ahead." This excites Minnie greatly, for she has never before met a man who would have been interested in such things, and who would understand her desire to learn. That she can have a meeting of the minds with such an attractive man, who is so fascinatingly different, causes Johnson to appear well nigh perfect in her eyes. Puccini expresses all these ideas about rising up and catching the stars in Minnie's aria, "Io non son che una povera fanciulla" (I'm nothing but a poor girl), in which she admits she doesn't understand some of the fine things Johnson says to her, and longs to raise herself up to his level.

The ascending music of the aria's concluding line, "...up, up, up, high as the stars," is the fourth of the finale themes— it is the Aspirations Theme — and this glorious, shimmering music, which culminates on a high B for the soprano, is not only related to the Brotherhood Theme of the waltz, it also, when employed in the finale, provides the cathartic resolution towards which the second prelude theme — the Anguish Theme — is always striving.

Here, however, "Io non son che una povera fanciulla," like all the other arias, has no definite end. Rather, it is followed by two lines of monotone chant from Minnie. This chant trails off inconclusively, then the thread is picked up by Johnson, singing to the music of the waltz, on lines invented by the librettists. The love duet will have to await the second act, but Puccini obviously felt the need to have Johnson here affirm his own feelings for Minnie, and he admits that when dancing with her, he felt a strange, indescribable sense of joy and of peace.

His final note is in turn picked up by Minnie, who in a rapid chant begins to tell of the delight and fear filling her heart. Before she can finish, however, she is interrupted by the entry of Nick, who warns that another ugly-looking Mexican has been seen lurking around the camp. This is Ramerrez' man Antonio, who is just about to give the Whistle, signaling that the gang is ready to descend on the Polka.

Asking where the man was seen, Minnie moves toward the door as Nick exits, revolver in hand. Johnson tries to stop her. The orchestra is silent as the piercing Whistle is now heard from a little ways off. To himself Johnson says, "The signal!" This creepy sound makes Minnie nervous, and she moves toward Johnson, as if for refuge. "What can that whistle mean?" she asks fearfully, then she points toward the whiskey keg and confides that the barrel holds a fortune. Puccini's Johnson has already decided not to steal the gold, but Belasco's has not. The latter Johnson is excited by the knowledge of how much gold lies within his grasp, and he goes to the keg and examines it. "In there?" he asks, trying to conceal his agitation.

Minnie tells him the boys guard it at night, but he points out that with them gone now, it seems a careless place to leave it. Her eyes flashing, Minnie assures Johnson that anyone who tried to steal that gold would have to kill her first. This leads him to assume that it must be hers. She corrects him, saying it belongs to the boys. Belasco's Johnson is relieved to hear this, for it means he can steal it without remorse, and so he cheerfully says, "Oh, that's different. Now, I wouldn't risk my life for that."

Puccini picks up some of this for the opening portion of an *arioso* for Minnie, one that features multiple repetitions of a sequence of four descending notes. This is the four-note motif from the first prelude theme, which as I commented earlier appears to relate to the lust for gold, and the consequences of giving in to that lust.

Minnie describes how the miners guard the gold day and night, except tonight they have gone off "after that damned bandit." The sequence of four descending notes is heard for the first of four times as Minnie begins to speak of the miners, who reached out their hands for gold, and despite their good motives have suffered the inevitable consequences. "Poor men," says Minnie, "So many of them have left a family far away, a wife, and children, and they've come here to die in the mud like dogs, just to send a little gold to the dear old ones, and the children, far away." The passage concludes with a sustained high B flat as Minnie vows that if anyone wants this gold, he will have to go through her first.

The four-note motif is now incorporated into a melancholy phrase, played by almost the full orchestra, during which time Johnson absorbs Minnie's words as to what will happen to the man who reaches out his hand for this particular stash of gold. The likelihood that the four-note pattern has its origin in the first prelude theme is reinforced by the music that follows Johnson's promise, "Oh, don't worry, no one will dare!" It's the second prelude theme — the Anguish Theme.

"How I like to hear you talk like that," he adds, and as the Anguish Theme trails along inconclusively, carrying the rest of Johnson's lines and the beginning of Minnie's response, we find our ears straining for the musical resolution that will only come in the finale, when the Anguish Theme is succeeded by a final version of the Aspirations Theme of "Up, up, up" (high as the stars).

Johnson knows he must be on his way. He has seen himself through Minnie's eyes, and can no longer continue on his old path. He has found, says Belasco, "new ambitions and desires awakened, and he looks downward as if it were impossible to meet her honest eye.... Impulsively the road agent's hand went out to her, and with it went a mental resolution that so far as he was concerned no hard-working miner of Cloudy Mountain need fear for his gold!" He tells Minnie he must leave as soon as the posse returns and he knows she is safe, although he would have liked to call at her cabin.

"Must you really go?" asks Minnie. The first prelude theme returns as she adds that the boys will be back soon, and then she will go home. Perhaps he could come up to the cabin then, "...an' we could talk o' reachin' out up there." Against his better judgment, Johnson agrees. With delight Minnie hands him a lantern, and tells him to follow the straight trail up the mountain. (It's likely this is an allusion to the "straight and narrow" path that a righteous person must walk to reach heaven.) A moment later, though, her eyes fill with tears and she warns him not to expect too much of her—"I've only had thirty-two dollars' worth of education. Perhaps if I'd had more, why, you can't tell what I might have been. Say, that's a terrible thought, ain't it? What we might a been—an' I know it when I look at you."

Minnie doesn't mean what she and Johnson might have been as a couple; she is referring to all of humanity, and the things we all might have accomplished in life, but didn't. It is a lament for the chances we all have had to reach up, up, up, high as the stars—chances that we let slip away. "What we both might have been," answers Johnson, his voice near to breaking in sorrow. "I understand it when I look at you."

"Do you mean it?" she asks wonderingly. But then, lapsing into despair, she breaks down completely, sobbing that it is no use—she is ignorant, and she never knew it until tonight. Johnson touches her hand sympathetically, saying, "No, Minnie, don't cry." Minnie's Theme is sounded in the strings, and fifteen tenors hum the tune off stage as Johnson tells her that her heart is all right—that's the main thing. And as for her looks, why, "you have the face of an angel!" (In Belasco, this comment relates purely to Minnie's physical appearance, but Puccini makes something more spiritual of it. "Face of an angel" always seems to be harkening back to the Bible reading scene, and Minnie's line, "...set within my breast a pure heart, and renew in me an elect spirit....")

As Minnie's Theme continues, Johnson picks up his saddle and the lantern. Two emotions, Belasco tells us, are struggling within him. It is a struggle between his two identities—Johnson and Ramerrez—for he mutters to himself, "Johnson, what the devil's the matter with you?" before he walks out of the Polka and into the night.

Nick reenters and puts out the light over the bar. He glances at Minnie, who sits, bewildered, in the middle of the darkened room. Nick leaves and Minnie, as though in a dream, murmurs, "He said.... What did he say? The face of an angel!" Minnie covers her face with her hands, utters a prolonged sigh, like a lament. "Ah!..." she sighs, and as the orchestra concludes on an unresolved chord, the curtain slowly drops.

Belasco now takes us to the saloon that's attached to the Palmetto. It's a seedy place, where the riffraff of Cloudy Mountain gather. Such men are not welcome at the Polka, and their presence has made the Palmetto "...a drab, squalid, soulless place with nothing to recommend it but its size." Ashby did not go with the posse on the wild goose chase led by Jose Castro. Ever since he left the Polka he has been here at the Palmetto, in the private parlor, awaiting the arrival of Nina Micheltoreña. A bottle of whiskey stands on the table in front of him, and as the minutes tick by he steadily draws on the bottle.

At length Ashby hears a step outside the parlor door, but he knows it is not that of Nina. His keen senses tell him Jack Rance is approaching. In silence the sheriff enters and helps himself to a drink. Though pleased that his rival has failed to catch the road agent, Ashby says nothing, and he even banishes the glint of satisfaction from his eyes.

For a long time the two men sit across from one another, neither saying a word. Rance hopes Nina will not show, for he has no desire for Ashby to succeed where he has failed. Finally he declares, "This woman isn't coming, that's for certain." Annoyed by Rance's cynical smile, Ashby says she will indeed come, and within ten minutes. "You evidently," responds Rance, "take no account of the fact that the lady may have changed her mind. The Nina Micheltoreñas are fully as privileged as others of their sex." This earns Rance a sharp look from Ashby, whose intuition tells him there is something bothering the sheriff. No doubt the Girl dealt his ego a blow tonight. In an indulgent tone the Wells Fargo man repeats his belief that Nina will come. The two lapse back into silence, and Rance entertains himself by thinking hard thoughts about Ashby. How ever had the man acquired such a great reputation? He certainly boasts enough. Goodness knows the boys have him on a high enough pedestal. Truth be told, Rance is jealous of Ashby.

At last the two men hear a door open quietly. Nina enters the parlor, throws back her mantilla, and takes a cigarette from a little case. As she lights the cigarette, Ashby cannot help but admire her voluptuous beauty. And yet something about Nina seems pitiful. Ashby knows the history of this former belle of Monterey, and it seems a shame she can be bought by any man with money.

Nina looks straight ahead, into space. In her heart there is nothing but hatred for Ramerrez. She sees a vision of herself in Mexico City, or Spain, living the fabulous life that five thousand dollars will buy. "Ramerrez was in Cloudy Mountain tonight," she says. Rance examines the sheen on his boots, while Ashby gazes at Nina. "Where was he?" Before Nina can answer the sheriff says, "Oh, come, Ashby! She's putting a game on us!" Nina wheels about and advances on the sheriff with a look so tigerish that Rance pushes back his chair in alarm. "I am not lying, Jack Rance," she says, and there is an evil glitter in her eye as she adds that Ramerrez was in this camp only two hours ago. The men question her eagerly, but first she asks about the reward. Ashby assures her he is playing fair.

"Is he an American or a Mexican?" asks Rance, and Nina tells him that tonight Ramerrez is an American; that is, that he is dressed and appears like an American. Ashby and Rance look at the woman, about whose mouth and eyes there is now an ugly expression. "Try to recall, Señor Ashby," she prompts, "what strangers were in the Polka tonight?" At first they consider Jose Castro, but in no way did he resemble an American. "Ah!" cries Rance suddenly. "Johnson, by the Eternal!" Ashby sees the corroboration in Nina's eyes, but has no idea who this "Johnson" might be. "You weren't there, explains Rance, when he came in and began flirting with the Girl...."

"The Girl!" snaps Nina. "So that's the woman he's after now!" With a bitter laugh she says, "Well, she's not destined to have him long, I can tell you!" She reaches for the whiskey and pours out a glass, which she downs in a swallow. The desire for vengeance burns in her, and she draws a photograph from the bosom of her dress, saying, "There—that will settle him for good and all! Never again will he boast of trifling with Nina Micheltoreña— with me, a Micheltoreña in whose veins runs the best and proudest blood of California!" Ashby looks at the photograph, then passes it to Rance. It is an excellent likeness of the man we saw on the road from Monterey. There can be no doubt about it; he and Johnson are one and the same.

Rance puts the photograph in his pocket, then looks with disgust at the degraded woman standing before him, who has sold for money a man she once loved. But soon his pale face grows a shade more white, as he realizes the danger the Girl is in. He and Ashby hurry into their coats, and only now do they become aware that a fierce storm — the first snowstorm of winter — has descended on Cloudy Mountain.

Rance pauses at the threshold of the Palmetto and calls savagely back to Nina, "You Mexican devil! If any harm comes to the Girl, I'll strangle you with my own hands!" He does not wait to hear her mocking laughter, but heads out into the storm, followed by Ashby. They are going to the Polka, and then they will gather some men, and see if they can pick up Ramerrez' trail in this blinding storm.

When the curtain rises for Act Two, we see the interior of Minnie's cabin. There are animal skins on the floor, a wooden rocker by the fireplace, a bed with a canopy and curtains around it, a table and chairs, a small dressing table, and a little bookcase filled with books. Above is a loft, accessible by a ladder that swings up to the ceiling. The wind whistles outside, and the glass in the windows is covered with frost. Although the effect is primitive, it is snug and homey.

A nine-bar introduction is played prior to curtain rise. Orchestrated for upper woodwinds and strings, the introduction has a faintly mysterious tone. Pieces of it will be used in the following scenes up until the arrival of Johnson.

There is a fire in Minnie's fireplace, and on the table is a glowing lantern. The moon is shining brightly through the window. Sitting by the fire is Wowkle, an Indian woman whom Minnie employs to keep house. Wowkle says little, but her presence will allow Minnie to voice her thoughts to the audience. Slung on Wowkle's back is her baby, a six-month old boy, and in a soft monotone the mother sings to him a lullaby that Puccini based on authentic Indian music.

Billy Jackrabbit, the baby's father, enters. Described by Belasco as lazy, shifty, and beady-eyed, Billy was seen in Act One, but did little more than skulk about the Polka, stealing whiskey and cigars. If, in this opening scene with Wowkle, it appears we came in during the middle of a conversation, there is a reason for that. Traditionally cut is an undignified exchange between Billy and Minnie in Act One, in which she orders him to go up to the cabin and arrange to marry Wowkle.[9]

Using music from the introduction and the lullaby, the two have a desultory conversation in which they discuss the marriage. They then sing a brief, mournful, and beautiful duet apparently based on Psalm 103, verses 15—16: "As for man, his days are as grass; as a flower of the field, so he flourisheth. For the wind passeth over it, and it is gone; and the place thereof shall know it no more." Puccini's version is, "Like a blade of grass are the days the Lord gave to man: Winter descends on the plain, and man droops and dies."

Minnie enters in a flurry, and looks around the cabin. What sort of impression will it make on Johnson? Billy leaves after assuring Minnie that he and Wowkle will be married the next day. To Wowkle's astonishment, Minnie tells her there will be two for dinner. This is the second of the three favors Minnie grants only to Johnson. Wowkle sets out plates and cups. (Although only "biscotti e crema" is mentioned for dinner, there is actually more. Minnie had the sweets sent up from the Palmetto, but the bulk of the meal, which she already had, was chipped beef and biscuits. Along with the coffee, it's far from being a bad meal.) Minnie excitedly asks Wowkle what time it is. (She doesn't answer, but it's about 1:00 A.M.) Minnie then asks where Wowkle has put the red paper roses, that she got in Monterey. They are in a chest of drawers, and Minnie takes them out and fixes them in her hair.

After tossing Wowkle a ribbon for the baby, Minnie decides to put on her best shoes, a pair she got in Monterey. They are terribly tight, and after hobbling about for a moment, Minnie asks Wowkle whether she thinks "he" will like them. Love is taking hold in Minnie, for when she declares she is going to dress as for a day of celebration, her words are carried by the Anguish Theme, which is music she and Johnson both use to express their painful doubt regarding their own worth. The Anguish Theme continues as Minnie throws a colorful shawl around her shoulders and decides, "I'm not so bad looking." She puts on a pair of gloves she hasn't worn in a year. And to complete the ensemble: a splash of cologne.

One can imagine the reaction of poor Rance, if he were to see how Minnie is getting herself up for the Sacramento shrimp.

A shout of "Hello!" announces the arrival of Johnson. The flustered Minnie bids him welcome, and seeing her attire, he asks whether she is going out. As Minnie stands confused, the oboe gives out a four-note motif of three rising notes and one falling note. The sequence is G sharp, A sharp, D sharp, A sharp. This motif, after being raised by nearly an octave and tweaked on the third note, will be employed on numerous occasions during the act, especially during the scene in which Rance and the others arrive at the cabin and reveal Johnson's true identity to Minnie. The motif seems to be a capsule version of the strutting Ramerrez Theme, and it is basically employed as a musical accusation against Johnson.

"Yes," stammers Minnie. Then, "No." And finally, "I don't know." Embarrassed, she invites Johnson in. "How pretty you look," he says as he enters and tries to embrace her. Wowkle closes the door with a grunt, surprising Johnson, who had not noticed her.

Seeing Minnie is offended, Johnson apologizes for the liberty he has taken, and asks whether he can stay. The music of the waltz is heard — the Brotherhood Theme, that represents friendship — and Johnson asks, "Are we friends?" His elegant style comes through even in this brief exchange, and she accepts his apology. They sit down at her table, and begin to talk.

Foremost in Minnie's mind is whether he is what she hopes — a man with a virgin heart. A new and rather uneasy theme is heard, interwoven with the waltz, and it represents Minnie's suspicions as to the state of Johnson's heart. She asks him why he came to the Polka tonight, for it wasn't for her. As the harp plays a series of ravishing arpeggios, Minnie asks whether it's true, as Rance accused, that he lost his way while taking the back trail to Nina Micheltoreña. Johnson doesn't answer the question, only looks innocent and tries to take her hands in his. Minnie rises to escape him, and calls for Wowkle to bring the coffee.

In Belasco, Minnie isn't put off so easily. When Johnson tells her it was Fate that brought him, she answers, "You're a bluff! It may have been Fate, but I thought you looked a little funny when Rance asked you if you hadn't missed the trail...." Johnson turns a bit pale, but recovers his composure. "Was it Fate or the back trail?" Minnie demands. Johnson looks her straight in the eye and calmly says, "It was Fate." The cloud disappears from Minnie's face, and she calls for the coffee. The uneasy theme of Minnie's suspicion continues for a few bars as Johnson looks smilingly about the cabin, but it vanishes as he remarks on how strange it must be to live so high on the mountain, away from the world.

His comment launches Minnie into an unusual arietta, "Oh, se sapeste" (Oh, if you knew). Its gay acrobatics are very unlike Puccini's normal style, but he meant it as a revelation of this Girl of the Golden West. The song expresses her intense happiness at living where she does. The countryside at the base of the mountain has fields of flowers, and there are rivers with banks perfumed with jasmine and vanilla. It's summer at the base, but she can ride up the mountains and find winter in the lofty, pine-scented Sierras. The best of all is Cloudy Mountain itself, the top of which is so high one feels he could knock on the door of heaven to be let in. The aria features a pretty *ostinato* from solo violin, and a harp, tambourine, and triangle description of the knocking on heaven's door, before Minnie ends the song with a brilliant and sustained high B on the word "enter," at which point the music trails along inconclusively for three bars before the four-note Ramerrez motif transitions to a question from Johnson.

"Oh, se sapeste" shows us Minnie's love of Cloudy Mountain — a place we are meant to recognize as Eden. It shows us what Minnie will be giving up when she later chooses to go with Dick Johnson, turning her back on Cloudy forever. Johnson is impressed by the song, and in Belasco he notes, "When you die, you won't have far to go." He then asks what it's like in winter. To a wisp of the first prelude theme Minnie proudly tells him that is when the Academy is open — the miner's school, in which she is the teacher.

The music of the upcoming love duet plays softly as Minnie offers Johnson some of her *biscotti e crema*, and it continues as the two begin to talk of books. The libretto communicates essentially nothing of the true meaning of this passage, so it's necessary to go to Belasco to understand what's happening.

In the play, Johnson offers to send Minnie a souvenir of this night — "something you'd love to read in your course of teaching at the Academy." He knows she isn't well educated, but with his characteristic gentility he speaks of her teaching with respect. Not wanting to embarrass her by naming something over her head (or worse, something insultingly simple), he doesn't suggest a book. Instead, he asks what she has been reading lately.

Minnie says she has been reading "...an awful funny book, about a couple. He was a classic, and his name was 'Dant.'" She rises to get the book from her shelf. Johnson is well acquainted with Dante's *Vita nuova*, a difficult book of thirty-one poems linked by a prose narrative in which the author's love for the (literally) divine Beatrice is celebrated, and he urges Minnie to continue talking.

Minnie explains that Johnson made her think of the book back at the saloon, when he spoke of living "so you didn't care what come after." In Puccini, this came out in Johnson's talk of how he loved life, and was sure Minnie loved it too, only she hadn't lived long enough to see right into the things of the world. Belasco's rendering was, "I mean life for all it's worth ... to the utmost ... to the last drop in the cup ... so that it atones for what's gone before, or may come after."

This sounds hedonistic, and it is not until the novel that Belasco makes his meaning clear. In the novel he has Minnie read aloud a passage from the book, and that happens during the week Johnson is in Minnie's cabin, recovering from his bullet wound. It is only at that point, after love has taken hold of Minnie, that she is able to understand the passage Johnson tells her to read. In that passage, Dante speaks of his awareness of the power of love using terms that might be used in describing a religious awakening. To Dante, the coming of love is a stunning event that leaves him shattered, trembling, and fully aware he is in the grip of something infinitely stronger than he.

As a result of Belasco's decision to incorporate *Vita nuova* into *The Girl of the Golden West*, Dick Johnson believes in the rightness of a man's devotion and submission to his lady, a divine and all-powerful being with the ability to guide him along the path of redemption. And this is a plot element tailor-made to inspire Puccini. As we will see in this act and in the last-act finale, the most powerful pieces in the score are Johnson's Masochism Aria, "Or son sei mesi," and the choral finale, in which Minnie assumes the role of a Beatrice-like redeemer of her literally captive lover.

Here in Act Two, Minnie has not yet been seized by love, so she does not understand what Dante felt when, as she describes it to Johnson, he wrote that "...he made up his mind that one hour of happiness with her was worth the whole outfit that came after. He was willin' to sell out his chances for sixty minutes with her." Minnie tells Johnson she put the book down at that point and hollered with laughter.

Johnson declares this was perfectly natural, and yet, he adds, at the same time she knew Dante was right. (In other words, Johnson accepts the *romance* male's role of submissive to his divine lady.) Minnie refuses to believe any man could be so wound up over a woman that he would say, "Jest give me one hour of your society — time ain't nothin' — nothin' ain't nothing — only to be a darn fool over you." But she thinks about it for a moment — thinks perhaps about her parents, who loved each other so — and she admits that maybe there are people who feel that way — people who love "...into the grave, into death — and after." It fascinates Johnson to see Minnie's mind beginning to open up, and Minnie in turn is delighted at the effect Johnson's conversation has on her. As she puts it, he gives her ideas.

In setting this scene of Belasco's, Puccini can use only a small amount of the conversation, and it must be simple. As the music of the upcoming love duet plays, describing the couple's growing feelings and preparing our ears for the duet in full force, Puccini has Johnson offer to send Minnie some books. She accepts, asking for "love stories." With passion she declares that for her, love is something that lasts forever. She can't understand how a man can love a woman, but be satisfied with only an hour. Johnson assures her there are some women whom a man would be willing to have for only one hour, and then die. (As usual in Puccini, the word "die" is sung on a thrilling note by the tenor — a high A, with a crescendo to *forte*.)

The two are talking about different things, for Minnie is talking about a sexual relationship — a one-night stand — while Johnson is expressing a reverent, non-sexual, Dantean worship of a divine woman. Minnie is still suspicious as to the state of Johnson's heart, and when he declares there are women one would be glad to have for an hour, and then die, the love duet music ceases. To the uneasy music with which she questioned him earlier about the "back trail," Minnie laughingly asks, "And how many times have you died?" She is speaking, of course, of "the little death," which is orgasm. In other words, how many women has he had?

Johnson doesn't answer, and Minnie doesn't press him. Instead, she offers him one of her best cigars. Johnson tries again to embrace Minnie, and she retreats, taking refuge in her roses: "Oh, my roses! You'll squash them!" He suggests she take them off, and pursuing her, pleads for a single kiss. She demurs, declaring if you give a man a hand, he'll take an arm. Endearingly, Johnson urges, "Your lips say no, but your heart says yes!"

Minnie is about to give in, and anyone but Puccini would have her say, "To heck with the roses," and go from there. But here she takes the roses from her hair, and puts them away in a drawer. By doing this, she loses the protection they seem to have given her against Johnson/Ramerrez. Whether Puccini intended this or not is impossible to know, but Minnie's removal and putting away of the red roses marks the point at which she loses her power to defend herself against this secret Vacillator. Minnie now orders Wowkle to go home. From off stage, the wind machine starts up, and as Wowkle opens the cabin door and sees a storm has begun, the orchestra describes the falling snow. Minnie again tells Wowkle to go, saying she can go sleep in the hay. (Wowkle is actually on her way to meet Billy.)

Johnson again pleads for a kiss, and strings and upper woodwinds make an urgent attempt to warn Minnie, giving out the accusing Ramerrez motif. Bereft of her roses, Minnie can't hear it. As she throws herself into Johnson's arms, the orchestra desperately sounds the Ramerrez motif one last time. A great, upwards rush is given out by woodwinds, harp, and strings, as the lovers embrace and kiss. A turbulent version of the Anguish Theme is heard, as the cabin door is thrown violently open by the wind and snow swirls into the room.

Little by little, the violence abates. The cabin door swings shut, and calm returns. The Anguish Theme continues to sound, but now it is slow and dreamy, played *ppp*. As Johnson murmurs Minnie's name, a harp plays arpeggios. The Anguish Theme expresses doubt about the fulfillment of love, and so it is that just as Johnson is telling Minnie he has loved her since the first moment he saw her, he suddenly recalls what he is, and how she would despise him if she knew. In despair, he tells her this is nothing but an empty dream. Johnson's dream is the waking dream that all Puccini lovers long to make real — the dream of a life and a love that can survive the short and blissful Night.

As always, Minnie misinterprets his words. She thinks he means she isn't good enough for him. Humbly, she pleads with him to teach her, and tells him that day on the road from Monterey, they recognized each other. "I said that day: 'He's good — he's grand — he can have me!'" As Minnie sings, the Anguish Theme struggles painfully, groping for the resolution it will not find until the finale.

Johnson looks at Minnie longingly, but with sudden resolve he cries, "Bless you! Goodbye!" With this, the theme abandons its struggle. An unresolved chord hangs in the air as Johnson kisses Minnie, grabs his hat and coat, and opens the door. But to his shock, there is a blinding snowstorm in progress. A gust of wind blows in, and snow swirls in the orchestra. Johnson closes the door. The Anguish Theme resumes and begins a crescendo from *pp* as Minnie assures the distraught Johnson the storm has wiped out the trail. He couldn't possibly get down the mountain tonight. "It's destiny!" she cries, the theme climbing higher and higher in both pitch and volume.

Three rapid gunshots are heard, and muted trumpets sound the full Ramerrez Theme. "Maybe it's Ramerrez!" Minnie cries. "What do we care?" Johnson repeats this question grimly and Minnie again urges him to embrace his destiny and stay. The two themes — Anguish and Ramerrez — contend with each other, describing Johnson's mental struggle, then he makes up his mind. Over the crying of the wind, Belasco's Johnson asks Minnie, "Suppose we say that's an omen — that the old trail is blotted out and there's a fresh road.... Would you take it with me, a stranger — who says: 'From this day on I mean to be all you would have me?' Would you take it with me? Far away from here — and — forever?"

This is a proposal of marriage, and it succeeds, temporarily, in silencing the doubt-filled Anguish Theme. Joyfully, Minnie answers, "Well, show me the girl who would want to go to heaven alone." The love duet begins as Johnson, throwing down his hat and coat, swears to Minnie he will never leave her.

In words that sound like they come from Wagner's *Tristan*, but whose real source is Dante's *Vita nuova*, the two sing of how sweet it is to live and die, and never part again. Puccini continues with the brief but passionate love duet, giving Johnson the language of a tortured knight of *romance* as he rapturously cries, "Can you tell me what is this suffering? I can bear no more...."

The love duet does not reach resolution, and as it trails away on the word "eternally" it is succeeded by the uneasy music to which Minnie previously asked Johnson what had caused him to come to the Polka. Was it Fate, prods the orchestra suspiciously, or the back trail toward Nina?

As the "back trail" music continues, Minnie offers Johnson her bed, saying she will sleep by the fire. Johnson's refusal silences the "back trail" music, then Minnie explains she often sleeps by the fire when it's very cold, curled up in a bearskin rug. The waltz, which represents friendship and deep affection, gently resumes as the two prepare for sleep. A rippling harp contributes to the suggestion of sleep. Johnson lays his hat and coat on Minnie's bed, and puts his revolver under the pillow, while she goes behind a curtain and changes into her nightgown.

Just as the waltz reaches its conclusion and is about to resolve, it segues into a few notes of the "back trail" music — "...this evening, at the Polka ..." — which seems to represent the uneasy state of Johnson's mind. Minnie blows out or turns down most of the lanterns. Johnson's cigar is sitting on the chest of drawers, where he placed it some time before.

Johnson starts to go to bed, but some faint sound disturbs him. He goes to the door and listens, while Minnie kneels by the fire and says a brief prayer. As Johnson listens at the door, an eerie version of the Polka Theme begins, informing us of what Johnson has heard. Somewhere out there in the snowstorm are Rance, Ashby, Nick, and Sonora, calling to one another, and fighting their way toward the cabin. "What's that?" asks Johnson softly. From her bed by the fire, Minnie yawns. "It's the snow sliding." Johnson thinks it sounds like someone calling, but Minnie tells him it's only the wind. Very uneasy, the outlaw goes to bed. Suddenly it occurs to Minnie that she doesn't know her fiancé's name. Dick, he tells her, from behind the bed curtains. Flute, horns, and solo viola hold a long note as Minnie asks, straight out, "You never knew Nina Micheltoreña?"

"Never," says Johnson miserably, and the satisfied Minnie wishes him a good night. Suddenly a cry of "Hello!" is heard. The voice is Nick's, and it is followed by a knocking at the door. Johnson is out of bed in a flash, revolver in hand. He orders Minnie not to answer. She listens at the door, and hears the voices of Rance, Sonora, and Ashby. It is the jealous Rance she is worried about — it never occurs to her the situation is compromising, but she fears what Rance would do if he saw Johnson.

Nick cries that they have seen Ramerrez on the trail, and Minnie whispers the men have come to help her. Oboe and solo bassoon sound the accusing Ramerrez motif. Minnie hides the outlaw behind her bed curtains, then opens the door and lets in the posse. The first one in is Jack Rance.

"You're safe!" cries Sonora, deeply relieved. Rance goes to the table and turns up the flame on the lantern. The men are eager to tell her the news, and Rance gets it out first: "Your beau at the dance — he was Ramerrez!" As he pronounces the name with venomous pleasure, the bandit's strutting theme is heard, recalling his bold entrance into the Polka.

"What are you saying?" Minnie gasps, and with satisfaction Rance declares her perfect Mr. Johnson is a highway robber. Minnie refuses to believe it, but as she and Rance talk, the orchestra repeatedly backs up the sheriff, confirming his accusation with emphatic soundings of the four-note Ramerrez motif.

A strangely tender melody (probably expressive of the men's sincere affection for Minnie) now begins, played by flutes and clarinets, as Rance, Sonora, and Ashby assure Minnie that Johnson and Ramerrez are one and the same, and he came to the Polka to rob it. Sid, Rance declares, told Nick he saw the man heading toward her cabin. Minnie looks toward Nick as Rance demands he confirm the statement, and Nick suddenly realizes he may have made a mistake in bringing the others here.

Nick did not come here as a bandit-hunter. He came up the mountain to help Minnie. And help her he will. Suddenly he sees the cigar Johnson left on the chest of drawers. He catches Minnie's eye, and a look passes between them. Nick slips the cigar into his pocket, and says he must have been mistaken. That Sid is such a liar!

There's one thing Minnie doesn't understand, and that is who told them that Johnson was the bandit. The orchestra falls silent as the triumphant Rance answers, "His woman! Nina!" "Nina Micheltoreña?" asks Minnie fearfully. "Does she know him?" Rance gleefully says the two are lovers. As he describes how Castro led them on, and how he went to the Palmetto to meet Nina, a solo flute plays the gang's signal whistle. Rance takes the photograph of Ramerrez from his pocket, and shows it to Minnie. As she looks at the back and sees it is inscribed to Nina with love, woodwinds emphatically play the Ramerrez motif.

Minnie gives a wild laugh, that puzzles Rance. She is laughing at the way she was taken in. Imagine her, thinking she had attracted a real gentleman, and all the time he was a bandit with Nina Micheltoreña as his lover. A man with a virgin heart, indeed! A man who would love into the grave, and beyond! What a fool she's been! Minnie gives the photograph back to Rance, and as she does, the Ramerrez motif begins to shrink. Solo flute, clarinet, and bassoon drop the first note, and play a three-note version, *piano*.

Seemingly calm, Minnie asks the men to go. Softly, Nick asks if she would like him to stay. "No," she says briefly. The Ramerrez motif loses more ground, as a solo bassoon drops the fourth note, and plays a two-note version, *pp*. What a comedown from the bold, brassy, *forte* strut of the road agent's entrance theme! This tiny little two-note whimper seems to represent Johnson's current, diminished state — writhing in shame behind Minnie's bed curtains.

The wind machine cranks up as the posse exits, but as they close the door the wind ceases, replaced by a soft but ominous rumble in the timpani. Boiling with rage, Minnie yells at the road agent to come out. The full orchestra plays one bar of the Anguish Theme as Johnson emerges from behind the curtains. The stage directions describe him as "vanquished; defeated."

Minnie accuses him of having come to rob her, and when he denies it she calls him a liar. Belasco's man tries to explain, saying, "I admit that every circumstance points to...." This elegant "style," so appealing to Minnie a short time before, now infuriates her, and she shouts, "Don't you give me any more of that Webster Dictionary talk!" A sweeping melody surges in the orchestra as Minnie rages at Johnson, ordering him to "Go! Go! Go!" She moves swiftly to the door, but he stops her with a gesture. It's time for his Masochism Aria, "Or son sei mesi."

It begins with a passage of ferocious *arioso*, marked with an extended and trumpeting high G as the road agent vows not to defend himself. Johnson admits he is a scoundrel (at which point lower woodwinds begin playing the Ramerrez Theme), but he swears he would not have robbed Minnie. Johnson hints at the back story Belasco will provide in his novel, saying he was born a vagabond, "But while my father lived, I never knew it." With that dramatic utterance complete, the aria proper begins.

In the play, Belasco gives no reason for the elder Ramerrez having taken to banditry, and Johnson's explanation reads as follows: "I lived in Monterey — Monterey where we met. I lived decently. I wasn't the thing I am today. I only learned the truth when he died and left me with a rancho and a band of thieves — nothing else — nothing for us all — and I ... I was my father's son — no excuse ... it was in me — in the blood ... I took to the road. I didn't mind much after — the first time. I only drew the line at killing. I wouldn't have that."

He goes on to tell Minnie the moment he kissed her (note that — he attributes redemptive power to the kiss), he vowed to go straight, and take Minnie with him, when he could do so honestly. Minnie asks him if that is all, and in what is surely a deliberate parallel with her embarrassed greeting when he first entered the cabin (he asked if she was going out, and she said, "Yes. No. I don't know. Come in."), he answers, "No. Yes. What's the use? That's all."

At this point Minnie is half-crying, and she tells Johnson what she has against him is that he took her first kiss under false pretences. He had said he had been thinking of her ever since Monterey, but in truth he had gone off and been kissing that other woman. "It's that damned Nina Micheltoreña that I can't forgive." She kicks him out of the cabin, saying they can kill him for all she cares. Ramerrez looks at his pistol for a moment; then, not caring himself, he puts it in his pocket, and goes out of the cabin empty-handed.

Puccini had to give more explanation as to why Johnson "took to the road," so he invented a mother and siblings for him to support. Using the same music to which Minnie, Johnson, and Rance conversed after the outlaw first strode into the Polka, the orchestra provides a low and throbbing accompaniment as Johnson gives his agonized description of "how it was."

"It's been six months since my father died," he begins. The only wealth the old man left was a gang of highway bandits. "I accepted it," he admits heavily. "It was my Destiny." Scrambling the sequence of events, Johnson goes on to say that when he met Minnie, he dreamed of going away with her. And where he wanted to go was, of course, *lontano* — far away.

The far away place is not, as Mosco Carner thought, an idyllic little country place invented through a foible of Puccini's. *Là lontano* is that longed-for place that is *not here* — a place where people love you unconditionally, and troubles cannot follow. It is the place where hope need no longer struggle with melancholy. It is the place where the waking dream becomes reality. As Johnson summons the image of *là lontano*, Minnie raises her head from her hands. She does not look at him, but seems absorbed by a vision of lost happiness.

The idea of redemption is now introduced, as Johnson adds he intended to redeem himself in a life of work and love. His error was in thinking that he, a mere male, was capable of redeeming himself. Dante knew better. Only Minnie, the first of Puccini's redeeming women, can accomplish Johnson's redemption.

As the aria moves into its close, the Anguish Theme enters. It is heard both in the vocal line and in the orchestra, as Johnson describes how his lips murmured an ardent prayer. The last time we heard the theme this strongly, Johnson was trying to leave the cabin before it was too late, only to find that a storm had blotted out the old trail.

Johnson's ardent prayer had been, "Oh God! May she never know, never know my SHAME!" An upwards rush in the violins at the start of the word intensifies the tremendous impact of "shame," which the tenor sings on an extended, trumpeting, high B flat. Typical of Puccini, this masochistic cry is far and away the most glorious vocal moment so far in the opera.

Ratcheting the aria downwards to its close, Johnson cries alas— alas for his shame. The vocal line walks down the scale in tiny steps as he mourns his lost dream. "Now," he says miserably, "I'm finished." Johnson attempts to end his song on a note of resolution, but the instant he stops singing Minnie picks up his closing note and uses it to begin a passage of *arioso*. She answers as she does in Belasco, saying bitterly that it is his theft of her first kiss she cannot forgive. She had believed he was a man with a virgin heart, who would love only once, and forever. "I thought you were mine, mine alone," she sings mournfully, and mechanically, she orders him to go.

Johnson moves to the door with a sense of *muoio disperato* — "I die despairing." His stage directions are: "Desperately, determined, unarmed, he opens the door ready for the sacrifice, like a suicide." The wind machine starts up as Johnson bids Minnie goodbye, then leaves quickly. The Girl wipes her eyes, and declares it's over. An instant later, a shot rings out.

Softly, the full orchestra begins to play a dry, staccato, nearly monotone pattern of notes. "They've shot him..." Minnie gasps. She steels herself, asking, "What do I care?" Something strikes the door of the cabin, and Minnie rushes to open it. Johnson staggers in, bleeding from a wound in his chest. He tries to go, saying he won't hide behind a woman, but Minnie refuses to let him leave. In a line of tremendous significance, Belasco's redeeming Girl cries, "If you can't save your own soul, I'm going to save it for you!"

The two argue fiercely about whether Johnson should go or stay. He wants urgently to face Rance, for he has had enough of being humiliated, and is determined to die like a man. (He did not knock on Minnie's cabin door, he fell against it.) Minnie repeatedly urges him to stay, but what settles things is her cry, "You're the first man I ever kissed. You can't die!" There is a sharp rap at the window. It is Rance, but with relief Minnie realizes he cannot see Johnson from where he is. Rance moves to the door and begins knocking loudly.

Johnson ceases to resist, and as the harp plays an upwards glissando, Minnie climbs on top of a chair to lower the ladder to the loft. As she returns to Johnson, who is now holding a handkerchief against his bleeding wound, an eerie, snaking melody, representative of Minnie's determination to save Johnson's life, is heard in the full orchestra. This Rescue Theme is dominated by a compelling sequence of four notes that shift incessantly, and it expresses intense effort, and pain.

Johnson is reeling from his wound, and as Minnie urges him up the ladder with cries of, "Courage! Up! I love you!" he contributes a few deep, moaning protests. At last he reaches the loft, where he collapses, still holding the handkerchief to his chest. Minnie swings the ladder back, then looks up. The cracks between the planks are wide, and she urges Johnson to move the handkerchief away, for its whiteness is clearly visible. Johnson obeys, and the blood flowing from his wound begins to pool on one of the planks.

Rance has been hammering on the door, and when Minnie finally opens it he pushes his way in and looks around quickly. The eerie music of Johnson's rescue ended as Minnie moved to the door, and Rance enters to a four and a half bar reprise of the melody that carried his first conversation with Minnie in Act One: the melody to which, after telling her he loved her, he offered her a thousand dollars for a kiss. Rance's love for Minnie is, via this music and that of Rance's Theme, always fatally associated with gold and death.

That music of Rance's gold-poisoned love ends as Minnie greets him coolly, calling him Jack. "I'm not Jack," he declares roughly. "I'm the sheriff, chasing that infernal Johnson." The split between the tenor character's two identities becomes remarked on now, for while Rance needles Minnie by calling the man he is chasing "your Johnson," she snaps back that she is sick of hearing about "your Ramerrez."

Rance begins to search the cabin. Not finding Johnson immediately, he demands to know where he is. Belasco's Minnie lies to him, but Puccini's does not; rather, she evades the question. Impatiently, Rance says he wounded the man, and he must be here. He takes off his hat and coat, and puts them on the table.

Angrily, Minnie tells him to go ahead and search the cabin, but then to get out — forever. Rance is startled by her anger, and fears she means to end what relationship they have left. The sheriff is not a villain, and in Belasco he now says pleadingly, "I'm crazy about you. I could have sworn I saw — You know it's just you for me — just you — and damn the man you like better! I — I — Even yet I — I can't get over the queer look on your face when I told you who that man really was. You don't love him, do you?"

Puccini condenses this into one line: "Oh, well. My mistake. But tell me you don't love him!" The music that carries this plea is from Rance's bitter, Act One aria, "Minnie, dalla mia casa," in which he told her of his loveless life, and how he'd give a fortune for her kiss. Again the music fatally ties Rance's words of love to the thought of gold. Minnie reacts with scorn, and the unhappy Rance tries to take her in his arms, telling her he loves her.

As in the play, Minnie struggles violently to get away, then grabs a whiskey bottle and threatens Rance with it. Rance is shocked, his pride deeply wounded. His worst fears have been confirmed: Minnie loves someone else — an outlaw! With a nasty laugh the sheriff picks up his hat and coat, and stretching out a hand for emphasis, he promises Minnie that man will never have her.

A puzzled look comes over the sheriff's face. There is blood on his hand. Her voice trembling, Minnie says she must have scratched him as they struggled. Rance wipes away the blood with a handkerchief: there is no scratch. And then, "Look! Blood again!" The harp plinks twice, describing the blood dripping down from the loft. Rance looks up, and with a shout of joy and hatred he cries, "He's there!" A scene far more violent than in Belasco now ensues, as Minnie struggles to hold Rance back. To a ferocious musical accompaniment, she grabs his arm, but he pulls free and shoves her to the floor.

The snaking music of the Rescue Theme returns, darkened by a key change and by having been pulled down the scale by an octave. As it plays mournfully, Rance positions the ladder and savagely orders Johnson to come down. Slowly and painfully, Johnson drags himself to the trapdoor, and begins to descend. Minnie, in the same urgent accents with which she pleaded with Johnson go up the ladder, now pleads with Rance to see that he can't come down it.

With a supreme effort, Johnson descends the ladder. He is pale and suffering, but according to Puccini the expression on his face is dignified and fierce. There is virility in his appearance, but he says not a word and makes not a gesture to defend himself. Rance has his pistol trained on the outlaw, and he laughs loudly at the sight of him, saying, "What a change!" Minnie helps Johnson down the last few steps, then guides him to the table. He manages to sit down, then pitches forward onto the table, unconscious, where he will remain for the rest of the act.

This is the big turning point for Johnson. When he entered the opera, he was a confident and strong man — the pistol-wielding leader of an outlaw band. The moment Rance spotted him in the loft, however, he ceased to be a man, and became property. In a few minutes, Minnie will suggest that Johnson serve as the bet in a poker game between her and Rance, and so it is quite right for him to be slumped over on the card table. That's where the bet is usually placed.

The elements of the sadomasochistic relationship between Minnie and Johnson originated in Belasco's play, but Puccini greatly intensified them. His Johnson is far more clearly a piece of property than Belasco's—not only in the final moments of this act, when Puccini has Minnie repeatedly exult, "He's mine! He's mine!" but in the last act, where Johnson, his hands tied, is passed from one man to another like a piece of meat, until Minnie claims ownership of him again. The situation is similar to that of the bound, helpless Cavaradossi and the powerful Tosca, only greatly intensified.

With each successive opera, Puccini has strengthened the female and weakened the male. In *Manon Lescaut,* the relationship of Manon and Des Grieux was described by the latter as that of mistress and slave—he was "dirt in dirt," her "slave and victim." But that was an emotional slavery, which Des Grieux could have ended had he wanted to. The heroine's power over her lover has steadily grown, until here in *Fanciulla* her ownership of him has become an actual fact, confirmed in the opera's last moments when Sonora unties Johnson, releases him from the noose, and tells Minnie, "On behalf of us all, I give him to you."

Now, observing the unconscious Johnson, Rance gives a nasty laugh, and sneeringly asks "Mr. Sacramento" what his choice is—the rope or the pistol? Determined to save her lover, Minnie picks up her own pistol. Her wonderful line in the play, spoken to Rance in a quiet but tense voice, is, "You better stop that laughing, or you'll finish it in some other place where things ain't quite so funny."

The entire scene in Puccini is far more violent and exciting than in the play, and part of that stems from the transforming of Rance—the "cool, waxen, deliberate gambler"—into a fierce and frightening adversary, quite different from the determined but calm Rance of the play. To a pounding accompaniment by woodwinds and strings, Minnie calls Rance a devil, and orders him to stop tormenting the outlaw. "Look at him!" she cries, on an extended high A. "He's fainted!" Johnson is "out of it," and so Minnie takes charge of his life, just as Tosca took charge of Cavaradossi's life when he was out of it.

Muted horns, timpani, double basses playing pizzicato, and violins and viola playing *col legno,* mark Minnie's desperate search for an idea. She finds one, and to communicate this to the audience, she touches the side of her head. As a matter of fact, she has thought of not one idea, but two. Minnie is smarter than Tosca was, and when it comes to saving her lover's life, she means to leave nothing to chance.

The full orchestra plays a surging accompaniment filled with exciting bits of melody as Minnie, calling on a voice of near–Wagnerian power, tells Rance the three of them are the same—all "bandits and cheats." This is a garbling of Belasco's line. What she means is that all three of them are gamblers. Rance is a card player, and Johnson is an outlaw, who gambles with his life every day. As for Minnie, she lives off of card-money, and the gold the miners find by chance. As all three are gamblers, she tells Rance, they two should be willing to gamble now, for Johnson's life.

A solo oboe sounds the Rescue Theme as Minnie makes Rance an offer she knows he won't refuse. "Una partita poker," she suggests: a game of poker. Speaking of Johnson as property, she tells Rance she offers him this man, and her own life. If Rance wins, he gets both of them, and if she wins, "This man is mine. Ah! he's mine." The offer made, the oboe falls silent. Rance has been studying Minnie closely, and in a line that seems to recall *Tosca's* Scarpia ("How you hate me!"), but actually originated with Belasco, he marvels, "How you love him!"

Burning with desire, Rance accepts the bet. Knowing Rance's weak point—his desperate need to be thought of as a gentleman—Minnie insists on his word of honor as to the outcome. If she wins, he leaves, and says nothing to anyone about Johnson being in her cabin. Rance agrees, saying, "I can lose like a gentleman." He immediately follows this, however, with a line Puccini renders as, "I'm all burned and destroyed, wanting you so much. But if I win, I'll have you." The savage voice of the operatic Rance makes Minnie shudder. Rance is calmer in the play, but his line is even more brutal: "I can lose like a gentleman. But, my God! I'm hungry for you — and, if I'm lucky, I'll take it out on you so long as God lets you breathe."

A new theme begins as Rance moves to the table, where he yanks the tablecloth from under the unconscious Johnson. Played by oboes, clarinets, and solo bassoon, the melody sets the opening mood of the poker game, and it is pure Puccini in its inimitable combination of drooping melancholy and rising tension.

Seated at the table, Rance has pulled a deck of cards from his pocket, and is shuffling them. In the meantime, we have seen Minnie take another deck from her cupboard, and extract five cards, which she furtively hid in her stocking. Now she sits down at the table, opposite Rance, and offers him the short deck, which he accepts. They should use this new deck, she says, for there is a lot riding on the game.

Two bars of orchestral silence announce the start of the game, as Rance says, "I'm ready. Cut. To you." Rance deals the first of the three hands. The players discard, and while they study their hands Rance broodingly asks Minnie what she sees in Johnson. The clarinet sadly brings back the Anguish Theme, which for the first and only time expresses the unfulfilled love of Jack Rance. Minnie gives the only answer possible; that is, what does Rance see in her? The melancholy Poker Theme resumes, but as Minnie anxiously asks what cards Rance has, the double basses begin a soft, pizzicato throbbing that will, by the third hand, swell to a roar.

Minnie wins the first hand with high cards of a king and a queen, then it is her turn to deal. Every instrument in the orchestra except the throbbing double basses cuts out as the players discard. Rance draws one card, and wins with a pair of aces. (He says, "Due assi e un paio," which may suggest to English speakers that he has a pair of aces and another unspecified pair. What he says in Belasco is that he has, "One pair — aces." The Italian should be translated as, "Two aces, and that makes a pair.")

The double basses describe the players' pounding hearts as they play out the deciding hand. Swiftly, Rance deals the cards, and Minnie has a moment to read her fate in a handful of nothing. Filled with shame at what she is about to do, Minnie apologizes to the man who had been her friend — a man who loves her, and who cannot suspect her of being capable of dishonesty. The apology is clearer in Belasco, where she softly tells Rance she has always thought of him the best she can "... and I want you to do the same for me."

Rance pays little attention to Minnie's veiled apology, so concentrated is he on his cards. "Three kings!" he cries exultantly. "See: I've won!" The double basses begin their great crescendo, which upper woodwinds, muted trumpet, and upper strings punctuate with a stabbing motif of three falling notes. Minnie, sacrificing the thing she once held dearest, cries that she is ill, and wildly begs Rance to get her something.

Rance runs to the cupboard for a bottle of water. The pounding in the orchestra reaches a point of almost unbearable tension as he searches frantically for the bottle and glass. It takes him a moment to find them, but that is enough. While his back is turned, Minnie thrusts her losing cards into her blouse, and pulls out the ones hidden in her stocking.

Rance hurries back, and as the orchestra seems to hold its breath via a long, swelling chord, he gloatingly cries he knows why she was fainting: "The game is lost!" Minnie rises

triumphantly, the orchestra falls silent, and as she shows her winning hand to the astonished Rance she shouts, "You're wrong! It's joy! Three aces and a pair!" The sheriff stares
at her cards for an instant. He is a gambler, and now he proves himself a gentleman. He
gives Minnie a searching look, then picks up his hat and coat. Coldly he bids her good night,
and leaves.

The tension is burst by a great, upwards *glissando* from the harp. Minnie gives a hysterical laugh, and the Rescue Theme roars back, *tutta forza*, as Minnie, wild with joy, gathers the cards and throws them into the air. "He's mine!" she cries, her voice rising to
extended, punishing, high Bs and B flats. "Ah! He's mine!" Drawing on Puccini's superior
ending to this tremendously exciting act, Belasco's subsequent novel finds Minnie, as the
cards fall about her, crying," Three aces an' a pair, an' a stockin' full o' pictures—but his
life belongs to me!" The hysterical laughter changes to tears, and as Minnie embraces the
unconscious Dick Johnson, the curtain swiftly falls on one of the most thrilling acts in all
of opera.

In his novel, Belasco tells us that in the moments after the curtain is dropped, Minnie pulled herself together and dragged Johnson to her bed, where she cut away his shirt
to examine the wound in his chest. To her great relief, the bullet had not lodged inside him.
She did what she could to clean and bandage the gash, then drew up her rocker, and prepared to spend the night watching over him.

Outside, the blizzard raged. Hours passed, and the storm did not abate. For three days
the snow fell, and Minnie watched over her lover. There was plenty of wood for the fire,
and enough food to last for a week. On the third day he slipped into a delirium, and began
to talk. Try as she might, Minnie could not make out what he was saying, but she could
tell he was calling someone, and the name he called was not hers. The jealousy that tore at
her was like nothing she had ever known, and mixed with it was hot shame at the way she
found herself straining to understand words he did not mean for her to hear. On the fourth
morning he awoke, just before dawn. Minnie was asleep, and too weak to get up, he waited
for her to rise. They were both embarrassed and awkward at first, but finally he asked her
what had happened, and how long he had been there, and embarrassment passed with the
realization of how much they loved each other.

After a time, Minnie had to attend to some chores, and this gave Dick Johnson a chance
to reflect on his life, and how he had come to this point, lying in bed with a lawman's bullet wound in his chest. It seemed to him there had come a stronger claim on him than the
oath he had made to his father, and that was the duty he now owed to Minnie. Although
she had been vague about what had taken place between her and the sheriff, Johnson realized she had saved him from Rance. Not only love, he told himself, but honor, demanded
he put an end to his outlaw ways, and devote the rest of his life to making her happy.

Soon after, he heard Minnie talking to someone. It was Nick. The bartender had begun
wading through the snow the minute the storm let up, to bring news of the camp, and some
supplies. So far, four people knew of Johnson's presence in the cabin: Rance, Nick, and the
two Indians. Minnie was certain none of them would tell.

As the hours went by, Johnson began to grow restless, and he asked Minnie if she
would read to him. Something from the Dante she had told him about. She took the volume from her bookcase, and began to read the passage he indicated. She stumbled over the
words at first, but gained confidence when she saw he enjoyed listening to her.

To Johnson's surprise, none of what Dante had written regarding his passion for Beatrice seemed funny to Minnie now, although she had told him that first night it had made her laugh. She made no comments at all, until she came to the following passage:

> At that moment, and what I say is true, the vital spirit, the one that dwells in the most secret chamber of the heart, began to tremble so violently that even the least pulses of my body were strangely affected; and trembling, it spoke these words: "Here is a god stronger than I, who shall come to rule over me."[10]

At that point the book fell from Minnie's hands, and with an expression of love so intense that it awed and humbled him, she told Johnson, "That Dante ain't so far off after all. I know just how he feels...."

With the passing of a few more days, Johnson began to lose his sense of danger. But one night, Jose Castro came to the door. Castro had learned that Ashby suspected the outlaw was in Minnie's cabin, so he had come to warn him. It was one week since Johnson had been shot, and the idyll was over.

Castro left to fetch two horses, which he was to bring to a place across a ravine some distance from Cloudy Mountain, where Johnson would meet him a few hours later. Johnson promised Minnie he would return in two weeks, for it would take that long to settle things at his rancho, with the men who had faithfully served his father and him. Silently the two embraced, and then he left her.

The final act of Puccini's opera is set in a clearing in a great forest of the Sierras. It is the dawn, the hour of greatest peril. It is the morning after Johnson left Minnie's cabin, and in the orchestra bassoons, horns, and double basses paint a somber picture of the grandeur of forest and mountains. Beside a fire sit Nick and the brooding Jack Rance. Ashby, some of the miners, and Billy Jackrabbit lie sleeping nearby. A solo clarinet describes the morning song of some bird.

Rance's face is drawn and tired, and for the first time since we have known him, he looks messy. His hair is uncombed, and his clothes are disordered and dirty. In a low and mournful voice, Nick tells the sheriff he'd give ten weeks' tips to turn back the clock one week, before that damned Johnson showed up.

In hatred and gloom, Rance curses Johnson, whom he had thought would surely die of his wound. We hear a reminiscence of Rance's gold-poisoned request for a kiss, and the sheriff seethes to think that while they've been out here freezing in the snow, "...he's been in there, warmed by Minnie's breath, caressed, kissed...." Nick is sickened by the obscenity implied, and he protests, "Oh, Rance!"

"A thief like that!" the sheriff mourns. "Oh, I could have shouted what I knew, for everyone to hear!" Nick knows how deeply hurt Rance has been by Minnie's rejection, and how well he's behaved in spite of it, so he says the kindest thing he can think of: "And you didn't do it. You've behaved like a real gentleman." But this no longer means what it once did to Rance, who asks bitterly what Minnie can possibly see in that puppet.

In a tone of whimsical philosophy, Nick sings of the heaven and hell that love is. Love eventually comes to everyone in the whole damned world. And now it's Minnie's turn. We hear a brief reminiscence of Minnie's Theme: "You have the face of an angel." The sun begins to rise, and little by little the terrible light of Day begins to penetrate the scene. At this exact moment, distant voices are heard shouting, and the turbulent music of the manhunt begins. The miners and Ashby's men are after Dick Johnson. Ashby wakes, elated by the shouting, certain it means his men have found their prey. "You're luckier than I am," says Rance bitterly, and Ashby looks at him wonderingly, puzzled by his strange behavior of late.

A group of armed miners bursts onto the scene, shouting that their quarry is on the other side of the hill, and Ashby, running to join the pursuit, warns them to take him alive. All but Rance and Nick race off in pursuit of Johnson. The ferocious music of the manhunt subsides, and as the music of Rance's plea for Minnie's kiss returns, the sheriff raises both arms, and in a tone of "cruel joy" vows it is Minnie's turn to cry. Night after night he's suffered for her sake, while she laughed at his misery. But now it is he who will laugh, and she who will weep. The music of the refused kiss mixes with that of the manhunt, as Rance exults that the man Minnie loves will never return.

Miners enter and excitedly report the outlaw is surrounded and it will soon be over. But a moment later Harry, Joe, and Bello shout he has gotten away, having knocked one man out of the saddle and taken his horse. In an instant he was streaking away like lightning. The Wells Fargo men are after him. Shots are heard, and the miners give a triumphant cry. Bassoons and horns play a baying version of the love duet, which gives a cruel reminder of Johnson's promise to Minnie: "I swear I'll never leave you!" If these men have anything to say about it, the music suggests, he may be forced to. Rance stares at the ground, reminding himself he kept his promise. As the others yell in glee, Rance continues to talk, as though speaking to Minnie. "What good did it do you? Your pretty beau will swing from a tree in the piercing wind."

Billy Jackrabbit has been preparing the noose, and now Nick grabs him and thrusts a pouch of gold into his hands. The gold is for him, Nick says, if he stalls in getting the rope ready. "But if you betray me, my word on it. I'll kill you." And with that he hurries away. Ashby reappears, smugly escorting the captive Johnson, whose hands are bound, and who has clearly been through a terrible struggle. He has been roughed up, and is bleeding. "Kill him!" shout the miners. "Hang him!"

What a contrast there is between Belasco and Puccini in the entrance of the captured outlaw, and his handover by the Wells Fargo man. The stage directions in Belasco read, "This entire scene is played easily and naturally — no suggestion of dramatic emphasis." Johnson's hands are tied in the play, but he hasn't been injured. Ashby is triumphant but cool, and there is no howling for the outlaw's blood. There is also no formal "handing over" by Ashby.

Puccini, on the other hand, does everything he can, not only to increase the excitement, but also to turn the final scene of the opera into the most sadomasochistic display he has yet presented on a stage. Roberto kneeling in terror before the murderous Anna — Des Grieux kneeling and weeping in the street of Le Havre — Cavaradossi, bleeding and sobbing as he awaited execution — all these are as nothing before the exquisite degradation to which Puccini subjects the bound and bleeding Dick Johnson in this final scene of *La Fanciulla del West*.

The moment Johnson began to descend the ladder in Act Two, he ceased to be a man, and became property. But he was unconscious during most of that scene. Now, he must acquiesce to his status as property, and stand in silence while his ownership is debated. This debate begins when Ashby formally addresses Sheriff Rance and announces, "I consign this man to you, to be given to the community."

In the play, the scene of Johnson's judgment by the miners takes place in a small room attached to the Polka. Minnie has been giving the boys a reading lesson, and while she is away for a moment, Ashby brings Johnson in. When Minnie is heard in the other room,

Johnson pleads to be allowed to speak to her before he is executed. The miners grant the condemned man's last request.

They untie Johnson's hands, and leave him alone except for Nick. The Girl enters, and is shocked to see Johnson, whom she had hoped had already gotten away from Cloudy Mountain. Johnson tells her goodbye, which strikes fear in Minnie's heart, though she doesn't know why. The words Minnie speaks during this scene are reminiscent of some of Butterfly's lines—not as heard in Belasco's play, but as in Puccini's opera. The distraught Johnson asks Minnie not to forget him, and she answers, "Every day that dawns I'll wait for a message from you. I'll feel you wanting me. Every night I'll say: 'Tomorrow'—and every tomorrow I'll say: 'Today.' For you've changed the whole world for me."

Johnson urges her not to be afraid, for in a few moments he'll be quite free. These words seem so foreboding that Minnie says, "A strange feelin' has come over me. A feelin' to hold you, to cling to you—not to let you go. Somethin' in my heart says, 'Don't let him go.'" Johnson walks out of the room, and a moment later Minnie realizes what is going on. She begins to sob, and to cry out that they mustn't kill him. To her shock, the miners, led by Sonora, immediately decide to let Johnson go, telling Minnie they hadn't realized what he meant to her. Minnie rushes outside to tell Johnson, and the men look at one another in silence. Says Nick, "The Polka won't never be the same, boys. The Girl's gone."

So there's no real threat of a hanging in Belasco, and no physically heroic role for Minnie, such as Puccini gave her. Belasco did give Minnie the role of redeemer, however, making her the means of Johnson's spiritual salvation, similar to the way in which, according to Dante, Beatrice served as the agent of his spiritual salvation.

In the play, during Johnson's farewell he tells Minnie he saw her praying that first night in her cabin. He tells her he doesn't know whether he believes in it, but he wants her to pray for him. Knowing in a few minutes he will likely be dead, he kneels before Minnie, and she silently prays over him. Sonora and the others are guarding the door and windows of the room, and they see this. It is the sight of Minnie praying over Johnson that causes them to decide to let him go, and in this way Belasco completes the link between his play and *Vita nuova*—between Johnson and Minnie, and Dante and Beatrice.

Puccini, as we know, decided to make Minnie the agent of Johnson's physical salvation as well, and so the threat of hanging is quite real. Ashby hands Johnson over to Rance, then turns to go, pausing for a moment to say mockingly to Johnson, "Good luck, my handsome gentleman."

Rance approaches the hated Johnson, and blows cigar smoke in his face. In a tone of irony he asks how Mr. Johnson is feeling, and begs him to excuse them if they've caused him any inconvenience. Johnson answers with studied indifference, telling them to just get it over with. Unimpressed by his courage, the miners taunt and curse him, accusing him of every crime they can think of, including several murders. "No!" denies Johnson hotly. "I was a thief, but never a murderer!" The men begin a new round of accusations, and as they do, a two-note *ostinato*—a rapid death-march—begins in the lower strings.

The miners now reveal what has kindled their rage the most. "We'll make you pay for Minnie's kisses!" they shout. (From this and other hints it appears it became public knowledge that Johnson was in Minnie's cabin. It appears the miners were waiting for him to come out, and ambushed him.) The death-march slows to a drag as Rance smiles ironically and tells the "caballero" not to worry, for hanging is really just a trifle. As the death-march saws away slowly and heavily, Johnson proudly tells the men to save their insults, for he isn't afraid to die. Masochistically, he cries, "If you untie one arm, I'll cut my throat with my own hand!"

He has one request before dying, however, and it relates to the woman he loves. His saying this infuriates the miners, who howl for his death — all except Sonora, who pushes to the front and declares the man has a right to speak. Sonora doesn't like Johnson, but he can't help feeling admiration for him. And some envy. Sonora's defense surprises Johnson, who thanks him in tones of touching graciousness.

Johnson's final aria, "Ch'ella mi creda," is based on lines from Belasco, but with two significant additions by either Puccini or his librettists. From Belasco came Johnson's plea that before the men hang him, they take him some distance away, so Minnie will not discover what became of him. "...and when she grows tired of looking for letters that never come, she will say, 'He has forgotten me.'" Mixed with this is the passage quoted above, in which Minnie spoke of how every night she would say, "Tomorrow," and every tomorrow she would say, "Today." Added by either Puccini or his librettists was the longing for *là lontano* — the far-away place where there are no troubles — as well as Puccini's near-mystical language of flowers.

"Let her believe me free and far away, on a new path of redemption!" the aria begins. According to Puccini's stage directions, Johnson's face bears a look of exultation, and he seems almost to smile. Solo flute, solo clarinet, bass clarinet, solo horn, and muted strings play the melody "like an organ," says Puccini, and the aim seems to be a religious effect.

Employing two stunningly beautiful high B flats, Johnson goes on to sing of how the days will pass, and he will never come back. "Minnie, you who have loved me so much! Ah, you, who of my life, were the only flower!" Perhaps it is that final word "flower" that does it. The furious Rance punches his bound prisoner in the face, while the orchestra simultaneously wrenches away from Johnson the musical resolution he had reached in his final note. The miners utter a chorus of disapproving cries, and Rance asks Johnson whether he has anything else to say. Haughtily, Johnson says, "Nothing. Let's go."

As Johnson begins his walk to the noose, a fanfare is heard, first in trumpets and trombones, and then in woodwinds and horns. The rumble of a funeral drum punctuates the fanfare. Sonora rolls a stone to the base of the hanging tree, and touches Johnson on one shoulder. With a steady step, the calm and stoic Johnson climbs onto the stone.

Having kept faith with Nick, Billy Jackrabbit has not prepared the rope. Billy is kicked by Rance and manhandled by Sonora, then the rope is snatched from his hands. The noose is put around Johnson's neck, and the free end thrown over a branch. From a distance we hear the voice of Minnie, wordlessly singing a four-note sequence she repeats three times. Nick had hurried off to warn her, and now she is galloping in on horseback to save her beloved. The miners shout Minnie's name, not paying the slightest attention to Rance, who is urgently ordering them to hang Johnson.

Seven times, Rance shouts, "Hang him!" but when Minnie gallops in and flings herself from her horse, she moves in front of Johnson to defend him with her own body. Throughout the scene, Johnson remains silent and immobile, his hands bound, the noose about his neck. Facing down Rance, Minnie calls him an old bandit, while to a curious sweeping figure in the strings, Rance essentially tells her to watch her mouth. Contemptuously Minnie says she isn't afraid of him.

Some of the miners move threateningly toward Johnson, and Minnie draws her gun, which brings in Minnie's Theme in the full orchestra, *fff* after a brilliant upwards rush, and launches the great choral finale. Again and again Rance orders the men to drag Minnie away, but in the face of Minnie's Theme — "You have the face of an angel" — they can't do it.

Minnie clings to Johnson, and as her theme continues, she threatens to murder her lover. As the miners attempt to pull her away, she points her gun at Johnson's head, and swears that if they don't let go of her, she will kill Johnson, and then herself. Minnie's threat to kill herself shocks Sonora, who forces his way through the yelling mob. Reaching her side, he shouts at the men to let go of her. Minnie's Theme, which is the first of the six finale themes, softens.

As Minnie cries that none of them ever said "Enough!" when, amid their curses and fights, she shared their troubles, we hear a reminiscence of the "tribute" music, to which the miners gave her the flowers, the ribbon, and the handkerchief. (This music seems meant to recall the fight that took place between Rance and Sonora, and the way Minnie stopped it.) The "tribute" music continues as Minnie declares, "Now this man is mine, as he is God's! God in heaven has blessed him!" She insists he had intended to seek new horizons, far away, and a bit of the Anguish Theme is heard as she says the bandit that he had been died up there beneath her roof.

Tearfully she pleads with the men not to kill Johnson, and the Anguish Theme, which represents unfulfilled, tormented love, continues as Sonora — "in a shout that is like a sob" — answers, "Oh, Minnie, more than gold has he robbed us of! Your heart!..." A long note is held by divided double basses as the miners murmur that it isn't possible for them to release Johnson.

The second of the finale themes — the Loneliness Theme of *lontano* (Echoes From Home) — steals in as Minnie puts a hand on Joe's shoulder and reminds him who she is: Puccini's Lady of the Rose. "Wasn't it you who offered me flowers, like those of your home?" She turns to Harry, and as she touches his hand she recalls the time he was sick and almost died, and she sat up with him. "In the delirium, you thought I was your little Maud, the sister you love, come from far away...." Harry puts a hand to his face, and weeps.

Sonora is won over by the utterance of that mighty word, *lontano*, and he tells the miners they must give in. Minnie turns to Trin, her voice sweet, and reminds him of how she taught him to write, so he could send his first letters home. As she sings, the resisting Happy is urged by Sonora to be quiet. Gradually, more of the miners' voices enter, and the finale shifts into a choral prayer as the men contend with each other. As the Loneliness Theme swells, slowly climbing towards resolution, more of the miners are won over by the pleas of Minnie and Sonora.

"Behold!" cries Minnie, throwing down her gun. Divided strings start a slow crescendo, beginning one of those great passages, as in the first-act finales of *Tosca* and *Turandot*, in which the listener — hypnotized, or even narcotized — feels himself pulled back and forth, as if by the waves of the sea. Having renounced violence, just as Johnson renounced theft, Minnie tells the men she is again what she had been: "your friend, your sister, who once taught you the supreme truth of love...." With those last four words, we may hear in the Anguish Theme the sound of Johnson, singing in "Or son sei mesi" of how his lips murmured an ardent prayer.

The miners have all given way, but they sing disjointedly, in twos and threes. As Minnie continues her climactic line, she sings, "...my brothers, there's not a sinner in the world to whom is closed...." Sonora removes the noose from Johnson's neck, and unties his hands. The miners make gestures of assent. And with this, the Anguish Theme slides into the fourth of the finale themes: the glorious and exultant Aspirations Theme. The final word of Minnie's plea for forgiveness—"...the path of **redemption!**"—culminates in an extended high B for the soprano, *fortissimo*, supported by the voices of all of the miners, and this at last provides that emphatic musical resolution towards which we have been striving since the opening notes of the prelude. The music to which Minnie sings the word "redemption" is that of her desire to rise up, up, up (high as the stars), and as she sings, for the first time all of the miners are with her, singing in unison, "We can't refuse any more. No! No!"

Johnson has knelt at Minnie's feet, and she has made a gesture of blessing over his head. One can't know exactly what the act of kneeling on the part of the tenor character meant to Puccini. As I noted above, it was taken from Belasco's play. It may be that Puccini simply thought the kneeling made for an effective stage picture, and that the gesture of blessing, which he added to the scene, conveyed the idea of Minnie praying for Johnson, and capped the Dante/Beatrice theme of a man's redemption via the intercession of a powerful woman.

On the other hand, this submissive action on the part of the tenor character is something Puccini employs in almost every one of his operas. That there is a masochistic impulse behind the posture is obvious in the kneeling scenes in *Le Villi*, *Manon Lescaut*, *La Rondine*, and *Turandot*, and here in *Fanciulla* Puccini will, in just a moment, drop Nick to his knees as well.

Although Sonora has already freed Johnson, he now formally hands ownership of the kneeling man over to Minnie. The fifth of the finale themes, the Brotherhood Theme of the waltz, now enters, and to it Sonora tells Minnie, "...on behalf of us all, I give him to you." Johnson rises, and in a gesture recalling his welcome by the miners back at the Polka, he extends a hand to Sonora, saying emotionally, "Thank you, brothers."

Minnie embraces Sonora, who bids her a heartbroken farewell. The music of *lontano*—the Loneliness Theme—returns as Minnie extends her hand to each of the miners, who mourn that she will never return. Nick, who entered the scene some time back, is overcome with emotion, and he kneels at Minnie's feet, sobbing. She caresses his head.

Their voices singing an identical line, Minnie and Johnson bid this sweet land goodbye, and as they do, the sixth and last of the finale themes—the love duet music—enters. The melody is given to the voices, upper woodwinds, and strings, with the harp contributing ravishing *glissandos*. The sound swells as Minnie and Johnson, continuing to sing an identical line, say goodbye to their beloved California, rising to an extended high B, *fortissimo*, before it subsides like a receding ocean wave.

The full orchestra holds a long, soft note as Minnie embraces Johnson, and they turn to leave. Singing together in a monotone chant, the lovers say farewell to the mountains of the Sierra, then the miners bring back the Loneliness Theme as they resume their mournful cry that the two will never return. The final bars are sung over a harp playing harmonics, a triad from the celesta, a high, sustained chord from divided violins, and the lightest possible tap on the bass drum.

The lovers are united, and have survived the rising of the sun. And yet this gray, frigid, winter scene is one of the most grief-stricken in all of Puccini, and has the flavor of death. The miners stand in various postures of grief. Jack Rance is nowhere to be seen, for when the tide turned against him he slowly exited. The only one unmoved is Billy Jackrabbit, who all the while has sat at one side, playing solitaire, smoking, and paying not the slightest attention to the incomprehensible doings of the whites.

10

La Rondine

Libretto by Giuseppe Adami, based on an original libretto in German
by Alfred Maria Willner and Heinz Reichert
First performed at the Monte Carlo Opera, March 27, 1917

The libretto of *La Rondine* has been derided as a poor imitation of Verdi's *La Travi-ata*. There certainly are similarities between the two, but I believe the model for Puccini's heroine Magda was not Verdi's Violetta, but a real person: Elisabeth-Céleste Venard, later Comtesse de Chabrillan, and better known as "Mogador."[1]

Céleste Venard was born in 1824. She was the illegitimate child of a poor mother, and never knew her father. After one of her mother's drunken lovers attempted to rape her, she was put in the women's prison of Saint-Lazare, supposedly as a refuge. At the age of 16, she legally registered herself as a prostitute. Céleste liked to go to the Bal Mabille (the dance hall spoken of in *La Bohème*), and one night a professional dancer called Brididi asked her to dance with him. She must have done well, because after a day of lessons Brididi invited her to take the place of his regular partner, who was consumptive. Partnering Brididi, Céleste made a tremendous impression on the crowd at Mabille, and men practically fought to dance with her. Said Brididi in the face of this competition, "It would be easier to defend Mogador than my partner!" (Mogador was a Morrocan fortress that had recently been taken by the French.) The name stuck.

After the season ended and the dance halls closed, Céleste went on to become an equestrienne at the circus at the Hippodrome. Soon afterward she became a courtesan, kept by a rich Italian. In his absence, she took an Italian tenor as her lover. After a time, Céleste became the mistress of Gabriel-Paul-Josselin-Lionel de Chabrillan, who seems to have truly loved her. His was an old and wealthy family, but he was arrogant, and a spendthrift. His family despised Céleste as a prostitute, and that probably influenced the couple's decision to end their relationship. By 1852, however, de Chabrillan had been disowned by his family. Penniless, he decided to go to Australia and look for gold. Still in love with Céleste, he asked her to marry him, and through his connections her name was removed from the official role of prostitutes. The two sailed to Australia on a ship called the Croesus, and owing to the length of time it took the vessel to reach Melbourne, the press reported it had been lost at sea, and the famous Mogador had drowned.

Céleste Venard had a long and fascinating life, and after the premature death of her husband she began a successful career as a writer. In addition to her autobiography, she wrote novels, plays, poems, songs, and operettas. She died in 1909, about four years before Puccini began working on *La Rondine*.

Puccini's opera uses a well-worn plot that covers some of the same ground as *La Travi-ata*: a beautiful, high-class prostitute with a loving heart sees the error of her ways when a handsome young man comes calling, but ultimately she gives the fellow up for his own good. Some of the elements of *La Rondine* that mirror the life of Céleste Venard could be coincidence, but there are three that I think give evidence in favor of my theory that she, not Verdi's heroine, was the inspiration for Puccini's Magda.

First is the name Magda, which seems too close to Mogador to be coincidence. The second is a passage in Céleste's *Memoirs*, which tells of an event similar to the one related by Magda in her Act One aria, "Ore dolci e divine." In her song, which is a waltz, Magda tells her friends of a romantic night when she went to the Bal Bullier. She danced with a young man, and their "spirits were filled with joy." After that night, she never saw him again. When Magda finishes the song, she adds, "The exquisite perfume of that strange adventure, friends, is always with me."

In Céleste's *Memoirs*, she tells of a night she went to the Café Anglais. A man insulted her, and another man, about 20 years old, took her part, and was kind to her. She asked him to see her home. Céleste wrote, "'Yes,' he said.... 'But first, I would like to dance with you.' A waltz was starting. He had me twirling on the dance floor before I could answer. I was nimble and his arm was tense. I felt a flash of happiness that passed through me as quick as lightning, but which I can still remember."[2] Finally, Puccini's Magda describes during the aria how her partner tipped their waiter a tiny amount, that was for him an extravagance, since he was so poor. One of her friends laughs, and says, "What a Croesus-like gesture!" Croesus was the name of the ship on which Céleste and her husband sailed to Melbourne, and which was widely reported to have been lost at sea.

I went over *La Rondine* extensively in Chapter Three, summarizing the plot, and showing how in this opera, Puccini had lifted material not from the librettos of Verdi's *La Traviata* and Strauss's *Die Fledermaus*, but rather from Wagner's *Parsifal*. Increasingly desperate in his later years for material that would inspire him musically, Puccini would again borrow material from *Parsifal* for *Suor Angelica*, and again for *Turandot*.

Puccini dropped his "family of motifs" technique for *La Rondine*, which lies somewhere between an opera and an operetta. In composing this light work, he seems to have given himself permission to take a break from advancing his technique with recurring music. No piece of music in *La Rondine* grows out of or is meaningfully related to another, either melodically or rhythmically. The majority of the rhythms are of popular dances, such as the waltz, the fox trot, the polka, the one-step, and the tango.

The character Lisette could be said to have a personal motif in the music to which she first sings, but aside from that no one has music that identifies him personally. Almost all recurrences are done with the intention of summoning up the original words or mood. The most important pieces of recurring music are the Amore Theme, Magda's Adventure, the *Lontano* Theme, the Heart Theme, the Rondine Theme, and the Act Two love quartet.

As for the close, it finishes with music original to the scene. (Perhaps that could be considered an advance for Puccini.) The only nod to former practice is the tolling bells that are heard in the seconds before the final curtain. Allegedly they are issuing a call to prayer, but in fact they are the typical Puccini bells that toll for death and disaster.

There are two symbolic elements in *La Rondine*, and both of them relate to the major subject of the Rose Cycle, i.e. the hope of the young lovers that they might live and love forever, and never die. These elements are the rose, which we have encountered in every opera since *La Bohème*, and the swallow — *la rondine*. Like the rose, the swallow is a symbol of rebirth in many cultures, and was considered a sacred creature as far back as ancient

Egypt. In medieval Christian belief, the swallow was a resurrection symbol because it mysteriously disappeared in winter, and just as mysteriously reappeared in spring. By bringing in the swallow, for the first time in the Rose Cycle Puccini employs two elements that symbolize the rebirth of love in spring.

Warring against this hope for a rebirth of love is the element of Alberich's Choice. The Alberich character in this opera is Rambaldo, a cold-hearted banker who is keeping the soprano heroine as his mistress. Having succumbed to the temptation of gold, Magda is a Vacillator, unfit for the love of the tenor character, the ardent and innocent Ruggero. The question is whether it is possible to turn back the clock; or rather, whether it is possible for Magda to escape the consequences of her error — escape to the place called *là lontano*, storied as the land where time stands still, and love never dies.

In *Fanciulla*, numerous characters expressed an intense longing to go far away, to where people love you, and there are no troubles. Here in *La Rondine*, Puccini allows his young lovers to reach that place. Is *là lontano* all it was cracked up to be? We shall see. Before getting to the opera itself, let's take a moment to look at the numerous plot elements and characters borrowed from earlier Puccini operas, because a couple of them are remarkable.

The students in the Bal Bullier scene are essentially the same group as in Act One of *Manon*. Both groups are eager for wine, love, and revels, and both are curious and watchful as to the love affair of the principal couple. *Manon*'s students back off on their pressuring of Des Grieux after he seems to have displayed the correct attitude toward love, in singing "Tra voi, belle," and *La Rondine*'s young men back off on their pressuring of Magda after they conclude she has an assignation with Ruggero.

Both Manon and Magda are Vacillators who give up the love of a poor and ardent young man for the wealth of an older and unsatisfying man. Manon's regretful aria on this subject is "In quelle trine morbide"; Magda's regretful aria on this subject is "Ore dolci e divine." The subject of the Lamplighter's Song in *Manon*— of a king who tried unsuccessfully to tempt the heart of a poor maid — is the identical subject taken up by Prunier in his "Chi il bel sogno di Doretta."

Both operas feature a male principal beginning a song with the declamation, "Paris!" In both operas, the tenor character initially refuses to speak to the pushy young revelers. Des Grieux tells Manon he feels a strange attraction to her — that he seems to have met her before. Ruggero tells Magda he feels a strange attraction to her — that he seems to have met her before.

In Act Two of *Manon*, the heroine's dancing elicits whispered expressions of delight from the onlookers. In Act One of *La Rondine*, the heroine's singing elicits whispered expressions of delight from the onlookers. In Act Two of *Manon*, the heroine applies makeup, and asks her brother for approval of her dress and looks. In Act One of *La Rondine*, Lisette applies makeup, and asks Prunier for approval of her dress and looks.

The roll call of the twelve women in Act Three of *Manon* is mirrored in Act Two of *La Rondine* when the girls who are trying to flirt with Ruggero demand to know his name. Pestering him for an answer, they call out twelve men's names. In *Manon*, Lescaut goes to the heroine (between Acts 1 and 2) and urges her to leave her poor and ardent lover for the wealthy older man. In *La Rondine*, Prunier goes to the heroine in Act Three and urges her to leave her poor and ardent lover for the wealthy older man. Both operas end with the tenor character, having been "left" by his lover, helplessly wracked by grief. Des Grieux is unconscious; Ruggero has "thrown himself down, sobbing."

As for the material from *Bohème*, Prunier appears to be Rodolfo, older and rather jaded, but still a poet. With his hopes of a career as a great writer gone, he is reduced to the status of a hanger-on in the world of the *demi-monde*. With his beloved Mimi long dead, he is now in love with another lower-class girl: Magda's housemaid, Lisette. When Lisette appears to notice anyone else when they are out together, he exhibits the same annoyance he did with Mimi.

Prunier even refers to "the vulgar crowd," just as his old friend Colline did that long-ago night at the Café Momus. And as of old, he cannot complete his art — in this case, the song of Doretta — without the aid of the soprano character. Previously he had simply needed her near, to inspire him, but by now the heroine has grown so powerful that the poet cedes his chair to her and she finishes the job herself. Combined with all this is material from *Parsifal*, which surely makes the libretto of *La Rondine* the strangest amalgam in all of opera.

The prelude consists of two pieces of music that will recur frequently during the opera. The first is the melody to which Prunier will, as soon as the curtain rises, describe the malady racing through Paris: the malady called "sentimental love." The second is a four-bar melody easily recognized in its first three notes, which carry the word "Amore." In contrast to the Malady Theme, which is cheery and brilliant, owing in part to its rapid tempo, strong accents, and the use of the glockenspiel and cymbals, the Amore Theme is warm and lyrical, moderate in tempo, and heavy on sighing strings and woodwinds, and rippling harp.

The curtain rises on the elegant Paris salon of Magda de Civry, in Second Empire France. At back right is a conservatory. At right center is a grand piano, on top of which is a vase of red roses. The first soprano to revere roses was Mimi. Then came Tosca. Then Butterfly. Then Minnie. Five in a row is too many to be a coincidence. And while we're at it, what time is it?

"The curtain rises," Puccini tells us, "on the last reddish rays of the fading sunset." With the setting of the sun, life begins to quicken in Puccini's World. Near the piano is a floor lamp with a large shade, but it isn't on yet. Other, smaller lamps, with shades of diverse colors, cast a light that is intimate and subdued. It is the *prima séra* — the hour of waking dreams, when hope struggles with melancholy.

An after-dinner party is in progress. In attendance are the lovely Magda and her poet friend Prunier, and Magda's wealthy patron, the banker Rambaldo Fernandez. Three male friends of Rambaldo's are also present, as are three female friends of Magda's — Yvette, Suzy, and Bianca. (Perhaps the latter six people are three couples, but we don't know for certain.) The other person present is Lisette, Magda's housemaid and a critically important character.

Prunier is leaning on the piano, holding forth to the women about the latest Paris fad. Magda is pouring coffee, which Lisette bustlingly serves. Rambaldo and his friends are in the background, talking about some boring business matter. This is the first time since *Le Villi* that the soprano is on stage at curtain rise. There will be no powerful entrances in the opera, no erotic passion, and no hint of violence. There is not even much in the way of comedy. The only thing in abundance is sentiment. These are all big disadvantages to one who would write an engaging opera, and Puccini will do his best to make up for them with charming and skillfully orchestrated music, and a variety of interesting stage pictures.

The girlfriends scoff at Prunier's claim that the latest rage in chic, sophisticated Paris is "sentimental love." To one of several "Lisette" themes—this one sprightly, and marked by some silvery notes from the glockenspiel—the impertinent maid interrupts to declare that what the poet says is nonsense. According to her, it's a matter of, "You want me! I want you!" And that's all there is to it. (Much of the music that carries this introductory conversation will be replayed in Act Two, during the opening conversation of Prunier and Lisette with Magda and Ruggero.) With exaggerated irritation, Prunier complains about Lisette to Magda. Actually, he and Lisette are having a clandestine affair, and this complaining is a little game. Prunier knows Magda likes Lisette tremendously, and nothing will come of his words.

Magda excuses Lisette's interruption as the sort of thing that takes place in her abnormal household, then tells the girl to go away. Magda's voice is habitually warm and wistful, and marks her out as a romantic and melancholy woman. She sits near Prunier and urges him to continue. Prunier explains that the rage in Paris is for romance: glances, embraces, sighs, kisses, but nothing more. (This means the opera will not feature the erotic passion needed for a great love duet.) The girls find Prunier's report absurd, and to the Amore Theme, they use the words of courtly lovers to mock the idea of romance: "Amore!" "O heaven!" "I suffer." "I swoon." "I surrender." "I die." "Give me some moonlight...."

Romance isn't a joke to Puccini, and it isn't a joke to Magda, either. She uses the music of the Malady Theme to interrupt her friends, saying, "Don't joke!" Prunier is quick to notice her tone, and asks if she's interested in the new fashion. She might be, she allows, and she asks him to continue telling about it.

The stage directions tell us that in the back, one of Rambaldo's friends has been leafing through a newspaper, and has noticed an interesting article, which he shows to the other men. The other two friends appear to read the article and talk about the matter. Rambaldo seems unconcerned. What may this interesting article be? The stage directions tell us it concerns a financial crash that does not affect Rambaldo's affairs. Only Puccini would put this sort of bizarre stage direction into one of his librettos. It is completely irrelevant to the plot, and the actors are completely incapable of communicating it to the audience. But it was important to Puccini to know that the four men are in business—that they are gold-poisoned Alberich-types who have no interest in the subject of romance.

Prunier responds to Magda's urging with the Malady song: "È un microbo sottile" (It's a subtle microbe). To the music of the first prelude theme, he tells of the malady, the epidemic, or rather, the madness, that has hit the feminine world. It's a subtle microbe, against which the heart has no defense. As Magda listens, her friends take the second verse, exclaiming in mock terror over the subtle germ that spares no one. "No one!" Prunier assures them. "Not even Doretta!" The girls ask who Doretta is, and to a subdued version of the Malady Theme Prunier explains she is the heroine of his new song. He pretends reluctance when the girls ask to hear it. "Don't make us beg you!" they cry. The use of the word "beg" seems deliberate, for this gives Magda the opportunity to speak as the imperious lady of *romance*, saying to one who is essentially her troubadour, "I order you to sing!"

Magda draws the attention of the businessmen, telling them in an achingly beautiful vocal line to be quiet, for, "The poet Prunier, the nation's glory, deigns to give our ears a new song." The words seem exaggerated, but Magda and Puccini are serious. Though Magda is a Vacillator, mistress of the wealthy and cold-hearted Rambaldo, she hasn't forgotten the respect due to an Artist in Puccini's World. Her call for the group's complete attention is no more than the poet's right.

Rambaldo begins to rise from his chair, asking the subject of the song. When Prunier declares that it is love, Rambaldo sits back down, saying the theme is rather withered. His friends nod agreement, but Magda, continuing with the Amore Theme, insists love is always new. (In other words, love is always being reborn.) Her friends urge Prunier on, so he lights the floor lamp near the piano and sits down.

The reason Prunier lights the lamp is that several minutes have gone by since the opening at sunset. Prunier will sing one verse of "Chi il bel sogno di Doretta" (Who can explain Doretta's beautiful dream?), and by the time he has finished, Puccini tells us, Night has fallen. The stage will be dark, except for the light coming from the lamp, that makes Prunier visible to us.

The subject of "Doretta's beautiful dream" is the same one addressed in the Lamplighter's Song in *Manon*: that of a beautiful and poor girl, who is wooed by a king, and refuses him. In the first verse, sung by Prunier, the king says not one word about love; he only offers the poor girl gold if she will "surrender" to him. Prunier plays the opening chords of the song on the piano, but not long after he begins singing, the orchestra takes over and provides a warmer and more romantic accompaniment.

Prunier modeled his Doretta on Magda herself. Although Magda succumbed to the lure of the loveless king's gold, and left the community of Artists in favor of this palace in which Rambaldo has installed her, Prunier knows that at heart she is still one of them. Finishing the first verse, he sings of how the girl refused the king, saying, "But as I am, so I will remain, for gold cannot give happiness!" The room is dark now, and Prunier stands up. Magda asks him why he does not continue, and he tells her he doesn't know the end of the story. If she can supply it, "I will cede my glory to you!" Magda sits at the piano, and sings the second verse, the words of which come from her heart.

Doretta's dream is of course the waking dream of endless love in endless night. Doretta's dream is Magda's dream, and so the end of Doretta's story — the end of her "mystery"— comes easily to Magda. One day, she sings, "a student kissed her mouth, and that kiss was a revelation. It was passion. Mad love! Mad intoxication! Ah, my dream! Ah, my life! What do riches matter, if at last happiness has bloomed again?" (We must remember the closing measures of this music, for the passage recurs at the end of the act.)

The word used was *rifiorita* — reblossomed, and it is meant to contrast with Rambaldo's use of the word *appassito* — withered. Magda's verse is a Spring Song, an anticipation of the rebirth of love in the season of flowers, and it also carries the *romance* element of Love as Madness. The word "student" is Puccini shorthand for a man who is young, ardent, poor, and a believer in the waking dream.

The six friends (but not Rambaldo or Prunier) uttered whispered praises while Magda was singing. The song concludes with the orchestra playing the Amore Theme, and to this music Prunier pays Magda the highest tribute he knows: he takes the red roses from the vase on the piano, and scatters them before her. "At your feet," he says solemnly, "all the abundance of spring." When she accepted Rambaldo's gold, Magda ceased to be Puccini's Lady of the Rose, but she has sung an Artist's song, and Prunier thinks a tribute of red roses is fitting.

Magda is not so sure she is worthy of roses, so when she gets up from the piano she says, "No, don't make fun of me." Everyone assures her the song was exquisite, and even Rambaldo says, "What heat!" Magda is amazed to hear such a comment from "the practical man," but he shrugs and says he was carried along by the current. It's clear what sort of sexual relationship these two have. It must be even worse than that of Manon and Geronte, for in that case the old man's spirit was willing, even if his flesh was weak.

With irony, Magda blames Prunier's genius for everyone's ruin. The poet disclaims the credit, however, saying, "In the depths of every soul is a romantic devil who is stronger than I, than you, than everyone!" Rambaldo loudly rejects this claim, saying his romantic devil is asleep. When Yvette asks how this can be, Rambaldo says, "I arm myself with holy water and defeat him. Would you like to see it?" He then takes a jewel case out of his pocket and opens it, revealing a pearl necklace, which he gives to Magda. (Starting with Rambaldo's offer of the necklace, the *parlando* is carried by a melody that sounds as if it might have some significance. It doesn't. It is only utility music, and we'll hear it on other occasions where it does nothing but carry conversation.)

I noted in Chapter Three that with so much of the *La Rondine* libretto having been taken from *Parsifal*, it was obvious Rambaldo was Puccini's version of Klingsor, the evil magician in *Parsifal*. Klingsor longed to be a member of the Grail community, so he castrated himself to destroy the sexual urge that made him unfit to be a Grail knight. The Grail community would not accept Klingsor after he had mutilated himself, but his action somehow enabled him to become a magician. Rambaldo's declaration that he arms himself with holy water to defeat the powerful romantic devil inside him only makes sense if we realize the reference is to Klingsor. Of course, Rambaldo is also one of Puccini's Alberich characters, and since he has deliberately killed his sexual passion, he is the worst one yet — a man in possession of the soprano heroine, and yet passionate only about gold.

Magda is "somewhat surprised" at the gift. Rambaldo says he had meant to give the necklace to her before dinner, but had forgotten. Giving it to her now, it is in obvious contrast with Prunier's tribute of the red roses. To Puccini Artists, jewelry is anathema. Eyes are more beautiful than the most stupendous jewels, and the only proper adornment for a young and beautiful woman is a flower in her hair. To Puccini, Rambaldo's gift is an insult, but a deserved one, since unlike Doretta, Magda accepted the king's offer of gold. Magda is unenthusiastic as she takes the necklace from Rambaldo, and she gets rid of it at once, handing it to her friends, who look at it admiringly.

Rather cryptically, Magda tells Rambaldo — to a bit of waltz music that will follow her upcoming aria, "Ore dolci e divine" — that her only reply is that she cannot change her opinion. (The waltz music, which is rather childlike in character, is identified with the one romantic night of Magda's life — a night she describes in the aria.) What she means by her reply to Rambaldo is that she has no intention of trying to put her own romantic devil to sleep. With irony, and to her own music, Rambaldo says he doesn't require her to.

The necklace has passed to Rambaldo's three friends, who according to the stage directions examine it not with an eye to its beauty, but rather with the goal of gauging how much it cost. Here again is a stage direction that was important to Puccini, but which the actors cannot possibly be expected to carry out.

During all this, Prunier has stood to one side, observing Magda. He is an Artist, and has no interest in touching the necklace, but he is very interested in Magda's reaction to it. To a few soft and thoughtful bars of Doretta's Theme, he comments to himself that the Doretta of his fantasy would not be disturbed (by the king's offer of riches), but the real Doretta seems to be vacillating. This is of course exactly what Magda is — a Vacillator, who reached out her hand for gold and lost her right to love — but her Spring Song showed us she is ripe for repentance.

Another "number" begins as Lisette races in to the sound of a strange, bitonal passage in 3/4 time. Its rising triplets communicate haste and agitation. Pulling Rambaldo aside, Lisette rapidly reports that some man who has been trying to see him for hours has come back again. So quickly does she chatter to her darting music that Rambaldo can't understand a word. Lisette gives an "Ouf!" of exasperation, and slowing her pace a little she explains over a pretty and lyrical melody in the strings that the young man has been pacing up and down in the street, has returned seven times since she first told Rambaldo of him, and is now demanding to know whether Rambaldo will or will not see him.

Rambaldo asks Magda's permission to receive this young man in her home. He is the son of an old school friend, and has been waiting for two hours now. In other words, he has knocked on the door every fifteen minutes. Is our interest in this offstage character being piqued? A little perhaps, but the picture being drawn is of somebody's son — a boy — who is in an inferior position to Rambaldo and is an importuner. We're probably not going to have much respect for a boy who has been hanging about in the street for two hours, hat in hand, waiting to see a wealthy man who has been inside enjoying a leisurely dinner with his mistress.

It would have been easy for Puccini to have given Lisette something else to bustlingly report about the young man, who is Ruggero, the lead tenor. She could have reported that he had just knocked for the first time, and then gone into raptures about how handsome he was, how well dressed, and how well mannered. Puccini presented Ruggero as he did because he wanted the young man to be seen as totally out of his element in the company of Rambaldo and the others. Ruggero is the "student" of Magda's song, and it would undercut his status as poor and ardent if he were welcomed by Rambaldo, and shown to be at ease in his company.

Almost always in Puccini there is a threat of serious violence when the tenor lover and the baritone villain meet and clash over the woman they both want. Here, the baritone has already made the soprano heroine his mistress, and the tenor doesn't even know her. This business of Ruggero being made to wait out in the street for two hours seems to be Puccini's attempt to show the tenor and the baritone at odds with each other during their one and only encounter.

Magda assents to Rambaldo's request, using a now old-fashioned phrase that is gracious, not literal: "You are in your own home." Lisette leaves to invite Ruggero in, and Rambaldo moves toward the conservatory. A slow and wistful waltz melody begins to sound in the strings. This melody — a vague and misty piece, reminiscent of Debussy — is the *Lontano* Theme. It is meant to evoke the sea, and it will be heavily featured in the opening of Act Three, which is set on shore of the Côte d'Azur. At that point the music will take on swell-and-subside dynamics that will offer a musical representation of ocean waves.

Just as important as its musical evocation of the sea is the fact that the *Lontano* Theme is — here in its first appearance — tied to the idea of Lisette. As the passage begins, Prunier asks Magda how she can put up with that giddy Lisette. Kindly, but in melancholy tones that droop and drag, Magda defends her maid as a good girl — "A ray of sunshine in my life."

Lisette is a far more important character than she appears, and the reason she is important is that she is a working class girl. As such, she is one of Puccini's Night people — poor, and therefore good and worthy of passionate love. Lisette represents Magda's only contact with the Night people, and as we will soon see, it will be Lisette who leads Magda back to that world. It is Lisette who is about to bring Ruggero into this house, and it will be Lisette who will provide the two other critical links in the chain between Ruggero and Magda. Only with the help of Lisette will Magda have a chance at finding a rebirth of love. That is why Lisette's name is spoken during the first sounding of the *Lontano* Theme. But notice what Magda said: that Lisette is a ray of sunshine. Sunlight is a deadly thing in Puccini. It kills hope, and it kills people. Why does Puccini have Magda say this?

The answer is that Puccini has begun to deal with sunlight in a new way. The lovers in *La Fanciulla del West* apparently accepted that the passion-filled Night must come to an end. They were able to survive the dawn, and at the end of the opera Puccini attempted to send them off eastward to live in Day — not as Night-intoxicated lovers, but as a respectable married couple. Whether they made it we don't know, but so heartrendingly sad were their goodbyes at the final curtain they certainly seemed afraid of facing the rising sun.

Here in *La Rondine*, Magda, who has grown discontented with her life as Rambaldo's mistress, is going to make an attempt to leave him for a more satisfying man — one who has not put his romantic devil to sleep. But where will they live? It no longer seems possible for her to live in the Night. With Lisette's help she will visit Night, in Act Two, but she can't stay there, because eventually dawn does come. Night is over at the end of Act Two, so where on earth can she and her newfound lover go? As it happens, Prunier has the answer to this, and he will give it to Magda in a few minutes, when he reads her future in her palm. Right now, however, he leaves to join the other men in the conservatory.

In the meantime, Magda's friends, singing wistfully to the music of the *Lontano* Theme, compliment her on her good fortune. Rambaldo is generous, Yvette sings to a notable bit of melody, and Bianca comments sadly on how much it costs one to get hold of money. The girls sing these words to the *Lontano* Theme because they have convinced themselves that money is happiness. When Act Three opens, and we hear this music as we see Magda with her lover, far away at the Côte d'Azur, we will be shown what Magda's happiness is.

Magda sits down in an armchair. Her friends sit around her on footstools, listening as she sings, still to the *Lontano* Theme, that she is certain they are like her, regretting she is no longer a poor shop girl, happy with her lover. Says Bianca significantly, "Those are dreams!" The Amore Theme is now heard, providing a transition to the next number.

Magda can't forget a night when she was young, and experienced for herself the waking dream of love. She remembers an evening when she slipped away from her elderly aunt, and went to a dance hall called Bal Bullier. It seems to her it was only yesterday; and if so, why could it not be tomorrow as well?

The soprano's best aria comes now: "Ore dolci e divine" (Sweet and divine hours), which is another waltz. In a voice made ardent by the recollection of that magical night, Magda describes in the introductory section the happy confusion of the dance hall, filled with students and little seamstresses. She knows neither how she got there nor how she left, but as she moves toward the second section of the aria she recalls a distant voice that spoke a warning. The music of the refrain is a recurring theme of great significance, and it is played mostly by a harp and plucking strings that give a charming impression of a guitar. "Girl, love has blossomed! Defend your heart! The magic of kisses and smiles is paid for with teardrops!" Let's call this lovely melody the Heart Theme.

Magda next describes how she and an unknown young man sat down from their dancing, tired and thirsty, but filled with gaiety. Her partner called for two beers, and when they were brought he tossed down twenty *soldi* and grandly told the waiter to keep the change.

The friends laugh at Magda's description of how she watched, amazed, as her young man made this extravagant gesture. Twenty *soldi* is a tiny amount, but it was obviously all the money the boy had. This act of tossing away one's small store of money as though it were nothing has tremendous significance in Puccini's World. To Puccini, no one could be more worthy of love than this poor, ardent, nameless young bohemian who bought Magda a glass of beer and gave away the rest of his tiny all.

Magda goes on to tell of how the young man tenderly asked her name. She wrote it down on the table, and he wrote his name next to hers, then the two looked at one another without saying a word. Yvette and Bianca are intrigued, but then Magda says that for some reason she does not know, she fled the dance hall. She repeats the line of the recurring music: "Girl, love has blossomed! Defend your heart! The magic of kisses and smiles is paid for with teardrops!" She rises from her chair, and concludes her song in tones of sheer rapture as she wishes she might experience the joy of that hour again.

The girls are disappointed at the conclusion of Magda's adventure, and Bianca calls to Prunier, telling him she has a subject for him. As Yvette and Bianca describe the action— "A flight, a party, a little beer, at home all alone, the old aunt waiting"—the waltz melody that was first heard when Magda told Rambaldo she could not change her opinion is sounded more forcefully. The music seems to represent Magda's Adventure. There's no sense of romance in it, only of fun. What represents sincere romance is the Heart Theme.

With mock self-importance, Prunier now describes himself as a man who is interested in women who are refined, elegant, and perverse. The one who "conquers" him must answer to his artistic tastes. He names four women from literature who would be worthy of him— Galatea, Berenice, Francesca, and Salome—and as he speaks the last name we hear the eerie Salome motif from Richard Strauss's opera.[3]

Magda wonders aloud how Prunier discovers women's qualities, and to the same utility music we heard at the presentation of the necklace Prunier says he reads their palms, in which the goal of a woman can be found. As the poet suggests a palm reading, the music turns exotic, heavy on flutes, harp, and the pings of a triangle. The poet tells the ladies that if they would like to try it, they should fetch the screen that is positioned upstage. There must be an air of mystery for the palm reading, and Magda needs to be shielded from the view of Ruggero, who is just about to enter.

The girls run to get the screen, which they place near the piano to form an intimate recess. The women sit in a circle around Prunier, who, gesturing first at the men in the conservatory and then at the ladies, declares that over there is the profane mob, while here is "beauty and science." It's no wonder he's so popular with the women—and so unpopular with the men. The girls laugh appreciatively, but Magda, quickly gaining a reputation as a killjoy, asks them to please be serious. (We'll hear demands of "Don't laugh," and "Be serious," from several other people as well.)

Magda extends her hand to Prunier, and her friends urge him to reveal all. At this point, Lisette runs in with a salver, on which is a visiting card. She offers the salver to Rambaldo, who reads the card aloud—"Ah! Ruggero Lastouc"—and orders Lisette to show the visitor in. Lisette raises the door curtain, and Ruggero enters. Unfortunately, he does so to the sweeping strains of "Girl, love has blossomed!" from Magda's "Ore dolci e divine."

Owing to the heavy accent and the long-held first note of the word "Fanciulla" during the aria's refrain, that word—Girl—attacks our ears when we now hear the Heart Theme reprised. Since Magda is behind the screen and does not even see Ruggero, and since our eyes are held by the person entering the room, the word seems to us to apply to him. It seems as though Ruggero, who will turn out to be an emotionally fragile virgin, is being addressed as a maiden and warned to defend his heart. Puccini's attempt to connect Ruggero with Magda's dream of romantic love has made a fine start at emasculating the tenor character, who by the end of the opera will have been reduced to the status of a crying infant, with Magda as his mother.

As the melody of "Girl, love has blossomed. Defend your heart!" continues to sound in the sighing strings and rippling harp, Rambaldo welcomes Ruggero as his young friend, and asks his forgiveness for making him wait. Ruggero, who the stage directions tell us is "embarrassed and timid," says it is he who should ask forgiveness. He offers Rambaldo a letter of introduction from his father, and asks him to read it. Rambaldo takes the letter and asks his guest to sit down.

This is the second scene of the opera in which something from *Parsifal* can be detected. Parsifal came to Montsalvat, while Ruggero comes from Montauban. Parsifal was "the guileless fool" who knew almost nothing about anything, while Ruggero is an utter naïf who has come here seeking guidance. When Parsifal first enters, he speaks of his mother, while Ruggero has spoken of his father. Both characters are virgins. Had sections of the *Parsifal* libretto not been incorporated into the second and third acts of *La Rondine* it would have been idle speculation to claim that in this scene, Puccini was thinking of Ruggero as Parsifal. But with the benefit of those other two acts, we can see he definitely was, and that he was thinking of Rambaldo as Klingsor during the scene of the pearl necklace.

During the few seconds in which Rambaldo and Ruggero were talking, Prunier had been examining Magda's palm. It seems quite rude for the five people behind the screen to ignore Ruggero, and for Rambaldo not to formally introduce Ruggero even to the other men, but we should probably imagine that with the placing of the screen, we have two groups of people in two separate rooms. Essentially, Rambaldo is receiving Ruggero privately, for some personal business between the two of them. That is of course not what would happen in real life — Rambaldo would introduce his friend's son to everyone — but we need to willingly suspend disbelief and imagine that is what we are seeing.

Puccini segues very neatly from the Heart Theme back to the exotic music of the palm reading as Prunier declares Magda has revealed herself through her palm, and her future is grave and mysterious. Excitedly, the girls urge him to reveal Magda's future, and like a good showman the poet again pretends reluctance, saying it is too sibylline. Magda asks him to tell what he's seen.

Suddenly serious, Prunier uses one of Puccini's key words, saying Destiny draws Magda on. The Rondine Theme, another ravishing melody from strings and harp, begins as Prunier begins to prophesy for Magda. It is a prophesy of rebirth, symbolized by the swallow. We hear the twittering of swallows in the flutes, and a beautiful depiction of breaking waves as the poet says, "Perhaps, like the swallow, you will migrate over the sea, toward a bright land of dreams, toward the sun, toward love."

Again Puccini has raised the possibility of his heroine and her lover being able to live in Day, in sunlight. What does it mean in the context of the Rose Cycle? It means that Puccini — in terms of his characters and his drama — has come to believe that his young lovers, who live and love in the Night and die when the moon and thus the soprano heroine lose their power, might be able to survive the dawn and live in sunlight if they can get to that place that everyone longed for in *La Fanciulla del West*. Prunier the poet is telling Magda she might be able to find rebirth — new love and new life — if she can find *là lontano* — the far away place where there are no troubles. Perhaps *là lontano* is where the waking dream becomes reality. We see now why Prunier and Lisette are a couple. "And perhaps..." Prunier continues. Magda interrupts him, asking if he sees an ill omen. No, says the poet. "Destiny has a double face. A smile or anguish? Mystery."

Rambaldo has finished reading the letter, and he asks Ruggero if this is his first visit to Paris. Originally, his response was simply, "The first," and then attention went back to the palm reading. Some years after the opera's premiere, however, Puccini decided to insert an entrance aria for Ruggero, whose sole vocal contribution to the act after this point is, "Thank you!" The aria begins with the declamation, "Parigi!" (Paris!).

Ruggero's aria, which is rarely performed during the rare performances of *La Rondine*, began life as a song called "Morirè?" — "To die?" It's quite possible the title alone was what prompted Puccini to use the music for Ruggero's entrance aria, for many of his best musical moments occur when the word "death" is being sung. "Morirè!" is not a very good song, but Puccini's instinct was to try to raise the level of excitement in his operas by bringing in ideas of death.

Even if the music of "Parigi!" isn't much, the words Ruggero sings during his melancholy song are absolutely fascinating. He is a young man, come to the great city from a rustic place, and here is what he sings:

> Paris! It is the city of desires ... which opens to the luminous dream of fascinations, of hopes! It is the goal of all! It is the siren! From the timid simplicity and quiet of the countryside, this disturbance catches us and leads us astray in a bewilderment, since our soul is honest and happy. Here, among the crowd, it is like walking within the sweetness of enchanted dreams, and peace is swept away in the new anxiety of desire.

This should remind us of someone. This is Roberto, from *Le Villi*. This is the simple and honest young man, come in all his innocence to the city, where he will be devoured by the *cortigiana vil* — the vile courtesan who will corrupt him, wring him dry of his inheritance and then cast him aside, a pitiful ruin, unfit for the stainless flower of a girl he left behind. The parallels are practically perfect, because of course Magda is a "courtesan," and there is a moment in the final act when Ruggero confesses he is out of money — indeed, he pulls a stack of demand letters out of his pockets and shows them to Magda, who expresses guilt over his situation — and then a few minutes later Magda tells him they are through.

Puccini had Ruggero sing these words, and have these thoughts, because the only thing that interested him dramatically was *romance*, with its powerful, devouring heroine, and her submissive, adoring, frightened lover. I said in the chapter on *Le Villi* that if Fontana's "vile courtesan" had slunk onto the stage, Puccini wouldn't have known what to do with her. Well, here's the courtesan, and we can see what Puccini made of her: she is his beautiful, beloved heroine — the only character in the opera he has any real interest in. She is the sexually independent woman, and the only thing wrong with her in Puccini's eyes is that she reached out her hand for gold, and so lost the right to love.

In productions that don't include Ruggero's entrance aria, his answer to Rambaldo's question (yes, it's the first time he has visited Paris) is followed by a return to the palm reading. Prunier examines Bianca's hand, and tells her the lines suggest "Et ultra." This is Latin for "And beyond," and it's the sort of motto one would find on a knight's shield in a tale of chivalry.

Lisette now enters with a tray, on which is a glass of champagne, which she puts down on a table in front of Ruggero. He makes a gesture of thanks and picks up the glass, but the stage directions say he barely touches it to his lips. He does not drink the champagne — not even a drop. He only avoids insulting his host, by making a gesture of acceptance. What is the meaning of this? Is it a recollection of Dick Johnson, who didn't drink in the presence of a lady? No, for Ruggero has no problem at all drinking champagne in Act Two. In fact, he's the one who orders it. It seems likely Puccini was trying to paint a picture of Ruggero as someone who is not at all at ease in this luxurious environment.

Rambaldo calls to Prunier, asking the "cultivated poet" where one might send a young man who wants to spend an agreeable evening. (Note that it is still early — the Night of Love is yet to come.) In a response that is perhaps more humorous to us now than then, Prunier answers, "To bed!" Apparently Rambaldo has more in common with Magda than we might have thought, for he answers this with an irritated, "Don't joke!" With an air of superiority, Prunier moves toward Ruggero and declares that all that stuff about one's first night in Paris is a legend, and it's high time it was debunked.

Lisette is still in the room, and she explodes in indignation, delivering herself of an impassioned defense of Paris as a city of fascinations, surprises, and marvels. One's first evening in Paris, she cries, is like seeing the ocean for the first time. Offended at being contradicted so publicly and so loudly, Prunier shouts that these are all fairy-tales, and he demands that Lisette be ejected. Puccini has been careful to keep Magda out of the sight of Ruggero (she's been *tête-à-tête* with one of Rambaldo's friends since Prunier left the screened area), and now she follows Prunier, who stalks off into the conservatory, and attempts to soothe him. The two of them will stay in the conservatory until Ruggero has gone, watching what is happening in the salon.

Rambaldo now says to Lisette, "Come now! You recommend the goal!" People complained to Puccini after *La Rondine* came out that it was absurd to show wealthy people putting up with antics from a servant girl, and including her in their conversations. They didn't understand Puccini. In this world of his, only a poor person such as Lisette would be capable of directing the steps of Ruggero toward a night of real, passionate romance. It MUST be Lisette who suggests the place. The first link in the "Lisette" chain between Magda and Ruggero was the girl's bringing Ruggero into the house. Her recommendation of the night spot is the second link.

So it is that Magda's three friends agree with Rambaldo, saying to Lisette that it is up to her to suggest a place. Lisette takes a pencil and paper from a table and gives them to Ruggero, telling him to write down the recommendations. Puccini uses a polka rhythm for the pretty quartet during which the four women circle about the hapless Ruggero and name one after another of Paris's glittering dance halls. Lisette suggests the Bal Bullier, and the friends concur. None of the ladies offers to escort the handsome boy from out of town, they merely let Lisette send him out the door with the assurance that among the lights and flowers of Bal Bullier, love sings more ardently.

As Ruggero exits, the Malady Theme recurs — the music of the subtle microbe that has attacked the women of Paris, and against which even Doretta's heart had no defense. Magda and Prunier come out of the conservatory as the theme begins. Magda is holding the pearl necklace in one hand, twirling it about nonchalantly. So far Magda has exhibited no interest at all in Ruggero, and as he goes out the door she comments that her friends seem to have stunned the poor boy. When Bianca declares that Bullier's works miracles, Magda repeats the dance hall's name vaguely, looks at the pearl necklace for a moment, then drops it negligently on a table.

As the Malady Theme continues, Prunier makes a telling remark about Ruggero: "He had all the perfume of youth. The air is filled with lavender. Don't you smell it?" Prunier sniffs the air comically, and Rambaldo agrees with what seems like a sneer, but Puccini is of course not joking. He is trying again to show that Ruggero is totally outside this corrupt, money-drenched society, and there is no better way to do that than by remarking on the boy's youth, and on the scent of flowers that fills the air where he had been standing.

Prunier's remark about the scent of lavender halted the Malady Theme, and now the utility music first heard during the necklace presentation returns as Rambaldo and the others bid Magda a good evening. (Note once again that it is not late enough to be called night. Night belongs to the Artists and the Students, and we will live through it with them in Act Two.) As soon as Magda is alone, the orchestra gives us her thoughts. She walks across the room slowly, thinking, to the music of Magda's Adventure ("An escape, a party, a little beer...."), of that romantic night she spent at Bullier's. She rings the bell for Lisette, then sits in an armchair. Lisette enters to a wisp of one of her themes.

Magda orders her to have the carriage brought around, but then she changes her mind. She tells Lisette to light the lamps in the boudoir, and the girl reminds Magda she won't be around later, since tonight is her night off. Magda agrees, and Lisette puts out the lamps in the salon and exits. The stage directions tell us the room is now illuminated only by the dim light coming from the conservatory. In other words, this is moonlight, entering through the greenhouse where the flowers are growing.

Magda sits and thinks for a moment, then repeats the words of Prunier's prophecy. Very softly, the Rondine Theme sounds as Magda recalls the poet's words: "Perhaps, like a swallow, I will migrate across the sea, toward a bright land of dreams, toward the sun, toward love." She walks toward the chair where Ruggero had been seated. Her eye lights on the paper, which he left behind, and she picks it up and reads Lisette's recommendation. "Bullier's," she says softly. Her face is lit up by a smile, then she runs into the boudoir and shuts the door behind her.

There is a brief silence, then six soft notes—three from the oboe, and three an octave lower from the bassoon—introduce the strange little love duet of Prunier and Lisette, "T'amo! Menti!" (I love you! You lie!). Lisette enters first, from the conservatory, stepping cautiously on tiptoe. In her hand is a fancy hat, and over one arm is a silk coat. She stops to listen at the door of the boudoir, and the sound of Magda undressing satisfies her. She comes back across the floor where she meets Prunier, who is wearing an overcoat with an upturned collar. To a soft and insinuating melody played by oboe and bassoon, Prunier embraces Lisette, and declares he loves her. Struggling against him, Lisette, who hasn't forgotten how he spoke of her during her paean to the city of Paris, calls him a liar.

With one foot in the world of the Alberichs, Prunier is still a member of the Artist community. He originated the song of Doretta, and knew what the pearl necklace represented. He spoke not one word to Rambaldo's friends, and it's obvious Rambaldo dislikes him. Final proof that he is one of Puccini's good people lies here, in his choice of a working class girl—not as a toy, but as a lover. He assures Lisette he does indeed love her, but before they go out on the town he wants her to change that hat. It may be Magda's best, but it doesn't go with the rest of the ensemble.

As Lisette runs off, Prunier makes a little prayer to the nine Muses, asking them to forgive him. "I love her and cannot reason," he says, and as he does, we hear a thrumming in the double basses that seems to depict the poet's throbbing heart. Lisette returns with a hat that passes inspection, but now Prunier rejects the silk coat. Again the girl runs off, and Prunier continues his prayer to the Muses. Having exchanged the coat for a black cape, Lisette is pronounced exquisite. Prunier gives her the purse she dropped, and she begins to make up her face. Using Puccini's language of flowers, the poet urges his sweetheart to let her lips flower, and to make two roses of her cheeks. A touch of mascara, and she is done.

The two go off slowly, murmuring of love, Prunier's arm about Lisette. In an exit reminiscent of Rodolfo and Mimi, they sing, to the lightest of accompaniment, "I am yours, I am yours!" One more kiss, and they go, leaving the unresolved chord of their final word hanging in the air. A moment later, however, a solo violin takes up the note, and with the aid of a harp and *pizzicato* strings turns it into the opening of the Heart Theme.

Magda enters from the boudoir, the violin gently telling her via the lilting waltz that love is in the air, and she'd better defend her heart. Here is the third and final link in the Lisette chain, for Magda is wearing one of Lisette's dresses. Magda now looks like a *grisette*, and so she has arranged her hair very simply, and taken off every piece of jewelry she might have been wearing. The repulsive pearl necklace lies where she dropped it, and now she goes to the piano and takes one of the red roses from the vase. She approaches a mirror on the wall and places the rose in her hair. She studies her reflection, and seeing her disguise seems perfect, asks herself, "Who would recognize me?"

Magda thinks she can pass. She thinks that with a servant girl's clothes and a red rose in her hair, no one will realize she is one of the Vacillators, tainted by gold, and unfit to mingle with Artists and Students, seeking love in the Night. She vocalizes the opening of "Doretta's beautiful dream," and drapes a shawl over her shoulders. The final touch in place, she happily asks herself, "Who can divine Doretta's mystery?"

As she walks toward the door, the orchestra slowly plays the final section of Doretta's song, its crescendos and decrescendos reminding us of breakers on the shore: "Ah, my dream! Ah, my life! What do riches matter, if...." Suddenly uncertain, Magda pauses. She goes back to the mirror and studies her reflection again. The sight of the rose reassures her, and she repeats, "But really! Who would recognize me?" She leaves quickly, and the orchestra brings down the curtain by softly finishing the question: "...if happiness has blossomed again?"

The Bal Bullier is the setting for Act Two. Like the Bal Mabille, mentioned in *La Bohème*, the Bullier was a real place—a Paris dance hall frequented by Puccini's favorite people: artists, students, and shop girls. These dance halls were huge—palaces of pleasure featuring open-air restaurants, gardens, fountains, roller skating rinks, and of course pavilions, where bands played waltzes, polkas, and the newest dances like the fox trot and the tango. A passage in Somerset Maugham's *Of Human Bondage* gives a description of Bullier's as of about 1914, which is contemporary with Puccini's composition of *La Rondine*:

> Bullier was not the resort of fashion. It was Thursday night and the place was crowded. There were a number of students of the various faculties, but most of the men were clerks or assistants in shops; they wore their everyday clothes, ready-made tweeds or queer tail-coats, and their hats, for they had brought them in with them, and when they danced there was no place to put them but their heads. Some of the women looked like servant-girls, and some were painted hussies, but for the most part they were

shop-girls. They were poorly dressed in cheap imitation of the fashions on the other side of the river. The hussies were got up to resemble the music-hall artiste or the dancer who enjoyed notoriety at the moment; their eyes were heavy with black and their cheeks were impudently scarlet. The hall was lit by great white lights, low down, which emphasized the shadows on the faces; all the lines seemed to harden under it, and the colors were most crude. It was a sordid scene.[4]

Act One closed on a quiet note: Magda exiting her dimly lit salon to the gentle strains of "Doretta's beautiful dream." Act Two could not provide a greater contrast, for the curtain rises on an eye-stunning scene of light, color, and confused movement, at the same time the orchestra begins a shockingly loud waltz, studded with shouts of merriment from the patrons of Bullier's, who are swarming around like bees in a hive.

We see an elaborate staircase at left, which leads into the dance hall that is before us. The garden is in the rear, and it is lit with small lamps. In the left-hand wall are two big windows, facing onto the street. The hall is filled to the bursting point with flowers.

That Bullier's is filled with flowers is only to be expected — this is a Rose Cycle opera, and the Night of Love is best set in the outdoors, in a garden filled with flowers. Since we are indoors, we must bring the garden inside, as Butterfly did when preparing for the return of Pinkerton. But we've already seen bits of *Parsifal* in Act One, and here in Act Two we see Puccini's version of the scene in Klingsor's garden, where first the Flower Maidens, and then Kundry, sexually tempt the innocent hero.

Although the stage directions call for a profusion of flowers in vases, Flower Girls mingle with the crowd. The girls speak the first words in this act: "Fresh flowers! Fresh flowers!" The cry continues as a babble of conversation is heard from the customers, who argue, call out orders for drinks, and try to pick one another up. "Violets?" the girls offer. "Beautiful roses?" "Fresh flowers!"

A group of Artists and girls uses Puccini's language of the magic of sunset to invoke the hour of waking dreams, during which hope struggles with melancholy in the hearts of young lovers: "Come, let's drink! Youth, eternal laughter, fresh flowers that crown the sweet faces of women! You are a divinity if you can chain the illusions of lovers!" Sitting alone at a table is Ruggero, who looks extremely out of place amid these wild revelers. Three girls (usually doubled by those singing the roles of Magda's friends) and some other *grisettes* decide that Ruggero looks lonely. They go to his table and try to pick him up.

This is Puccini's version of the Flower Maidens' attempt to seduce Parsifal. The girls call Ruggero "a lily — a mimosa," and complain that he doesn't give them a smile or a look. The stage directions say Ruggero "looks at them, half-annoyed and surprised." What an odd reaction, for anyone but Parsifal. Ruggero is just what a Puccini heroine longs for — a young man with a virgin heart, destined to love only once, and forever — but the surprise and annoyance of Ruggero at being importuned by this gaggle of girls comes from Parsifal.

The girls come nearer to Ruggero, and noisily demand to know his name. Parsifal did not know his name, and here, Ruggero refuses to speak to the girls, who call out twelve men's names in a fierce and dissonant attempt to guess Ruggero's. The Flower Girls continue their cry of "Fresh flowers! Fresh flowers! Violets! Beautiful roses!" Ruggero drives the friendly girls off with a gesture of irritation, just as Parsifal did the importuning Flower Maidens. Wagner's Maidens had cried of Parsifal, "We give him up for lost!" Puccini's girls go off saying, "He comes from distant shores! He refuses our beds!"

Now Magda appears on the staircase. Nervous and uncertain, she looks around, while a few men begin to look her over. They observe her hesitation, and wonder if she is an "honest woman." One comes over and offers his arm, which the embarrassed Magda refuses. Others swarm around her, describing themselves to the Malady Theme as students, rich in kisses, but short of cash. Normally, a Puccini heroine would be delighted to be approached in this way, and to this music, and in truth we have no idea what Magda wants, for she has not come here looking for Ruggero, whom she scarcely noticed at her house.

Magda tries to get rid of the students by telling them she has a date. The Malady Theme mixes with the conversational music as the men continue questioning her. When they demand to know whom she is meeting, she looks around helplessly, and her eyes light on Ruggero. The students "very politely" escort her to Ruggero's table. Baffled, the young man looks back and forth as the students, sounding like a fraternity choir, sing, "Lovers, enjoy your young life!" before they go off, laughing.

The Rondine Theme sounds as Magda asks Ruggero's forgiveness. She tells him, truthfully, that she was trying to get rid of the students by claiming she was meeting someone. She promises to leave as soon as they have gone, and she sings this last line, strangely enough, to the music of the opening of Ruggero's entrance aria, "Parigi!" Perhaps it is meant to describe Ruggero's thoughts about the wonders of Paris as he looks at Magda and hears her speak.

Ruggero is won over by this pretty girl's desire not to inflict her company on him, and he urges her to stay. She is, he says, very different from the other girls here. Magda naturally wants to know what he means, and to the rhythm of a one-step dance the young man begins to tell her about the girls back home in Montauban. She seems shy and lonely, he says, thus she is like the girls of Montauban, when they come to dance to the music of an old song. The Montauban girls "are very beautiful, and simple, and modest. They are not like these. All they need for jewelry is a flower in the hair, like you." (In other words, eyes are more beautiful than the most stupendous jewels.)

Magda wishes she could dance like the girls in Montauban. Ruggero offers his arm. Magda takes it "languidly," which suggests Puccini is leading her into a dream state in which she will live again that romantic night she sang of in "Ore dolci e divine." Half to herself, she remarks on what a strange adventure this is, like those of long ago. Ruggero asks what she means, and she merely says, "I am happy to be in your arms."

A lovely waltz begins, "Nella dolce carezza della danza" (In the sweet caress of the dance). As the lovers first sing to it, we hear little more than harp and strings supporting their voices. Soon the chorus takes a verse, however, and a marvelous, silvery chiming is heard from the glockenspiel as the music segues into a reprise of the music of Magda's Adventure: "An escape, a party, a little beer...."

Shouts, laughter, and a crash of cymbals signal a new and fiery phase of the dance. Soon the voices of Magda and Ruggero are heard from the garden, singing, to the Amore Theme, many of the words associated with the Night of Love: Sweetness! Enchantment! Intoxication! A dream! Forever! Eternally! At this point, the stage directions tell us, pairs of dancers representing spring enter, and the focus of both sight and sound changes from Night to a celebration of Spring. With others, the three girls who tried to seduce Ruggero sing of the perfume of an April night. "Flowers and love blossom in spring's warmth!" The waltz is now sweeping and lyrical, and it has become a Spring Song, representative of the rebirth of love.

The crowd dances off to the garden, leaving the stage fairly clear for the entrance of Prunier and Lisette, who are arguing. It annoys her greatly that he tries to stop her from socializing with others. He assures her he is only trying to improve her education. As they quarrel, we hear a recollection of the music to which Prunier gave his description of the woman who would conquer him. When their argument is done, a whirling figure is heard in the orchestra, and the couple dance off, lost amid the crowd.

Magda and Ruggero return, tired and hot from dancing, but full of high spirits. They plop into their seats. Fanning herself with a handkerchief, Magda says she is thirsty. Immediately Ruggero orders two bocks from a passing waiter. (Bock is a dark beer usually drunk in spring.) Although she is having a good time with Ruggero, it appears Magda is still focused on her fantasy. The music of "Ore dolci e divine" is heard as, "Joyfully, as if reliving a memory," she asks Ruggero to give the waiter twenty *soldi*, and let him keep the change.

Ruggero smiles, unaware he is being asked to help Magda play out a fantasy. The harp ripples dreamily as Magda happily sings the words of Magda's Adventure: "An escape, a party, a little beer...." Uncomprehending, Ruggero asks her what she is saying. Her answer is, "Fantasie! Fantasie!"—Waking dreams! Waking dreams!

The waiter brings the beer, and Ruggero toasts Magda's health. She raises her glass and toasts, "To your many loves!" Ruggero is shocked by this, and instantly puts his glass down with a gesture of vexation. "Don't say that!" he orders her. Puzzled, Magda asks him why and with great seriousness he declares, to the Amore Theme, that he is a man with a virgin heart, destined to love only once, and forever. "Because if I were to love, it would only be once, and for all my life!" It is Magda's turn to be shocked, and as she looks at him she repeats his last words. This seems to be a turning point for her, for she did not come here looking for him, and nothing so far has suggested he has made any great impression on her.

Ruggero looks carefully at Magda's face, and her reaction to his words pleases him. Very sweetly, to the music of "my little adored one" from "Ore dolci e divine," he asks her name. It might have been a good idea if Puccini had had Magda start to go on with her fantasy—begin to write her name on the table as before—but then stop, put down the pencil, and speak her name. It would have suggested she had let go of the young man of her memory, and had turned to Ruggero as himself. But the fantasy continues, for Magda gets a pencil from Ruggero and writes "Paulette" on the tabletop. The name pleases Ruggero, who writes his own next to it.

Puccini's lovers are always aware that the clock is ticking, so Magda points at the names and says the writing is something of the two of them that will remain. Ruggero disagrees, saying the marks will be wiped away. Yet there is something that will remain with him: her "mystery." "Mystery" is one of Magda's key words, first appearing in "Doretta's beautiful dream," and returning during the palm reading. Magda's "mystery" is her destiny. Will she find a rebirth of love? Will she, like the swallow, find her way to the bright land of dreams? There is no telling as yet, for Fate has a double face: a smile and a frown. As for Magda, she urges Ruggero not to attempt to find out her mystery, but simply to take her as destiny has brought her to him.

Her answer is the beginning of a love duet, "Perchè mai cercate di saper" (Why should you try to discover), sung to the rhythm of a slow fox trot, but it isn't a very good one. The problem is the old one: no passion. This is a romantic duet, rather than one inspired by erotic feelings, and as a result it is placid and limp. Puccini tried to throw fuel on the fire by employing some of his magic words. Magda cries, "Let me dream!" and Ruggero uses the words of romance's tortured knight: "I feel a strange torment, sweet, infinite." But it's no use. Puccini just didn't feel it. And neither do we.

Their last words—which are broken off by a kiss—are sung to the Amore Theme, then a violin sweetly reprises the main melody of the love duet as a mob of students and other young people notice and comment on what seems to be a shocking sight: two people kissing in Bal Bullier. To the Amore Theme, the onlookers urge one another to be quiet, and respect Love.

The stage clears as the mob tiptoe away, and now Prunier and Lisette appear. Lisette is startled to see her employer, and her outcry causes Ruggero and Magda to break off their long kiss. Prunier catches the signal thrown by Magda, and promptly tells Lisette she must be drunk. He takes her toward the table, and she is again startled when she recognizes Ruggero. Prunier bids Ruggero a good evening, and as he does we hear the music of Magda's Adventure. Evidently the poet realizes Magda is living out her fantasy, and Ruggero is the stand-in for the young man who had charmed her.

Numerous pieces of music from the first act are heard as Prunier and Lisette talk to Magda and Ruggero. We hear a bit from the Prunier/Lisette love duet, then much of the music from the opening of that act, including Lisette's declaration that the report of sentimental love being the rage was nonsense. Then we hear the music of Prunier's claim of being annoyed at that, then the music to which Prunier told the girls that it was true, and a few other scraps, none of which seem to have any significance as recurrences. Puccini seems to be reusing the music because of its association with light conversation about love.

Prunier introduces his friend Lisette to Ruggero, and Ruggero introduces his friend Paulette. He then introduces Prunier to Magda, calling him a friend of a friend of his father's. To the music of, "In Paris, they love," Prunier completes Ruggero's sentence, saying, "And therefore a friend of yours."

Magda asks Lisette why she keeps looking at her, and the girl (who has indeed been drinking) declares that she (Magda) looks just like her mistress. Ruggero asks if this mistress is charming, and Lisette points at Magda and says that if she were elegantly dressed she would look like her. Magda teases Lisette about her own attire, and the girl confesses proudly that everything she is wearing she has sneaked away from her mistress. The glockenspiel chimes as Magda teasingly says she shouldn't say that—it's too imprudent. Prunier laughs, and in what must be the most repeated phrase of the opera, Lisette tells him not to laugh.

In a low voice, Ruggero places an order with a waiter. In a moment we will see it was for champagne—the drink he would barely touch to his lips at Magda's house. The champagne arrives, and Ruggero introduces the love quartet by singing, rather powerfully, and unaccompanied by music, that since chance has united them, they should drink a toast to love. The introduction is completed by the four people singing, still unaccompanied, that they should drink to life, which gives us love. A series of harp arpeggios then launches the song.

The love quartet, "Bevo al tuo fresco sorriso" (I drink to your fresh smile), has a ravishing melody line, and is considered by many to be the high point of the opera, both musically and visually. But it's repetitious—first the tenor sings the melody to a light accompaniment, then the other three join him to sing the melody to a moderate accompaniment, then the chorus joins them to sing the melody to a loud accompaniment. The song is almost criminally undeveloped, considering the beautiful melody and Puccini's talent for writing passionate love songs.

The words sung by Prunier and Lisette aren't important, but those sung by Ruggero and Magda have great significance, for they express an intense and frightened hope that love might succeed in warding off death. Ruggero says he has given Magda his heart, and she should guard it so it may live forever in her. Magda sings that this is the fulfillment of her dream, and she hopes it might never die. Ruggero then assures her that, "No, this moment cannot die.... Nothing greater can I ask of life than to revel in the infinite joy your kiss gives me!" This is the concept that underpins the Rose Cycle, and has done since the curtain went up on *Manon Lescaut*: the lovers' hope — which always deceives — that the intensity of their love might cause their dream of endless love in endless night to come true.

Another thing to notice in the quartet is the Puccini Mixture of joy and sadness. In a few minutes it will be dawn, and Magda will sing the following words to a reprise of the love song's melody: "I am so afraid. I am too happy. This is my dream, do you understand? But I tremble and weep." After one has heard the opera several times, he may find himself thinking of these words of sadness and fear during the love song, and he will hear the words of the love song during Magda's expression of sadness and fear. When Puccini sings of love, he thinks of sadness, and when he sings of sadness, he thinks of love.

At the point where the chorus joins in the quartet, the opera's focus on flowers and the rebirth of love in springtime becomes all-encompassing. Some of the girls begin to weave a crown of flowers, which they place on the head of Prunier, who, being a poet, is the most deserving of such a tribute. The chorus sings, "Flowers! Flowers! Flowers! Our flowers, our flowers! Ah, with flowers! Fronds and flowers! Let us smother the four loves with flowers! With flowers!" And with that, they begin to throw flowers onto the four lovers from all directions — sides, back, and above.

The intense focus on flowers in *La Rondine* rivals that of *Madama Butterfly*, which also addressed the *romance* theme of love being reborn in spring. The love quartet is, on the part of the principals, pretty much a straightforward love duet (except of course for the Puccinian, dream-inspired hope of undying love), but the chorus's contribution is infused with the sentiment of a Spring Song. (This is, incidentally, the opera's third Spring Song so far.) The celebration of love is brought to an end when Prunier suddenly notices Rambaldo coming down the staircase. The orchestra blares excitedly, and Prunier warns Magda: "Rambaldo!"

Rambaldo has brought a very pretty melody with him. The party is over, not just for the four lovers but for everyone at Bullier's. Dawn is only minutes away, and this new melody, which will carry most of the dialogue from now until Rambaldo leaves, is the first part of the Dawn Song. The second part, which has words, will be heard after Rambaldo has gone.

As the crowd makes preparations to leave, Prunier ensures that Ruggero will not encounter Rambaldo. Loudly, he tells Lisette her master is here. The girl is terrified, presumably because she doesn't want to be caught wearing Magda's clothes. Vehemently, Prunier tells Ruggero he is entrusting Lisette to his care, and he urges him to take her out of here. Poor Ruggero looks like a dunce as he solicitously urges Lisette to trust him and not to be afraid. Completing the young man's humiliation, Prunier puts Lisette in the know, whispering to her to take Ruggero away. Even the servant girl knows what Ruggero does not. Prunier urges Magda to leave before Rambaldo sees her, but Magda has already decided to break with the banker. Prunier thinks she is being foolish, but there is no arguing with her.

There is a pause in the dawn music as Prunier goes to meet Rambaldo and attempts to keep him from spotting Magda. The banker extends his hand politely, and as Prunier takes it he comments on Rambaldo's ring. "Oh! What a big emerald!" This remark really annoys Rambaldo, who tells the poet to go away. There is no better way of insulting someone in Puccini's World than by accusing him of possessing wealth. As Rambaldo is on his way to see a beautiful young woman, Prunier might just as well have looked at his head and said, "Oh! What a big bald spot!"

Unable to help Magda, Prunier gives up and exits, undoubtedly circling around to the garden to pick up Lisette. In between the dialogue of the principals, conversation is heard from other customers of Bullier's, all of which deals with dawn, and the idea of things having come to a tiring end. "It's late, almost dawn. I've had enough. What else are you waiting for?" People put on their coats, pay their tab (or not), and begin to clear out.

The music of the coming dawn resumes as Rambaldo approaches Magda, who is leaning against a table. Quietly but firmly, he asks for an explanation. He is surprised when she declares, in a passage that manages to be simultaneously overwrought and lifeless, that she is staying here, and that she loves "him." The more excited she gets, the more her music wrenches itself upwards, until finally her excitement is spent. Her vocal line sags and droops as she tearfully tells Rambaldo to let her follow her "destiny."

Once again the dawn music resumes as Magda, upset and sorry, offers Rambaldo her hand and apologizes for hurting him. Expressing a hope that she won't come to regret it, Rambaldo bows politely and exits. The final passage of the first part of the dawn music ends as first oboe, then flute, use the main motif of the melody to effect a climb up the scale that gives the impression of bird calls. (Morning has broken.) A transitional passage is then played by the bassoon—a low-voiced variation of the same motif.

Much of the rhythm and melody of that motif is carried over into the second part of the dawn music—the actual Dawn Song—as an offstage female voice, accompanied by someone whistling the same melody line, sings of the peril of dawn. As she listens to the voice, Magda drops limply into a chair. She is alone, and Bullier's is a dismal sight. What is sadder than the lonely mess left behind after a wild party has ended and all the guests have gone? Glasses are overturned, and tables disordered. Flowers, wilted and stepped on, are all over the floor. The lights in the garden have been extinguished. From outside, the sounds of Paris waking up can be heard.

Accompanied by the whistling and by the bassoon reiterating its motif, the offstage voice sings, "In the uncertain light of morning, you appeared to me garlanded with roses, and I see you lightly gliding, strewing the heavens with petals. Will you tell me who you are? I am the dawn that was born to put to flight the magic of the night moon." As the voice utters the word "moon," we hear a "bong" in the orchestra. This is a single note of the tolling bell that always signals disaster and death. (Act Three will close with tolling bells. Ostensibly they are ringing for vespers, but we know what they really mean.)

The bassoon and the bass clarinet finish off the song, then Ruggero enters, carrying Magda's shawl. He brings with him a warm and comforting reprise of the love quartet, and in his youth, innocence, and sincerity, he seems like a ray of hope. He calls to "Paulette," telling her their friends have gone. And then he utters the most frightening words a Puccini heroine can hear. "You know, it's dawn." Magda knew that already, which is why her face has a "mortal pallor." She starts when Ruggero speaks to her, and he runs to her anxiously, asking what is wrong.

Magda seems to "suddenly awake from a dream," and she reaches out to Ruggero. As the reprise of the love song continues to play, she speaks in tearful and cryptic terms of her terror of dawn, which brings death — the death of dreams, and physical death. The glockenspiel chimes as Magda sings, "It's nothing. I love you! But you don't know! You see, I'm afraid! I'm too happy! This is my dream, do you understand? But I tremble and weep."

Ruggero is not one of Puccini's Artist characters, who live and love in the Night. Although Puccini gave him a few stock phrases from the tortured knight of *romance*, he is not a *romance* character. Ruggero is an ordinary and respectable young man of Day, and he has no idea Magda is not a respectable young woman of Day. Her words are a mystery to him. The two link arms, and as they stroll towards dawn, their voices rise to a gorgeous high B flat as they bring down the curtain with a cry of, "My life! My love!" Perhaps these mismatched lovers can find a place that is neither Night nor Day, where they can live eternally on love. Perhaps they can find that Shangri-la Puccini calls *là lontano*. We can hope, anyway.

As the curtain rises on the final act, we see a small summer-house on the Côte d'Azur. The little house is on high ground, and it slopes down to a grass-covered clearing. In front of the house is a terrace, with table and chairs. Tea is on the table. This is a more elegant setting than usual for a pair of Puccini lovers, but the idea is the same: a small place, high up, that serves as little more than shelter to a couple who basically live out of doors.

Slender, blossoming trees dot the landscape. At back is a wall with a gap in the center. The wall is covered with ivy and climbing roses. Beyond are olive trees, and through the branches we glimpse a bit of the Côte d'Azur. A path goes down to the sea. It is late afternoon on a magnificent day in spring. Swallows circle the distant sky. So this is what *là lontano* looks like. Time seems to stand still here. This place of roses and swallows seems like a land of eternal springtime. Magda and Ruggero stand, surrounded by the symbols of regeneration, and enjoying the intimacy of the time and place.

The music opens with a recurrence of the *Lontano* Theme, which we first heard in Act One, subsequent to the scene of the pearl necklace. Magda answered Prunier's complaint about Lisette by saying the girl was a ray of sunshine in her life, then her friends congratulated her on her enviable life. "Rambaldo is generous," said one, thinking luxury was Magda's happiness. Here, as the theme replays, we see what her real happiness is. The only problem with the recurrence of the theme is that those words—"Rambaldo is generous"—received such emphasis that we might recall them here. Listeners may wonder whether the music is meant to suggest Rambaldo is financing this summer place.

Although Puccini at one point considered having Rambaldo appear in the last act and give Magda some money, it is not the case that he is paying for this place. The music simply describes Magda's happiness, which Prunier predicted would be linked with the sea. The ocean's swell was scarcely audible when the *Lontano* Theme was heard in Act One, but it is unmistakable now, in the repeated crescendos and decrescendos. The harp seems to describe ripples in the water, while the timpani gives us the crash of waves on the shore. "Do you feel it?" Magda asks. "Even the sea breathes quietly. The air drinks the perfume of the flowers."

Every movement and utterance in this opening scene is slow, languid, and mysterious. That we are in a magical and timeless place, like the land of the lotus-eaters, is suggested by Magda's slow-waltz arietta, "So l'arte strana" (I know the arcane art). After slowly handing Ruggero a cup of tea, Magda moves gracefully to his side and softly sings that she knows the strange art of compounding a philter that will banish all weariness. Ruggero smiles, and after being urged he tells her that everything about her pleases him. He denies being bored by the solitude of this place, saying he isn't alone, not when her love "awakens each day more passionate, more intense, more sacred."

That last word was "santo," and it could also be translated as "holy," or "saintly." Puccini wrote to a friend of his, Sybil Seligman, that he believed *La Rondine* would do well in London because its subject was a moral one.[5] Combined with Puccini's identification of Ruggero with Parsifal, the word "santo" suggests that Ruggero and Magda have not consummated their relationship. Let's not forget that the opening conversation in the opera focused on Prunier's declaration that the latest rage was sentimental love, featuring kisses and sighs, "but nothing more." Certainly none of the couple's music contains anything in the way of fiery passion. (Incidentally, Ruggero never addresses Magda by name during this act, but clearly he still believes her to be "Paulette.")

Magda is "overcome with grateful emotion" at Ruggero's characterization of her "sacred" love, and she enfolds him in her arms. Without a hint of eroticism, Ruggero murmurs that nothing can destroy her tender embrace. Hugging him more tightly, Magda lightly asks, to the polka music of the "night spot" suggestions of Lisette and the three friends, if he remembers their first meeting, where "I saw you and dreamed of Love!" The Act Two music of the coming dawn is briefly heard, as Ruggero says they fled to this place to hide their love. Indeed, this place —*là lontano*— is not a place of Day, where sanctified, married love can thrive. It is a hiding place that is neither Day nor Night. The question that remains is whether the lovers can stay in *là lontano* forever.

Magda and Ruggero exchange sentences that sound saccharine to the untrained ear, but which are focused on the theme of the rebirth of love, of undying love, symbolized by roses. "Our love was born among the flowers! I live among the flowers! Engarlanded with songs and dances! Engarlanded with spring!" A wisp of the love quartet music carried that last line, along with a wisp of the music of romance in Paris, and now Magda runs to gather roses, and gracefully, with "languorous abandon," she showers Ruggero with the petals. To the music of their first dance together, Magda offers again to crown their love with garlands, and Ruggero cries, "Blessed be love, and blessed be life." Almost always, his remarks have a seriousness and a religious tone that have nothing to do with sexual love.

Ending the little duet, Ruggero declares Magda deserves something special today. Magda guesses it might be a prize, and during the pause that precedes Ruggero's answer — not a prize, but rather a secret — the love quartet music begins in earnest. The secret is that three days ago Ruggero wrote to his parents, asking for money to pay their mounting debts. He pulls a stack of demand letters from both pockets and shows them to Magda, who blames herself. (The parallel with *Le Villi*, that I noted earlier, really is remarkable. The poor rustic has gone through all his money living with the big city courtesan, and soon after he admits he's out of money, she'll tell him they're through, at which point he will presumably go back to his home, a broken man.)

The love quartet music continues as Ruggero laughs off their financial problems, saying, "Let's go begging!" One might think it incredible that Puccini would not realize how contemptible this would make his tenor character appear to the audience, but in Puccini's World, poverty is a highly positive trait. Along with his youth, Ruggero's lack of money is what makes him worthy of love. His cry of, "Who will open their door to two impoverished lovers?" is distressing to Magda, but anyone who thinks Ruggero might consider getting a job does not understand Puccini at all. His romantic characters do not fritter away their youth sweating in exchange for pieces of metal. They are like the lilies— or rather, the roses— of the field.

At last Ruggero is persuaded to tell Magda the rest of the secret. His letter to his parents also included a request for their permission for him to be married. (The music to which he announces this is amazingly childlike, a tone that is heightened by the silvery tapping of the glockenspiel.) Magda is quite naturally shocked by Ruggero's statement. *Là lontano* is not a place for married people. If they two were to be married, they would have to leave this place of roses and swallows, and go where the people of Day live.

The love quartet music turns lush as Magda demands that Ruggero tell her everything. But there isn't anything to tell. In one of his most heroic-sounding passages, Ruggero sings that it should be forever, "If I love you and you love me!" The Amore Theme is hinted at as Magda remembers what he said after she offered him a toast to his many loves.

In what is undeniably the worst aria Puccini ever wrote —"Dimmi che vuoi seguirmi alla mia casa" (Tell me you will follow me to my house)— the tenor character tells his beloved she should come live with him in his parents' house, where "Our love will find in those shadows its own light, more pure and more serene, the sacred protection of my mother against all anguish and away from all pain." He goes on to anticipate there might one day, in the early morning light, "sweetly appear the tiny hand of a little child."

Ruggero's focus on his mother begins here, in this dull aria, and in the final scene he will become the most humiliated of all of Puccini's tenor characters, reduced to the status of a sobbing child, crouched at the feet of the lover who has taken on the role of his mother. At this point, however, it is Magda who is sobbing. Ruggero "gently frees himself" from her clinging arms, kisses her on the head, then goes off to see whether an answer to his letter has come. As he exits, the Heart Theme is heard, reminding Magda of the need of those who would fall in love, to defend their hearts.

The stage directions tell us Magda is overcome with confusion, almost to the point of terror. To some anguished and uninteresting music, she wars with herself as to whether she should keep quiet or tell Ruggero everything about her past. She says nothing at all about what she would confess, but it's clear from the rest of the libretto that her sin is not her sexual experience. As will be made clear in her upcoming confession, Magda is unfit for romantic love because she has been tainted by gold.

Sunk in grief, Magda walks to the summer-house and goes inside. As soon as she does, Prunier and Lisette appear, arguing. Lisette seems gripped by terror, and it soon comes out that she was persuaded by Prunier to get up on a stage in the city of Nice and sing. Her performance was a disaster, paid with whistles of disapproval, which Puccini comically reproduces in the orchestra. To Prunier's disgust, Lisette can't wait to return to being Magda's servant. In a telling line, Prunier describes this place where Magda and Ruggero live as a secret, placid oasis, where "lovers rejoice far from the world." This is indeed *là lontano.*

Poor Lisette is terrified when she sees a man approaching, for in her state she thinks anyone at all might be one of those awful whistlers. Fortunately, Prunier knows the fellow.

He's the maître d'hôtel, and he is carrying several letters on a salver. (No doubt one of them is for Ruggero.) He guesses Prunier has come to see Magda, and goes off to tell her that she has visitors. While waiting for Magda to come, Prunier and Lisette go at each other like cats and dogs. "I despise you!" shouts Lisette at last. When Magda comes out they instantly calm down, and go to meet her.

The three greet one another gladly, and Prunier asks whether Magda is still happy here. With sadness, she says she is. To the *Lontano* Theme, Prunier tells her they still talk about it in Paris, and in fact they don't believe it. Musically, this means they don't believe that what she has in the Côte d'Azur is her happiness, they think that that is what she had in Paris.

Prunier is a Puccini Artist, who lives in Night. He has no liking at all for the people of Day, which is what he is talking about when he now says to Magda, "...this is not the life for you, with trivial renunciations and nostalgia, with the vision of an honest home in which to bury your love in a tomb." Very upset at this, Magda changes the subject, asking what has brought them here. Prunier tells her about Lisette's disaster, and Lisette asks for her job back. Of course Magda gives it to her.

Lisette has returned to the place she belongs, the place she held originally. Prunier draws a parallel between her and Magda, saying that, "Even you, like her, Magda, will have to abandon an illusion that you think is real." The illusion is the belief that *là lontano* is anything more than a temporary hiding place.

It seems Rambaldo asked Prunier to suggest to Magda that she was welcome to come back to him. Indeed, Prunier says that Rambaldo is willing to help her out in any way. (This is a remnant of Puccini's idea that perhaps Rambaldo would appear in this act, and give Magda some money.) Magda flatly rejects this suggestion, and so Prunier makes ready to leave. After an exaggeratedly courteous claim that he will have nothing more to do with "certain people," he whispers a question to Lisette: What time does she get off this evening? She tells him the time, and he exits. After quickly fetching her maid's apron, Lisette also exits.

The final scene begins with Ruggero's entry, to the Amore Theme. Unfortunately, his first words are, "My love! My mother!" This is the first indication of the coming, deliberate confusion between Magda, and Ruggero's mother. Ruggero is carrying a letter, and as the Amore Theme plays he reports that his mother — not his father, whom we know is living — has answered his letter asking permission to marry.

Terrified, Magda staggers, her face pale. Ruggero hurries to support her, and asks why she is trembling. Did she think his mother would not consent? All Magda can say is, "Your mother! Your mother!" A new passage of music begins as Ruggero makes her sit down and then offers her the letter. Again Magda says, "Your mother!"

Ruggero insists she read the letter, and after making a great effort to control herself, she does. It is extremely significant that Magda is now speaking the words of Ruggero's mother, for she quickly takes on other aspects of his mother, putting herself into the place of his mother, figuratively *becoming* his mother. At the same time, this is an enactment of two of the major incidents in *Parsifal*— the Initiating Kiss of Kundry, and the Redemption of the Sinner.

The words of the mother, now spoken by Magda to a soft string accompaniment, are, "My child, you have told me a sweet creature has touched your heart. May she be blessed, if she be sent by the Lord...." Magda stops, and the stage directions tell us her eyes are welling with tears. Ruggero urges her to continue reading. She goes on: "I think with eyes

wet with tears that she will be the mother of your children. It is motherhood that renders love sacred."

To a rather ominous, low thrumming in the strings, Ruggero interrupts with a cry of, "My love!" and Magda continues, speaking in what are surely the identical accents that would have been used by the tearful mother herself: "If you know she is good, mild, pure, and has all the virtues, may she be blessed! Now I anxiously await your return. The honorable old house of your ancestors will be bright with joy to receive your chosen bride. Give her my kiss!"

As was explained in Chapter Three, this "mother's kiss" was quite clearly inspired by the "mother's kiss" that Kundry bestows on Parsifal. Both recipients pull away in horror — Parsifal because the kiss awakens his sexual urge in an incestuous manner, and Magda because she knows herself unworthy of the kiss. So far Puccini has had Ruggero enact the role of Parsifal, the naïve boy who didn't give his name to the Flower Maidens but was fascinated by Kundry. And he has had Magda enact the role of Kundry, the beautiful and sexually experienced woman who had all the knowledge Parsifal lacked, and who was the only one who could awaken the "tormenting flame of love" in the virgin youth.

Now, though, Puccini has his two characters switch roles. As the bestower of the Mother's Kiss, Ruggero begins to enact the role of Kundry, who is the sinner in need of redemption, while Magda, the recipient of the Kiss, begins to enact the role of Parsifal the redeemer. Magda now accepts that she wrongly drew Ruggero into sin, and she decides to right that wrong.

Ruggero of course does not understand why Magda cannot receive his mother's kiss (which he offered with the music to which he first told Magda that he had written for permission), and he is utterly baffled when she begins to speak, to the Amore Theme, of her past that cannot be forgotten. Demanding to know who she is and what she has done, he is further baffled when she declares, to a thoroughly uninspired piece of new music, that she came to him "contaminated." He declares he doesn't care, but then Magda admits all: "Triumphantly I passed between shame and gold!" The key word here is "gold." To Puccini, who loves the sexually liberated woman, Magda's shame is not that she has had sexual experiences, it is that she reached out her hand for "gold." She is not the Lady of the Rose — she has been masquerading as her. "But really! Who would recognize me?" Now is the time for the unmasking.

Ruggero alternately demands that Magda tell, and not tell, what she has concealed, and at last she declares she can never be the wife his mother expects and believes in. In other words, it is what Ruggero's mother wants that matters most to Magda, not what he wants. She has put herself in the place of his mother.

Desperately, to the agonized music to which Magda earlier warred with herself over whether she should confess, Ruggero says he is in agony. Magda's response is that "Your mother is calling you today." Speaking as an incredibly strange combination of herself, the mother, Parsifal, and Kundry, Magda insists that she must leave him, "...because I love you, and will not be your ruin!"

Ruggero is now reduced to the status of a sobbing infant, crying "No! Don't leave me alone! No!" Interestingly, the music suddenly gets much, much better in the form of a duet, "Ma come puoi lasciarmi" (But how can you leave me?). Magda holds her beloved close during this lovely duet, which begins with Ruggero's declaration that he is consumed in tears. He begs her not to shatter his heart.

Now entirely dominant in this relationship, Magda sings her verse in masterful tones, telling him not to despair, but to listen to what she has ruled will be. It is Parsifal speaking when she says, "Remember that the sacrifice I offer in this hour I make for your sake." The duet, though not its lovely music, ends with Ruggero's childlike plea, "No! Stay! Stay! Never leave me!"

Magda's self-identification with Ruggero's mother becomes complete as she takes his face in her hands and gazes at him intently. Accepting her decree, the grief-stricken boy bows his head, and Magda says, "Let me speak to you as a mother would to her own dear little son." She "gently caresses his hair," and tells him that after a while, when he has healed, this will only be a memory. "You return to your serene house, and I to my [swallow's] flight and my pain."

The last, gulping words of Ruggero are, "My love..." and these are cut off by the masterful Magda. "Say nothing more," she commands. "Let this pain be mine." The music of the lovely duet makes its soft, shimmering close, and as the Puccini bells that always herald death and disaster begin to toll for vespers, Magda—like Parsifal leaving the ruins of Klingsor's garden—slowly exits to follow a path of pain.

The first evening shadows have begun to fall. It is the *prima séra*. Hope has lost its struggle with melancholy. Looking like Kundry, who slowly sank to the ground dead after being redeemed from sin by Parsifal, the thoroughly emasculated Ruggero lies before us, crumpled in a heap, sobbing.

11

Il Tabarro

Libretto by Giuseppe Adami, based on the play
La Houppelande, by Didier Gold
First performed at the Metropolitan Opera,
New York, December 14, 1918

Many of the elements of Puccini's World are present in this one-act opera. It opens at sunset, and the characters live as Puccini's "good" characters all do: out of doors, under a starry night sky, and without money. The only thing that matters to any of these people is love, or the lack of it.

Basically *Il Tabarro* (The Cloak) is a related short story, rather than a chapter in the Rose Cycle, because despite the sadomasochistic *romance* relationship that exists between its soprano and tenor characters, it focuses on their fear, sadness, and anger, rather than their hope for endless love in endless night. In fact, it is the baritone character — the soprano's cuckolded husband — who expresses that desire. It is he who loves Night and the shining moon, and who longs to experience a rebirth of romantic love. The tenor character, on the other hand, is an unhappy and frustrated man. Our baritone has the soul of a tenor; our tenor, the soul of a baritone. The result is that *Il Tabarro* is a horror story — a nightmare version of a Rose Cycle chapter.

While *Il Tabarro* was based on a play by the Frenchman Didier Gold, it is very close in spirit to another work Puccini had long considered adapting: Oscar Wilde's *A Florentine Tragedy* (left uncompleted, and finished by Thomas Sturge Moore). It's obvious why Puccini was drawn to Wilde's play, and it's just as obvious why he never used it.

A Florentine Tragedy is a nasty little *fin de siècle* sex fantasy featuring a Florentine merchant named Simone, his wife Bianca, and her lover, a nobleman called Bardi. The husband knows perfectly well he is being cuckolded, and without bringing the matter into the open, the three spar verbally for a while, until finally Simone and Bardi draw swords.

Bianca had considered her husband a weakling, but when he kills Bardi she is deeply impressed, not to mention aroused. Beside the dead body of her lover she opens her arms to her husband and asks, "Why did you never tell me you were so strong?" His response is, "Why did you never tell me you were so beautiful?" Mosco Carner claimed the play was meant to show that people often do not value what they have until they see it through the eyes of others who are more perceptive.[1]

In a November 1906 letter to his friend Sybil Seligman, who had provided him with a copy of the (then unpublished) play, Puccini expressed unqualified praise for *A Florentine Tragedy*, calling it "beautiful, inspired, strong and tragic."[2] Giulio Ricordi showed far more sense, telling librettist Luigi Illica in a December 11 telegram, "Absolutely necessary for the future good of [Puccini] to throw Florentine stupidity into fire."[3]

Puccini considered using works even more sexually perverse than Wilde's, the most graphic of which was Pierre Louÿs' *La Femme et le Pantin* (The Woman and the Puppet), also known as *Conchita*, after the heroine who sexually dominates and mentally tortures her besotted suitor, until he at last turns the tables and beats her within an inch of her life, causing her great joy. Far less shocking but just as unstageable was Giovanni Verga's *La Lupa* (The Wolf Woman), an atmospheric short story by the author of *Cavalleria Rusticana*, that features a sexually devouring peasant woman.

There is an obvious parallel between *Il Tabarro* and *A Florentine Tragedy* in that both feature a love triangle of husband, wife, and wife's lover, that is smashed when the husband kills the lover. The obvious difference is that Giorgetta in *Il Tabarro* does not fall happily and amorously into her husband's arms after he strangles her Luigi. Nevertheless, the two works are even more similar than they appear at first glance.

Even a cursory look at Puccini's libretto reveals the typical sadomasochistic *romance* relationship between the soprano and tenor characters. The lovers speak of being bound hand and foot, of being tortured, of being in chains, but Giorgetta says their difficulties— the fact that this is a classic, illicit, *romance* relationship involving danger, terror, and the possibility of murder — renders their lovemaking more exciting and pleasurable to her than it otherwise would be. It is very significant that Giorgetta is five years older than Luigi— twenty-five to his twenty. She, not Luigi, runs this relationship, and she subtly tortures him in their first scene alone, arousing him by recalling their lovemaking of the night before, yet insisting he not act on his arousal because her husband might appear at any moment.

While it would be ridiculous to suggest that Giorgetta "likes it" when her husband murders Luigi, there is an atmosphere of subtle depravity in *Il Tabarro*, just short of complicity between the husband and wife in their mutual, fierce tormenting of the lover, that must have satisfied any lingering desire Puccini might have had to set *A Florentine Tragedy* to music.

In respect to music, Puccini accomplishes in *Il Tabarro* a wonderful advance in his use of themes and motifs. The first theme we hear is that of the River, during the prelude. This River Theme consists of two motifs, the first of which is a pattern of three rising notes: dotted quarter notes. The second motif, which immediately follows the first, is a pattern of three falling notes: a triplet. This River Theme, only slightly altered, will later serve as the whirling theme of the Joined Fates of the baritone and tenor characters.

There is more, however, for after the prelude the River Theme will be split into its two component motifs. The first one — the rising notes— will be transformed into the Luigi Motif, and the second one — the falling triplet — will serve as Michele's murderous Cloak Motif. Luigi will deserve to be associated with the river because of Michele's intention of hurling his dead body into the water. Presumably Luigi gets the rising notes because he is young, and he is striving towards something: he is trying to win Giorgetta and get away with her to some place where they can be happy. Michele is already associated with the river because as a barge owner he lives his life on the Seine. Presumably he gets the falling notes because he is old, and he is the agent of Luigi's death.

The Luigi Motif is sneaky-sounding, and suggestive of the stealthy footsteps of a lover coming to call on a married woman. It consists of six rising quarter notes— the first three covering the span of an octave, and the second three embedded within that octave. Michele's Cloak Motif is the falling triplet, and it speaks the word "ta-bar-ro." To repeat, the Luigi Motif suggests the first parts of the River Theme and the theme of the Joined Fates, while

Michele's Cloak Motif duplicates the second parts of the River Theme and the theme of the Joined Fates.

The Joined Fates is the most important theme in the score, for it brings together the motifs of the two men, musically demonstrating their coming fight. Prior to this opera, Puccini used recurring music to remind us of something, or to predict something, or to reveal someone's thoughts. Here, the motifs *do* something; they *illustrate* something that is going to happen: the coming together of the motifs' owners, in a physical fight to the death.

We saw Puccini's skill in unifying a score via a triplet pattern in *Le Villi*, and his skill is even greater in *Il Tabarro*. The triplet is the main rhythm of this opera, and Puccini surely chose it for the same reason he chose it for *Le Villi*; that is, it is a dance rhythm with storytelling ability. Luigi and Giorgetta dance to a waltz rhythm in the first part of the opera, and later on Michele and Luigi will engage in their own sort of waltz — a fight that will whirl these two men whose fates are joined, down, down, down, "into the deepest pit."

Another interesting motif is that of Michele's Love, heard during a long scene between the barge owner and his wife, during which he tries to win back her heart. The motif shifts from tender and loving to frighteningly dissonant and sawing whenever the conversation approaches a dangerous subject, then reverses itself when the dangerous subject is pulled back from. This dangerous subject, of Giorgetta's infidelity, never comes out openly in the words, but the secret thoughts of both husband and wife are terrifyingly revealed in the music.

As for the opera's close, Puccini brings back for the final scene a passage of music that wonderfully reveals Giorgetta's thoughts as she nears her husband, who is concealing Luigi's corpse beneath his cloak. The music reveals she is lying to her husband, pretending to seek his forgiveness when in fact she is trying to get him out of the way so he won't encounter her lover. There was something of this sort near the end of *Tosca*, in the motif of the Fully Charged Rifles, that told us the truth about the supposedly sham execution, but the musical recurrence in *Il Tabarro* provides much more information, laying Giorgetta's shameful thoughts completely open. In composing *La Rondine*, Puccini gave himself permission to take a break from trying to find new ways to work with motifs and themes. Whatever the weaknesses of *La Rondine*, the score of *Il Tabarro* shows his imagination was far from exhausted.

The curtain rises on *Il Tabarro* before the music begins. We see a barge moored in a bend of the Seine. *È il tramonto*, says the stage direction— "It is sunset"— and the barge's 50-year-old owner, Michele, is leaning against the rudder, watching the sun go down. There is very little hope here, in this hour of waking dreams, to struggle against a great deal of melancholy. Michele's wife is Giorgetta, and at 25 she is half her husband's age, and restless. We see her now busy at various tasks that reveal the barge is her home. She takes down laundry, waters her geraniums, and cleans the canaries' cage. The barge has been hauling cement, and on shore is a horse-drawn cart, onto which stevedores are piling sacks they've been unloading from the hold.

The prelude begins: a melancholy piece in 12/8, played *ppp* mainly by woodwinds and muted strings, with delicate contributions from glockenspiel and harp. Some have identified the theme with the endless flowing of the Seine, while others believe it only evokes a mood. As noted above, the River Theme is the source of the Luigi Motif and Michele's Cloak Motif. The River Theme describes not only the Seine, but also Luigi, Michele, and the joined fates of the two unhappy men. One can hear encapsulated in the prelude the entire story that is about to be told, and within it are hints of Michele's beautiful aria, "Resta vicino a me."

The music of the prelude continues, punctuated now and then by the sound of automobile horns, and the moans of a tugboat siren. Giorgetta asks her husband whether he isn't tired of watching the sun set. "Is it so spectacular?" she asks. A foolish question for one who lives in Puccini's World. The sight of the sun vanishing is beautiful — so beautiful the enraptured Michele has allowed his pipe to go out. It is Giorgetta who observes the pipe has gone cold, and her comment hints at her dissatisfaction with her husband. In her eyes, there is no flame remaining in him.

Indicating the stevedores, Michele asks his wife whether they have finished unloading the hold. Eagerly Giorgetta offers to go below and see. Michele refuses, saying he will go himself. The stevedores (tenors, baritones, and basses) are nearly finished, and they sing a melancholy work song that punctuates the conversation of their boss and his wife. If they work hard, "...afterwards you can rest, and Margot will be happy."

This is a bitter verse for Michele to hear, for although he has not really lost his flame, he has lost his youth, and his wife's love. Giorgetta suggests offering the men some wine as thanks for the special effort they've put in on clearing the hold. Michele is touched by her thoughtfulness. There is kindness in her; perhaps there is some there for him. But when he moves toward her affectionately and asks, "And me, haven't you thought of me?" she pulls away and coolly asks, "Of you? What?"

Michele puts his arm around his wife, saying that if his pipe has gone out, his passion hasn't. "One of your kisses, O my love...." As he assures her his passion is not spent, we hear a frightening, whirling figure in the flutes, that will become increasingly significant. (This whirling describes Michele and his wife's lover, grappling in mortal combat, plunging down, down, down together.) Giorgetta endures her husband's kiss, managing to deflect it to her cheek, instead of receiving it on her lips. Michele goes into the hold to see how much cargo remains.

A young and handsome stevedore — Luigi, aged 20 — comes onto the barge from the dock, and complains to his boss's wife about the heat. Unwittingly speaking of his own death, what he actually says is, "It's suffocating, padrona." This is the first of several times the strangulation of Luigi is foreshadowed. (Notice, too, how he is required to humbly address Giorgetta as *padrona* — mistress.)

It may be that Giorgetta suggested a drink for the men because she wished to give one to Luigi, for she casts a significant look at him and says, "I have what's needed. Taste this wine!" She goes into the cabin to fetch the bottle and glasses, and as she disappears another stevedore comes up from the hold carrying a sack. This is *Il Tinca*, whose name means "The Tench" (a kind of freshwater fish). Tinca is 35, and very unhappy, and now he curses his heavy sack and the wretched world.

Another stevedore appears—*Il Talpa*, meaning "The Mole." At 55, he is the oldest. Complaining of his sack and the heat, he urges Luigi to make another round (between the cargo hold and the shore). "Here's your other round!" laughs Luigi, gesturing at Giorgetta, who has come out of the cabin with wine and glasses. At last the music of the prelude ceases. Everyone rushes for the wine, which Giorgetta pours out generously, and a little triple-time *brindisi* is sung: "Eccola la passata." There is wine for everyone, even a glass for the cart driver. Everybody seems happy enough, yet as Tinca offers a toast he adds, "My only pleasure is here in the bottom of the glass."

A poor organ grinder is passing by on shore. Luigi hails him as "Professor," and with a chuckle assures the others they will hear what an artist the man is. As always when Artists arc brought in by Puccini, the words of praise are serious, even if spoken laughingly. Though only by turning a crank on a machine, the organ grinder brings music into the hard lives of working people.

Luigi's seemingly innocent remark, along with Giorgetta's response that she only understands music for dancing, are in fact anything but innocent, for in it we hear two motifs. The first is the sneaky-sounding Luigi Motif, played *piano* by *pizzicato* strings, and the second is the murderous Cloak Motif, given out here as two sets of falling triplets heard in Giorgetta's voice. According to the stage directions, Giorgetta's response is made to Luigi, "as if luring him to dance with her." The word is *sedurlo*, which means to seduce him, to lead him astray. All of these things—the Cloak Motif in Giorgetta's vocal line, the description of Giorgetta leading Luigi astray, and her veiled invitation to him to waltz with her, are leading us toward a dance of death between Luigi and Michele, in a scene filled with reiterations of the Cloak Motif. The organ grinder's machine is badly out of tune, and the waltz it plays (which Puccini based on a popular tune of the time) has at the start an almost nightmarish tone.

The younger of the other two stevedores, the unhappy Tinca, has been made momentarily cheerful by the wine, and he offers his services as an expert dancer. Giorgetta laughingly accepts. Talpa and Luigi cover their ears against the discordant wailing of the hurdy-gurdy, and as they watch Giorgetta struggling with the clumsy, foot-dragging Tinca, Luigi laughs, "The music and the dance are in accord. You look like you're cleaning the floor!"

A moment more and Tinca has trod heavily on Giorgetta's foot. Luigi pushes him aside and confidently takes his place, and in the space of a few breaths the music has lost its discordant quality. And yet somehow it is still frightening. The handsome young man and the slightly older woman dance well together, and their attraction to each other is very obvious, especially to old Talpa, as Giorgetta seems to lose herself languidly in Luigi's strong arms.

The nightmarish tone returns to the waltz as muted strings play a rising figure descriptive of the couple's growing excitement. Michele climbs up from the hold, and Talpa quickly warns, "Boys, here's the boss!" At once the couple stop dancing. Luigi tosses some coins to the organ grinder (a payment for art that we never see in the Rose Cycle proper), and the three stevedores return to the hold, leaving Michele and his wife alone.

With an air of nonchalance, Giorgetta pats at her hair and asks Michele his plans. Are they to leave next week, and will Tinca and Talpa stay on? Suspecting nothing at this point, Michele says he is keeping the two, and Luigi as well. Concealing her delight, Giorgetta engages Michele in an unimportant conversation about Luigi, and as they talk we hear from a ways off the voice of a Song Seller, pitching his latest, with words and music. As the Song Seller comes closer, he repeatedly cries, "Who wants it?"

The music of the prelude returns. Apparently rather excited, Giorgetta comments on the evening, with its rosy September sunset. She likens the sun to a great orange dying in the Seine. Giorgetta sees in the distance a familiar figure: *La Frugola* (The Rummager). She is a rag-picker, and the wife of old Talpa.

A pointless argument between Michele and Giorgetta begins as the Song Seller enters onto a street near the river. With him is a man carrying a small harp. Several seamstresses emerge from a shop, and gather around to hear the latest song. This song is the story of Mimi, who lived and died for love. As the Song Seller sings of lovers in springtime, and the orchestra quotes the opening of "Mi chiamano Mimì," Michele and Giorgetta continue to argue. It seems this may be a reenactment of the wonderful Act Three quartet of *La Bohème*. The Song Seller is singing the part of Rodolfo and Mimi, who vow to love each other until springtime, and Michele and Giorgetta are taking the parts of the quarrelling Marcello and Musetta. It also seems clear that the Song Seller is Puccini himself, taking a cameo role in his own opera, selling the sheet music to *La Bohème*. Some of the girls buy the song from the peddler, and they go off singing it. (As the Song Seller is Puccini, this payment of money to the greatest of all of Puccini's Artist characters may be a little joke on his part. Notice how the only persons in all of his works to receive money for art are an organ grinder and the Maestro himself.) The street clears, then Frugola appears and crosses onto the barge. On her shoulder is an old sack, filled with the harvest of this day's rag-picking.

Frugola greets Giorgetta and Michele, calling them "eternal lovers," and bidding them good evening, but while the former gives her a friendly answer the latter merely waves and retires to the cabin. Frugola asks after her husband, for whom she obviously feels affection, then puts down her sack and begins to rummage through it. She comes up with a brand-new comb, the nicest thing she found today, and offers it to Giorgetta.

The rag-picker has a song about the contents of her sack, "Se tu sapessi gli oggetti strani" (If you knew the strange objects). Usually Puccini looks at love through the eyes of Youth, but in Frugola's song, which is sung over a pulsing triplet pattern in the strings, we get a view through the eyes of Age, where joys and torments, "the documents of a thousand loves," are seen to have found their way into a rag-picker's sack.

Among Frugola's possessions is a beef heart, intended for her tabby cat, Caporale of the strange eyes, who keeps her company when Talpa is out. (Muted cellos describe the mewing of the cat.) There are what seem to be possible further references to *Bohème* in this second part of Frugola's song, and she seems to have within her a bit of Musetta, whose favorite food was hearts, according to Marcello. Frugola declares her cat's philosophy is, "It is better to live on two slices of heart than to tear at your own with love." This could easily be Musetta's advice to Marcello, but the music that supports the line marks it as advice for both Luigi and Michele, both of whom are tearing their hearts for love of Giorgetta.

Frugola's music segues into a reprise of the River Theme as Talpa and Luigi emerge from the hold. Tinca brings up the rear. He is heading off for a night at the tavern, and when Frugola chides him for his drunkenness he snaps at her. The waltzing music of the *brindisi* returns as he cries that wine is good for him. "If I drink I don't think, and if I think I don't laugh!" His barking laughter is filled with despair, and at the sound of it Michele goes into the hold.

"Hai ben ragione" (You're right), declares Luigi, who a moment ago accepted Michele's offer to load some iron tomorrow. Gloom settles over the little group as the tenor sings his Masochism Aria—a lament for the hard lives they all lead. In respect to the rest of the score the aria is unimportant. No motifs appear in it in any significant way. The song is there because a Puccini tenor must have an aria in which to express his sense of *muoio disperato*—"I die despairing." "If you look up," Luigi cries, "watch out for the whip." He then gives his aria the faint flavor of a Dawn Song, singing, "The day is already dark at morning." At the song's gloomy conclusion—"It's better not to think. Just bow your head and bend your back"—Tinca suggests they take his advice, and drink. Rebuked by Giorgetta, he exits.

The exhausted Talpa would like to go too, but first his wife, now in a melancholy mood, has a song. Frugola dreams of having a little house in the country where her husband can stretch out in the sun, and she, with her cat at her feet, can wait for that remedy of all ills: death. This strange song is an expression of the longing for *lontano*, and it inspires Giorgetta to reveal her own dream, which is a return to the Paris suburb where both she and Luigi were born: Belleville.

The word "suburb" suggests, at least to Americans, a place of two-car garages and manicured lawns. That's not what it means here. Belleville was a slum, populated by artisans and the working poor, who during the Second Empire had been forced out of central Paris. Belleville was the place where the Paris Commune was born, in March 1871, and it was the place where it died, that same May, its barricaded citizens mounting the last valiant resistance by the revolutionaries to the imperialist forces. With one word — Belleville — Puccini is giving us a character sketch of Giorgetta and Luigi. They come from a race that is artistic, hard working, poor, proud, and willing to fight to the death for its rights.

The Belleville duet is Giorgetta's and Luigi's love duet. Their other duets, sung when they are alone, express erotic longing, frustration, and fear, and Puccini must have felt the need to give them a duet that would bind them together in a song of love untainted by any negative feelings. They don't speak of one another during the song, but that doesn't matter. What matters is that Giorgetta and Luigi sing together, and become almost transported by shared feelings of passionate love.

It is revealed in the Belleville duet how discontented Giorgetta is with her current life. We already know Luigi excites her far more than the husband who is old enough to be her father, and now she tells Frugola and Talpa that she can't stand life on the barge, living in a tiny cabin almost filled by the bed and the stove. (The stage directions at the start of the opera describe the cabin's exterior as very neat, freshly painted, with green window shades.)

Puccini began work on *Il Tabarro* right after he finished *La Rondine*, and the Belleville duet, with its ecstatic, almost hysterical praise of the unending fascination of the Paris suburb, seems linked to the outburst of *La Rondine*'s Lisette, who passionately praises Paris as a city full of "fascinations, surprises, and marvels."

By the time Giorgetta and Luigi have finished singing of their love for Belleville, their hands are clasped. It takes them a moment to come back to themselves, and to realize the others are looking at them. Then they separate. There is nothing Frugola can say in response except, "Now I understand you. Life is different here." Talpa (who wasn't much interested in the praise of Belleville) invites Luigi to come eat with them, but the young man refuses, saying he has to talk to the boss. Arm in arm the older couple leave, with Talpa joining his wife in a reprise of her song of the little house in the country, where one waits for death.

At last the lovers are alone. As the two stare hungrily at one another, the voices of another pair of young lovers are heard from off stage, wordlessly vocalizing the River Theme. The carefree couple pass out of hearing, a tugboat sounds its siren, then the Luigi Motif begins: six soft notes, played *pizzicato* by lower strings. We heard it first when Luigi summoned the organ grinder, and it seemed out of place in that cheerful scene, sounding as it did like stealthy footsteps. Again the meter is triple-time: 6/8 now.

Luigi begins to move toward Giorgetta, but she stops him with a gesture. Passionately, but softly, Giorgetta speaks first, calling, "O Luigi, Luigi!" (Note the way Puccini has her torment her lover, ardently calling him yet gesturing him to stay back.) Although eager to embrace him, Giorgetta urges Luigi to keep far away, for "he" might appear at any moment.

"Stay there, lontano," she whispers. Throughout this scene the orchestra concentrates on the Luigi Motif, but in this first part of the scene, while the lovers are fearful, their voices conclude almost every line with the three descending notes of the murderous Cloak Motif. (This motif is not identified with the cloak until later, during the scene between Michele and Giorgetta.)

The aroused and frustrated Luigi asks why she calls him in vain — "Why make the torment worse?" Determined to increase his desire and his torment, Giorgetta tells him that when she thinks of the passion of his kisses, she throbs all over. The lovers whisper of *lontano*, the far-away place where they would be alone, and always together. Giorgetta adds, "...and always in love! Say you won't fail me!" This music will return at the end of the opera, in a moment of horrid irony.

The thought of *lontano* drove away the Cloak Motif. Overwhelmed by his passion, Luigi is about to rush to Giorgetta, but again she stays him with a warning, and an instant later Michele emerges from the hold. He is surprised to see Luigi hasn't gone yet. Bassoon and muted horns play soft chords as the two men begin to chant their *parlando*. As always, Luigi addresses his boss respectfully. He says he stayed behind, first to thank Michele for having kept him on, and second to ask him to take him to the river town of Rouen and leave him there. Michele is startled by this request, saying, "Are you crazy? There's nothing there but poverty. You'd be worse off."

Perhaps Luigi really had intended to end his affair, but even this slight resistance is enough to derail his resolve. And now, as he answers Michele, the orchestra reveals his thoughts. "All right...." Luigi agrees, and on the final word the stealthy notes of his motif are heard. "...So I'll stay," he finishes. Michele heads toward the cabin where he will prepare the lanterns that must be mounted on the barge during the night, and the two men bid each other a morose good night.

With her husband gone, Giorgetta feverishly demands to know why Luigi had asked to be left off at Rouen. The tormented young man answers that he can't stand sharing her any longer. (This was a change Puccini made in Gold's story, increasing the suffering of the tenor character. Gold's young man decided to try to break off the affair out of principle.) Another foreshadowing of the strangulation occurs as the two sing, "The joy is stolen amid spasms of fear, in an anxious grip, amid smothered cries...." The lovers grow more excited. They sing ardently of kisses, of vows and promises given and received in *lontano* — far away, all alone, far from the world. But a noise, real or imagined, startles Luigi out of his passionate lyricism. "Is it him?" he cries, his words choppy and nervous, and sung over a *forte* reprise of the Luigi Motif. Giorgetta reassures him, but when she asks him to come back later that night, her request ends with those three descending notes that mean *ta-bar-ro* — the cloak.

The lovers agree to meet as they did the previous night. Giorgetta will leave the gangplank in place, and when it is safe she will signal with a lighted match. Using the language of Puccini's World of Night, Giorgetta remembers how, last night, she lit the match, and "It seemed I was lighting a star, flame of our love, star that never sets." As she sings the words "lighting a star," we hear the Cloak Motif — an eerie, almost ghostly bit of music played *pp* by flute and clarinet. (The reason her words summon the Cloak Motif is that when Michele later strikes a match to light his pipe, Luigi will mistake it for Giorgetta's match.)

The young man has a final, jealous outburst in the lyrical arioso, "Folle di gelosia!"

(Insane jealousy!) He sings of his frustration and suffering, of his rage at the thought that anyone else may touch Giorgetta's divine body, and as he pulls out his knife in a passion, the orchestra begins to thunder the Luigi Motif.

On a ringing high G sharp, at top volume, Luigi vows he would not fear to use his knife, "...and with drops of blood, make for you a jewel!" The song ends in a dizzying fall of "Cloak" triplets that evokes an image of the two men, locked in mortal combat, spiraling into that black and bottomless pit Michele will sing of in his upcoming monologue.

Giorgetta looks fearfully at the cabin, and pushes Luigi toward the gangplank. Urged onward by her, he runs into the night. Tired and sad, Giorgetta passes a hand over her face and murmurs, "How difficult it is to be happy!" It is full night now. Under normal circumstances it would be time for the Night of Love. But things are mixed up in this horror story, for the soprano is married to the baritone, whom she cannot love. As Giorgetta utters that last word, "happy," Michele comes out of the cabin, accompanied by a new melody. A gently rocking piece in 6/4, sounded by muted horn, viola, and cello, it expresses Michele's love for his wife. At this point the melody is tender and comforting, but it won't stay that way long.

Michele sets down the lanterns he has readied, and asks Giorgetta why she hasn't gone to bed. She turns the question back to him, and as he answers evasively we hear the motif of Michele's Love begin to alter, as it does every time the couple's conversation approaches dangerous ground. Apparently out of the blue, Giorgetta comments, "I think it's good that you kept him." She means Luigi, and as she sings this line the motif of Michele's Love moves from the strings to the bassoon, which plays a sawing, obsessive-sounding figure, frighteningly dissonant.

Shifting to the clarinet, the motif returns to its original, gentle form as Michele wonders whether he really needs more than two men, but Giorgetta suggests he fire the drunken Tinca, and the musical shift begins again, as a dangerous subject approaches. This time the viola sounds the obsessive, dissonant figure as Michele bitterly explains the reason for Tinca's drunkenness: "He drinks to calm his grief. He has a whore for a wife! He drinks so he won't kill her!"

Giorgetta excuses her nervous reaction by saying those stories don't interest her. Michele approaches her, and the motif of his love again returns to its gentle form. Filled with a "sweetly sad" emotion, he asks, "Why don't you love me anymore? Why?" Coldly, Giorgetta denies it. She insists she loves him, then adds lamely, "You are good and honest." If it weren't so sad, it would be funny — hearing the poor man damned with a "nice personality." Trying to end the conversation, Giorgetta adds, "Now let's go to sleep." But that last word — sleep — is another dangerous subject, and the horrid, obsessive figure takes over in the bassoon. Angrily, Michele responds that *she* never sleeps.

A long passage of conversation, grim with double meaning, begins as Giorgetta insists she can't sleep in the cabin: "I suffocate in there!" Michele thinks she is referring to the heat, but that isn't it at all, and again the word "suffocate" foreshadows the coming murder.

Tenderly Michele reminds his wife that a year ago, "we were three under that roof — there was the cradle of our baby...." There were indeed three of them a year ago, and there are three of them now. As Michele speaks lovingly of the baby, distressing Giorgetta terribly, he is simultaneously, unwittingly, speaking of Luigi. "You reached out and rocked him," sings Michele, "sweetly, slowly, and then, on my arm, you fell asleep." Giorgetta begs him to stop, but which meaning upsets her? Her sweet, slow rocking of the baby last year, or her sweet, slow rocking of Luigi last night? "Those were evenings like these," he continues. "If a breeze stirred, I wrapped you together in my CLOAK." As he finally utters that word, the orchestra sounds the haunting theme of the Joined Fates, which ends with the three falling notes of the Cloak Motif.

"I wrapped you together in my cloak," sings Michele, and the ominous music declares that whether he knows it or not, he is speaking of Luigi. "As though in a caress. I felt on my shoulders your blond heads. I felt your mouths close to my mouth." His words recall a passage of the whispered conversation of Giorgetta and Luigi: "In an anxious embrace ... and kisses without end."

A new and lovely melody, again in triple-time, is introduced as Michele cries, "I was so happy, ah, so happy!" He is sure his 50 years and his gray hair have killed Giorgetta's love for him, but again she refuses to admit any problem. Michele makes a last attempt to win back his wife with his achingly beautiful aria, "Resta vicino a me!" (Stay near me!). Trying to draw Giorgetta near, he lays his heart bare and woos her as ardently as any 20-year-old Luigi could. "Don't you remember other nights, other skies, and other moons? Be what you once were," he pleads. "Back when you loved me, and kissed me! Stay near me!" Using Puccini's magic words—the words that will persuade her if any words known to man can do so—Michele cries, "The night is beautiful!"

His plea ends in a series of shimmering, hopeful triplets from clarinet and viola. As though offering an alternative to the death threatened by the descending notes of the Cloak Motif, these shimmering triplets rise, pulsing like the rippling of water. They begin strongly, *fortissimo*, but as Giorgetta spurns her husband's plea they begin to fade.

"What do you expect?" Giorgetta asks. "We're older. I'm not the same now. You've changed too, you're suspicious; what are you thinking?" From a distant church, the Puccini bell that presages death and disaster begins to toll. Ostensibly it is striking the hour of nine, but we know what it really means.

The shimmering triplets weaken, growing slower and softer as Michele, his hope at an end, responds, "I don't even know myself." Again pleading exhaustion, Giorgetta moves toward the cabin. When she passes him, Michele tries to kiss her, but she evades him. As the cabin door closes behind her, the hopeful triplets come to a stop and Michele cries, "Strumpet!"

A pair of Puccini's normal young lovers passes down the street as Michele picks up his lanterns and fixes them in their posts. "Mouth like a fresh rose," the tenor sings. The soprano answers, "Oh perfumed evening ... there's the moon!" The lovers bid each other a sweet good night, "...until tomorrow, my love!" In the distance, a bugle call is heard from a military barracks.

A terrifying rumble is now heard from the timpani, then woodwinds and lower strings sound the theme of the Joined Fates as Michele cautiously approaches the cabin and strains to listen. "Nothing!" he mutters, beginning a scene that Verdi might have relished for one of his own operas. "Silence." He creeps along the cabin wall and peers inside. Giorgetta is in there, not doing anything at all. What does she wait for, he wonders, and then a thought strikes him: "Perhaps she's waiting for ME to sleep!"

Michele moves to the center of the barge, and filled with grief he asks himself who could have changed her, who has made her stray. This is classic Puccini, and one can easily imagine how different a Verdi baritone's musings would have been at this moment. We should note that after the explosion of "Strumpet!" Michele does not utter a single word against his wife. He knows she has been with another man, but instead of threatening her and demanding the name of her lover, he tried with great tenderness to win back her heart. There is no doubt that had Puccini written a scene to follow the revelation of Luigi's killing, whatever happened it would not have involved Michele hurting his wife.

Certain he has been betrayed, Michele turns over in his mind the names of possible suspects. Talpa! No, he's too old. Tinca, perhaps? No, he drinks. There is a brief pause, then it hits him. "Luigi!" he cries, as cello and double bass hammer the Luigi Motif. But no—it can't be Luigi, for why then would he have asked to be let off in Rouen?

Michele can think of no further suspects, and in frustration he turns to thoughts of what he would do to the man, if he could only grasp him. The theme of the Joined Fates takes over Michele's vocal line and, joined with a whirling figure in the strings, is fleshed out into a complete thought: "Share this chain with me! Join your fate with mine, down together into the deepest pit! Peace is only in death."

Crushed and worn, his great monologue finished, Michele takes out his pipe and strikes a match to light it. (This is a nice touch. That Michele's pipe had gone out was, in the opening scene, related to a loss of vigor. Now that he has struck a match to relight the pipe, his vigor will be recovered.) The lighting of a match is the signal Luigi has been waiting for. Strings play a soft but agitated version of the theme of the Jointed Fates of Michele and Luigi, indicative of pounding hearts and rapid footsteps.

Michele sees the intruder's shadow, starts in surprise, and waits in ambush. Recognizing Luigi, he grabs him by the throat. "I've got you!" he cries. Luigi struggles, and denies he's looking for Giorgetta. He pulls his knife, but the older man forces him to drop it, taunting, "You wanted to go to Rouen, didn't you? You'll get there dead, in the river!"

Beginning to weaken, Luigi cries, "Murderer!" Michele demands that he confess, promising if he does, he'll let Luigi go. The young man resists for a moment, then briefly, grudgingly, says, "Yes." Michele wants complete submission, however, and Luigi gives it to him. "Yes—I love her!" he admits faintly, singing the three descending notes of the Cloak Motif. He has joined his fate to that of Michele.

The vengeful barge owner continues to throttle Luigi, demanding that he repeat the confession again and again. Four times in all, his voice weaker each time, the stevedore sings his confession to the notes of the Cloak Motif. But just as the motif of the humiliated Dick Johnson shrank in Act Two of *Fanciulla*, notes of the Cloak Motif drop away as Luigi weakens. He sings his second and third confessions on only two notes, and the final one is sung on one note. Luigi then gives a death rattle and sags, clutching at Michele "in an extreme contortion of death." At that very moment, Giorgetta's voice is heard, calling from inside the cabin. "I'm afraid, Michele!" Quickly Michele wraps his voluminous cloak around the dead Luigi and sits down. His voice is calm as he speaks, but beneath it lower strings are softly plucking the Luigi Motif.

If we listen only to Giorgetta's words, we will wonder if she means what she says: that she is sorry she made Michele unhappy, and wants to be forgiven. If we listen to the melody she sings, however, we will know she is lying—trying to get her husband off the deck and into the cabin. She sings the music of the scene that began, "O Luigi, Luigi!" in which she and her lover whispered endearments, and fretted that he—Michele—might appear at any moment and catch them. The music puts Giorgetta in a shameful light as, looking around anxiously, she seductively coos to her husband, "Tell me I'm forgiven. Don't you want me closer?"

Michele would have given anything to have heard that an hour before, but now his wife sings the music to which she first said to Luigi, "If we could be alone, far away." Michele is playing with Giorgetta now, and when, in a terrifying voice, he inquires, "Where, inside my cloak?" he uses the music of Luigi's response, "And always together!"

"Yes," Giorgetta answers, "close, close." ("And always in love," she told Luigi.) The replay ends with her next line, as she says to her husband, "You once said to me...." (The music is that of her, "Say you'll never fail me." Poor Luigi's response had been, "Never!") What Michele had once said to Giorgetta was that everyone wears some kind of cloak. Woodwinds and horn softly whisper the Cloak Motif as Giorgetta recalls the rest of what he had once said: that sometimes this cloak hides joy, sometimes sorrow.

A crescendo begins as Michele adds savagely, "...and sometimes a crime! Come to my cloak! Come! Come!" He stands up and sweeps open his cloak, and the corpse of Luigi falls at Giorgetta's feet. She screams in horror and steps back, but Michele grabs her and forces her down on the deck, against the face of her dead lover. As he does, the orchestra thunders out a final version of the theme of the Joined Fates, crying, "Join your fate with mine, down into the deepest pit!"

12

Suor Angelica

Original Libretto by Giovacchino Forzano
First performed at the Metropolitan Opera, New York, December 14, 1918

Many critics consider this opera a saccharine piece, made monotonous by an all-female cast dressed in nuns' habits. It's a matter of taste. Those whose preference is for "masculine" subjects will probably not like it, but there are many people in the world who have lost a child, or can sympathize with that, and surely they can be allowed one or two operas out of all those in the repertory. *Suor Angelica* (Sister Angelica) is a lovely and delicate piece, and what a production needs most in order to succeed is distinctive voices for the principal and solo singers.

The libretto was based on an original sketch Forzano reportedly wrote for a touring company. No one knows with any detail what this original sketch was like, but Puccini's opera, which is set in a Catholic convent in the late 1600's, is deeply infused with the feminizing elements of medieval Christianity; that is, Bridal Mysticism, the Cult of the Virgin Mary, and Maternal Mysticism.

I discussed in Chapter One how the first two of these forms of Catholic worship, which were promoted by influential 12th century theologians like Bernard de Clairvaux, helped to shape the literary genre called *romance*. These forms of worship sublimated the sex drive, eroticizing religious devotions via the concept of a quasi-sexual relationship between the female soul and God, and the male soul and the Virgin Mary.

Originally the Church itself was considered to be the bride of Christ, but St. Bernard promoted the idea that the individual soul was the bride. The reasoning behind this feminization of the soul was that while it is (according to the theory) the nature of the male to be aggressive, strong, and independent, it is the nature of the female to be yielding, weak, and dependent. By this logic the female stands in a position superior to the male when it comes to a relationship with God, for she is malleable and receptive — open to God's embrace. St. Bernard referred to himself as a woman, and urged his monks to be "mothers" — to "let your bosoms expand with milk, not swell with passion."[1] (A peculiar remark indeed, especially considering that St. Bernard was a major force behind the Second Crusade.)

Medieval mystics such as Margaret Ebner (1291–1351) eagerly embraced such teachings, writing what seem to us to be astonishingly raw passages about their imagined physical relationships with Jesus. Margaret wrote of how she felt Jesus' "wondrous powerful thrusts against my heart," and declared that "Sometimes I could not endure it when the strong thrusts came against me for they harmed my insides so that I became greatly swollen like a woman great with child."[2]

Men who recoiled from the idea of being a receptive, yielding, bride of Christ, or a mother whose bosom was swollen with milk, were encouraged by St. Bernard to an eroticized worship of the Virgin Mary, an infinitely superior and matchlessly beautiful woman. Prior to the 11th century, Mary had been a relatively minor figure of worship. As an increasingly personal relationship between the individual and the deity began to be preached, however, Mary began to be seen as the main intercessor between mankind and God. The teachings of St. Bernard helped to fix that role.

Bridal Mysticism thus encouraged women to think of themselves as having a special and deeply intimate relationship with God, that men did not share, and the Cult of the Virgin encouraged men to worship a superior female figure. These ideas were greatly appealing to wealthy, aristocratic women like Eleanor of Aquitaine and her daughters and granddaughters, and so the medieval troubadours who were dependent on the patronage of these powerful ladies were quick to incorporate that material into their verses. In combination with other influences, such as the love poetry of Ovid, these elements of Christian worship caused *romance* literature to became focused on a religious/erotic relationship between an unmarried couple, in which the female was a strong, beautiful, and superior figure to be devoutly worshipped by the subservient male.

The libretto of *Suor Angelica* only briefly mentions Bridal Mysticism, but it is utterly infused with material from both the Cult of the Virgin, and, more subtly, Maternal Mysticism. Maternal Mysticism refers to the maternal/erotic relationship of women to the infant Jesus. Medieval convents frequently contained dolls that represented this figure, and since the maternal longings of many of the nuns must have been intense, it is not a surprise to learn from their writings that they tended to lavish attention on these dolls. (One such doll figures in the Poulenc opera *Les dialogues des Carmélites*.)

There was on occasion a strong erotic component to this devotion to the infant Jesus, that is described quite openly in the writings of some of the women mystics. Gertrude of Helfta (1256–1301), for example, wrote of a vision she had of the Child, saying she watched Mary swaddling the infant, and asked "...to be swaddled with you, so as not to be separated, even by a linen cloth, from him whose embraces and kisses are sweeter by far than a cup of honey."[3]

While there is none of this sort of dubious material in *Suor Angelica*, what we do find is the soprano heroine, a young woman who was forced into a convent after she gave birth to an illegitimate boy, longing passionately for the child, whose father is never mentioned. Angelica's beautiful aria "Senza mamma" (Without your mother) is a love song, sung by a woman in a mystic trance, and in it she addresses her dead son as, "amore, amore, amore," and sings, "You're here. You kiss me and caress me."

In itself, there is nothing at all unseemly about Angelica addressing such words toward her son. It is, however, important to recall that at the end of *La Rondine*, the soprano's childlike lover was essentially transformed into her "dear little son." Here in *Suor Angelica*, there is no tenor character, and the person the heroine loves actually *is* her dear little son.

There are very clear parallels being drawn in *Suor Angelica*: parallels between Angelica and the Virgin Mary, and between the two women's sons. That may be part of the reason why the father of Angelica's son is never mentioned; that is, the equation of Angelica with Mary is strengthened by the *appearance* of a virgin birth on Angelica's part. (Mentioning the father would also have been distracting, and would have blunted the focus on Angelica's longing for her son.)

Note the two women's names and titles, as well. Mary is the Queen of the Angels, while

Angelica had been a Princess. Mary is the Queen of Heaven, while Puccini always thinks of his heroines as being linked with the starry night sky. As Angelica is dying, the chorus of angels call on Mary as "the most glorious of virgins, sublime among the stars."

The parallel between Mary and Angelica is further strengthened by the date chosen for the setting. Almost immediately after the curtain rises we are told the day is *quindena*. This is a day of celebration for Catholics, and it comes 15 days after Easter. Puccini set this opera on a day linked to Easter because he wanted to link the death of Angelica's son to the death of Mary's son. "Senza mamma" clearly references the Crucifixion and the grieving Mary in the opening section, during which the grieving Angelica sings, "Without your mother, O child, you died. Your lips, without my kisses, paled, cold, cold! And you closed, O child, your beautiful eyes! Not being able to caress me, you placed your little hands in a cross!"

Puccini set the opera on *quindena* so the idea of Good Friday and Easter, and the death and resurrection of Mary's son, would be evoked, and yet would not fill the air and take over the action. Puccini's celebration, which he turns into a three-day event via the nuns' "three evenings of the golden water," is presided over by the Virgin Mary, who in medieval times became for Catholics the primary intercessor between mankind and God. In this opera it is Mary whom the nuns worship. It is Mary who judges peoples' lives. It is Mary who grants salvation, and Mary who resurrects the dead. In Puccini's World, it cannot be otherwise, for males have no real power here. They can kill, like Scarpia and Michele do, but they cannot do the truly great things Puccini's women can do. If there are any wonders to be performed during a Puccini opera, women will do them.

It is surely a coincidence that the actual date on which *Suor Angelica* is set is one determined by the phase of the moon. Easter is what is called a "moveable feast," taking place on the first Sunday following the first full moon occurring on or after the spring equinox. As *quindena* takes place 15 days after Easter, it too falls on a date determined by the appearance of the full moon. Puccini surely chose *quindena* because of its tie to Good Friday and Easter, and yet — how perfect this is! This is precisely how things should be arranged in Puccini's World, where the beauty, the power, and the life-force of his soprano heroines is so often linked to the moon. And in conjunction with that coincidence of *quindena*, Puccini does indeed link Angelica's life-force to the moon. Her act of suicide takes place under a night sky, and the stage directions say that once she has swallowed the poison, and awareness of what she has done grips her, "The clouds now cover the moon and stars; the scene is dark." This is not a coincidence, and it is not done solely for theatrical effect. We have seen too much proof that Puccini's Rose Cycle heroines are born at sundown, and die when the moon disappears.

The other Rose Cycle elements are here as well. Again there is the life lived without money, in a natural setting filled with flowers. Angelica had been a Princess, and when she chose love — that is, her son — she instantly lost her wealth and her high position. Angelica's Aunt is extremely rich and powerful, and a more loveless woman can scarcely be imagined. The Aunt is the Alberich figure.

There is also the longing for *là lontano*, which has been seen in every opera since *Tosca*. Having learned to our sorrow in *La Rondine* that the ideal of *lontano* cannot be found on Earth, we see that Puccini has now located *là lontano* in heaven. Angelica believes that is the place where love never dies — up in the starry night sky.

Again red roses are featured, and there is even a nun, lately deceased, whose name was

Bianca Rosa — White Rose. The suggestion is given that there is a rosebush planted on her grave. Angelica has a deeper and more personal relationship with flowers than any other Rose Cycle heroine, for she spends her life caring for them, and intimately knows their properties, and when she calls on them for help, they bring her the death she longs for. Listen to the music with which Puccini describes the flowers' poison rippling through Angelica's system. It's a beautiful sound. There is no way Puccini would make the suggestion that flowers might cause his heroine pain, and the music of the rippling poison could just as easily have been used to describe the scent of a lovely, if narcotic, perfume.

Moving on to the score, what does Puccini do with recurring themes and motifs? He reduces them to a minimum. There is the Son Theme, that expresses Angelica's anguish at being separated from the boy, but the most important piece of recurring music is the theme of the Virgin's Justice. This is first heard in the prayer chanted by the nuns after Sister Osmina is assigned penance, and it is last heard when the chorus of Angels chant their final prayer to Mary after Angelica is saved. The theme is derived from a line in Angelica's aria, "Senza mamma" — the line, "Now that you are an angel in heaven...."

Some critics have complained that Puccini plays the music of this aria through too many times during the course of the opera, and indeed, it does get quite a workout. The composer had a technical problem to deal with; that is, the subject addressed in "Senza mamma" is the only thing on Angelica's mind. Puccini was pretty much forced to use the music over and over, but he was careful to vary it in accordance with the tone of each scene.

The first time we hear a long passage of "Senza mamma" is during the scene in which Angelica frantically questions one of the other nuns, begging for a detailed description of the rich-looking carriage the woman saw outside the convent. It could be her family's carriage! It could be that her son has been brought to see her! In this scene, "Senza mamma" is rapid, urgent, and there is a little passage, almost an *ostinato*, that is remarkably beautiful and insinuating.

Some time later, after Angelica's hopes have been brutally destroyed, we hear the aria itself, with its words. Now it is a love song — a grief-stricken lament for the dead son. Another time we hear a long passage from "Senza mamma" is during Angelica's gathering of the flowers and herbs from which she will brew a poison with which to kill herself. The music is calm and peaceful then, because in a few minutes — Angelica believes — she will be united with her son, and everything will be all right.

There are no artistic breakthroughs in Puccini's handling of the recurring music, yet the score is a bit different from anything he has done before. We hear more animal noises than usual (a bird, a lamb, some wasps, and a donkey), and for the first time Puccini attempts music that evokes the supernatural. This include the mystic trance described by the Aunt, who often communes with the spirit of Angelica's dead mother, and the mystic trance of Angelica herself, which grips her part way through "Senza mamma" and does not pass off until she realizes that by swallowing poison, she has committed a mortal sin. Both the music and words of Angelica's mystic trance suggest Puccini had been dipping into the "Liebestod" of *Tristan und Isolde.*

In addition to the heroine's one-track mind, Puccini had another technical problem: how to stage Angelica's death. The Virgin Mary grants Angelica salvation, and appears before her with the son. What now? If Angelica embraces the boy, which the audience of course wants her to do, should the two stay frozen in that tableau until the curtain drops? If they do, the audience is sure to ask questions. "Does this mean Angelica doesn't die?"

"Has Mary restored the child to life?" Another option is for the two to embrace, after which Angelica sinks to the ground, dead. This is worse the first idea. "Does this mean Angelica is separated from the boy again?" "Has she been sent to Purgatory?" "Is the boy upset at having his mother fall from his arms?"

One wonders whether Puccini thought longingly for a moment about what would have been done in the old days. In the Baroque Era, all three people — the Virgin, the child, and Angelica — would have climbed onto a cloud and been wafted up to heaven. As this would have been laughed to scorn in the 19th century, let alone the 20th, Puccini's only real option was to do what he did: the boy approaches his mother slowly, not showing any eagerness, and Angelica dies blissfully without touching him.

The opera is divided into seven vignettes: The Prayer, The Penances, Recreation, The Return From Alms-Collecting, The Princess-Aunt, Grace, and The Miracle. The orchestra includes an offstage group including bells, and these bells play for four bars before the curtain rises. Are these the famous Puccini bells, that presage death and disaster? Are they in imitation of the bells in *Parsifal*'s Grail Hall? No. They are just convent bells, which toll for the nuns' prayer.

When the curtain rises we see the interior of a convent — the chapel and cloister. At back right is the cemetery. At back left is the vegetable garden. Center stage: cypress trees (a traditional symbol of mourning), a cross, and growing herbs and flowers. Back and to the left is a patch of irises, in the midst of which is a fountain. Its jet of water spills into a basin on the ground.

What time do you suppose it is? *Tramonto di primavera*, says the stage direction: spring sunset. This is the hour of waking dreams, but there is scarcely a thread of hope here, to struggle with even more melancholy than was seen in *Il Tabarro*.

The Prayer

The nuns are at chapel, and as the curtain rises we hear them singing a gentle Hail Mary. Two lay sisters cross the stage. They are already late, but even so they stop to listen to a bird singing in a cypress tree. The bird's song, which provides a more decorative element than would otherwise be allowed in church music, is played by the offstage piccolo, supported by bells. The lay sisters will be punished for their lateness (actually, for not making an act of contrition) but Puccini carefully arranges for us to see their "sin" as their having stopped to listen to the lovely birdsong. Puccini, who has repeatedly shown us he has no religious faith, is out to portray the convent as a place where even the most innocent pleasures, such as the enjoyment of birds and flowers and laughter, are punished.

The two lay sisters enter the church, then Sister Angelica enters at right. She too is late, but when she opens the chapel door she makes the required act of contrition, kneeling and kissing the ground. (Angelica is in the convent as a punishment, and she is shown as entirely submissive to that punishment. As a perfect penitent for seven long years, she surely deserves forgiveness.)

The offstage chorus of nuns continue to sing the Hail Mary, and Angelica's voice is raised in a highly significant solo line addressed to the Virgin: "Pray for us sinners, now and at the hour of our death." (This opera lasts less than an hour, and so Puccini doesn't waste any time getting to the word that, along with "love," inspires him most: "death." And this is, quite literally, the hour of Angelica's death.)

The prayer to the Virgin is of course very meaningful in its entirety. Except at rare and dreadful moments, men have no power in Puccini's World. They do not even exist in *Suor Angelica*. God is mentioned a few times in passing, and so is Jesus, but in this opera the great deity is the Virgin Mary, the Mother of Mothers. The prayer declares that the Lord is with Mary, and she and her son are blessed. Already we are receiving a subtle suggestion that Angelica and her son should be blessed as well. As Mary suffered the cruel death of her son, we will equate her with Angelica and her suffering. Mary will be able to sympathize with Angelica, whose opening line launches another of Puccini's bracketings. The first thing we hear from Angelica is her prayer for Mary's intercession at the hour of death, and that is the last thing we will hear from her as well.

When the prayer ends, the nuns emerge from chapel, two by two. The Abbess pauses before the cross, and the sisters bow to her as they pass by. The sisters form a semi-circle, and Sister Zelatrice (appropriately, her name means "zealous") comes into the middle to hand out punishments to those who have sinned.

The Penances

Sister Zelatrice scolds the two lay sisters who were late. They lost a day of *quindena*! She observes that Angelica was also late, but she made a full act of contrition. (Notice: Angelica has paid for her sin, and doesn't merit further punishment.) One of the lay sisters humbly admits her guilt, and asks for a great penance — the bigger the better. Zelatrice orders the two to recite twenty times, "the prayer for the afflicted, for slaves, and for those in mortal sin."

One of the lay sisters agrees "with joy and fervor" to do so, and in the opera's one mention of Bridal Mysticism, the two sing, "Christ our Lord, Bridegroom of Love, I wish only to please Thee, now and at the hour of my death! Amen!" The two lay sisters withdraw to the arches, and Zelatrice moves on to the punishment of Sister Lucilla. Her sin was to laugh in choir this evening, and to make others laugh, and for that Zelatrice orders her to go work with the distaff, and observe silence.

Next is Sister Osmina, who stands accused of having concealed two small red roses in her sleeves in chapel. (We can imagine what Puccini must have thought of this sin.) Osmina is defiant, and denies having had the roses. Zelatrice sternly orders the girl to go to her cell, but Osmina simply shrugs. Zelatrice tells her to go along, and she adds, to a liturgical cadence, "The Virgin is watching you!"

Without a word, the angry Osmina goes to her cell. Six of the sisters chant in Latin, "Virgin queen, pray for her...." Osmina slams her cell door hard. With the Latin chant, we hear a very important musical theme: the Virgin's Justice, which is derived from the line in "Senza mamma" on which Angelica sings, "Now that you are an angel in heaven...." We will hear this theme repeatedly, and it will recur during the opera's closing moments, when the chorus of angels pray for Mary to save Angelica.

Recreation

Now that punishments have been meted out, it is time for recreation. Zelatrice tells the others that since it pleases the Lord, and makes them work for Him more gaily, the sisters should now enjoy themselves. Violas, cellos, and a solo, muted horn begin a sweetly sad melody, and the sisters scatter through the cloister, while Angelica begins to care for the herbs and flowers. She will later call the flowers her friends, and we see here that caring for them is her recreation.

Sister Genovieffa now distinguishes herself from the other sisters. In a delicate and pretty song, "O sorelle, sorelle" (O sisters, sisters), she points out that a ray of sunlight is striking the iris plants. Soon it will reach the water of the fountain. "The three evenings of the golden fountain are beginning!" Pings from the triangle and a pulsing figure in wood-winds and harp describe the jetting water and the sparkle of sunlight. Other nuns exclaim at the sight, saying Mary's lovely smile comes with the beam, and they thank her as the Queen of Mercy.

The Novice Mistress tells an inquiring novice this is a sign of God's goodness. Once a year, for three evenings in a row, God allows the sisters to see the sunlight strike the fountain and turn the water gold. All days of the year except these three, the women emerge from choir either too early, so the sun is still up, or too late, and the sun is down. In other words, this three-day period is the only time during the year in which the nuns emerge at sunset. This is clearly a very special day to Puccini. Angelica will later scoop up some of the golden water and use it to brew her poison. The suggestion is thus made that the poison is to some degree a gift from Mary and from God.

We see the Puccini Mixture of joy and sadness now, as, in a tone of great melancholy, some of the nuns observe that the joyous event means another year has passed. Others add sadly, "And a sister is gone." They are speaking of Sister Bianca Rosa (White Rose), who recently died. The nuns assume an attitude of silent and sorrowful prayer, then Genovieffa, in an almost merry tone, suggests taking a pail of the golden water to Bianca Rosa's grave. (Presumably there is some plant growing on or by it, and the most likely one would be Latin culture's traditional rosebush.)

The sisters like Genovieffa's suggestion, declaring the sister who reposes would surely wish that. Angelica quickly disagrees. She knows too much about wishing for something, year after year, and she doesn't like to think people continue to wish for things after death. In an achingly sad voice she refers to wishes as "the flowers of the living." She says these flowers don't bloom in the realm of the dead, for the Virgin Mary knows what everyone wants, and grants their wishes even before they have blossomed. Angelica calls Mary the Mother of Mothers, and cries, "O sister, death is beautiful life!"

As she sings these last words, the full orchestra gives out a passionate melody that will recur when Angelica drinks the poison. (Her line seems to mean something like, "death is life made beautiful," and it should be noted that the highly stressed final words, "beautiful life," mirror Angelica's first highly stressed word, during the Hail Mary: "death.")

Zelatrice, whose job it is to keep everyone in line, answers Angelica's comments about blossoming wishes by saying primly that nuns are not allowed to have wishes, even in life. (Here again, Puccini is depicting the convent as a place devoted to punishment, empty of all joy. The enjoyment of birdsong is forbidden, along with laughter and red roses. One can't even silently wish for things.)

This doesn't seem right to the cheerful Genovieffa, who asks why they should not have wishes, if they are simple and innocent. She is the only one who will admit to having a wish, and she describes it in a little song, "Soave Signor Mio" (My Sweet Lord), that is charmingly accompanied by a solo bassoon, sounding quite pastoral, with punctuations from oboe, cor anglais, and clarinet. Genovieffa sings of how she had once been a shepherdess, and has not seen a lamb in her entire five years in the convent. She asks whether it would displease God for her to stroke a little lamb and hear it bleat. (The bleating is of course described musically, via adorable little honking noises made by woodwinds.) Singing a liturgical cadence, Genovieffa humbly asks forgiveness of the Lamb of God if her wish is a sin.

Now Sister Dolcina eagerly admits to having a wish. She is a plump and ruddy girl, and as the oboe gives a little chuckle, the nuns declare they already know what her wish is—some tasty morsel. "Greed is a serious sin!" they say to the mortified Dolcina (whose name means "sweet one"). When Genovieffa began to talk about wishes, Angelica moved quickly away. Now Genovieffa and some of the others approach her, and ask whether she has a wish. Angelica denies it, and turns back to her flowers. The nuns form a group a little ways away and begin to murmur that she told a lie. They know Angelica has an intense wish.

A novice questions them, and they eagerly tell her Angelica longs for news of her family. Gossiping furiously, they confide that Angelica has been in the convent for seven years without a word from her people, and although she seems resigned, she is actually tormented. (Having depicted Angelica as a perfect penitent, Puccini's message is plain: the convent is a place of neither justice nor mercy. In fact, it is hell: a place of eternal punishment, where no amount of atonement is ever enough.) The nuns describe Angelica's former life to the novice. She was rich and noble, the Abbess told them. She was a Princess. Her family chose to punish her by making her a nun. What the sisters don't know is what Angelica did to deserve this.

The sisters scatter, and the Sister Infermaress comes running in, calling for Angelica. Sister Chiara was adjusting the trellis of roses, and she disturbed a wasps' nest. Many wasps came out and stung Chiara on the face, and now she is in her cell, moaning. Angelica knows the properties of flowers and herbs, and the Infermaress begs her to relieve Chiara's pain.

The music to which the Infermaress describes the wasp attack is unusual for Puccini, and quite fascinating. (The closest thing to it in the rest of the canon is the palm reading music of *La Rondine*.) Muted trumpet, triangle, and pizzicato strings first accompany the chanting voice with a strange and pulsing melody, until the Infermaress reaches the part about the wasps attacking. At that point, piccolo, flute, glockenspiel, and harp describe the darting, angry wasps. The passage concludes mournfully, as the Infirmaress speaks of the pain tormenting Chiara, and the sisters sympathize with the poor girl. Angelica runs to pick an herb and a flower, and as she does the Infermaress declares she always has a good remedy from flowers and herbs, that relieves suffering. (Angelica will repeat this line while preparing the poison that will relieve her own suffering.)

Handing the Infermaress some spurge, Angelica tells her to bathe the swelling with the milk that oozes from it. She gives her another plant as well, saying she should make a potion of it and have Chiara drink it. To that same pulsing music the Infermaress used, Angelica says the potion will be bitter (hint, hint), but will do her good. The darting, musical wasps return as she adds that Chiara should not lament about the pain. Wasps' stings are a small pain, Angelica observes, and lamenting increases the torments.

The Infirmaress promises to tell Chiara that, and when she thanks Angelica we hear in her response what sounds like a line from *Parsifal*: "I am here to serve," says Angelica, evoking Kundry in the final act of Wagner's opera.

The Return from Alms-Collecting

From rear left, two alms-collecting sisters enter with their little donkey, who is laden with goods. "Mary be praised!" they cry in a liturgical cadence. The sisters gather around the donkey and watch as the Collectors unload the donated food and hand it to the Sister Procuratrix. Dolcina cannot resist interjecting remarks as the Collectors unload oil, nuts, flour, cheese, lentils, eggs and butter. One of them offers the "greedy sister" a small bunch of currants, which Dolcina invites the others to share. They form a little group at right, plucking the currants and giggling softly.

One of the Collectors now asks who has come to the parlatory this evening. The nuns are unaware of any visitor, but the Collector says there is a sumptuous carriage outside the gate. As though seized by a sudden uneasiness, Angelica questions the Collector. A carriage is outside? Sumptuous?

An up tempo, rocking version of "Senza mamma" begins as the Collector declares the carriage worthy of great lords. It surely awaits someone who has come to the convent, and perhaps in a moment they will hear the sound of the parlatory bell. (As soon as the Collector says this, bass clarinet, muted trumpet, celeste, and harps play a two-note figure that sounds like a postillion's horn.)

The music of "Senza mamma" continues as Angelica feverishly questions the Collector, asking whether the carriage had an ivory coat of arms, and an upholstered interior of pale blue silk embroidered in silver. (Blue and silver are colors associated with the Virgin Mary.) Dumbfounded, the Collector says she does not know — she only saw it was a carriage, and beautiful. With this, the music of "Senza mamma" briefly halts. The other nuns have been watching Angelica curiously, and as the timpani begin to pound like a heartbeat they comment sympathetically on how pale she was a moment ago, and how red she now is. (This a reference to the lily and the rose.) They know she hopes the visitors are her people.

From off stage, bronze bells begin to chime. Nuns run in from all sides, wondering who the visitor is. The music of "Senza mamma" begins again as each one expresses hope that the visitor is one of her own relatives, bringing a gift. The pitying Sister Genovieffa points out the distraught Angelica to the others, and they look on as Angelica raises her eyes to heaven and prays to the Mother to turn a smile to the Savior for her.

The tone of "Senza mamma" turned ardent and pleading with Angelica's prayer, and it continues so as Genovieffa steps out from the group of nuns that have approached Angelica, and with great sweetness tells her they pray to the Star of Stars (Mary) that the visitor is for her. Moved, Angelica thanks her, and "Senza mamma" fades away.

From the left, the Abbess enters to summon the nun who is to go into the parlatory. In that tense moment, all the sisters make the sacrifice of their wishes in favor of Angelica, who is suffering most. Angelica stands as if her life were in suspense, her eyes again raised to heaven. "Sister Angelica!" calls the Abbess, and the nuns let out a collective sigh. The Abbess motions the others to leave, but as they are going they notice the jet of water from the fountain has turned to gold. (As I noted in Chapter Three, the fountain of water that turns gold when a ray of light from heaven strikes it seems very much like the Holy Grail in *Parsifal*, which turns crimson when a ray of light from heaven strikes it.) The nuns take a small bucket of the golden water, and head for the cemetery to pour it on the grave of Bianca Rosa — the White Rose, whose name suggests purity, and rebirth.

Played by solo violin, "Senza mamma" briefly returns as Angelica pleads with the Abbess to tell her who is waiting to speak with her. "For seven years I've been waiting, waiting for a word, a note...." She says she has offered everything to the Virgin in full atonement. The Abbess interrupts the distraught young woman, telling her to offer the Virgin the anxiety that has made her lose her composure. Obediently, Angelica kneels and collects herself. From the cemetery, the nuns chant a *requiescat* for Bianca Rosa: "Give her eternal rest, O Lord: and may perpetual light shine on her. May she rest in peace. Amen! Amen!"

Angelica raises her eyes, saying she is calm and submissive now. The dark and ominous Aunt Theme—a climbing, twisting figure in the full strings, followed by a sustained chord from muted horns—begins to sound as the Abbess tells Angelica her Aunt, the Princess, has come to visit her. Angelica makes a little cry, and the Abbess sternly tells her that in the parlatory, one says no more than is required by obedience and necessity. "Every word is heard by the Blessed Virgin," she warns. Angelica's response, sung to the theme of the Virgin's Justice, is, "May the Virgin hear me. And so be it."

The Abbess exits. Angelica rises and goes anxiously to the arches of the parlatory. The Sister Janitoress unlocks the door from within. Horns play soft chords over pizzicato strings as a figure in black—the Princess Aunt—passes the Janitoress and the Abbess, who bow slightly in respect. The elderly woman leans on an ebony cane, and holds herself in an attitude of aristocratic dignity. She looks at Angelica coldly.

Angelica is filled with emotion, but she restrains herself because the Janitoress and the Abbess are still there. Then the door is closed, and Angelica, almost stumbling, goes to her Aunt. The old woman extends her left hand, allowing only a submissive kiss. Angelica kisses the hand, and the Aunt sits. Her eyes filled with tears, Angelica looks at her Aunt pleadingly. The Aunt looks straight ahead.

At last the Aunt begins to speak, chanting in a near-monotone that twenty years ago, when Angelica's parents died, they entrusted her with their children and the entire family patrimony. At this, double basses softly begin to reiterate the menacing Aunt Theme. The Prince and Princess, the Aunt continues, left it to her to divide the estate when and how she thought appropriate, and with full justice. She has brought Angelica the paper dividing the inheritance, and she is to read it, discuss it, and sign it.

After seven years apart, Angelica cannot bear to discuss business—the business of money. A thrumming begins in the harp as she pleads with her Aunt to be inspired by this holy place, and in the brief pause that follows, the theme of the Virgin's Justice is played by muted trumpets. "It's a place of mercy," Angelica urges. "It's a place of compassion." As though passing sentence, the Aunt coldly responds, "Of penance." Continuing with her business, she tells Angelica the reason she has arrived at this division: "Your sister Anna Viola is to be a bride."

The music turns tender as Angelica exclaims with joy at this news of her younger sister, who was a child when she saw her last. She prays that her little blond sister will be happy, and asks who it is who will "bejewel" her. The Aunt's response is, "One who for love forgave the sin with which you stained our white escutcheon!"

For the first time, Angelica flares up. Emphasizing the entirely female orientation of this opera, and reiterating two of the most important words in the libretto, she addresses the Aunt as "sister of my mother," and accuses her of being inexorable—unrelenting. This angers the Aunt, who briefly loses her composure. How dare Angelica mention her mother's name? How dare she bring her mother into this, against her?

Let's pause here, because something seems a bit familiar. Do we remember somebody else named Anna, who was to be a bride? And wasn't there something about a long separation, during which the heroine grieved for her absent beloved, and when he didn't return she closed her eyes in eternal sleep? Women chanted a *requiescat* for a dead woman, singing, "Like a lily cut down, she lies in her coffin, her face as pale as the moonlight. O purest maiden, rest now in peace." There is a lot in *Suor Angelica* that may remind us of *Le Villi*, including the final scene, in which the nuns—virgin women in white who seem not to touch the ground as they walk—come to Angelica from the cemetery. Doesn't that seem a lot like the band of Villi?

That said, this scene of Angelica's meeting with her Aunt seems too much like one of the scenes in *Parsifal* for it to be a coincidence. As was pointed out in Chapter Three, Angelica appears to have been modeled on the *Parsifal* character Amfortas, who like Angelica lived in a single-sex religious community, and was sentenced to an agonizingly long and painful period of atonement, in punishment for having committed a sexual transgression. The one who passed sentence on Amfortas was God, and Angelica's Aunt appears to be Puccini's version of God—a harsh and relentless figure who requires eternal penance. We already saw the similarity of Angelica's fountain to Parsifal's Holy Grail—both the fountain and the chalice miraculously change color when struck by a divine light from above—and in a moment we will hear something that sounds so much like the agonized cry of Amfortas that it can't be explained away.

Angelica's Aunt, having regained her composure, begins to speak in mystical terms, describing for Angelica what happens when she prays in the family chapel. This is the first time Puccini has attempted music evoking the supernatural, and he calls on muted horns to provide a haunting, authoritative, and otherworldly sound.

Considering the numerous cult elements of medieval Catholicism that exist in this libretto, it should perhaps not be too startling to hear this cold fish of an Aunt suddenly begin to speak like an entranced mystic. "In the silence of those prayers my spirit seems to leave me and join your mother's in secret, ethereal communion. How painful it is to hear the dead mourn and weep."

The words "mourn and weep" are sung to a motif of three rising chords—very eerie ones—played by muted violins. This is an important motif that will soon be featured in the introduction to "Senza mamma." There too this Communion Motif suggests the pain of the living, at the thought of pain felt by the dead. These eerie, rising chords seem to describe the living spirit leaving the body, rising upwards to join in communion with the spirit of the dead.

The Aunt concludes, saying that when the mystical trance passes, "I have only one word to say to you: Atone! Atone!" Her cry in Italian is "Espiare! Espiare!" and as was observed in Chapter Three, the word is pronounced, pitched, and drawn out almost exactly like the cry of Amfortas—"Erbarmen! Erbarmen!"—in *Parsifal*'s first scene in the Grail Hall. Addressing God, Amfortas was begging for "Mercy! Mercy!" The answer, from Puccini's God-figure of the Aunt, is an unrelenting, "Atone! Atone!"

Angelica says she has offered everything to the Virgin, and with that we hear again the theme of the Virgin's Justice. There is but one thing, she says, she cannot give. She cannot promise the Mother of Mothers to forget, "My son! My son! My son! My son!" She is almost hysterical now, and oboes, clarinets, violins, and violas begin to sound the agitated Son Theme, which will be played 17 times in sequence. Angelica demands to know how her son is, and what he looks like. Has he a sweet face? What color are his eyes? She saw and kissed him only once before he was torn from her, and for seven years she's been praying for word of him.

The Aunt stands unmoved, saying nothing even when Angelica cries that another moment of silence will damn her for eternity. But then Angelica hauls out the big gun: "The Virgin hears us, and She will judge you." In the face of this awesome threat, coldly sung to the Virgin's Justice, the Aunt obeys. (Recall that the threat that the Virgin was watching was what caused the rebellious Sister Osmina to submit to punishment.) To a soft, uneasy twitching in the strings, the Aunt, cold as Angelica, says that two years ago the child was stricken with a severe illness. "Everything was done to save him...."

"He's dead?" asks Angelica. The Aunt bows her head, and says nothing. Angelica gives a heartrending cry, and flutes, oboes, clarinets, and violins give a great upwards rush as she falls to the ground. The Aunt believes she has fainted, and rises to assist her. But then she hears Angelica crying, and restrains herself. The Aunt turns to a holy image on the wall, and prays for a moment.

The three rising chords denoting mystical Communion with the weeping dead are heard three times, then the Son Theme begins to play in intervals. A funeral march is heard in the lower strings. The Janitoress comes in with a lamp, that she sets on the table. At a word from the Aunt, the Janitoress goes out, then returns with the Abbess, carrying a table with an inkwell and pen.

Angelica understands what is wanted, and she drags herself to the table and signs the paper. The nuns go out. The Aunt takes the paper, and begins to approach Angelica, who draws away. The Aunt then raps on the door; the Janitoress returns and takes the lamp, and leads the Aunt out. The Aunt stops at the threshold and looks back at Angelica for a moment. Then she leaves, and the Janitoress locks the door.

Evening has fallen, and in the cemetery the sisters are lighting votive lamps on the graves. As soon as the Aunt has gone, Angelica bursts into desperate sobs. Woodwinds play the Communion Motif, twice, as the prelude to "Senza mamma."

Grace

On her knees, her voice desolate, Angelica sings an apostrophe — a love song — to her son, who died without his mother. Drawing a parallel between her son and Mary's, Angelica sings of how, unable to caress her, he folded his hands in a cross.

In the B section of the aria, we hear the source of the theme of the Virgin's Justice. "Now that you are an angel in heaven," sings Angelica, to the soft plucking of a heavenly harp, "you can see your mother." (The music of this passage and the lines that follow was used during Angelica's anxious questioning of the Alms Collector, though it was very different in tone from this sweet and weeping lament.)

By now, Angelica has been gripped by a mystic trance. She asks her son when she will see him in Heaven. "When shall I die?" she asks, and on that word, a throbbing heartbeat begins in the horns, timpani, harp, and full strings. Angelica concludes "as if in ecstasy," singing to her little boy to tell her when she will be able to die, and to communicate this message in the faint sparkle of a star (illustrated by three soft pings on the triangle). "Speak to me, speak to me, my love, love, love!" On this last word, sung *pp* on a high A, the harp describes an upwards ripple, as though Angelica's soul were leaving her body. Three pulses more, and the musical heartbeat stops. The sisters have finished lighting the votive lamps, and they come from the cemetery into the darkened cloister, where they approach Angelica. Puccini tells us "it seems as if the white figures, as they walk, do not touch the ground."

Genovieffa and some of the nuns congratulate Angelica. The Virgin has heard her prayer, and shown her Grace. "Angelica stands as if in the grip of a mystic exaltation." Sounding very much like Isolde singing over the body of Tristan, Angelica rapturously sings, "Grace has descended from heaven; everything, everything enflames me; it shines, it shines! Already, sisters, I see the goal!" The orchestra swells as the voices of the sisters join in, praising the Holy Virgin.

Now the signal of the clappers is heard, ordering the nuns to their cells for the night. More nuns enter, from all sides. Each one, including Suor Angelica, enters her cell and closes the door, still singing praises to the Virgin. "Let us praise!" sings Angelica, floating a sustained high C. The scene is empty for a moment, as full night falls. A dome of sparkling stars begins to twinkle, and the moon appears. From her cell, Angelica sings that Grace has descended from heaven. The sweetly sad music of the B section of "Senza mamma" is heard, asking when Angelica will be able to kiss her son — when she will be able to die.

Now Angelica comes out of her cell, carrying a bowl. As "Senza mamma" continues, she sets it down near the cross that is among the cypress trees, and makes a small hearth from some stones. She gathers twigs and branches, and sets them on the hearth. Then she goes to the fountain, and fills her bowl with golden water. Returning to the hearth, she lights a fire and sets the bowl down to boil the water. Now she goes to the flowerbed.

Remembering the words of the Infirmaress, she softly sings that Suor Angelica always has a good remedy made with flowers. With that word — flowers — a heartbeat begins again in the full strings. The music of the B section of "Senza mamma" returns as Angelica calls the flowers her friends — friends who have drops of poison enclosed in their little bosoms. (The heartbeat grows softer here, as the violins and violas drop out.) She has given them so much care, and now they will repay her. "Thanks to you, my flowers [and here the heartbeat stops], I will die." Making a little bundle of the herbs and flowers she has picked, Angelica drops them into the simmering water. For a moment she watches the poison form, then she takes the bowl from the fire and sets it at the foot of the cross. A soft and solemn chord is heard.

Now Angelica turns to the cells at right, and happily bids her sisters farewell. As violins play a lighthearted melody, she explains her son has called her from heaven, his smile appearing in a beam of stars. A heavenly harp ripples as she tells of how he called his mamma to come to Paradise. She says goodbye to the chapel where she prayed so much, and as she does we hear the music of the sisters' prayer to Mary, which is also the theme of the Virgin's Justice. Her voice rising in ecstasy to a sustained high B, she sings that Grace has descended. "I die for him and I'll see him in heaven!" Utterly entranced by her mystic vision, Angelica embraces the cross and kisses it, then picks up the bowl and drinks the poisoned, flower-filled water. As she does this, the orchestra plays the melody that was heard much earlier, after she cried, "Death is beautiful life!"

Angelica leans against one of the cypress trees. She presses her bosom with her left hand, feeling the poison course through her in exquisite little ripples described by flute and harp. We can tell by the sound the poison does not hurt. Angelica's right arm falls, and the bowl drops to the ground. A dark and ominous figure is heard in the clarinet, bassoon, and double bass as Angelica's mystic trance leaves her, and she realizes what she has done. An expression of anguish comes over her face, and the moon and stars disappear behind a bank of clouds. No light shines from the sky.

"Ah! I am damned!" cries Angelica, and the anguished Son Theme begins to play. Terrified of dying in a state of mortal sin, Angelica falls to her knees and begins to pray to the Madonna to save her. "For the love of my son!" she begs.

The Miracle

The chorus of Angels is heard in the distance, chanting prayers in Latin, imploring the Queen of Virgins, the Chaste Mother, the Queen of Peace, on Angelica's behalf. The Angels slowly approach, singing their prayers to the theme of the Virgin's Justice. Between their lines, to the music of the Son Theme, Angelica wildly cries that she has lost her reason, and pleads with Mary not to make her die in damnation. "Give me a sign of Grace!"

The Angels reply to this plea, "raising the hymn to the Mother of Mothers." In Latin they sing, "O most glorious of virgins, sublime among the stars, who created you, and nursed you as a baby with a milk-laden breast." This is sung to the music of Angelica's first mystic ecstasy, when, Isolde-like, she sang that everything enflamed her, everything was shining.

The full orchestra sounds as Angelica's voice is joined with that of the Angels. Still desperate, her voice harmonizes with the mystic melody, but she sings a different line as she pleads as a mother for the Madonna to save her. As she sings this, the Angels pray, "That which Eve sadly took away, you restore to the precious seed. Let the mourners enter the realm of stars. Open the gates of heaven. Most glorious of virgins, hail Mary!"

The chapel is now filled with blazing light, and Angelica sees the miracle achieved. A door opens, and the Queen of Comfort appears. She is solemn and sweet, and before her is a small blond boy, all in white. For the last time, Angelica cries, "A mother implores you! O Madonna, save me!" And as she does, she joins her vocal line to that of the Angels, bringing the choral prayer to its cathartic climax with a unison singing of the mystic melody. With a gentle gesture, not touching the child, the Virgin urges him to go to the dying woman. Angelica cries "Ah!" much as she did when she learned her son was dead, and she reaches out to the child, filled with the renewed ecstasy of her mystic vision.

To the theme of the Virgin's Justice, the Angels praise the most glorious of Virgins, the Pure Mother, the Tower of David, and as they do the child takes three slow steps toward Angelica. The precious, lost thing has been recovered, and so Angelica, like Amfortas, can die now. With the boy's final step, Angelica falls back gently, and dies without having touched him. The orchestra and the chorus hold a long chord, played as softly as possible, while, "The miracle shines forth."

13

Turandot

Libretto by Adami and Simoni, based on a play by Carlo Gozzi
First performed at the Teatro alla Scala, Milan, April 25, 1926

Turandot is a retelling of the Regeneration Myth, which celebrates the endless cycle of life, and is surely one of the oldest stories known. The subject of this myth is a kingdom fallen into chaos as a result of the weakening of its ruler. Perhaps he has become too old to defend the land, or maybe he has offended a deity. Many bold champions have attempted to dispel the chaos—to kill the monster, lift the curse, placate the god, rescue the king's daughter, halt the plague, recover the lost talisman, or whatever—but all have failed, dying in the attempt. The people are desperate, for without help they will soon perish.

At the height of the crisis, a young man appears. He is a stranger, come from far away. Strong and brave, the young man offers himself as champion. Many beg him not to sacrifice himself needlessly; for how can it be that he might succeed, where so many others have failed? The young man insists, and he undergoes a fearful trial of his wits, strength, and courage. After a terrible struggle, he prevails. The chaos is dispelled, and the land returns to a state of peace and plenty. With the acclamations of a grateful people ringing in his ears, the young man ascends the royal throne that is now rightfully his.

It is most unlikely Puccini was aware he was beginning a continuing story when he composed *Le Villi*, but there can be little doubt he knew he was ending one when he began work on *Turandot*. Chaos has come to the World of Night, for the moon has become an evil presence, and the impossibly beautiful heroine has spurned love. For the first time the leading soprano character has wholeheartedly chosen as Alberich did, reveling in the cruel ecstasy of supreme power, and the result is of course infinitely worse in Puccini's World than when mere, puny males made the dark choice.

The rose has all but disappeared, for the soprano character scorns love. Flowers still exist, but until the final scene they are confined to the royal garden, where Calaf will spend what may be his last night of life, dreaming that love might be born in the heart of the fierce Princess Turandot. The moon, symbol of the heroine's strength and beauty, has grown monstrous. No longer does she shed a warm, silvery light that inspires love. Rather, she emits a cold, white light that illuminates the graveyards of Peking. The moon is now "the bloodless one," "the severed head," "the gaunt lover of the dead."

Puccini is attempting to regenerate his World in *Turandot*, and so the story begins with a world that is old and sick, and should end not with a world that is healed, but rather with a new world. *Turandot* begins with the same sadomasochistic dynamic that has existed between the Rose Cycle characters ever since *Le Villi*, and we soon see that things have come full circle—back to the point of the ritual murder of the male by the female. This has to stop. Enough is enough. Puccini will not do as his misogynistic contemporaries did, showing that a powerful woman is a force of irredeemable evil. There will be no more passionate lovers, tearing their tormented hearts under the Night sky. Instead there will be spouses, living peacefully and respectably in the golden light of Day.

As the story opens, 25 champions have already fallen, and at the rising of the moon the 26th — the Prince of Persia — will lose his head. It will join those of the others, mounted on spikes on the palace wall, and when it does the pale and silent moon will kiss it. It is sunset when the curtain rises on the execution; "the sweet hour of dreams." As the dazed-looking Prince advances toward the block, the boys of Peking sing, "From the desert to the sea, don't you hear a thousand voices whisper, 'Princess, come down to me! Everything will flower, everything will shine!'"

Soon the ghosts of the 26 dead champions will appear on the ramparts, begging for another sight of the Princess Turandot — for another sight of she, "who makes us, dead men, dream." It is sunset, the hour of waking nightmares, and at long last the dream of a love that will never die has come true. But even as the Prince of Persia kneels before the sword, a new champion enters the lists. It is the Unknown Prince, Calaf. As he sees among the milling crowd his father, the blind and ruined one-time King Timur, Calaf cries out to him, "Father! Look at me! This is no dream!"

At first horrified by the cruelty of a princess who would do as Turandot does to one who only sought her love, Calaf too becomes spellbound at the sight of her unearthly beauty. Despite the pleas of his father and the slave girl Liu, who cares for the old man, Calaf strikes the gong to summon Turandot and bring on the Contest of the Riddles. Failure to answer the riddles means death, but success means the winning of Turandot, and an end to the blood in which Peking is drowning.

Physically, the Princess dominates Calaf totally during the Contest scene, and Calaf accepts this as only right. For the first riddle, she towers above him at the top of a tall staircase. Angry and nervous after he succeeds in answering, she moves for the second riddle to the middle of the staircase, where she continues to stand above him. Almost frantic after he again answers correctly, she runs down to the bottom of the staircase, yet she still stands over Calaf, for he drops to his knees and gazes up at her with terrible anxiety to receive from the Princess the riddle of that which, "...if it allows you your freedom makes you a slave; if it accepts you as a slave, it makes you a king!" Clearly, the ushering in of a new world of equality and friendship between male and female will be no easy task on either side!

As discussed in Chapter Three, Puccini's heroines early on developed three conflicting urges in respect to their tenor lovers: the urge to dominate them, to love them, and to redeem them. His heroines expressed these urges more and more intensely as Puccini aged, to such a point that by the time he began composing *Turandot*, it was impossible for all three urges to be contained in one character. The heroine's urge to dominate had metastasized into the urge to devour, as a black widow spider devours, and thus had become totally incompatible with the other two urges.

The solution for *Turandot* was to split both the soprano and the tenor characters into two people. This resulted in a cast that features two couples — Liu and Timur, and Turandot and Calaf — both with powerful females and imperiled males. One soprano, Liu, loves and redeems, while the other, Turandot, devours. Timur was given all of the tenor lover's helpless dependency, and Calaf was allotted his youth and ardor.

The immediate objection to this argument is obvious. Of these four people, the only one who dies is Liu — a young girl who is also a slave — so how can she possibly be considered a powerful person rather than an imperiled one? Conventional wisdom has always had her as a frail waif who suffers and dies for the unrequited love of Calaf. The answer to that objection is that in drama, it is necessary to look at what people *do*, not at what they *say*. One has to look at what a character *is*, rather than at what he *claims to be*.

Liu calls herself, "Nothing — a slave." But who rescues people in this opera? Liu, who preserves the lives of both Timur and Calaf. Who redeems in this opera? Liu, whose martyrdom redeems the soul of Turandot, who had apparently sinned beyond forgiveness. Who wins the hand of Turandot for Calaf? Liu, who under torture refuses to reveal the Prince's name, which would result in the victory of Turandot over Calaf. No other character in the opera accomplishes any such heroic tasks as these. It would take a shallow reading indeed for one to accept Liu as a helpless little waif.

Since the character of Liu was invented by Puccini (she doesn't exist in the Gozzi play on which the opera was based), there has been some speculation about how she was conceived. Many writers on opera have expressed a fondness for the theory that she was based on Doria Manfredi, the young servant girl whom Puccini's wife Elvira drove to suicide via her evidently unfounded accusations that Doria had been having an affair with the composer. This theory seems unworthy of credit, for not only is it redolent of the armchair psychoanalyst, it ignores the fact that Liu is the most powerful of all of Puccini's heroines.

Let's look at Liu and Timur for a moment. We have here a young, unmarried girl — little more than a child, really — and her self-appointed task in life is to lead about and take care of a helpless, blind, elderly man — a dispossessed king who, having once been at the height of power, has fallen to about as low a state as he could possibly reach. And the girl willingly dies for a noble cause relating to the king's son. Doesn't this scenario sound familiar? Liu and Timur are Antigone and Oedipus.

I don't mean that literally, of course; nor even that Puccini and his collaborators ever consciously thought about Antigone and Oedipus. What I mean is that there is so much overlap in literature — it's all but impossible to find something that hasn't been done before — and we so much want to have all our questions answered about how a plot or a character developed, that it's very easy for us to convince ourselves that because an attractive explanation of a writer's inspiration is *plausible*, it must be true. We've seen so many totally inaccurate claims about "borrowings" in Puccini's librettos, particularly in respect to alleged borrowings from Wagner for *La Fanciulla del West*, that we should be extremely cautious about concluding that we "know" the source of any character or plot element or device.

That said, I feel safe in saying that without a doubt Puccini lifted large sections from the libretto of *Parsifal* and incorporated them into *La Rondine*, *Suor Angelica*, and *Turandot*. The scenes in the three Puccini operas that correspond with scenes in Parsifal are too many and too closely matched for it to have been a coincidence. We know for a fact that Puccini was seeking a conclusion for *Turandot* in the libretto of *Parsifal* because he himself *said* he was, in the letter to Renato Simoni I quoted in Chapter Two.

While *Suor Angelica* contains a scene inspired by *Parsifal*'s first scene in the Grail Hall, *Turandot* uses material from the same three scenes from which Puccini borrowed for *La Rondine*: those of *Parsifal*'s encounter with the Flower Maidens, the Initiating Kiss of Kundry, and the Redemption of the Sinner. In her role as redeemer, Liu is *Turandot*'s version of Parsifal. (*Parsifal* is also a version of the Regeneration Myth: kingdom in chaos, weakened ruler, young champion, how succeed? fearful trial, prevail at last, ascend throne rightfully his, acclamations grateful people!)

Having discussed these scenes in *Turandot* in Chapter Three I won't go over them at length in this introduction, but I do want to offer further evidence about Liu's role as the redeemer, beginning with a line in the libretto that comes immediately after the exit of Timur with the body of Liu. That is the point at which Puccini's music stops, for it was at that time that he went to Brussels for treatment of throat cancer, which treatment was followed by a fatal heart attack. Without having had the opportunity to examine the notes Puccini left behind, I don't know for an absolute fact that he knew of this particular line and approved it before he died, but I'm willing to wager that he did.

Attempting to melt Turandot's heart just after Liu's suicide, Calaf says to her, "Look ... look, cruel one, at that purest blood that was shed for you!" This is an allusion to the Crucifixion. And Calaf is telling Turandot that Liu died for *her*, not for *him*. The words of Liu's martyrdom aria, which had been addressed to Turandot, include the following: "Such secret love, and unconfessed, so great that these tortures are sweetnesses for me, because I present them to my Lord ... I give him your love ... I give him you, Princess, and I lose all!... Give me torments and pains! Ah! as the supreme offering of my love!"

The word "Signore"—Lord—is capitalized, and as such it means "God." The word does not refer to Calaf. The characterization of Liu as a weepy little waif who suffers and dies for the unrequited love of Calaf is absolutely wrong. She is Puccini's version of the mighty Parsifal, whom Wagner deliberately and notoriously confused with the figure of Jesus.

As for the score, there are several recurring themes in the opera, and the most important of these is the Spring Song, "Là sui monti dell'Est" (There on the mountains of the East). This number is first heard during the execution procession for the Prince of Persia, sung by a chorus of boys. Since the melody returns in the processional music that opens and closes the Contest of the Riddles, and also precedes the torture scene (not to mention numerous other recurrences), some have concluded it is imperial music representing the power of Turandot. That is incorrect.

The words sung by the boys during the first playing of the Spring Song express the hope that Turandot will heed the voices that call her, and that as a result, April will flower — love will bloom. This is the crux of the opera: the question as to whether regeneration will take place; whether there will be a birth of love in spring. Appropriately, the Spring Song is first sung by boys, who have themselves not yet blossomed. When the Song returns after the melting of Turandot's heart, the voices of the boys are joined by tenors.

No character in the opera has a personal musical motif except Turandot herself, who has two. By now, a widespread labeling of people and objects is much too old fashioned for Puccini. There is also no use of his "family of motifs" technique. But while no piece of music seems to be thematically related to any other, Puccini does make some subtle and interesting musical connections via rhythm, especially in Liu's final aria, "Tu che di gel sei cinta" (You who are girded with frost). This slow and mournful aria references, through rhythm alone, a fast and savage piece of music from the first act.

The most important rhythm of the opera is our old friend the triplet, which Puccini has always had a special fondness for and a special touch with. The triplet was an obvious choice for emphasis in *Turandot*, not only because the title character's name has three syllables, but also because this opera has a fairy tale plot, in which three is a magic number.

There are astounding quantities of "threes" in *Turandot*. There are three riddles, three attempts by the Emperor to dissuade Calaf, three ministers (who have three lanterns and three servants), and three bribes offered to the Prince. There are numerous occasions on which a song is finished with a word uttered three times ("Gloria," for example, or "Vincerò!"), and scenes begin and end with three repetitions of a chord. Time and time again there is a hypnotic chant of Tu-ran-dot! or Pu-Tin-Pao! (the Executioner).

There is no telling exactly how Puccini would have musically concluded the opera had he lived, but it's obvious he wanted a "Liebestod"-type ending, on a far greater scale than anything he had ever done before. Among the pile of notes he left behind at his death was the famous scribble, "Then, 'Tristan.'"

The ending Franco Alfano gave it — a full-throated reiteration of the "Nessun dorma" music, sung to by the chorus alone — would, I think, have displeased Puccini very much. He never once ended an opera with an extended replay of an earlier melody, for this is boring to the ear, and prompts audiences and critics to go off grumbling that the composer must have been too lazy to write one more piece of music. My guess is Puccini would have written a shimmering finale that featured spectacular parts for Calaf and Turandot, backed by prayerful lines for the chorus, and that it would have been a new piece of music that included quotations from both the Spring Song and "Nessun Dorma" (which is actually an anti–Dawn Song).

Turandot is the last chapter of the Rose Cycle, and in it a decisive conclusion to this long story is reached. There are frequent references to Calaf's intention to leave behind the Romantic World of Night, and one of the most pointed ones comes when he sings "Nessun dorma." As he approaches the song's final climax Calaf cries, "Disappear, O night! Set, stars! Set, stars! At dawn I'll win!"

One can almost hear the collective gasp of horror from the many previous pairs of young lovers, who lived so happily beneath Puccini's starry night sky, and died at the rising of the sun. Calaf knows exactly what he is saying when, after being savagely threatened to abandon his quest — or else! — he declares firmly, "Should the world collapse, I want Turandot!" And no mistake about it — the World is indeed about to collapse.

The opera begins with a harsh, five-note theme that will be heard on several occasions during the work. The first three, descending, notes of the theme — two quarter notes followed by a half note — are the most prominent, and they speak the name of Turandot. The Princess has two motifs, and this one — that of the three descending notes— we might refer to as "Savage Turandot." Following the harsh theme, an upwards rush is heard in the woodwinds, then woodwinds and horns begin a series of sharp and vicious pulses, descriptive of the blows of the Executioner's sword. (The upwards rush in the woodwinds will be brought back, transposed down, to open Act Three, subtly reminding us of the horror we are now about to witness.)

The curtain rises on the seventh bar, and as it does we see the walls of the great Violet City of legendary times. The massive ramparts enclose almost the entire stage in a semicircle. Only on the right is their movement broken — by a great loggia, entirely sculptured and carved with monsters, unicorns, and phoenixes. The pilasters stand on the backs of giant tortoises. At the foot of the loggia, supported by two arches, is a gong made of highly sonorous bronze, and which is capable, at the appropriate moments, of glowing with a mysterious light.

There are poles set on the ramparts, and they bear the skulls of the executed suitors. (Obviously, these are in various stages of decay.) Three gigantic gates are in the walls at left and back. Peking, which slopes away in the distance, shines like gold. (This "gold" color is equated with the sun, for when the moon rises the stage directions will tell us that the color of the distant city has changed to silver.)

The square is filled with a picturesque crowd of motionless Chinese, waiting to hear the words of a Mandarin. From the summit of the rampart, where the red and black Tartar guards flank him, the Mandarin reads a "tragic decree." Need we ask what time it is? The stage directions declare that, "When the curtain rises, we are in sunset's most golden hour."

The xylophone plays a skeletal melody, and on the twelfth bar, the Mandarin begins the ritual speech that precedes both the Contest of the Riddles, and the subsequent execution of the failed contestant. (This is another of Puccini's bracketings, and a very effective one. Preceding the Act Two Contest, along with the ritual speech we will hear the skeletal xylophone melody and the musical sword-slashing.)

The vicious blows of the sword continue in the orchestra as the Mandarin chants exposition to the people of Peking: Turandot the Pure (i.e. the Virgin) will be the bride of any man of royal blood who can answer her three riddles, but he who attempts the trial and fails must submit his proud head to the sword. The crowd exclaims, and the musical sword-blows move into the bass clarinet, bassoon, and lower strings, where they become a death march. The Mandarin continues: Fortune was against the Prince of Persia, and at the rising of the moon, "at the hand of the executioner let him die!" The rhyme on these last lines is lovely. *Fortuna* is rhymed with *luna* (both of which are changeable and wanton), and *boia* (executioner) is rhymed with *muoia* (let him die). The words "die" and "love" are the ones that most excite Puccini dramatically, and some form of "die" is heard an incredible number of times during the opera.

The Mandarin steps back, and the crowd seethes with excitement. It demands the Prince's immediate death, and calls for the Executioner, Pu-Tin-Pao, to come forth. The eager mob threatens to rush the palace, and at this the guards step forth and thrust them back, calling them "dogs." Many people fall, and we hear shouts and protests from people frightened for a mother or a child. These cries for mercy are sung to a lamenting theme — the Plea for Pity Theme — that will continue until the crowd again begins to shout for the death of the Prince of Persia. (This theme will recur near the end of Act Two.)

Now the high and piercing voice of Liu is heard, crying, "My old one has fallen!" Everyone is busy with his own troubles, so the crowd ignores the girl pleading for help in lifting up her old one. A moment later, however, a young man runs up, and bends over to help the fallen one. The Plea for Pity Theme continues, but softened and sweetened, and it now takes on a second function as a Recognition Theme when the young man utters a shout: "Father! My father!" As the guards continue to brutalize the milling people, this Unknown Prince pleads with his dazed father to look at him, to see that this is no dream.

Liu recognizes Prince Calaf, then the old man, Timur, opens his eyes. According to the stage directions, he can scarcely believe what he sees: "Oh, my son! You! Alive?" (There is obviously a problem here, since Timur is meant to be blind. The confusion over Timur's blindness will persist in the stage directions until his final scene.) In terror, Calaf tells his father to be silent. He whispers that the one who usurped Timur's crown is seeking them both, and there is no refuge for either of them in the world. What this means, of course, is that despite being a royal prince, the young and handsome Calaf is penniless, and homeless. In other words, he has all the qualities needed for a romantic hero in Puccini's World!

It also establishes for all three of these people an atmosphere of immediate and terrible danger. They are not carefree tourists in the Violet City, they are fugitives, one of them old and blind, and another an apparently helpless young female.

Timur and Calaf exchange tearful greetings, but by this time the crowd has recovered its ferocity and gathered near the ramparts. They see the Executioner's servants at the top of the walls—grotesque figures horridly dressed in bloodstained rags and dragging an enormous sword. As the excited crowd repeatedly shouts, "Let him die!" the Executioner's men prepare to sharpen the sword on a huge whetstone.

Still on the ground, Timur tells his son how, after the last battle was lost, he—an old king without kingdom and in flight—escaped capture. "I heard a voice that said, 'Come with me, I'll be your guide....' It was Liu!" An unnerving drumbeat throbs beneath Timur's voice as the Executioner's men position the sword. Calaf interjects a blessing on the girl, and Timur goes on to describe how, later on, when he would fall, exhausted, "...she would dry my tears, she begged for me...." Deeply moved, Calaf asks Liu who she is, and as he speaks her name, we hear a lovely, blooming figure from two harps. Humbly, Liu answers, "I am nothing ... a slave, my lord."

As the crowd excitedly urges the Executioner's men to turn the whetstone, Calaf asks Liu why she has shared his father's anguish. With ecstatic sweetness, culminating with a high B flat, she answers, "Because one day, in the palace, you smiled at me." As the soprano spins that high B flat on the word "smile," muted trumpets, celesta, and divided violins play a simple yet magical figure—four soft chords that descend in tiny steps before they are lost in a low but terrifying ostinato played by the timpani.

As the ostinato swells, attention shifts to the ramparts, where the Executioner's servants have cleaned the sword's blade, and are about to sharpen it. They make it move and shriek on the whetstone, which dizzily turns. Sparks fly, and the work becomes fiercely animated. To a pounding dance, the servants sing a raucous song, which the crowd echoes. The people shout *Gira! Gira!* which might remind us of the feverish "Gira!" waltz of *Le Villi*, and of the excited cries of the bloodthirsty Villi as they pursued the hapless Roberto.

The men oil and sharpen the blade, and call on it to spurt fire and blood. Using a line that will be sung by the Princess herself, they cry that the riddles are three, and death is one. The crowd urges sweet lovers to come forth, and he who strikes the gong will see the beautiful Turandot appear, white as jade, as cold as that sword. To a recurring theme—the Execution Theme—they howl, "Work never languishes where reigns Turandot!"

At the end of the final repetition of the Execution Theme we hear a *tutta forza* reprise of the opera's opening; that is, of the Savage Turandot Theme. This reprise neatly brackets the opening section of the opera. The first act is arranged in a series of contrasting blocks of music, and following the block of savage music that has just ended will be a block of calm and dreamy music, as the people sing their invocation to the moon.

The sword is sharp now, and as the Executioner's men go off to take it to him, the people forms picturesque groups here and there. With "fierce impatience" they examine the sky, "which little by little has grown dark." Turandot and the moon are one, thus it is only when the moon has risen that the luckless Prince of Persia can be executed. Eager to witness the death, the people urge the moon to show herself in the sky.

Puccini employs the chorus beautifully during the invocation to the moon, with the voices of the men trading off lines with those of the women. They call the moon "wan face," "severed head," "bloodless one," "pale lover of the dead." At first this invocation music is all soft chords and long sighs, but as moonlight begins to appear and spread, we hear narcotic twitterings from the clarinet, flute, and celesta, descriptive of shimmering light. The volume rises and falls, rises and falls, delaying and thus enhancing our satisfaction.

By now, what had been a golden background, equated with the setting sun, has begun to turn an intense silver, equated with the rising moon. The crowd grows excited, and as the music swells to *fortissimo* they chant the name of the Executioner, Pu-Tin-Pao, rhythmically linking it to the name of Turandot (via two short notes followed by a long-held note). There is a quick decrescendo to *piano*, and now the offstage boys' chorus takes over. Although the choral number continues, the boys' thin, childish voices contribute a block of music with a tone entirely different from the savage opening and the dreamy invocation, as they sing a melody based on a Chinese folk tune called *Moon-Le-Wha.*

Their voices sweet and innocent, the boys tell of how the stork sang on the mountains of the East, "but April did not rebloom...." If the Princess will heed the thousand voices that call her, they say, "Everything will bloom, everything will shine!" As the boys sing, piccolo, flute, and oboe introduce another three-note Turandot motif, which is also played as two short notes followed by one long note. As played by the oboe, it is B flat, C, B flat. Unlike the first, hammering motif, this one is rather pretty—friendly, even.

As was mentioned in the introduction to this chapter, the boys' song is a Spring Song, and its melody is by far the most important and frequently recurring piece of music in the opera. The Spring Song expresses the hope that Turandot will heed the voices that call her, and that as a result, April will flower—love will bloom. Let's call the second three-note Turandot motif, first heard here in the Spring Song, "Turandot in Love."

The men who sharpened the sword are next in the procession, and following them are priests, carrying funeral offerings. Next come the mandarins and the high dignitaries. "And finally, very handsome, almost childish, appears the young Prince of Persia." His look is dazed, dreaming, and his white neck is bared. The crowd is seized with pity at the sight of him. While the Prince is on the stage, the gigantic Executioner appears, carrying his enormous sword on his shoulder.

A limping, drooping, funeral theme, led by muted trumpets, carries the fickle crowd's plea for mercy for the Prince of Persia. Again the men and women sing in contrasting groups. After the people have sung a few lines remarking on the sweetness of the boy's face, and the intoxication in his eyes, Calaf's voice is suddenly heard. With his voice following the melody of the funeral theme, he too cries for mercy for the condemned boy, but a moment later, overcome with horror, he demands that Turandot show herself so he may see the cruel one and curse her. By now, the most prominent part of the theme has emerged: three falling notes that remind us of the first, Savage Turandot motif.

As the music of the boys' Spring Song blaringly returns, the people turn toward the imperial balcony where the Princess will appear and pronounce final sentence on the Prince of Persia. Perhaps, the Spring Song music suggests, Turandot might prove to be Turandot in Love, and thus will pardon the Prince of Persia. The stage directions tell us "She comes forth, like a vision. A ray of moonlight illuminates her." Everyone prostrates themselves before this cruel moon goddess—everyone except the Executioner, the Prince of Persia, and Calaf, who is utterly stunned by the beauty of Turandot. These three alone remain standing.

Turandot makes an imperious, definitive gesture, and the Executioner assents with a nod. The hopeful Spring Song gives way to a resumption of the limping funeral theme, now played by piccolo, oboe, and English horn. As the cortege, followed by the crowd, moves off to the place of execution, the bass drum plays a death march for two measures—just long enough to escort the Prince of Persia off the stage.

His voice again following the melody of the funeral dirge, the dazzled Calaf praises the divine beauty, the miracle that is Turandot. (A harp glissando on the word "beauty" makes for a lovely emphasis.) Significantly, Calaf calls Turandot a *sogno*—a dream — and as he does, we hear a soft, drawn-out version of the Savage Turandot motif. Calaf's cry is answered by the deep voices of the White Priests of the procession: "O great Kouang-tze! May the spirit of the dying one come to you!" On the last words, oboe, clarinet, and cellos play a five-note, ascending figure that mimics the music the priests have been singing, and probably describes the spirit of the dying one rising to meet Kouang-tze. The voices of the priests die away, then there is a pause, during which strings play three soft chords. The ecstatic trance of Calaf justifies the pause, which marks a definite division between the first and second parts of the act.

Turandot has gone. The square is in semi-darkness now, and only Calaf, Timur, and Liu remain. Calaf stands motionless, ecstatic, "as if the unexpected vision of beauty had fatally riveted him to his destiny." The blind Timur approaches his son, and anxiously asks what he is doing. Calaf expresses surprise that his father cannot feel what he feels— the perfume of Turandot, which is in the air, and in his soul. Horrified at this demented answer, Timur exclaims that his son is lost.

Singing to a slight variation of the boys' Spring Song, Calaf marvels at the divine beauty, and cries that he is suffering. Liu's importance and power is now hinted at, as Timur urges the girl to speak to Calaf. Neither Timur nor Liu uses the music of the Spring Song, and significantly, Liu tries to tempt Calaf away from this place by uttering what had always been a magical phrase in Puccini's World: "Andiam lontano!"—Let's go far away!

Calaf was born to destroy Puccini's World, however, so the idea of *lontano* has no power over him. When his father eagerly agrees with Liu, saying they should go to *lontano*, because life is there, Calaf rejects that. He cries that life is here, and freeing himself from his father's grasp he rushes toward the brass gong that a man of royal blood strikes when offering himself as a suitor to Turandot.

As Calaf runs toward the gong, which is now glowing with a mysterious light, he shouts Turandot's name three times, culminating on a trumpeting high B flat. A moment later, however, his cry is echoed from off stage as the Prince of Persia — singing a half step lower — calls the name of Turandot, before his voice is stilled forever by the Executioner's sword.

From off stage, the crowd gives a quick and violent shout in what seems like exultation. The distraught Timur asks his son if he wants to die like that, and Calaf corrects him, saying he wants to conquer gloriously in the Princess' beauty. Calaf has been seized by Love as Madness, and as a very traditional *romance* hero, he speaks of love in terms of combat, and glories in his intense suffering. Nothing could be more painful than the suffering of Calaf, and the last thing in the world he wants is for it to stop.

In his rush towards the glowing gong, Calaf is suddenly intercepted by three weird figures— grotesque "masks" from the world of the commedia dell'arte. Ping, Pang, and Pong are, respectively, the Emperor's Grand Chancellor, Grand Purveyor, and Grand Cook. As they step between Calaf and the gong, the gong's strange light fades. The startled Calaf steps back, and Liu and Timur huddle together in the shadows, frightened.

In a vigorous and rather cheery block of music, employing a theme that references the

Chinese Imperial Hymn, the three ministers swarm about the Prince and bluntly warn him to leave this horrible place at once. It is a great butcher's shop, they assure him, where they garrote, impale, and behead you. And Turandot herself? She's just raw flesh, they declare — a female with a crown on her head. As is common in Puccini's *romance*-infused librettos, the lovesick young man is repeatedly declared "insane." Calaf's only response to the ministers is a violent demand that they get out of his way.

Calaf and the ministers have been making a lot of racket, and now Turandot's hand-maidens—a chorus of nine sopranos, appropriately dressed all in white, like a cluster of stars attendant on the moon that is Turandot—come out onto the imperial balcony. Another soft and dreamy block of music begins as the maidens reach out their hands in a gesture that calls for an end to the noise. The oboe plays a somewhat narcotic and creepy melody while three of the maidens softly demand silence. This is the sweet hour of repose, and now that the Prince of Persia has been put to sleep, Turandot would like to sleep as well. Adding to the sense of unease as the maidens sing is a soft, throbbing *ostinato*, played by timpani, drum, harp, and full strings.

The ministers sneer at the maidens, telling the "chattering females" to go away, but a moment later they realize their attention has strayed from the crazy young man. "Watch out for the gong!" they cry, but in fact Calaf is standing still, apparently lost in thought. The handmaidens have vanished, and Calaf absently repeats their final line: "The air is scented with her perfume!"

Sounding half amused, the three masks make another attempt to dissuade Calaf. Adopting grotesque poses, they gather around the Prince. A new and very tight, staccato melody begins as they warn him nothing is more obscure, nothing is more difficult, than the riddles of Turandot. Triangle, celesta, glockenspiel, and xylophone add to the marvelously weird sound, as does the peculiar, twittering figure played in the last four bars by piccolo and oboe, which seems to refer to the ghosts of the executed suitors.

The Prince, we are told, can barely react, for he has almost no strength remaining. But then the "shadows of voices" begin to spread out from the ramparts. Harp and divided strings play a ponderous, dragging accompaniment in 3/4, as little by little, the ghosts of the executed suitors appear, pale and phosphorescent. The ghosts' voices are produced by four contraltos and four tenors, off stage, and their message is that of the waking dream of undying love. The piccolo continues to twitter as the ghosts urge Calaf to summon the woman "...who makes us, dead men, dream!" They long to hear her voice again. After wailing, three times, "I love her!" the ghosts vanish.

The ghosts' declaration rouses Calaf, who is outraged to hear others claim to love the Princess. Angrily, he declares he alone loves her. Prancing about him, the ministers mock at this, insisting Turandot does not even exist. Nothing exists, they tell the "demented boy," but the Tao. Shouting that he wants the triumph, and love, Calaf again makes a lunge for the gong, but at that very moment the Executioner appears on the bastion, displaying the severed head of the Prince of Persia. "Fool!" mutter the ministers, "There's love!" As the twittering figure that represents the ghosts is heard in the piccolo, they chant, "Thus the moon will kiss your face!" (It's not difficult to find an echo of Strauss's *Salome* in this.)

A little upwards rush is heard in the violin, changing the focus to Timur, who now clutches at his son and begs him to think of his poor old father, dragging about the world alone in his tortured old age. He asks rhetorically if there is no human voice that can move his son's fierce heart, and significantly, Liu then begins to speak.

Her opening words, "Signore, ascolta" (Lord, listen), touch off the act's long, concluding passage that culminates in the great sextet — perhaps the most beautiful and hypnotic piece of music Puccini ever wrote. Liu's song is the first aria of the opera, a sweet and lamenting song in which she, weeping and imploring, approaches the Prince and begs him to have pity on her and Timur. If Calaf dies, she cries, Timur will lose a son, and she will lose "...the shadow of a smile." The word she uses is *ombra*, which should probably be translated as "ghost," rather than "shadow." The ghosts' voices are *ombre di voce*, the ghosts themselves are called *ombras*, and now Liu speaks of *l'ombra d'un sorriso*. She seems already to be mourning the smile's death.

Liu's aria is based on another authentic Chinese song, this one called *Sian Chok*. Oboe and strings take turns in softly supporting her as she pleads with Calaf to have pity, and as a harp makes delicate upwards ripples, she concludes with another gorgeous, luminous high B flat, before she crumples to the ground, sobbing.

The numerous pleas for pity are worth remarking on. First the crowd begged the Tartar guards to have pity and stop beating them, and the guards ignored the plea. Then the crowd and Calaf begged Turandot to have pity on the Prince of Persia, and she refused. Now Timur and Liu (and in a rough way, the ministers) have begged Calaf to have pity and give up the quest for Turandot, and he too will refuse. This Violet City is a town without pity, and Calaf clearly belongs here.

Although Calaf will not accede to Liu's plea, it does touch him. She is the only one who can reach him at all. So powerful is this supposedly insignificant little slave girl that she succeeds in pulling Calaf out of his ecstatic trance long enough for him to sing a gorgeous answering aria: "Non piangere, Liù." He focuses entirely on Liu as he tenderly asks her not to cry, but to stay with Timur, if only for the sake of that long ago smile. This request can hardly be counted on to cheer up Timur and Liu, who interject doleful predictions as to how they will surely die on the road of exile. Calaf ignores these, and concludes his aria by again asking Liu to take care of his father, for the sake of him "who smiles no more."

Timur's deep cry, "Ah, for the last time!" marks the beginning of the finale. As Liu pleads with Calaf to overcome the horrible spell, the three ministers approach and take part in the sextet, which is eventually joined by the chorus. Puccini's ensembles are best when there is a mass of deep male voices, and one soprano, knifing through like a streak of brilliant white light in the blackness. This is one of his hypnotic numbers, in which the music seems to drag the listener back and forth as though he were being rocked by the waves of the sea. The voices weave in and out like the threads in a tapestry, and it's quite difficult to follow any one thread without resorting to the score. Individual lines emerge, shimmer and gleam, then are submerged again in the web. The shimmering lines include the ministers', "La vida è così bella!" (Life is so beautiful!), and Calaf's plea for pardon for the one who smiles no more. This line, in which Calaf repeats both the words and the music of the final line of "Non piangere, Liù," marks the first climax of the ensemble.

Repeatedly calling the Prince a madman, the ministers try to help Timur drag Calaf away. "Let's take him away!" they cry, in another compelling line uttered three times. Calaf again wails his intense suffering, and as he cries that glory awaits him "over there," the gong again begins to glow with that mysterious light. Using more and more of the language of a *romance* hero, Calaf cries that he is in a fever, in a delirium, with every sense a fierce torment. "I follow my luck!" he sings.

The ministers warn that the shadow of the Executioner is over there, and with that the chorus begins to sing, off stage, warning that they are already digging the grave of the one who wants to challenge love. There is a final, wild plea from Timur, Liu, and the ministers, to which Calaf answers, "Every fiber of my soul has a voice that cries: Turandot!" Three times he shouts that name, climbing higher each time, and three times the other five respond: "Death!" The Prince rushes for the gong, seizes the mallet, and like a madman he strikes three blows. We now hear a full orchestra reiteration of the music of the Spring Song, *fff*, as the three ministers, holding up their hands, flee in horror, and the chorus again declares they are already digging the grave.

There is a reprise of the last line of the finale music, and then, as Calaf stands in an ecstasy at the base of the gong, and Timur and Liu huddle together in despair, the full orchestra brings down the curtain with five repetitions of a two-note flourish that was heavily featured during the ensemble, and which now essentially shouts, "The End!"

The second act curtain rises to reveal a great, tent-like pavilion, "strangely decorated with symbolic and fantastic Chinese figures." As there were three gates in the great wall of the first act's set, there are three openings in this pavilion: one in front, and one at either side. As woodwinds, horns, muted trumpets, and glockenspiel repeatedly play a sequence of three descending, syncopated notes, Ping looks out from the center opening. Looking first right, then left, he calls his companions. They enter, followed by three servants, who carry three lanterns, which they place symmetrically on a low table surrounded by three stools. One lantern is red, another green, the third yellow. The servants efface themselves in the background.

An extended, scherzo-like trio now begins as Ping tells the other two to prepare for either outcome of the stranger's striking of the gong. Pong happily promises to prepare for the wedding, and Pang gloomily volunteers to handle the funeral. The three then lament what poor China has come to since the birth of Turandot. Unrolling scrolls on which the suitors' deaths have been recorded, they count six in the year of the rat, and eight in the year of the dog. When this latest fellow has been dispatched, the tally for this terrible year of the tiger will reach 13.

The three are disgusted by their work, and as they sing of having been reduced to ministers of the Executioner, we hear the Execution Theme, to which the crowd, while watching the sharpening of the sword, had howled, "Work never languishes, where reigns Turandot!" There is a pause, then the ministers drop the scrolls, sink down, and indulge in the only form of escape possible to them: dreaming of *là lontano*, the far away place where there are no troubles.

Là lontano proved to be a fantasy in *La Rondine*, and in *Suor Angelica* Puccini located it, as a last resort, in heaven. It's not possible to live without hope, however, so here in *Turandot* the longing for *là lontano* on Earth is expressed again. But this is a realistic longing, for each minister wants to go to an actual place he knows and loves.

As softly as possible, flutes, clarinets, celeste, and harps play a dreamy and gently rocking accompaniment to each man's nostalgic recollection of his personal *là lontano*. Ping remembers his house in Honan, with its little blue lake surrounded by bamboo. Pong remembers his forests, than which there are none more beautiful, near Tsiang. And Pang remembers his garden, near Kiu. These men are obviously Puccini Artist–type characters, for they long not for palaces, but for unspoiled Nature: a lake, forests, a garden. In another time and place, they might have been Bohemians.

The ministers rise, and with broad gestures they exclaim at this world full of mad lovers. They recall several of the past suitors— the Prince of Samarkand, the Indian Sagarika, the Burmese, the Prince of the Kirghiz, and the Tartar — and as they do, the chorus, standing behind a special curtain, brings back the cruel words and savagely pounding music of the Execution Theme. Caught up in their own descriptions of how the suitors were killed, executed, decapitated, and slaughtered, the ministers take on the same brutal accents as the chorus.

A measure of calm returns as the ministers, sadly foreseeing the end of China, sing a lovely farewell to the *stirpe divina* — the divine race. Pang and Pong then sit down. Ping remains standing, and raising his arms he invokes the Tigress, the "great she-marshal of heaven," praying that the night of surrender might come. Having for years been required to see to the details of the suitors' funerals, the ministers dream of seeing to the details of Turandot's wedding night. One by one they speak of preparing the nuptial bed, plumping the pillows, perfuming the bedchamber, and carrying the light for the bridal pair. And then all three would stand in the royal garden and joyously sing of love until morning.

The garden is the place of flowers— it is where Calaf will go in Act Three, as he waits for dawn to come and bring him his bride — so it is the only appropriate place for the ministers to sing their love songs. As he did in *La Rondine* and in *Suor Angelica*, Puccini will be incorporating scenes from *Parsifal* into this libretto, and the first hint of that is this mention of the garden, where the love songs will be sung.

This garden will turn out to be Klingsor's garden of the Flower Maidens, where Calaf will be subjected to a series of three temptations, and the ministers now make reference to what should be recognized as the Initiating Kiss of Kundry, that kindled the tormenting flame of love in the previously ignorant Parsifal. The ministers sing, "Everything whispers in the garden, and golden campanulas tinkle. They whisper amorous words to one another.... Glory, glory to the beautiful, unclad body that now knows the mystery it was ignorant of." (The ignorant one here is of course Turandot, who will be introduced to the mystery of love via the Initiating Kiss of Calaf.)

The ministers have worked themselves into a state in which they almost believe the wonder has been accomplished, but now offstage noises, and the music of trumpets, trombones, and drum, awaken them to reality. This music is based on the opening notes of the Spring Song, and Ping says, "We are dreaming!" The great drum of the Green Temple is calling, the ceremony is beginning, and the three men, crestfallen, go off to enjoy what they call "the umpteenth torture."

Scene two takes place immediately, the second curtain rising to reveal the vast square of the royal palace. Near the center is a tremendous marble staircase, "which is lost at its summit among triple arches." The focus on the number three continues in the triple arches, the three broad landings of the staircase, the incense-spewing tripods at the top of the stairs, and the three silk scrolls carried by each of eight sages who appear at the top of the steps. These scrolls contain the answers to the three riddles.

To some processional music that heavily features various patterns of triplets, the crowd enters the square little by little, and blue-and-gold clad mandarins appear. The crowd, suitably awed, comments on the grave and mysterious appearance of the scroll-carrying sages, who are huge, and whose gestures are slow and simultaneous. The people observe the entry of Ping, Pang, and Pong, who are wearing their yellow ceremonial dress, and a jaunty version of the Spring Song is brought in. Up-and-down scale patterns played by piccolo, flute, clarinet, and harp, and especially the glissandos of the xylophone, lend a festive, holiday air to the proceedings.

The yellow and white standards of the Emperor become visible through the clouds of incense, and the Spring Song turns brassy and imperial. The incense slowly clears away, revealing the Emperor Altoum, seated on his ivory throne. "He is very old, entirely white, venerable, hieratic. He looks like a god who appears from among the clouds." The crowd chants a ritual blessing on Altoum: "Ten thousand years to our Emperor!" To the Turandot in Love motif they cry glory to the Emperor, then kneel and touch their heads to the ground.

The square is now enveloped in a rosy light. (The stage directions don't say so specifically, but it's pretty clear the time is the *prima sera* — the first hour of sunset.) The Unknown Prince stands at the foot of the marble staircase. Timur and Liu are at left, lost in the crowd. Offstage trumpets and trombones play a long fanfare that concludes with a flourish from woodwinds, brass, timpani, and percussion, including the gong.

His speech punctuated at intervals by gong-like tremolo chords, Altoum, in a thin and reedy voice, declares that a terrible vow forces him to keep to a grim pact. His holy scepter streams with blood. There has been enough blood. "Young man, go!" As usual in tellings of the Regeneration Myth, the hero is urged not to attempt the trial of his brains, strength, and courage, for how can he succeed, where so many others have failed? The other five members of the sextet having failed at dissuading Calaf, the Emperor himself will try his powers of persuasion.

Firmly, without any orchestral accompaniment, Calaf responds: "Son of heaven, I ask to face the trial!" Following his response, flutes, clarinets, glockenspiel, and celeste make a somewhat inquiring comment, that leads us to look toward the Emperor, to learn what he will say. Three times in all, using a different argument each time, Altoum begs the suitor to abandon the trial, and three times the young man gives his unchanging answer. Only his increasing emphasis — his first response is given "firmly," the second "more strongly," the third "with mounting strength" — shows his impatience to get on with the trial. The Emperor is filled with ire, but he accepts the inevitable. "Stranger, drunk with death! So be it!" The Chinese gong sounds, and the Emperor chants mournfully, "Let your destiny be accomplished!"

Harp and full strings play a lovely, *largo* version of the Spring Song, to which the crowd softly prays for ten thousand years to their Emperor, while white-clad women — the handmaidens — enter in procession from the palace and range themselves along the stairs. The Spring Song makes a quick transition as the mandarin steps forward, the tragic decree in hand, and the musical blows of the Executioner's sword suddenly begin their vicious slashing in the orchestra. The xylophone repeats its skeletal theme, then the mandarin rapidly recites the decree, all of which instills in the audience a fear that history is about to repeat itself.

From off stage, the boys' chorus now sings an abbreviated reprise of its Spring Song. "From the desert to the sea, don't you hear a thousand voices sigh: Princess, come down to me! Everything will shine, shine, shine!" The word *splenderà* — "will shine" — is sung to the gentle, Turandot in Love motif. ("Down" refers to her descending the staircase to her successful suitor.)

Turandot now appears at the top of the stairs, and moves to the front of her father's throne. Impossibly beautiful, utterly impassive, she looks with cold eyes at the Prince. There could be no more haughty and imperious lady in all of *romance,* and no more ardent and determined knight than Calaf, who at first is dazzled by the sight of Turandot, but gradually masters himself and looks at her with ardent determination. (He is surely the first of the suitors who was able to accomplish this feat of self-control.)

Turandot, the stage directions tell us, "is entirely a thing of gold." Puccini was extremely particular about such things, and I suspect he attired Turandot in gold, rather than the silver we might have expected, because gold is the color of wealth and power. Turandot is the Alberich-figure of this opera, and by dressing her in gleaming gold Puccini seems to be reiterating a critical law of his World: that one may have gold and/or power, or else love, but not both. Remember that Calaf, though a Prince, is a hunted, penniless fugitive. The other suitors entered the lists as royalty, but Calaf—the Unknown Prince—has not even offered his name. From where they are huddled in fear, Timur and Liu, according to the stage directions, "cannot take their eyes, their souls, from the Prince." (Again, being that Timur is supposed to be blind, the bass playing the role should probably not stick too closely to this direction.)

Everything that has so far been seen, done, and said in this scene has been part of the ritual, and the next phase of the ritual is Turandot's entrance aria, "In questa Reggia" (In this Palace), during which she relates the story of how she, who is the source of the evil in this particular telling of the Regeneration Myth, came to afflict the city. The story and the grievance are entirely hers, so there is no orchestral lead-in to the *arioso* with which she begins.

Turandot regards the Prince with her cold eyes, and solemnly, in an icy voice, she begins to chant her tale. A thousand, thousand years ago, in this very palace, a desperate scream rang out. Passing from descendant to descendant, that scream of the Princess Lo-u-Ling at last took refuge in the soul of Turandot. As she tenderly sings the beloved name of Lo-u-Ling, muted horns breathe a soft sigh, and muted violins and violas begin a slow and gently rocking figure that accompanies Turandot's loving description of her ancestress as a sweet and serene creature who reigned in dark silence, and in joy. She tells of how Lo-u-Ling defied domination. "Today you live again in me!" she sings, and the crowd softly murmurs that it was the King of the Tartars, unfurling his seven flags, who attacked the palace.

"Like something far away," Turandot, her pace quickening and her vocal line rising higher and higher, describes how the kingdom was defeated. Lo-u-Ling was dragged away, "by a man like you, like you, stranger, there in the atrocious night, where was extinguished her fresh voice." This is an accusation, and the ritual retelling of the outrage keeps it ever fresh. As Turandot has chosen to take vengeance for Lo-u-Ling, she likewise makes the murderer live again in each of the men who would dominate her. Again the crowd utters a reverential murmur.

Turandot addresses, in Calaf, all the princes who come here to try their fate. "I avenge on you that purity, that scream, and that death!" She sings that last line a second time, holding a piercing high B on the word "scream," so that it becomes the scream of Lo-u-Ling herself. This is the fourth time the Princess has uttered that word, and it is clear that the scream of Lo-u-Ling is an obsessive thought in the mind of Turandot.

The word "death" launches a new and very lyrical theme, played three times, rising by a major third with each repetition. This strong, proud theme is played first by violins, then by upper woodwinds, and last by the full orchestra. The first two times it plays, Turandot sings bits of the theme, as she vows no one will ever possess her, for the horror of he who killed Lo-u-Ling is alive in her heart. When it plays the third time, Turandot sings the full theme, swearing for the third time no one will ever possess her, and that in her is reborn the pride of Lo-u-Ling's purity. This is another important recurring melody. Let's call it the Determination Theme.

The Princess stares threateningly at Calaf, and using the monotone of ritual speech she warns the stranger not to tempt Fate. A new melody is heard as she cries, "The riddles are three, death is one!" Suddenly, like a hammer smashing through a sheet of ice, the powerful male voice of Calaf is heard, shouting, "No! No!" The tenor's voice is shocking after so many minutes of solo soprano, and it shatters to bits the cold waves of sound put forth by Turandot. Calaf wrenches her music up to a higher key, singing that the riddles are three, and LIFE is one!

Outraged at being so boldly challenged, Turandot wrenches the phrase still higher, but as she repeats the words as she first sang them, she finds to her shock that Calaf is singing *with* her, repeating his contradiction, both of them holding first a long high C, and then a long high A, and competing to see who can outlast the other. This theme too will recur, and since it is not yet certain whose version will prevail, let's call it the Death/Life Theme.

The crowd is thrilled at what Calaf has already accomplished, and to the Determination Theme they urge Turandot to offer the stranger the trial. The Determination Theme trails away inconclusively, then, after a few soft notes from the timpani, offstage brasses play a two-note flourish. There is a brief pause, and Turandot proclaims the first of the three riddles, all of which will be asked (and answered) to the Riddle Theme.

Turandot's first riddle takes us back to the very beginning of the Rose Cycle, to that which has animated every one of Puccini's ardent young soprano and tenor characters, who love life and one another passionately, and dread the loss of both. The first riddle addresses the waking dream of a life and a love that will never die — of a night that will never end.

> In the dark flies an iridescent phantom.
> It soars and spreads its wings over gloomy, infinite humanity.
> All the world invokes it, and all the world implores it.
> **But the phantom vanishes at dawn, to be reborn in every heart.**
> **And every night it is born, and every day it dies.**

This riddle cannot possibly defeat Calaf. Nothing could be more obvious than the answer to this riddle. With confidence he cries at once, "Yes! It is reborn! And in triumph it carries me away with itself, Turandot: La Speranza!" The thing that is born at sundown, and dies at dawn, is Hope.

Almost the first phrase uttered in the Rose Cycle, at the beginning of *Manon Lescaut*, was that sunset was "...the hour of waking dreams, when hope struggles with melancholy." The waking dream begins in the *prima sera*, when Puccini's young lovers are born. As the night advances, they try to persuade themselves— via a *hope* for love and life, that struggles with the *melancholy* fear of death, which they know will come at dawn — that through their ardent love, they can make the night last forever. How strange it seems, that Calaf wants to leave the Night, filled as it has always been with frenzied, illicit love. He and Turandot were both born at sundown, but her madness is such that there is no Night of Love — only nights filled with death.

The sages stand and examine the first scroll. Three times they chant the word "hope."

Calaf has answered the first riddle correctly. They sit, and a murmur runs through the crowd. Shaken for a moment by the stranger's success, Turandot laughs coldly, and again assumes her air of haughty superiority. "Yes!" she declares. "Hope, which always deceives!" She knows how things have worked all through the Rose Cycle; not once has the waking dream been fulfilled, not even for Minnie and Dick Johnson, whose last, mournful farewells in the chilly dawn of winter had the flavor of death. Turandot's unsuccessful suitors have always died at moonrise, for that is the moment when the Princess gains her killing power, but things will be different with Calaf. The moment in which his life will hang in the balance will be dawn.

Knowing how intoxicating she is, Turandot comes halfway down the marble staircase, to the middle landing. She hopes her nearness will dazzle and confuse the Prince as she proclaims the second riddle. She asks him what it is that is a flame, and yet not a flame. Sometimes it is a fever, but if you are lost or die it grows cold. If you dream of conquest it flames. This riddle also goes to the foundation of the Rose Cycle, in the final clue: "**It has a voice you listen to in fear, and the vivid gleam of the sunset.**" Calaf hesitates, uncertain, distracted by the gaze of Turandot. The Princess looks triumphant, but first the Emperor and then the crowd urge the stranger to speak. "It's for your life!"

Once again Liu's power is hinted at, for now she speaks, and as soon as she does Calaf hits on the answer. As much as he wanted to make Calaf the hero of this opera, it was totally against Puccini's nature to utilize a male in that role. It is at this point that Puccini begins to snatch the job of hero, and the task of winning Turandot, away from Calaf and to hand it over to the opera's heroine: Liu. "It is for love!" urges Liu, and when Calaf hears that, the uncertainty and confusion vanish from his face.

"Yes, Princess!" cries Calaf. "It flames, and it languishes, if you look at me, in my veins. Blood!" Blood's "vivid gleam of the sunset" refers to the Rose Cycle characters' birth at sunset, and its "voice you listen to in fear" refers to the fear of death — the fear that that voice will go silent. The sages open the second scroll, and three times they chant the word "blood." The crowd is overjoyed, and they hail the stranger as the solver of riddles. Furiously, Turandot orders her guards to beat the wretches.

As she gives this command, she runs down the steps, attaining the bottom landing of the staircase. If Puccini had not been so enamored of the domineering lady and the subservient male of *romance*, he might have had Calaf look Turandot straight in the eye for the third and final riddle, now that they are on the same level. True, a leap to the feet when the final riddle is solved is very exciting, but it must be admitted that the tenor character's favorite position has always been on his knees before the soprano, all the way back to Roberto in *Le Villi*, kneeling in terror before the murderous Anna. Whatever the basis of the impulse, the stage directions order Calaf to fall to his knees before Turandot.

The Princess leans over him like a bird of prey, her mouth right next to his face, and she hammers out the last riddle. What, she asks, is frost that sets him on fire, and that gains more frost from his fire? In a line that could have been taken straight from a 12th century *romance* she says, "**If it wants you free, it makes you more a slave! If it accepts you as a slave, it makes you a King!**" (In other words, no matter what the outcome, "you" will be a slave.)

By now Calaf has ceased breathing. He cannot answer, and Turandot continues to bend over him, demanding that he answer. For a moment Calaf feels himself defeated, and he bows his head in his hands. But an instant later he is filled with joy, and the stage directions declare, "he leaps to his feet, magnificent in pride and strength." This leap *should* mark the death of the subservient male of the Romantic World, and the birth of the new male, who will be equal partners with the female. We shall see.

Calaf trumpets his answer on two high B flats. "My fire thaws you: Turandot!" He sings her name, of course, to the Turandot in Love motif. The Princess staggers and steps back, and the sages unroll the third scroll. Three times they pronounce the answer to the third riddle: Turandot. The crowd is ecstatic, and as they echo the name of the Princess, the full orchestra rushes two octaves up the scale, in a flurry of joyful triplets. As the crowd exclaims, the Spring Song bursts into full bloom. The horrified Princess rushes up the marble stairs, and in a little girl's voice begs her August Father not to cast her into the arms of a foreigner. The Emperor declares the oath is sacred, and Turandot goes wild. She absolutely refuses to be given away like a slave, dying of shame. Like a child having a tantrum, she shouts, "I don't want to! I don't want to!" Barely noticeable under the exchange between Turandot and her father is the Plea for Pity Theme, played by oboe, flute, and strings.

The crowd and the Emperor insist that Turandot fulfill her promise, and Turandot continues to refuse. At last she addresses the Unknown Prince. Singing with the chorus, and to an ear-shattering rendition of the Spring Song, she asks if he wants her in his arms by force, reluctant, shuddering. In other words, she asks him if he is like the King of the Tartars, whose rape and murder of Lo-u-Ling she has punished on the bodies of 26 men.

Calaf is not like the King of the Tartars, of course. He wants Turandot to love him. "I want you ardent," he sings, with an optional high C on "ardent." "Courage!" urges the crowd, to the Turandot in Love motif. Calaf is an adherent to the laws of chivalry, so he offers the Princess a second chance to win. To the Riddle Theme he says he answered her three riddles, and now he will ask her one.

A new, warm, and slightly melancholy melody plays as Calaf tells Turandot that if she can find out his name before dawn, at dawn he will die. We who have been following the Rose Cycle know this is the bravest and most reckless thing Calaf could propose. How can a *romance* hero imagine he might be able to survive the coming of dawn? The melody to which Calaf makes his offer comes from "Nessun dorma," the aria to which he will, through the long night ahead, dream of his victory at dawn. A *hopeful* Dawn Song? Who has ever heard of such a thing? Perhaps Calaf has powers we don't suspect.

Turandot bows her head in agreement, and the old Emperor rises to his feet. In a heartbroken voice he softly prays that heaven might will that at first sunlight, Calaf will be his son. Everyone rises. The Spring Song returns, and the chorus begins to sing its melody. Trumpets sound, and flags wave. Calaf, his head high and his step firm, climbs the marble staircase, toward the throne that is rightfully his. The people sing glory to the Emperor, and wish him ten thousand years. "Glory to you!" they sing, and the curtain descends to the musical cry of, "Turandot in Love! Turandot in Love! Turandot in Love!"

The final act begins in the royal garden. It is night. As the one man who has succeeded in answering the riddles of Turandot, Calaf could no doubt command one of the finest rooms in the palace, but the Night of Love always takes place in a gardenlike setting, under a night sky. It is unprecedented for the tenor character to spend the Night of Love alone, but if all goes well he won't be alone tomorrow. As it is, Calaf plans to spend this night — Puccini's last Night — in the garden, dreaming of love.

Calaf is lying on the steps of a pavilion, listening to the voices of the heralds. According to the stage directions, it seems "...as if he were no longer living in reality." The musical atmosphere is mysterious and uneasy. The upwards rush in the woodwinds and strings, and the heavy pulses that follow it, seem meant to remind us of the opera's opening, when a similar rush started those musical sword blows slashing. A soft, slow, obsessive, rocking melody begins. It suggests time passing, slowly but inexorably. Perhaps the pinging of the xylophone is meant to evoke the chiming of a clock.

From a distance, the royal heralds are proclaiming the command of Turandot: This night, "nessun dorma in Pekino"—no one sleeps in Peking. Voices of the people echo the command: "Nessun dorma! Nessun dorma!" The stranger's name must be found out before dawn, or a lot of people will die. Dreamily, Calaf repeats the command. "Nessun dorma!" he sings softly. And with that he begins one of Puccini's most famous tenor arias. Calaf addresses the Princess, who no doubt is also awake in her cold room, "looking at the stars that tremble with love and with hope!" There's that word again. Hope. It's what one does at night, under the starry sky. One sinks into the waking dream of a life and a love that will never die, that will stay forever fresh and ardent, beneath a silvery moon. Yet Calaf is determined to destroy the Romantic World of Night, as he himself says openly in the aria's final lines.

Using the music to which he offered Turandot a second chance to win, he vows no one will know his name until he himself breathes it upon Turandot's lips, when the light shines. And then he sings the words it must have broken Puccini's heart to set music to. "Disappear, O Night! Set, stars! Set, stars! At dawn I'll win! I'll win! I'll win!" That triple declaration of "I'll win!"—*Vincerò!*—uses the notes to which Calaf had promised that if his name was discovered, "I'll die!"—*Morirò!*—except that he crowns it with a glorious high B on the final repetition.

This beautiful aria, loud and forceful, if slightly melancholy, serves for what would normally have been the tenor character's Masochism Aria. But Calaf has no sense of guilt and humiliation to display to the world. All that's left of the *romance* hero's masochism is the uncontrollable urge to kneel before his lady. An almost instantaneous musical transition takes place, and all at once the three ministers appear from out of the night shadows, followed by a crowd of people. Ping urges the Prince to tear his eyes away from the stars and look at them, for he has the power of life and death.

A bit confused, Calaf asks what they want of him. Obviously they don't demand to know his name—that would be ridiculous. What they want is for him to give up his quest. As some highly exotic music plays, marked by dramatic, swooping figures in middle woodwinds and middle strings, the ministers thrust a bevy of beautiful, half-naked women before the startled eyes of the Prince. These provocative creatures are all for him if he will abandon his quest.

These half-naked women, appearing so seductively in the royal garden, are surely the *Parsifal* Flower Maidens, making their second appearance in a Puccini opera. The Maidens surround the Unknown Prince, trying their best to make him forget his goal. When Calaf angrily refuses them "with a movement of rebellion," we might be reminded of *La Rondine*'s virginal Ruggero, who angrily refused the advances of that opera's tempting Flower Maidens.

The first bribe having failed, the ministers open sacks, coffers, and baskets, all brimming with precious stones—a king's ransom in sapphires, emeralds, rubies, and diamonds. Horns play an impressive little melody, while several other instruments, most notably the xylophone, describe the gleaming colors of the gems. This is Alberich's Choice being offered — the choice of riches over love — and naturally Puccini's tenor hero spurns the second bribe in disgust.

Perhaps it is glory the Prince would like! The ministers suggest that he flee, "E andrai lontano con le stelle...." To any tenor hero but Calaf these would be extremely tempting words: "And go far away with the stars...." But the third bribe of *lontano* holds no attractions for Calaf, and all he wants of the shimmering stars is for them to set forever. Calaf raises his arms to heaven and cries, "Dawn, come! Dissolve this nightmare!"

Their fear and despair increasing, the ministers huddle around the Prince. They and the crowd describe the horrible tortures they will be put to if they fail, and they plead with Calaf to have pity on them. (Puccini uses some urgent but unremarkable music for this moment. We might have expected him to use the Plea for Pity Theme, but we're too close to the torture scene, where that music will be employed in its second function, as Recognition music.)

Calaf dismisses their words as useless. There is dead silence in the orchestra, all except *tremolo* chords from the violins, as he warns the people of the Romantic World what he is about to do: "Should the world collapse, I want Turandot!" Naturally, Puccini's people go almost mad with fear when they hear this, and to the music of the precious stones they savagely yell, "You will die before us!" The crowd is "fierce and desperate," and they surround the Prince with daggers drawn, demanding he tell his name.

Shouts are suddenly heard nearby, and all turn their attention to the guards and hired assassins who are now dragging in Timur and Liu. The guards triumphantly report the name is here with these prisoners. The crowd falls silent, and the Prince rushes to his father and Liu, who are exhausted and bloody. They have been badly beaten, but so far they have not revealed Calaf's name. The Prince shouts that these two do not know his name, but the overjoyed Ping remembers them from last night's sextet. The guards tell Ping the prisoners were taken as they wandered near the walls, then the ministers run to the pavilion and call for the Princess.

A cluster of syncopated triplets is heard, then Turandot emerges from the pavilion, accompanied by the Spring Song. Singing to it, Ping tells her the stranger's name is within those mouths, and they have the tortures to extract it. Hearing this, Calaf makes a movement, but a look from the Princess stops him.

The Recognition Theme begins, played by the full orchestra, as Turandot says ironically, "You're pale, stranger!" Haughtily, Calaf retorts that what she sees on his face is dawn's pallor. It's a piece of deliberate irony that to the same music to which he had urged his father to recognize him Calaf now says to Turandot, "They don't know me."

The Princess turns her gaze toward Timur. Certain of her victory, she commands the old man to speak. He is dazed, dirty, bleeding, his hair disheveled, and the sight of a young woman treating an aged man with such disrespect really should distress the audience far more than it probably does. Timur says nothing in response to Turandot's command; he only stares at her mutely, imploringly, his eyes wide. (That Timur is indeed blind will be made certain in a few minutes.)

The Recognition Theme continues as Liu, in response to Turandot's furious demand that the ministers compel Timur to speak, advances toward the Princess and declares she alone knows the name. The crowd exclaims in relief that the nightmare is about to end. Calaf had been just a moment late in stepping forward to defend his father, and now, trying to protect Liu, he says to her haughtily, "You know nothing, slave!"

Old habits die hard, and as brave little Liu steps forward, Puccini hands over to her the tasks he knows she is far better able to accomplish than Calaf—the tasks of saving the lives of Timur and Calaf, winning Turandot for Calaf, and redeeming the sinful Turandot. In trying to promote his submissive *romance* male to co-equal with the soprano heroine, Puccini wound up erasing him from the picture completely. Calaf no longer matters at all.

Liu bestows a look of infinite tenderness on the Prince, then turning to Turandot says she knows the name. To the climax of the Recognition Theme she sings, "It is a supreme delight to me to keep it secret and possess it, alone!" This infuriates the crowd, who howl for Liu to be bound and tortured. A new and tender theme—the Martyrdom Theme—begins as Calaf shouts they will pay for her tears and torments. Violently, Turandot orders her guards to seize Calaf. They bind his feet, and grasp him firmly by the arms, thus Calaf is now in the same position of helpless prisoner as were Cavaradossi and Dick Johnson.

The Princess resumes a look of near-indifference. Liu assures Calaf she will not speak, and on her final word, two bars of the Spring Song are tenderly played by an oboe and two violas. The music appears to mean, "Don't fear, my lord. I will make her bloom for you." The Martyrdom Theme returns, its opening melody played once by solo violin, then by solo cello, but it vanishes in an upwards rush in the violas as Ping harshly demands that Liu give up the name. She refuses, and at a sign from Ping the assassins grab her and twist her arms. Liu screams.

Let's ponder this for a moment. Here in this Palace, a desperate scream is resounding. A scream from a sweet and serene girl. Here, in the atrocious night, her fresh voice is about to be extinguished. On whom will be avenged that purity, that scream, and that death? What an ironic thing this is, that in attempting ceaselessly to avenge the murder of the innocent Lo-u-Ling, Turandot is about to replicate it in Liu.

Timur has been sitting in a "terrible silence," but Liu's scream causes him to stir. He asks why she is crying, and Calaf demands that they release her. Liu sings to the Martyrdom Theme as she first swears to Timur that no one is hurting her, then begs the guards to gag her so the old man will not hear her cries. Spent, she then says that she can't stand any more.

The Princess orders the men to let go of Liu, who tells her she would rather die than speak. This puzzles Turandot, who stares at the girl and asks who placed such strength in her heart. The answer is, "Princess—love!" Turandot repeats the word as though it were unfamiliar, and Liu prepares to redeem the murderer Turandot by dying for her sins. She tells Turandot that the tortures are sweetnesses to her, because she offers them to her Lord. Liu calls on the guards to bind and torture her, as the supreme offering of her love.

Liu's speech had briefly upset and fascinated Turandot, but when it is finished the cruel Princess orders her guards to tear the secret from the girl. Ping calls for Pu-Tin-Pao to come forth, and the helpless Calaf struggles angrily and fruitlessly. The crowd howls for the Executioner, and suddenly Pu-Tin-Pao appears. The sight of this huge and frightful figure, flanked by his men in their bloodstained rags, terrifies Liu, and she emits a *grido disperato*—a desperate scream—precisely as Lo-u-Ling did. On Turandot's command, Pu-Tin-Pao is about to replicate on Liu the actions of the King of the Tartars on Lo-u-Ling. Almost mad with fear, Liu tries to force her way out, but the crowd blocks her path, demanding that she speak. In desperation, Liu runs to Turandot and begs her to listen.

Liu's last aria—the last aria Puccini ever composed, on lines he wrote himself—is "Tu che di gel sei cinta" (You who are girded with frost). Liu is Puccini's last *romance* heroine, and unlike Calaf, she has no intention of leaving the Romantic World of Giacomo Puccini. The aria addresses Liu's own death, which she is about to ensure will take place just before the breaking of dawn. It is she, not Calaf, who is meant to destroy the World, and bring a new one into being. For the sake of love, Liu will give both Calaf and Turandot the ability to break through the great barrier that divides Night from Day.

Liu's aria is another of those limping, drooping songs that the chronically melancholy Puccini was such a master of. A death march runs under much of it, as Liu tells the Princess that she, who is girded with frost, will be overcome by the Prince's flame. She too will love him. And "Before this dawn, I close, weary, my eyes, never to see him more."

Fascinatingly, the main rhythm of Liu's aria harkens back to the main rhythm of the pounding dance music to which the crowd savagely urged on the Executioner's men in their whetting of the sword blade near the start of Act One. This was of course deliberate on the part of Puccini, who took a master craftsman's care with such details. By repeating that rhythm in Liu's suicide aria, slowing and softening it, he is making the subtle musical statement that by her death Liu is putting an end to the executions. I'd go so far as to say he is making the statement that Liu is Redeeming not just Turandot, but all of the people.

Her aria finished, though the orchestra continues to play its death-march melody, Liu suddenly snatches a dagger from the belt of one of the guards, and plunges it into her breast. She looks at Calaf "with supreme sweetness," staggers toward him, and falls dead at his feet. As the music of her aria swells to *fortissimo*, the crowd shouts for her to speak the name. Filled with sadness, the Prince cries out. "Ah, you are dead! Oh, my little Liu!"

Silence falls over the now terrified crowd, and the music of Liu's aria sinks back to *piano*. In a rage, Turandot seizes a whip from one of the Executioner's men and strikes in the face the guard whose dagger Liu took. The man covers his face and falls back in the crowd. The guards release Calaf. Timur rises, crazed with grief. He staggers over to Liu, and according to the stage directions, "he kneels." Yes, it's what anyone might do, but...

Perhaps it's a coincidence, but Liu takes on an even greater resemblance to the Redeemer as Timur urges her to rise from the dead: "Liu! Liu! Rise! Rise! It is the bright hour of every awakening! It's dawn, Oh my Liu. Open your eyes, dove!" Noticing an expression of torment on the face of Turandot, Ping intends to roughly send Timur away. But when he approaches, he softens a bit, and merely tells the old man to get up, for the girl is dead.

As the music of Liu's aria continues, Timur warns of the soprano's great power, which we had received hints of before. "The offended spirit will avenge itself!" Timur cries. He sounds very much like old Guglielmo in *Le Villi*, praying that the legend of the Villi is true, that the offended spirit of Anna will avenge itself on her betrayer.

That Puccini was indeed thinking of his first opera when he wrote this last scene of his career seems likely, for the stage directions say the people are now filled with a superstitious fear that Liu, having died unjustly, might return as a vampire, and prey upon them. Like so many other comments he wrote in his librettos, this one has absolutely no significance to either the actors or the audience. Puccini put it in because it was important for *him* to know that was what his characters were thinking.

Two of Turandot's handmaidens cover the Princess' face with a white, silver-embroidered veil, and as they do, the supplicating crowd, using a rather hazy new melody, prays that the grieving spirit of Liu will forgive them, and not hurt them. Liu's melody returns, and with it are the famous Puccini tolling bells, striking triplet patterns. In a mood of religious piety, the crowd raises the body of Liu. Like Liu, Timur has no intention of leaving the Romantic World. As the funeral cortege begins to move, he takes his beloved's hand in his, and walking beside her he says he knows where she is going. "And I promise to rest beside you, in the night that has no morning." And this time, Manon will not stay his hand. Ping, Pang, and Pong utter expressions of grief and guilt, and as all but Calaf and Turandot go off, the crowd chants to the spirit of Liu to forgive, to sleep, and to forget. Puccini's life's work, and the Rose Cycle, ends here, and the last word spoken, by the crowd, is, "Poetry!"

Enlisted by the Ricordi Company and Puccini's heirs to finish the opera, composer Franco Alfano found himself confronted with 36 sheets of music paper scrawled with verbal and musical notes, and a major problem. Calaf and Turandot are standing on stage alone after Liu's suicide, staring at each other. Now what?

One author, writing about the creation of *Turandot*, noted that one of Puccini's verbal notes was "...puzzlingly, 'Then, "Tristan."'" In fact this isn't puzzling at all, for Puccini was obviously wanting to close his opera with a "Liebestod"-like finale similar to that of *La Fanciulla del West*—a shimmering, twinkling number for principals and chorus, giving a tremendous sense of catharsis, and of "two dissolving into one for eternity."

Alfano, who had been Puccini's friend, did what he could with the notes, but it must be admitted that the opera's final two scenes are not at all good. It's certainly worth looking at them, though, for hints about what Puccini was contemplating, for Alfano reportedly did his best to carry out Puccini's intentions, as he perceived them.

The full orchestra plays three chords, in the same pattern as the tolling funeral bells. It marks a sharp division between what just occurred, and what will follow. To a portentous and vaguely Chinese-sounding accompaniment, Calaf urges the Princess of death and frost to descend from her tragic sky — to lift her silver and white veil and look at the blood that was shed for her. In the first part of this we see the strongest equation yet of Turandot with the moon, and there seems to be a verbal reminiscence of the *Madama Butterfly* love duet, in which Butterfly spoke of the little goddess of the moon who descends at night from the bridge of heaven with her white cloak. The second part, addressing the blood that was shed for Turandot, is further proof that Liu was perceived as the redeemer of Turandot, not as one who was sacrificing herself for Calaf.

Calaf tears the veil from Turandot's face as he urges her to look at the blood. The orchestra noodles nervously as Turandot essentially declares she is a moon-goddess, for she says she is not human, that she is the daughter of heaven and her soul is on high. (Yes, her father is called the son of heaven, but that's not what's going on here. The Princess really means it.) The orchestra begins to work its way toward the melody of "In questa Reggia" as Calaf, well, sort of threatens to assault the Princess. He says her soul may be on high, but her body is here, and he intends to clasp the edges of her mantle and press his trembling mouth on hers.

As the orchestra continues to climb toward "In questa Reggia," the two essentially utter a series of "Yes! Yes!"—"No! No!"—"Yes! Yes!"—"No! No!" The aria's music bursts forth on the Prince's cry of, "It is a lie!" (her iciness), and to the music of the warning to the stranger that he not test Fate, Turandot sings, "Don't touch me, stranger! It is a sacrilege!" The next line in "In questa Reggia" was what I have named the Death/Life Theme (of how the riddles were three and either death or else life was one), and to that music Calaf answers, "No, your kiss gives me eternity!"

And now Calaf, "strong in the knowledge of his right and his passion," does indeed assault Turandot. There is a deep rumbling from the timpani as he grabs her and kisses her in a frenzy. The harp, supported by muted violins, does a mysterious little plinking run up and down the scale, the volume swelling and subsiding as Calaf kisses and then releases. The "incredible contact" of this kiss—the Initiating Kiss of Kundry—"transfigures her." Turandot has "no more resistance, no more voice, no more strength, no more will." In a low monotone she sadly asks what has happened to her. She is "lost."

Like his brothers before him, Calaf now brings in the reverent language of flowers. As an offstage chorus of women vocalize, he calls the Princess his morning flower, with breasts of lily. "My flower, I breathe you in!" We hear the faintest hint of "Nessun dorma" as he admires her, all white in her silver mantle. Narcotic night music is heard as the Prince sees his conquered Princess is weeping. The sun is rising, and with the waning of her power, Turandot shudders. "It is dawn!" she cries three times. The music of the Spring Song is heard, and offstage voices of the boys and some tenors sing to it, "The dawn! Light of life!" The message is that of the birth of love in spring.

With great sadness the Princess says, "Turandot tramonta!" This is often translated as "My sun is setting," but "tramonta" does not specifically refer to the setting of the sun. What she means is, "My moon is setting." Ecstatic at his victory, the Prince cries, "It is dawn! It is dawn! And love is born with the sun!" Turandot sings to the Spring Song as with sweet resignation she says, "My glory has ended!"

New music, which had been sketched out by Puccini, begins as the Prince declares her glory is just beginning, that it began with the first kiss and the first tears. Turandot has a last aria, featuring the music of Calaf's declaration, in which she confesses she was frightened when she first laid eyes on him, for she saw in his eyes the light of heroes. She felt love for him at once, and it terrified her.

The last of Puccini's race of powerful, domineering heroines, Turandot can conceive of no relationship between a man and a woman in which one is not the conqueror and the other the conquered. And she feels herself conquered now — not by Calaf's victory in the Contest of the Riddles, but by "this fever that comes to me from you." In other words, *romance's* mighty god, Love, and not Calaf, has conquered Turandot.

Turandot begs her Unknown Prince to be satisfied with his victory, and not desire a greater. She asks him to leave with his mystery (that is, his unknown name). Impetuously, wrenching his vocal line higher and higher, Calaf tells her his name. Now that she trembles at his touch, and pales at his kiss, he will give her his name and his life, and she can kill him if she wants to. "I am Calaf, son of Timur!" If Calaf had not done this, the two would always have wondered what would have happened if he had. Both of them need to know, and even more important, she needs to come to him voluntarily, not like "a slave, dying of shame."

The old feeling comes over her, and with a fierce cry Turandot exults that she knows the name. The Riddle Theme is heard as Calaf answers that his glory is her embrace. Trumpets blare, summoning everyone to the palace, and a replay of their vocal contest occurs as the two trade off belting, long held, *fortissimo* lines. Again singing to the Riddle Theme, the Prince vows his life is in her kiss. Turandot "draws herself up to her full height, regally, dominating," and in a piercing chant she orders him to come before the people with her. Calaf, unafraid but ultimately unable to break the chains, says in his final line of the opera, "You have conquered!"

The last, very brief scene is set before the imperial palace. We see the effect of Puccini's thoughts, expressed in that letter to Simoni, on the possibility of ending the opera "in a Chinese Holy Grail, full of pink flowers and full of love," when we look at the white marble walls of the palace. For the last time we glimpse the beloved red roses, for according to the stage directions, "on [the walls] the rosy lights of dawn are kindled like flowers."

The Spring Song plays as processional music, and the crowd cries ten thousand years to their Emperor. As Turandot walks up the stairs, the three ministers spread a golden mantle, evocative of the rising sun. There is silence, then Turandot exclaims to her august father that she knows the stranger's name. Fittingly, Calaf is at the foot of the stairs, the Princess looking down at him. "Finally, conquered, she almost murmurs in a soft sigh," which culminates on a high B flat, "His name is Love!"

As the final measures of the Spring Song play, Calaf impetuously climbs the stairs, then the two lovers—female and male, equal at last—embrace. The crowd throws flowers, and as the music of "Nessun dorma"—the anti–Dawn Song—thunders forth, they seem to express a new hope, for endless love in endless day. To "Nessun dorma" the chorus sings, "Love! O Sun! Life! Eternity! Light of the world is love! Our infinite happiness laughs and sings in the sun! Glory!" Their last words are sung to Calaf's triple-cry of "Vincerò," followed by a full-orchestra chord played three times.

And then the final curtain falls.

14

The Trouble with Turandot, and How to Fix It

The only real problem with the libretto of *Turandot* is Turandot herself, for Kiss or no Kiss, she is too horrible a person for the audience to accept her instant transformation into a heroine and a fit lover for Calaf. The situation needed to be changed so the Contest of the Riddles and the executions of those who failed it could be excused away as not her fault. In "In questa Reggia," Turandot declares that the desperate scream of her ancestress, Lo-u-Ling, passed from descendant to descendant, until finally taking refuge in her soul. Puccini would probably have had a much easier time with the opera had that claim been treated literally, so that his libretto followed a plan like this:

At the start of the opera, it is explained to the audience that the beloved Princess Turandot has been possessed by the vengeful spirit of her ancestress, Lo-u-Ling, who long ago was brutally murdered by a foreign prince. The chorus can sing this after the announcement of the failure of the Prince of Persia to answer the riddles. The audience is told that Lo-u-Ling's angry spirit sought out the body of a young woman of her blood so she could take revenge on men of royal birth, like the one who killed her. The sympathy of Turandot to her ancestress' sad history made her vulnerable to the spirit, who was thereby able to take possession of her body.

Lo-u-Ling, the chorus explains, convinced the Emperor to allow the Contest of the Riddles in exchange for her promise to release Turandot, and leave his kingdom in peace, if one of the suitors is able to answer her riddles. But all who fail must submit themselves to the Executioner's sword. Thus it is that the Emperor has promised his daughter's hand to any man of royal blood who can rescue her from the grasp of the bloodthirsty Lo-u-Ling.

Calaf hears this exposition, and is filled with pity for the gentle Turandot, whose only mistake was to be sympathetic to a poor murdered girl. Calaf will not have seen Turandot yet, so that when he does, his motivation in offering himself for the Contest will be something nobler than just Love as Madness. When he does see Turandot a few minutes later, however, the sight of such incredible beauty pushes him over the edge, and he decides to risk the Contest so he can rescue the Princess and win her hand. With minor changes in the text to account for these differences, all proceeds as in the opera until Calaf successfully answers the riddles.

At this point, Lo-u-Ling frantically refuses to leave the body of Turandot. The Emperor demands that she do so, for she gave her word. If she does not, he says, he will give her in marriage to the Unknown Prince anyway, for his daughter has been won in accordance with the rules. Lo-u-Ling vows to kill Turandot if the Prince so much as touches her.

Calaf offers the vicious Lo-u-Ling a second chance. If she can discover his name before dawn, she can have him executed. Otherwise, she must release Turandot and leave the kingdom. Lo-u-Ling eagerly agrees. (The audience will probably suspect that Lo-u-Ling has no intention of honoring this promise, but as we shall see, it will not matter whether she intends to honor it or not.)

All proceeds as in the opera until the torture of Liu. The young girl has admitted she knows the Prince's name, but vows she will not reveal it. She loves him, and knows that he loves Turandot. If Lo-u-Ling knew what love is, the girl says, she would understand why Liu wants the Prince to have his heart's desire. Lo-u-Ling seems deeply bewildered for a moment, but she shakes this off and angrily orders that Liu be tortured. Calaf is horrified, and shouts that he will reveal his name in order to keep Liu from being hurt. "I will tell you my name!" he cries. "My name is...." It is at this moment that Liu grabs the dagger from the soldier and kills herself.

As all look on in horror, Calaf rushes to Liu's side and cradles her dead body in his arms. Lo-u-Ling walks slowly toward them. On her face is a look of intense puzzlement, which slowly changes to one of peace, and happiness. She sings that Liu's deep, unselfish love for the Unknown Prince has touched her scorched heart. The self-sacrifice of this young girl has countered her own long-ago murder. Her thirst for vengeance has been satisfied, and at last her tormented spirit can rest. (This talk of her long psychic pain allows the audience to feels some sympathy for Lo-u-Ling.) As all look on in wonder, the spirit of Lo-u-Ling leaves the body of Turandot. This will need a brilliant stage effect — perhaps a column of blood-red light that spreads out, changing color and twinkling as it dissipates.

For the first time, Turandot sings as herself. Obviously she will have to use a very different voice from that of the icy Lo-u-Ling — a warm and human voice. (Perhaps she will, during Lo-u-Ling's final aria, have a chance to transition to the warm voice.) She will have to acknowledge Liu's sacrifice, but this can't go on too long, or else Calaf will fade into the background.

Turandot expresses her thanks to Liu in a few lines (during which the body is removed), perhaps promising to raise a monument in her honor, then she turns to Calaf and thanks, "You, my Unknown Prince, whose name is Love." This begins a choral finale, during which the chorus gives thanks that their beloved Princess has been restored to them, and all sing of the transformative power of love.

15

Conclusion

"Cio-Cio-San is a sister of Liu, a half-sister of Mimi, a cousin of Manon, and a not-too-distantly-removed cousin of the more self-assured Tosca. These frail, fragile creatures, these unheroic heroines who, loving wholly, are wholly broken by love, these are the ones who fired Puccini's mind."

— George Marek, author of *Puccini*, in liner notes to
1963 RCA Victor recording of *Madama Butterfly*

"...[Puccini's] standard heroine is frail and dies for love, whether in crinoline or kimono...."—Stanley Jackson, *Monsieur Butterfly: The Life of Giacomo Puccini*

"In his seven major works, seven beautiful butterflies—his pathetic heroines—are pinned quivering beneath the examiner's glass. Six of them die."

— M. Owen Lee, *First Intermissions*

"Now he would choose a subject with a frail, gentle, docile heroine, tinged with delicate poetic colours; to her he would apply a subtle, slow-working and insidious form of sadism, until he crushed her."

— Mosco Carner, in liner notes to 1978 Deutsche
Grammophon recording of *La Fanciulla del West*

"After all, she [Liu] is the direct descendant of his meek, devoted, beloved heroines Mimi and Butterfly and Angelica (and, before, Anna in *Le Villi*...)."

— William Weaver, in liner notes to
1973 Decca recording of *Turandot*

What on earth prompted these declarations, and so many others just like them? Why have so many critics and other writers on opera been, for a hundred years and more, so utterly, stupefyingly blind as to the awesome strength of Puccini's heroines? A significant part of the reason, I think, is that most writing on opera has been done by people who know a fair amount — sometimes a tremendous amount — about music, but very little about literature.

There are astounding riches contained in the librettos of some of the most popular operas—librettos that were written by talented poets and highly educated men — but one would never know that from today's newspaper articles, books, and recorded lectures on opera. Even the most respected critics simply do not know that these riches are there, and that the music is enhanced by them, and as a result, their readers and listeners do not know it either.

There is a little more to it than that, however; something more to the tremendous misunderstanding of Puccini's works than the focus of critics on music at the expense of words. It has to do with the difference between Puccini and Giuseppe Verdi. The plots used by the former seem "feminine," the latter "masculine." Even a Verdi love story, like *La Traviata*, seems somehow masculine in tone. But what do we mean by this? The answer to that lies, of all places, in ancient Greece.

Beginning with the playwrights of Greece's golden age, the 5th century BC, a major theme in Western theatre and literature has been the conflict between one's personal interests, and his perceived duty to society. The Greeks framed this as a conflict between the *oikos*, which refers to the home, and the *polis*, which is the city-state. The *oikos* encompasses one's home, relatives, friends, and anything else that is a purely personal concern. The *polis* is the larger society, and so it encompasses *all* of the community's homes, friends, relatives, and concerns. The Greeks conceived the home as the responsibility of women, and the city-state as the responsibility of men. The *oikos* is thus feminine, and the *polis* male.

The Greeks did not by any means disdain the *oikos*, nor think the woman's responsibility a trivial one. The *oikos* is, after all, the building block of the *polis*. But it was clear to the Greeks that no matter how painful it was for a man, if he was faced with a choice between his personal interests and those of the larger society, his decision had to favor the *polis* over the *oikos*. If society fell, they reasoned, so would all of the individuals in it. Thus: a man's got to do what a man's got to do.

That philosophy was what caused the Greeks to conceive a myth in which a king, Agamemnon, offers his own daughter as a human sacrifice, in exchange for winds that would blow his fleet to Troy. As painful as the sacrifice was for him personally, they believed, it was Agamemnon's duty to make it as the protector of the *polis*. The myth continues with Agamemnon's wife, Clytemnestra, killing her husband in revenge for her murdered daughter. As protector of the *oikos,* it was only natural for her to see things that way.

Almost all the operas written by Verdi address the *oikos versus polis* question, and Verdi stood with the Greeks. He loved melodramatic plots in which more or less attractive and honorable people find themselves in wrenching situations, and forced to take a stand. And no matter how painful the result is to them, Verdi's "good" characters know that in the end, their personal interest must be sacrificed on the altar of Honor and Duty. We see this theme in *Ernani, Un Ballo in Maschera, La Traviata, Don Carlo,* and *Aida*, to name just five.

As for Puccini, he had, both dramatically and personally, not the slightest interest in the wants and needs of the *polis*. Only personal interests matter to characters like Anna, Manon, Mimi, Tosca, Butterfly, Minnie, and Magda. And that's all that mattered to Puccini: my family, my friends, my home, my art, my royalties. When World War I started, the great question to him was, "How will this affect G. Puccini?" This is in marked contrast to Verdi, who had been the artistic voice of the Italian people during their struggle to free themselves from foreign rule, and who served as a senator (albeit as a self-described rubber stamp of a senator) after independence was achieved.

Verdi was also generous with his money, and this too is in great contrast with Puccini, who was a notorious tightwad. This does not mean Puccini was not a kind, decent, and thoughtful person, and indeed, biographers have related a number of stories about him going well out of his way to help someone who asked him for assistance. And one would search in vain through the biographies of Puccini for descriptions of the sort of nasty, emotionally abusive behavior toward wife and friends that is well documented throughout the middle and later years of the famously cantankerous and bad-tempered Verdi. But this sort of personal comparison of the two composers is outside the scope of this book, as is a comparison of them as musicians. The point of this discussion is the strange blindness of critics regarding the characterization of the heroines in Puccini's and Verdi's operas.

By the time Verdi was composing, women in popular fiction didn't do the sort of awe-inspiring things the ferocious women of Greek myth did. In 19th century fiction, to be a protector of the *oikos*—that is, to be the hero's love interest—generally meant you were frail, fragile, unheroic, and wholly broken by love. So it is that Verdi's heroines tend to settle their problems not by taking their fate into their own hands and striking back against their tormenters, but rather by giving up on life, or else submitting to the demands of the *polis*. They commit suicide, they droop and die of disease, they wearily retire to a religious life, or they meekly submit to murder.

It strikes me as extremely telling that Verdi has never been taken to task for the brutal treatment dished out to so many of his female characters. Gilda, for example, in *Rigoletto*, is kidnapped and assaulted, then willingly allows herself to be murdered in place of the utterly despicable man she loves. *She* is a real victim. Or how about the title character in *Luisa Miller*, who after suffering all sorts of horrible anguish and torment and fear, is at last deliberately poisoned by the man she loves, who has falsely accused her of having been unfaithful to him? Then there's the utterly wretched Leonora, in *La Forza del Destino*: bullied by her self-absorbed lover, cursed in the dying breath of her harsh father, and ceaselessly chased by her enraged brother, who finally succeeds in killing her. And there is the slave Aida, who is bullied and cursed by her manipulative father, until she collapses in tears and agrees to betray the man she loves. Subsequently she joins her beloved in a horrible death, since life holds nothing for her.

In no small part, the plots of Verdi's operas are judged to be manly and respectable because his frail and fragile heroines are tormented, bullied, and killed in the conventional, acceptable, 19th century way. And Puccini's operas are considered effete and suspect because his women are powerful and they die heroically. It's a perverted judgment, and to thank for it we have the viciously misogynist writers of the *fin de siècle*, and the oblivious music critics who for more than 100 years have unquestioningly followed them.

And yet Puccini's ravishing music and life-affirming characters have always appealed in a very positive way to women, who have traditionally made up the greatest part of the opera audience. If we could take his works back to the dawn of the *romance* era, to 12th century France and England, and perform them before Eleanor of Aquitaine and her contemporaries, those ladies would, allowing for changing tastes in musical style, undoubtedly adore them. Had Puccini been born in that time and place, he would surely have had a great career as a troubadour, and his female audiences would have easily seen through the youth and surface delicacy of his heroines, to the strength and courage that lies within them.

If we can judge him by his work, Giacomo Puccini liked and respected women as intelligent and competent beings, and was excited in a positive way by their beauty and their sexuality. He was inspired by thoughts of his female characters' loveliness, tenderness, and fierce bravery to compose some of the best operas the world has ever heard. One can never imagine him telling a friend, as Verdi once did, "Horses are like women. They have to please the man who owns them."[1]

Although Puccini's works are greatly loved, his strange genius has never been entirely appreciated. I hope this book will help to remedy that.

Appendix: The Operas of Giacomo Puccini

Le Villi (Teatro dal Verme, Milan. May 31, 1884.)
Edgar (La Scala, Milan. April 21, 1889.)
Manon Lescaut (Teatro Regio, Turin. February 1, 1893.)
La Bohème (Teatro Regio, Turin. February 1, 1896.)
Tosca (Teatro Costanzi, Rome. January 14, 1900.)
Madama Butterfly (La Scala, Milan. February 17, 1904.)
La Fanciulla del West (Metropolitan, New York. December 10, 1910.)
La Rondine (Casino Theatre, Monte Carlo. March 27, 1917.)
Il Trittico (Metropolitan, New York. December 14, 1918.)
Turandot (La Scala, Milan. April 25, 1926.)

Chapter Notes

Chapter 1

1. I am indebted to Bram Dijkstra's magnificent and exhaustively-researched book, *Idols of Perversity: Fantasies of Feminine Evil in Fin-de-Siècle Culture* (Oxford University Press, New York, 1986), for acquainting me with the vast quantity of misogynist depictions of women in the pictorial art of the *fin de siècle*.

2. On the subject of contraception, for example, Leo Tolstoy, author of *Anna Karenina*, wrote the following: "Every woman, however she may call herself and however refined she may be, who refrains from child-birth without refraining from sexual relations, is a whore." (Quoted in *Idols of Perversity*, p. 216.)

3. Mosco Carner's blanket description of Puccini's women is "gentle, tender, affectionate, and childlike, and they love to the point of self-sacrifice." A late Victorian at heart, and a disciple of Freud to the point of nuttiness, he goes on to describe Puccini's heroines in prudish and condemning terms that relate to their uninhibited sexuality and their membership in the lower classes, but he has nothing to say in respect to the moral and social status of the Puccini hero. Among Carner's most condescending labels for Puccini's heroines is "lights-o'-love." (Citations are from *Puccini: A Critical Biography* (Holmes and Meier, New York, 1988), p. 275.)

The most common descriptions of Puccini's heroines are like those of George Marek in his liner notes to the 1963 RCA Victor recording of *Madama Butterfly*: "These frail, fragile creatures, these unheroic heroines, who, loving wholly, are wholly broken by love...," and Stanley Jackson, in his *Monsieur Butterfly, The Life of Giacomo Puccini* ((Stein and Day, New York, 1974) p. 109): "...[Puccini's] standard heroine is frail and dies for love, whether in crinoline or kimono...."

One exception to the rule appears to be the late Ernest Newman. According to the liner notes by Remy Van Wyck Farkas to the 1952 London recording of *Madama Butterfly*, Newman considered Puccini "to be a strong feminist in his operatic writings." I have not myself found comments of that nature in Newman's books, but am willing to take Van Wyck Farkas' word for it.

4. *The Art of Courtly Love*, written in 1184 by the monk Andreas Capellanus, provides the only known codification of the conventions of courtly love. As with *The Art of Love*, scholars debate whether Capellanus intended a serious work or a parody.

5. Chapter 12 of this book, on *Suor Angelica*, includes a discussion of Bridal Mysticism, the Cult of the Virgin Mary, and Maternal Mysticism. My primary source on the teachings of Bernard de Clairvaux was Leon J. Podles' *The Church Impotent: The Feminization of Christianity* (Spence Publishing Company, Dallas, 1999).

6. Sidney Painter, *French Chivalry* (Cornell University Press, Ithaca and London, 1969) pp. 123–124.

7. Walter Scott's *Ivanhoe*, for example, features two women, both of them supremely desirable. Rowena, the beautiful blonde Saxon, is important only as a linear descendant of King Alfred. Rebecca, the lovely dark-haired Jewess, is nobly self-denying, and spends a great deal of time nursing people. After numerous importuning suitors and would-be rapists are disposed of, Rowena finally marries her beloved Ivanhoe, while Rebecca resolves to live the remainder of her days as the Jewish version of a nun.

8. Carner lists over 70 works that Puccini considered and rejected during his career. Among the ones that attracted him most were *Due Zoccoletti* (Ouida), *La Femme et le Pantin* (Pierre Louÿs), and *A Florentine Tragedy* (Oscar Wilde). All three are sadomasochistic works. Also sadomasochistic are the more briefly contemplated *Trilby* (George du Maurier), *La Lupa* (Giovanni Verga), *Notre Dame de Paris* (Hugo), and even *Oliver Twist* (Dickens), since what interested Puccini in this work — which he contemplated setting as an opera called *Nancy* — was the relationship between Nancy and her brutal lover, Bill Sykes. There were various reasons for Puccini's failure to set these and other, similar works, but in many cases the reason was undoubtedly that in addition to being sadomasochistic, the work was misogynist. In other words, it was too difficult to warp the story such that the heroine could be made the dominant sexual partner.

9. *Eroticism and Love in the Middle Ages*, ed. Albrecht Classen (American Heritage — Custom Publishing Group, New York, 1995) p. 96.

10. Wolfram Von Eschenbach, *Parzival*, trans. by Helen M. Mustard and Charles E. Passage (Vintage Books, New York, 1961) Book X.

11. *Eroticism and Love in the Middle Ages*, p. 111.

12. *Middle English Romances*, ed. A. C. Gibbs (Northwestern University Press, Evanston, 1966) p. 47.

Chapter 2

1. Carner and Jackson, among others, have described Fontana as stubbornly refusing repeated requests to make changes in the libretto of *Edgar*, but Ashbrook points out numerous examples of alterations, and Elphinestone cites a collection of letters from Fontana to Puccini, in which the poet comments on material that was dropped from the initial plan of the opera. In his increasingly desperate attempts to give coherence to the opera, Puccini himself made massive revisions to the score, but in its final form *Edgar* consists of a group of unmotivated and one-dimensional characters acting out a series of absurd scenes that do not logically follow one another.

2. Puccini's friend, mentor, and publisher, Giulio Ricordi, seems not to have shared the composer's attitude. On May 31, 1903, Ricordi wrote Puccini, who was unmarried at the time, an extremely long letter regarding an affair the latter had been having with a young woman named Corinna. Apparently unaware that Corinna was a teacher (or perhaps a law docent — the facts are unclear), Ricordi wrote in terms that sound like they were pulled from one of Fontana's librettos. Using such words as "whore," "corrupt woman," "foul vampire," and "obscene sensual pleasures," Ricordi tried to convince Puccini that his relationship with Corinna was a horror that would ruin his body, his morals, and his art. Puccini had, at the time, been undergoing a long and difficult convalescence after an automobile accident, and it seems likely that Ricordi feared that his protégé's slow recovery might be due to the effects of a venereal disease. The letter is quoted in its entirety in Claudio Sartori's book *Puccini* (Milan, 1958) pp. 62–68, and extensively in Howard Greenfeld's *Puccini* (Robert Hale, London, 1981), pp. 154–158.

3. The work was a five-act verse drama called *La coupe et les levres* (The cup and the lips). First published in 1832, it tells the story of a dissatisfied man who embarks on a long and complicated quest of spiritual self-discovery. It seems quite possible that Musset may have been inspired by thoughts of Goethe's *Faust*.

4. Edgar typically refers to Tigrana as demon, leper, filth of the world, useless plaything, etc.

5. In the liner notes to the 1972 Vienna Volksoper recording of Act 2 of *Edgar*, Robert Jacobson quotes the letter in which Puccini gave his final judgment on the opera: "In setting the libretto of *Edgar*, I have, with all respect to the memory of my friend Fontana, made a blunder. It was more my fault than his."

6. Vincent Seligman, son of Puccini's friend Sybil Seligman, quotes Puccini as having cried, "Sorrow, sorrow, sorrow! Sorrow is the very essence of life!" Mr. Seligman recalls that "...deep down in him a sense of melancholy permeated his whole being, just as it ran, like a strand of gold, through all his music." Vincent Seligman, *Puccini Among Friends* (The Macmillan Company, New York, 1938), p. 202.

7. N.B.: Killing a parrot, as *La Bohème*'s Schaunard did, is not art.

8. Maxence (1871–1954) was a French painter of portraits, landscapes, and still lifes. His specialty, however, was the vaguely religious or allegorical work featuring beautiful females in medieval dress. Though disdained by progressive critics, he was very popular with middle-class purchasers of art.

9. Resistance to the women's suffrage movement was intense in Puccini's time, with many opponents charging that the whole thing was a communist plot inspired by the teachings of Karl Marx. In chapter 5 of *The Puccini Problem* (Cambridge University Press, 2007), Alexandra Wilson details the savage and multi-pronged attacks on Puccini that were fueled by a monograph published in 1912, and written by Fausto Torrefranca, a virulent misogynist and nationalist who accused the composer of a sickening "effeminacy" and of writing music that was insufficiently "Italian."

10. The ancient Romans planted rosebushes on tombs with just this symbolic meaning in mind. In our own time, the Swiss refer to cemeteries as "rose gardens." In Arab culture, the rose has long been seen as a symbol of male beauty, and the flower is used by Christians as a symbol of the Virgin Mary. (*Facts on File Encyclopedia of World Mythology and Legend*, New York, 1988, pp. 560–561.) Jesus' crown of thorns clearly carries the same meaning of coming resurrection.

11. Edmund likens Manon to Proserpine, the girl who in Graeco/Roman mythology was abducted by Pluto, lord of the underworld, while she was picking flowers. Warning Des Grieux that an old libertine is about to steal away his girl, Edmund refers to Manon as a sweet flower that is about to be torn up by the roots.

12. At one point in the opera, the nuns decide to take a pail of water to their sister's grave. There is clearly *something* there that needs water, and a rosebush is the most likely choice.

13. Quoted by Howard Greenfeld in *Puccini*, p. 261.

Chapter 3

1. Puccini explained his needs in a letter dated July 18, 1894, written to Carlo Clausetti, who was acting as intermediary between Puccini and the celebrated Italian poet Gabriele D'Annunzio. Puccini wrote that what he wanted was "...poetry and again poetry, tenderness mixed with pain, sensuality, a drama surprising and burning, and a rocketing finale." (Quoted in *Puccini: A Critical Biography*, p. 120.)

2. *Letters of Puccini*, ed. Giuseppe Adami, trans. Ena Makin (Vienna House, New York, 1973) p. 270.

3. *Puccini: A Critical Biography*, p. 171

4. Ernest Newman, *Seventeen Famous Operas* (Alfred A. Knopf, New York, 1955) p. 242.

5. Charles Osborne, *The Complete Operas of Puccini* (Da Capo Press, New York, 1983) p. 27.

6. Mary Jane Phillips-Matz writes, "Drawing parallels between Puccini and Wagner, Michele Girardi brilliantly associates the importance of redemption in *La Fanciulla del West* with that in *Parsifal*, Puccini's favorite Wagner work." Acknowledging that Mosco Carner had previously made similar comparisons, she adds that Girardi had observed that, "Sieglinde and Siegmund embrace just as Minnie and Johnson do. ...Johnson's wound is related to Tristan's wound, both men having been injured by 'impotent rivals,' Rance and Melot. And as Tristan is run through after kissing Isolde, so Johnson is shot after he declares his love for Minnie. Girardi pairs *Fanciulla* and *Tristan*, 'two "fables" that are apparently so different.'" (*Puccini: A Biography*, Northeastern University Press, 2002, p. 188.) In fact, the two fables that are apparently so different are not Puccini's *Fanciulla* and *Tristan*, but rather Belasco's *The Girl of the Golden West* and *Tristan*.

7. In contrast to the numerous others who have pointed out false bits of "Wagnerisms" in Puccini's librettos, I am apparently the first to have noticed the large scenes lifted bodily from *Parsifal*, and used in *La Rondine*, *Suor Angelica*, and *Turandot*.

8. *Letters of Puccini*, pp. 204–205.

9. *Puccini: A Critical Biography*, pp. 434–435.

10. A brief description of the notes is given in *Puccini: A Critical Biography*, p. 487

Chapter 4

1. Of course, the theory ignored the simultaneous belief that men were also physically superior to women. The reader who is interested in seeing some of this artwork is directed to *Idols of Perversity*, pp. 243–248, in which a number of paintings representing the "swirling, suspect passions of women in the throes of dance" are reproduced.

Chapter 5

1. All citations from *The Story of Manon Lescaut and the Chevalier des Grieux* are taken from the translation by Helen Waddell (The Heritage Press, New York, 1935).

2. *Vita nuova* is a book of great importance to the lovers, and to the story, of *The Girl of the Golden West*. Although it was only after the Risorgimento that the Italian government began to promote Dante as a figure of national unity, librettists made use of him prior to that time. The aria *Voi che sapete* (You who know what love is), from Mozart's *Le Nozze di Figaro*, sung as it is to the Countess and Susanna, opens with words that were surely meant to recall the opening line of Dante's first important poem, and the one that helped launch what was called the "sweet new style" of late 13th century Italian poetry.

The first line of Dante's poem is, *Donne, ch'avete intelletto d'amore*—"Ladies, who have an understanding of love."

3. *Puccini: A Critical Biography*, pp. 286–287.

4. *The Complete Operas of Puccini*, p. 78. Osborne puzzles over the tone of the love duet music, and speculates that Puccini "may here be making use of music conceived to fit words of a different temper." We will hear this many times in the future: the opinion that the lazy Puccini must surely have tossed into his score some mouldering bit of cast-off music he found lying about his study. Puccini was in fact a true Artist, who took immense care with his scores.

5. Quoted in *Puccini: A Critical Biography*, p. 62.

6. Incredibly, Carner (p. 320) offers the opinion that Puccini contrived the Embarkation scene in order "to gratify his desire for the utmost humiliation of the heroine."

7. Interestingly, it is the desire to go legitimate that ruined Manon and Des Grieux. The same thing happens in *La Rondine*: the couple's unwedded bliss is destroyed when the tenor character decides that he wants to marry his beloved.

8. As it turns out in Prévost, Des Grieux and Manon were mistaken as to the outcome of the duel. Des Grieux was certain he had killed the governor's nephew, but it was later revealed that he was not even seriously injured.

9. Osborne (p. 79) faults this dramatically perfect recurrence of the minuet, declaring that "one would have thought neither Manon nor her composer would want [anyone] to be reminded at this solemn moment of her flippant, frivolous, amoral behavior." He adds "...at this stage of his career [Puccini] was still comparatively inexperienced, and apt to use whatever tune came into his head at any given moment."

Chapter 6

1. All citations from *Vie de Bohème* are taken from the translation by Norman Cameron (Hamish Hamilton, London, 1949).

2. The Bal Mabille was one of the many public dancehalls to be found all over Paris in the years between the Revolution and the end of the Second Empire. We will get a good look at the once-famous Bal Bullier in Act 2 of *La Rondine*.

3. Osborne comments that "...Murger leaves his readers in no doubt that Mimi had the instincts of a mercenary little tart..." *The Complete Operas of Puccini*, pp. 92–93.

4. An example is John Keats' *La Belle Dame Sans Merci*: "I see a lily on thy brow/With anguish moist and fever dew/And on thy cheeks a fading rose/Fast withereth too."

5. According to Newman, the "rose in the wind" is not a flower reference. Rather, "...its idiomatic meaning is the card beneath the magnetic needle,

showing the points of the mariner's compass." (*Seventeen Famous Operas*, p. 64.)

6. Ernest Newman, while conceding that "the dodge works to perfection," chides Puccini for having fastened, "one familiar tune to the tail of another ... without any conceivable rhyme or reason.... It is a brazen evasion of the problem of dramatic composition...." (*Seventeen Famous Operas*, p. 66.)

7. Carner (p. 168) reports that Puccini was distressed by reading programs that gave the date of his birth, quoting a woman who told him that Puccini had said, "I detest that 'Puccini *born*....' It always reminds me that in a few years will be added '*died*....'"

8. *The Complete Operas of Puccini*, p. 114.

9. Oblivious to the tender words summoned up by the final measures of "Vecchia zimarra," Carner declares that Puccini reprised the music "...manifestly for no other reason than that it happened to suit the mood at the close of this orchestral peroration." (*Puccini: A Critical Biography*, p. 346.)

Chapter 7

1. Carner (p. 363) declares that he has identified "some sixty leitmotives."

2. The 18 year old Pierre Louÿs, who later wrote the intensely sadomasochistic story *La femme et le Pantine*, that Puccini long considered as a subject for an opera, adored Sarah Bernhardt's performance as Tosca. Sounding very much like a love struck knight in a troubadour song, Louÿs rhapsodized in his diary: "Ah, Sarah! Sarah! Sarah is grace, youth, divinity! I am beside myself! My God, what a woman! ... When shall I see you again, my Sarah! I weep, I tremble, I grow mad! Sarah, I love you!" (Quoted in *The Divine Sarah—A Life of Sarah Bernhardt*, Vintage Books, New York, 1992, p. 232.)

3. Information on the plot of Sardou's play was drawn mainly from *Seventeen Famous Operas*, and *The Bernhardt Edition of the Argument of the Play of La Tosca* (F. Rullman, New York, 1891).

4. Evidently unaware that the motif signals the approach of the Sacristan, Osborn (p. 139) declares the recurrence to be incongruous.

5. Misinterpreting the import of Tosca's fierce battle cry, Carner (p. 363) translates the final line — "O Scarpia, avanti a Dio!"—as "Scarpia, God will be our judge," and declares that Tosca is "expressing a religious sentiment."

Chapter 8

1. While describing the character of Butterfly in complimentary terms, Spike Hughes cannot resist referring to her as one of "Puccini's Little Girls." He writes, "Puccini wrote musically greater operas than *Madama Butterfly*, but he created no greater, more sympathetic and moving character than that of the little Japanese girl who epitomized the composer's

favorite figure — the Little Girl who suffered for her devotion and love." (*Famous Puccini Operas*, Dover edition, New York, 1972, p. 138.)

2. All citations from John Luther Long's story *Madame Butterfly* are taken from The Century Company edition, published 1911. Those from David Belasco's *Madame Butterfly* are taken from *Six Plays* (Little, Brown, and Company, Boston, 1928).

3. Source: Ruth Benedict, *The Chrysanthemum and the Sword: Patterns of Japanese Culture* (Meridian, New York and Scarborough, Ontario, 1974) pp. 185–187.

4. Source: *The Chrysanthemum and the Sword*, Chapters 7 and 8.

5. Carner (pp. 385–386) identifies seven of the Japanese tunes that Puccini used, including the Japanese Imperial Hymn, "The Cherry Blossom," "The Nihon Bashi," and "My Prince." He doesn't give a title for the song used at the appearance of Butterfly and her friends.

6. Suzuki prays to Izanagi and Izanami, the brother-and-sister deities who are the universal parents and creators in Japanese mythology.

7. Surely this is the white veil that Butterfly wraps around her fatal wound in the last moments of her life.

8. *The Complete Operas of Puccini*, p. 169.

9. This business of Butterfly calling Sharpless "the best man in the world" stems from a touching situation in Long. In his story, Butterfly and Sharpless had a little game, in which she would tell him that he was the nicest man in the world, except for Pinkerton. Near the end of the story, after she learns what Pinkerton has done, Butterfly tells Sharpless one last time that he is the nicest man in the world — and she doesn't make any exceptions.

10. As has frequently been pointed out, the boy is called Trouble in Long's story, but Italian doesn't allow for the use of that word as a name. Significantly, the substitute word results in before-and-after names that are emotional opposites: Sorrow, and Joy.

Chapter 9

1. *Famous Puccini Operas*, p. 168.

2. "Minne" means love in German. The Minnesänger were the German courtly-love poets of the 12th and 13th centuries. Although Puccini did not name Minnie after Frau Minne, nor Dick Johnson after Richard Wagner, it is of course possible that David Belasco did.

3. A possible "true" *Fanciulla* Wagnerism, which I have never seen pointed out before, is the last-act manhunt, in which Dick Johnson's wild, offstage attempt to escape on horseback is described by secondary characters. Puccini himself invented that scene, and it is quite similar to Kundry's wild, offstage arrival on horseback, described by secondary characters, in the first act of *Parsifal*.

4. All citations from the play *The Girl of the Golden West*, by David Belasco, are taken from *Six Plays* (Little, Brown, and Company, Boston, 1928). All citations from the novel are taken from the Dodd, Mead and Company edition, (New York, 1911).

5. Despite being equipped with blonde hair and unstained purity, Minnie is not one of our typical 19th century madonnas. And her dark-haired counterpart, the evil Nina Micheltoreña, is not the clichéd whore, either. Although Nina does not appear in the play or the opera, she has a big part in the novel, where she is a vividly-drawn and extremely interesting character.

6. Note the highly feminine descriptions of both Ramerrez and Rance. Ramerrez is elegant of speech, beautifully dressed, and refined to the point that Minnie fears the miners' reaction to him. Rance is described in terms that would do credit to a beautiful woman: pale skin, fringed eyes, soft white hands, highly fashionable clothes, and expensive jewelry. Minnie and Nina, on the other hand, though very beautiful, are pretty tough cookies. Belasco and Puccini both appear to have been intrigued by the slight gender ambiguity of *The Girl*'s characters.

7. Considering all the accusations of plagiarism against Belasco, it seems surprising no one has accused him of having copied J. M. Barrie's *Peter Pan*, which premiered as a play in 1904, the same year Belasco began working on *The Girl*. The parallels are obvious: Minnie and Ramerrez (who leads a band of outlaws) are Wendy and Peter (who also leads a band of sort-of outlaws), the boys of Cloudy are the Lost Boys, and Rance is the menacing Captain Hook. Both Minnie and Wendy are motherly figures to their boys, there are Indians in both plays, and there is even a parallel in the significant matter of "the kiss."

8. The instrument that actually plays the part of Wallace's banjo is a harp with paper woven through the strings.

9. Those who wish to see that scene can find it on the Metropolitan Opera's 1992 video starring Placido Domingo and Barbara Daniels, available on Deutsche Grammophon.

10. Dante, *Vita nuova*, trans. by Mark Musa (Oxford University Press, New York, 1992) p. 4.

Chapter 10

1. Information on the life of Céleste (Mogador) Venard was taken from her autobiography, *Memoirs of a Courtesan in Nineteenth-Century Paris*, trans. by Monique Fleury Nagem (University of Nebraska Press, Lincoln and London, 2001), and from Joanna Richardson's *The Courtesans: The Demi-Monde in 19th Century France* (Phoenix Press, London, 2000).

2. *Memoirs of a Courtesan in Nineteenth-Century Paris*, p. 169.

3. In Greek myth, Galatea began as a marble statue carved by Pygmalion. When the youth fell in love with the beautiful figure, Aphrodite brought the statue to life. Berenice probably refers to the daughter of Herod Agrippa, who married her uncle and then had an incestuous relationship with her brother. Francesca is Francesca da Rimini, an adulteress whom Dante came across and pitied during his travels in the *Inferno*. Salome, of course, danced for her stepfather Herod in exchange for the head of John the Baptist.

4. Somerset Maugham, *Of Human Bondage* (Penguin Books, London, 1963) p. 238.

5. *Puccini Among Friends*, p. 275.

Chapter 11

1. *Puccini: A Critical Biography*, p. 150.
2. *Puccini Among Friends*, p. 95.
3. Quoted in *Puccini: A Critical Biography*, p. 149.

Chapter 12

1. Quoted in *The Church Impotent*, p. 104.
2. Ibid, p. 106.
3. Ibid, p. 120.

Chapter 15

1. Quoted by Mary Jane Phillips-Matz in *Verdi: A Biography* (Oxford University Press, Oxford/New York, 1993), p. 541.

Bibliography

Ashbrook, William. *The Operas of Puccini*. Ithaca: Cornell University Press, 1985.

Belasco, David. *The Girl of the Golden West*. New York: Dodd, Mead and Company, 1911.

_____. *Six Plays*. Boston: Little, Brown, and Company, 1928.

Benedict, Ruth. *The Chrysanthemum and the Sword: Patterns of Japanese Culture*. New York: Meridian, 1974.

The Bernhardt Edition of the Play of La Tosca. New York: F. Rullman, 1891.

Capellanus, Andreas. *The Art of Courtly Love*. Trans. by John Jay Parry. New York: Columbia University Press, 1960.

Carner, Mosco. *Puccini: A Critical Biography*. New York: Holmes and Meier, 1988.

Dante. *Vita nuova*. Trans. by Mark Musa. Oxford: Oxford University Press, 1992.

Dijkstra, Bram. *Idols of Perversity: Fantasies of Feminine Evil in Fin-de-Siècle Culture*. New York: Oxford University Press, 1986.

Eroticism and Love in the Middle Ages. Ed. Albrecht Classen. New York: American Heritage Custom Publishing Group, 1995.

Eschenbach, Wolfram Von. *Parzival*. Trans. by Helen M. Mustard and Charles E. Passage. New York: Vintage Books, 1961.

Gold, Arthur, and Robert Fizdale. *The Divine Sarah: A Life of Sarah Bernhardt*. New York: Vintage Books, 1992.

Gozzi, Carlo. *Five Tales for the Theatre*. Ed. and trans. by Albert Bermel and Ted Emery. Chicago: University of Chicago Press, 1989.

Greenfeld, Howard. *Puccini*. London: Robert Hale, 1981.

Hughes, Spike. *Famous Puccini Operas*. New York: Dover Publications, 1972.

Jackson, Stanley. *Monsieur Butterfly: The Life of Giacomo Puccini*. New York: Stein and Day, 1974.

Lee, M. Owen. *First Intermissions*. New York: Oxford University Press, 1995.

Letters of Giacomo Puccini. Ed. Giuseppe Adami, trans. Ena Makin. New York: Vienna House, 1973.

Long, John Luther. *Madame Butterfly*. The Century Company edition, 1911.

Louÿs, Pierre. *The Collected Works of Pierre Louÿs*, trans. by Mitchell S. Buck. New York: Liveright Publishing Corporation, 1932.

Maugham, William Somerset. *Of Human Bondage*. London: Penguin Books edition, 1963.

Mercatante, Anthony. *The Facts on File Encyclopedia of World Mythology and Legend*. New York: Facts On File, 1988.

Middle English Romances. Ed. A. C. Gibbs. Evanston: Northwestern University Press, 1988.

Mogador, Céleste. *Memoirs of a Courtesan in Nineteenth-Century Paris*. Trans. by Monique Fleury Nagem. Lincoln: University of Nebraska Press, 2001.

Mürger, Henry. *Vie de Bohème*. Trans. by Norman Cameron. London: Hamish Hamilton, 1949.

Newman, Ernest. *Seventeen Famous Operas*. New York: Alfred A. Knopf, 1955.

Osborne, Charles. *The Complete Operas of Puccini*. New York: Da Capo Press, 1983.

Ovid. *The Art of Love*. Trans. by Henry T. Riley. New York: Stravon Publishers, 1949.

Painter, Sidney. *French Chivalry*. Ithaca: Cornell University Press, 1969.

Phillips-Matz, Mary Jane. *Puccini: A Biography*. Boston: Northeastern University Press, 2002.

_____. *Verdi: A Biography*. Oxford: Oxford University Press, 1993.

Podles, Leon J. *The Church Impotent: The Feminization of Christianity*. Dallas: Spence Publishing Company, 1999.

Prévost, Abbé Antoine François. *The Story of Manon Lescaut and the Chevalier des Grieux.* Trans. by Helen Waddell. New York: The Heritage Press, 1935.

Richardson, Joanna. *The Courtesans: The Demi-Monde in 19th Century France.* London: Phoenix Press, 2000.

Seligman, Vincent. *Puccini Among Friends.* New York: The MacMillan Company, 1938.

Seven Puccini Librettos. Trans. by William Weaver. New York: W. W. Norton and Company, 1981.

Wilde, Oscar. *The Complete Oscar Wilde.* New York: Quality Paper Back Book Club, 1996.

Wilson, Alexandra. *The Puccini Problem: Opera, Nationality, and Modernity.* Cambridge University Press, 2007.

Index